DATABASES: IMPROVING USABILITY AND RESPONSIVENESS

Academic Press Rapid Manuscript Reproduction

Proceedings of The International Conference on
DATABASES: IMPROVING USABILITY
AND RESPONSIVENESS
August 2–3, 1978 at the Technion, Haifa, Israel

DATABASES: IMPROVING USABILITY AND RESPONSIVENESS

BEN SHNEIDERMAN

Department of Information Systems Management
University of Maryland

ACADEMIC PRESS   New York   San Francisco   London   1978

A Subsidiary of Harcourt Brace Jovanovich, Publishers

ACADEMIC PRESS, INC.
111 Fifth Avenue, New York, New York 10003

United Kingdom Edition published by
ACADEMIC PRESS, INC. (LONDON) LTD.
24/28 Oval Road, London NW1 7DX

Library of Congress Cataloging in Publication Data

Main entry under title:

Databases.

Sponsored by the Israel Institute of Technology.
1. Data base management. I. Shneiderman, Ben.
II. Haifa. Technion, Israel Institute of
Technology.
QA76.9.D3D363   001.6'4   78-18900
ISBN 0-12-642150-1

*This book is dedicated to the free pursuit of
scientific research in a peaceful world*

Contents

QUERY LANGUAGES

SIMPLIFYING DESIGN AND IMPLEMENTATION

DATA QUALITY, INTEGRITY, AND SECURITY

Contributors

Numbers in parentheses indicate the pages on which the authors' contributions begin.

NANCY D. ANDERSON (57), Computer Science Division, Department of Applied Physics and Information Science, University of California at San Diego, La Jolla, California

JOEL ARDITI (193), Computer Center, Weizmann Institute of Science, Rehovot, Israel

WALTER A. BURKHARD (57), Computer Science Division, Department of Applied Physics and Information Science, University of California at San Diego, La Jolla, California

MICHAEL F. CHALLIS (245), Departamento de Informática, Pontifícia Universidade Católica do Rio de Janiero, Rio de Janiero, Brazil

ERIC K. CLEMONS (371), Department of Decision Sciences, University of Pennsylvania, Philadelphia, Pennsylvania

E. F. CODD (3), IBM Research Laboratory, San Jose, California

DAVID COHEN (411), Computer and Information Science, The Ohio State University, Columbus, Ohio

JAMES P. FRY (151), Database Systems Research Group, Graduate School of Business Administration, The University of Michigan, Ann Arbor, Michigan

VIRGIL GLIGOR (295), Department of Computer Science, University of Maryland, College Park, Maryland

DANIEL GOLDSCHMIDT (131), Department of Computer Science, Technion–Israel Institute of Technology, Haifa, Israel

DAVID GREENBLATT (77), Department of Computer Sciences, Queens College, Flushing, New York

EHUD GUDES (319), Department of Computer Science, The Pennsylvania State University, University Park, Pennsylvania

MING T. LIU (411), Computer and Information Science, The Ohio State University, Columbus, Ohio

E. L. LOZINSKII (273), Department of Computer Science, Hebrew University, Jerusalem, Israel

DAVID MAIER (295), Department of Electrical Engineering and Computer Science, Princeton University, Princeton, New Jersey

JOHANN P. MALMQUIST (319), Department of Computer Science, The Pennsylvania State University, University Park, Pennsylvania

T. H. MERRETT (99), School of Computer Science, McGill University, Montreal, Quebec

T. WILLIAM OLLE (343), T. William Olle Associates, Ltd., West Byfleet, Surrey, England

G. PELAGATTI (399), Instituto di Eletronica-Politecnico di Milano, Piazza Leonardo da Vinci 32-20133, Milano, Italy

ALLEN REITER (131), Department of Computer Science, Technion–Israel Institute of Technology, Haifa, Israel

EDWARD L. ROBERTSON (319), Department of Computer Science, The Pennsylvania State University, University Park, Pennsylvania

JOACHIM W. SCHMIDT (215), Institut für Informatik, Universität Hamburg, Hamburg, West Germany

F. A. SCHREIBER (399), Instituto di Eletronica-Politecnico di Milano, Piazza Leonardo da Vinci 32-20133, Milano, Italy

TOBY J. TEOREY (151), Database Systems Research Group, Graduate School of Business Administration, The University of Michigan, Ann Arbor, Michigan

JERRY WAXMAN (77), Department of Computer Sciences, Queens College, Flushing, New York

MOSHÉ M. ZLOOF (29), IBM T. J. Watson Research Center, Yorktown Heights, New York

ELI ZUKOVSKY (193), Computer Center, Weizmann Institute of Science, Rehovot, Israel

Preface

How this book came to be

In the first weeks of 1977 as Allen Reiter was ending a three-month visit to the University of Maryland's Department of Information Systems Management we casually discussed the possibility of holding a database systems conference in Israel. In the last few days, just before he returned to the Technion's (Israel Institute of Technology) Computer Science Department, we hurriedly made phone calls and plans. Calvin C. "Kelly" Gotlieb of the University of Toronto informed us that the Third Triennial Jerusalem Conference on Information Technology was to be held August 6–9 of 1978, and our numerological instincts focused on the preponderance of threes and dates divisible by three. We realized it would be fortuitous to align ourselves with the JCIT and scheduled our conference for August 2–4, 1978. Allen Reiter became the General Chairman and I became the Program Chairman.

While I assembled the prestigious Program Committee consisting of Giampio Bracchi, Politecnico di Milano; Edgar Codd, IBM San Jose; Jim Fry, University of Michigan; Calvin C. Gotlieb, University of Toronto; Michael Hanani, University of the Negev; Jacob Katzenelson, Technion; Stuart Madnick, MIT; Jack Minker, University of Maryland; Howard L. Morgan, University of Pennsylvania; Seev Neumann, Tel Aviv University; G. M. Nijssen, Control Data, Belgium; Hans-Jochen Schneider, Technische Universität Berlin; Edgar H. Sibley, University of Maryland; and Dennis Tsichritzis, University of Toronto; Allen Reiter received supporting help from an organizing committee consisting of J. Raviv, S. Zur, and J. Wolberg. Publicity was supplied by E. Grinoch and P. Scheuermann.

The General Chairman of the JCIT, Anthony Ralston, and the Program Chairman, Aaron Finerman, gave us supportive advice. The Technion agreed to become our major sponsor with cosponsorship by the Israel Council for Research and Development, Israel Academy of Sciences, U.S. Army European Research Office, and University of Maryland. The Association for Computing Machinery agreed to be "in cooperation with" our conference. Further assistance was provided by the IBM–Israel Scientific Center and Elbit Computer Ltd.

The program committee was active and helped stimulate the submission of 40 manuscripts in response to our call for papers. Papers were received from Israel, the United States, Canada, Belgium, Germany, France, Netherlands, England, Italy, and Brazil. Four invited speakers—Edgar F. Codd, G. M. Nijssen, T. William Olle, and Moshé Zloof—provided papers that were the backbone of our program. Manuscript reviewing was conducted by the program committee and 29 additional referees: N. Ahituv, C. Beeri, H. Biller, B. Claybrook, E. Clemons, C. Cook, P. Elin-Dor, E. Falkenberg, D. Feigin, E. Gudes, M. Hammer, W. T. Hardgrave, L. Kerschberg, T. Klug, M. Lefler, D. Levin, F. Lochovsky, E. Lowenthal, E. Lozinskii, F. Manola, G. Marini, S. Navathe, H. Sayani, P. Scheuermann, F. Schreiber, G. Sockut, R. Taylor, R. Teitel, and M. Zloof.

An attempt was made to distribute the refereeing internationally and between program committee members and the additional referees. Each manuscript was read by at least three people. All comments were returned to the authors, unsigned. Fourteen papers were chosen for this volume and six were presented at the conference only: R. Demolombe, Centre d'Etudes et de Recherches de Toulouse, France, *A General Semantic Method for Efficiently Evaluating "AND" Operators in Relational DBMS;* D. Deutsch, National Bureau of Standards, *Database Management Standardization Issues in the United States Government;* W. Litwin, Institut de Recherche d'Informatique et d'Automatique, France, *Virtual Hashing: A Dynamically Changing Hashing;* J. L. Kolodner, Yale University, New Haven, Connecticut, *Memory Organization for Natural Language Data-Base Inquiry;* A. Shoshani, Lawrence Berkeley Laboratory, University of California, *CABLE: A Language Based on the Entity-Relationship Model;* and G. M. Nijssen, Software Research Department, Brussels, Belgium, *DBMS Gross Architecture and Conceptual Scheme Concepts: Status Report of IFIP WG 2.6.*

I derived a great deal of satisfaction from cooperating with so many people. Most of my repeated demands for punctuality were met. The helpful comments from the program committee kept me working harder and the detailed critiques from the referees enabled the authors to do better. Special thanks go to Edgar H. Sibley and Jack Minker who were close by and ready to help with some tough decisions. The staff of Academic Press was professional, prompt, and helpful.

Scientific research is an intellectual challenge yielding private satisfactions. Reporting results and risking insights require a supportive environment of competent, demanding, and yet sympathetic colleagues. The international community of scholars who contributed to this conference were united by their scientific interest, desire to share ideas freely, and willingness to give and take constructive criticism in an atmosphere of trust. I hope that those who participated were satisfied with the process and those who read this volume appreciate the product.

Why this book came to be

The sociologists and historians of science have frequently pointed out the smallness of the international clique that focuses on specific research topics, the importance of professional contacts, and the essentially conservative nature of scientific progress. These three factors may make it difficult for young scientists, geographically remote research centers, and new ideas to participate in the mainstream.

This conference was held in Haifa partly to give Israelis the opportunity to present their work and hear quality presentations directly from leading researchers. We hoped that this kind of interaction would stimulate database work in Israel, while giving "outsiders" a chance to see current Israeli progress.

The title of this book, which was the conference theme, was designed to draw attention to more practical issues and concentrate on database functioning from the user's point of view. Usability refers to the utility and ease of use of the database system. Responsiveness refers to how well the system responds to specific user requests and general needs. These topics are included in other conferences and books, but we wanted them to be the center of attention.

As expected, we received many papers proposing query languages or natural language front end facilities. Evolutionary refinement of query facilities is inevitable and, as in programming languages, we should not expect a universal or optimal language to emerge. Human diversity creates the need for a variety of styles and levels of complexity. Comparative studies conducted in a controlled psychological experimental environment will provide the data on human performance necessary to improve these facilities. Natural language front ends, which are portrayed by some researchers as the best facility for nonprogrammer database access, are the subject of several research efforts. The effectiveness of natural language systems, actual ease of use, utility, and cost are still unclear.

For a system to be usable and responsive, it must be accessible. Several papers in this volume deal with user facilities in distributed systems and the architecture of complex multiuser systems. Elaborate distributed systems have become economically viable due to cheap mini- and microcomputers and declining telecommunications costs. Coordinating the user community may prove to be more challenging than building the hardware and software components.

An acceptable database system must store data efficiently while preserving security, reliability, consistency, and integrity. Papers in this volume contribute new ideas for coping with these system quality issues.

None of the papers offers revolutionary approaches that solve all our problems with a radical departure from current practice. On the contrary, each paper has fresh ideas for evolutionary refinements to current practice and to proposals now under research and/or development.

By focusing on human aspects of database systems we sought to underline the notion that computers are merely tools with no more intelligence than a wooden pencil, hand calculator, or bulldozer. By making databases more usable and responsive we enable humans to apply their intellect and creativity to more ambitious tasks. The scientific discipline that we use does not include value judgments about applications, but every scientist must acknowledge the necessity of making such judgments. Scientists must be involved in politics, concerned about social issues, troubled by violations of human rights, and dedicated to creating a better world.

Computer-based information systems are often portrayed as contributing to alienation and repression, but the database tools that are the subject of this book can be applied to facilitating communication among individuals and nations, improving health care, stimulating education, increasing options in life choices, and protecting freedom. We trust that those who use knowledge will use it wisely.

Query Languages

DATABASES: IMPROVING USABILITY AND RESPONSIVENESS

HOW ABOUT RECENTLY?
(English dialog with relational data bases
using RENDEZVOUS Version 1)

E. F. Codd

IBM Research Laboratory
San Jose, California

The query HOW ABOUT RECENTLY? dramatically exhibits marked contrasts between natural language mode of expression and thought on the one hand and formal language mode of expression and thought on the other. A viable system for natural language interrogation of formatted data bases must be capable of 'talking back' to the user in natural language. RENDEZVOUS Version 1 is an experimental system intended as a query formulation front end for relational data base management systems. It differs markedly from other natural language query systems in the extent to which it talks back to the user about his query before any data base retrieval is executed. The system's ability to engage the user in clarification dialog and the analyzer's ability to cope with input that does not conform to its own built-in phrase transformation rules make this system far more robust than previous natural language systems for data base interrogation.

In this paper we discuss the types of dialog supported by this system and some of the lessons learned from tests conducted with subjects of widely varying capabilities interacting with a sample data base concerning suppliers, parts, projects, and shipments.

1. INTRODUCTION

To many people a natural language query system for retrieving data from a formatted data base is simply a combination of the following two components:

1) a front end which translates from input expressed in a natural language subset (e.g., restricted English) into a formal query language -- let us call this front end a <u>natural language analyzer</u>

2) a subsystem which interprets the formal query language and retrieves the requested data -- let us call this subsystem a <u>retriever</u>.

It is this somewhat narrow concept of a natural language query system which has given rise to much of the controversy over the relative merits of using natural language versus formal languages and menus for expressing

queries. It has been our contention for some time (1) that a natural
language system of this kind is essentially non-viable (except possibly
for a very limited class of dedicated professionals who use the system so
frequently that they remember its restrictions and who take great pains to
avoid ambiguous input and equally great pains to stay within the bounds of
the data base). However, it is entirely fallacious to argue that natural
language is non-viable as a query language simply because a particular
kind of natural language query system is non-viable. To have any hope of
being viable, a natural language query system must 'talk back' to the user
using the same natural language he uses, except that its style has to be
much more precise than that of the average user. Accordingly, there must
be a natural language generator as well as a natural language analyzer in
a viable natural language query system.

In this paper we provide an introductory description of a natural
language query system called RENDEZVOUS Version 1, which includes both an
English generator and an English analyzer, and which became operational in
April 1977. It is capable of conducting many different types of dialog
with its users. The main aim of this paper is to demonstrate (through
examples of actual user behavior) how essential it is to support these
types of dialog. We shall also discuss some of the lessons we learned
when subjects interacted with the system.

For information on recently-developed natural language query systems
with somewhat similar goals but apparently lacking any generator
component, see (5,6,7,8). Incidentally, very little work on the
generation of natural language has been published (see for example
(9,10,11,12,13)), and none of this appears to treat the problem in the
context of query formulation.

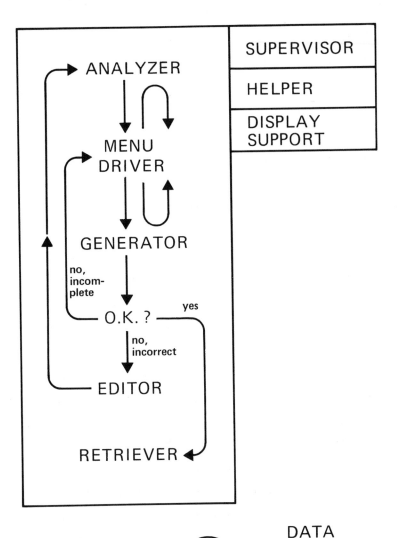

2. MAJOR COMPONENTS OF RENDEZVOUS VERSION 1

A block diagram of the system is shown in Fig. 1, and the first thing
to notice is that the system has many more components than the English
analyzer. We shall give a brief description of the services provided by
each major component.

The <u>analyzer</u> attempts to translate the user's query into a simplified
version of the data sublanguage DEDUCE (3). It also supports two kinds of
dialog: <u>clarification dialog</u> which consists of posing questions to the
user about his intended query in the context of the query he actually
entered (we do not assume that the query entered is a faithful
representation of the query intended); and <u>continuation dialog</u> which
allows a user to formulate a new query by specifying (perhaps very
indirectly) small changes to be applied to his immediately preceding
query.

The <u>menu driver</u> takes the analyzer output, tests its logical
completeness, and poses only those questions to the user that will yield a
logically complete formal query. This <u>menu-driven dialog</u> is conducted
without reference to the query actually entered by the user, and this is
what distinguishes it from clarification dialog.

The <u>generator</u> translates the logically complete formal query (output
by the menu driver) into a precise English re-statement. It then asks the
user if he is satisfied that this re-statement captures his intent.

The <u>retriever</u> is invoked only when the user has approved the English
re-statement. It then takes the logically complete formal query from the
menu driver and retrieves data from the data base in order to generate an
answer to that query. It also supports <u>output dialog</u> -- that is, dialog
with the user about the answer from the data base.

The <u>query editor</u> provides a menu-oriented means for the user to change
his query or the system's version thereof. The <u>helper</u> provides a

menu-oriented means for the user to obtain general information about the kinds of data stored in the data base. The display support provides a dynamic partitioning of the display terminal screen to facilitate user interaction. It also keeps a history of the user's interactions and allows the user to examine this history whenever the system is awaiting a response from him. The supervisor is responsible for invoking each of the components cited above whenever appropriate.

The knowledge base in Version 1 provides just enough time-independent semantic and linguistic information about the data base to allow the system to interact with reasonable intelligence concerning any English query whose formal counterpart lies within the class of formal queries supported as an internal interface. The knowledge base encompasses all the tables used by the analyzer, menu driver, and generator plus all the transformation rules used by the analyzer plus certain procedures which are domain-dependent (e.g., a procedure to compute differences between calendar dates would be applicable only to those data bases that have dates in them). Whenever a semantically new data base is installed, much of the knowledge base must also be replaced. A linguistic engineer is needed to plan and execute this task.

Version 1 supports queries whose DEDUCE representation is a conjunction of relational clauses wherein each attribute can be given a value along with a connective $(<, \leq, =, \geq, >, \neq)$, or it may be starred (for printing or counting), or it may be equated to a join variable. For example

```
FIND:   PART ( PNO=x1 *PNAME )
        SHIP ( PNO=x1 DATE=22/3/74 )
```

is the DEDUCE representation of the query: PRINT THE NAMES OF PARTS SHIPPED ON MARCH 22, 1974 (assuming a relational data base as outlined below). In this query PNO stands for part serial number and x1 is a join variable. Existential quantification is assumed where necessary (no other

QUERY
VIEWPORT

> YOUR PRESENT QUERY IS:
> NONEXCELLENT NON DETROIT SUPPLIERS SHIPPING PART P37
>
> IN ADDITION, THROUGH DIALOG YOU INDICATED THAT YOU WANT:
> TO PRINT INFORMATION ON SUPPLIERS:

HISTORY
VIEWPORT

> S 014   WHICH OF THE FOLLOWING ITEMS OF INFORMATION ON SUPPLIERS
>   DO YOU WANT PRINTED?
>   1   SUPPLIER NUMBER
>   2   SUPPLIER NAME
>   3   SUPPLIER LOCATION
>   4   SUPPLIER RATING
>   5   NONE OF THE ABOVE
>   SELECT ONE OR MORE ITEMS BY NUMBER

INPUT
VIEWPORT

> U 014   1,2,3,4

MESSAGE
VIEWPORT

QUERY
VIEWPORT

> YOUR PRESENT QUERY IS:
> NONEXCELLENT NON DETROIT SUPPLIERS SHIPPING PART P37
>
> IN ADDITION, THROUGH DIALOG YOU INDICATED THAT YOU WANT:
> TO PRINT THE SERIAL NUMBER, NAME, LOCATION AND RATING OF
> EVERY SUPPLIER;

HISTORY
VIEWPORT

> NOTE   THIS IS WHAT THE SYSTEM UNDERSTANDS YOUR QUERY TO BE:
>   PRINT THE SERIAL NUMBER, NAME, LOCATION AND RATING OF EVERY
>   SUPPLIER NOT RATED EXCELLENT AND NOT LOCATED IN DETROIT
>   WHO SENT A SHIPMENT OF PART NUMBER P37.
>
> S015   IS THE SYSTEM'S UNDERSTANDING
>   1   CORRECT AND COMPLETE
>   2   NOT YET COMPLETE
>   3   INCORRECT
>
>   SELECT ONE ITEM BY NUMBER

INPUT
VIEWPORT

> U 015   2

MESSAGE
VIEWPORT

Example A.

S 001 PLEASE TYPE IN YOUR QUERY:
U 001 I WANT TO FIND CERTAIN PROJECTS. PIPES WERE SENT
      TO THEM IN FEB. 1975.

no clarifi-   NOTE THIS IS WHAT THE SYSTEM UNDERSTANDS YOUR QUERY TO BE:
cation dialog   PRINT THE NAME OF EVERY PROJECT TO WHICH A SHIPMENT
                       OF A PART NAMED PIPE WAS SENT DURING FEBRUARY 1975.

verification   S 002 IS THE SYSTEM'S UNDERSTANDING
of single   1   CORRECT AND COMPLETE
rephrasing   2   NOT YET COMPLETE
                         3   INCORRECT
                       SELECT EXACTLY ONE ITEM BY NUMBER
                 U 002 1

* *** THE ANSWER TO YOUR QUERY IS:

         PROJECT
         NAME

         SAN LUIS
         HYDRO
         SONOMA

                 S 003 IN REGARD TO YOUR PRESENT QUERY, WHAT ADDITIONAL
                       INFORMATION WOULD YOU LIKE TO HAVE? IF NONE, JUST
                       HIT THE 'SEND' KEY.
target ellipsis U 003 GIVE ME THEIR LOCATIO ALSO

spelling   S 004 IS THE WORD 'LOCATIO' INTENDED TO BE: LOCATION?
                       (YES OR NO)
correction   U 004 YES

                 NOTE THIS IS WHAT THE SYSTEM UNDERSTANDS YOUR QUERY TO BE:

                       PRINT THE NAME AND LOCATION OF EVERY PROJECT TO WHICH
                       A SHIPMENT OF A PART NAMED PIPE WAS SENT DURING
                       FEBRUARY 1975.

                 S 005 IS THE SYSTEM'S UNDERSTANDING
                         1   CORRECT AND COMPLETE
                         2   NOT YET COMPLETE
                         3   INCORRECT
                       SELECT EXACTLY ONE ITEM BY NUMBER
                 U 005 1

* *** THE ANSWER TO YOUR QUERY IS:

         PROJECT   PROJECT
         NAME   LOCATION

         SAN LUIS   FRESNO
         HYDRO   SACRAMENTO
         SONOMA   SAN FRANCISCO

                 S 006 IN REGARD TO YOUR PRESENT QUERY, WHAT ADDITIONAL
                       INFORMATION WOULD YOU LIKE TO HAVE? IF NONE, JUST
                       HIT THE 'SEND' KEY.
qualification   U 006 HOW ABOUT RECENTLY?
ellipsis

fuzzy value   S 007 BY THE WORD RECENT(LY), DO YOU INTEND ONE OF THE
                       FOLLOWING:
resolution   1   WITHIN THE LAST FEW YEARS
                         2   WITHIN THE LAST YEAR
                         3   WITHIN THE LAST FEW MONTHS
                         4   WITHIN THE LAST MONTH
                         5   NONE OF THE ABOVE
                       SELECT EXACTLY ONE ITEM BY NUMBER
                 U 007 4

```
NOTE    THIS IS WHAT THE SYSTEM UNDERSTANDS YOUR QUERY TO BE:

        PRINT THE NAME AND LOCATION OF EVERY PROJECT TO WHICH
        A SHIPMENT OF A PART NAMED PIPE WAS SENT DURING
        JULY 1977 OR AFTER.

S 008   IS THE SYSTEM'S UNDERSTANDING
                    1   CORRECT AND COMPLETE
                    2   NOT YET COMPLETE
                    3   INCORRECT
        SELECT EXACTLY ONE ITEM BY NUMBER
U 008   1


* ***   NO OBJECTS IN THE DATABASE QUALIFY AS AN ANSWER TO
        YOUR QUERY.
        NOTE THAT IN THIS DATABASE
        THERE IS NO SHIPMENT SENT DURING JULY 1977 OR AFTER
```

explanation of
empty result

type of quantification is permitted). The only functions supported in
Version 1 are COUNT and EXIST. Although these limitations may seem highly
restrictive and certainly must be removed in Version 2, the majority of
queries encountered in practice probably fall within the class supported
by Version 1. It is important to note that the system completely protects
casual users from DEDUCE. On the other hand, experienced users may, if
they wish, use DEDUCE as their source language, or even DEDUCE freely
intermixed with English. Such users will still enjoy the benefits of
English feedback prior to data base retrieval.

A more detailed description of Version 1 is provided in (2), while
some supporting technology is described in (3,4). The code of Version 1,
excluding comments, consists of 10,500 APL statements.

3. TYPES OF DIALOG SUPPORTED

3.1. Sample Data Base

The behavior of the system will be illustrated using a sample data
base concerning water projects in California, parts for these projects
(such as pipes and valves), suppliers located in major cities of the

Example B

```
            S 001  PLEASE TYPE IN YOUR QUERY:
            U 001  NONEXCELLENT NON DETROIT SUPPLIERS SHIPPING PART 37.
```

value ambiguity   S 002 WHEN YOU USE THE PHRASE 'PART 37', WHICH OF THE
resolution   FOLLOWING PROPERTIES OF PARTS DO YOU INTEND BY
                         THE WORD '37'?
                           1 PART PART-SERIAL-NUMBER
                           2 PART QUANTITY-ON-HAND
                           3 PART QUANTITY-ON-ORDER
                           4 NONE OF THE ABOVE
                         SELECT ONE ITEM OR NONE BY NUMBER
                  U 002 1

value inconsis-   NOTE   BUT 37 IS INCORRECT AS A PART-SERIAL-NUMBER OF A PART;
tency notifi-   THE PART-SERIAL-NUMBER OF A PART MUST CONTAIN AT LEAST
cation   ONE DIGIT AND AT LEAST ONE LETTER

                  S 003 DO YOU WISH TO CHANGE YOUR QUERY? (YES OR NO)
pressed HELP   U 003 <HELP>
key

                  S 004 WOULD YOU LIKE
                           1 INFORMATION ON THE DATABASE
help mode   2 HELP WITH THE KEYBOARD
                           3 TO MAKE CHANGE(S) IN YOUR QUERY
                           4 TO ENTER A NEW QUERY AND RESTART
                           5 TO RESUME ACTION ON YOUR QUERY
                           6 TO END THE SESSION ALTOGETHER
                         SELECT EXACTLY ONE ITEM BY NUMBER
                  U 004 1

                  S 005 ON WHICH OF THE FOLLOWING DO YOU NEED EXPLANATION:
                           1 THE WHOLE DATABASE
                           2 SUPPLIERS
                           3 PROJECTS
                           4 PARTS
                           5 SHIPMENTS
                         SELECT ONE OR MORE ITEMS BY NUMBER
                  U 005 4

database   PARTS HAVE A SERIAL NUMBER AND A NAME.
information   THE SERIAL NUMBER OF A PART IDENTIFIES ITS TYPE UNIQUELY.
on parts   EXAMPLES OF PART SERIAL NUMBERS: P1, P13, P25, ETC.
                         PART NAMES DO NOT NECESSARILY DETERMINE THEIR PART SERIAL NUMBER.
                         EXAMPLES OF PART NAMES: SCREW, BOLT, PIPE, PUMP, ETC.
                         QUANTITY ON HAND SPECIFIES THE TOTAL QUANTITY OF A PART TYPE
                             IN STOCK.
                         QUANTITY ON HAND IS GIVEN IN NUMBERS, E.G. 5, 30, 100, 250, ETC.
                         QUANTITY ON ORDER SPECIFIES THE TOTAL QUANTITY OF A PART TYPE
                             ORDERED FROM ALL SUPPLIERS.

                  S 006 WOULD YOU LIKE
                           1 INFORMATION ON THE DATABASE
                           2 HELP WITH THE KEYBOARD
                           3 TO MAKE CHANGE(S) IN YOUR QUERY
                           4 TO ENTER A NEW QUERY AND RESTART
                           5 TO RESUME ACTION ON YOUR QUERY
                           6 TO END THE SESSION ALTOGETHER
                         SELECT EXACTLY ONE ITEM BY NUMBER
                  U 006 3

menu-driven   S 007 DO YOU WISH TO
editing   1 INSERT A WORD OR PHRASE BEFORE A WORD IN THE QUERY
                           2 INSERT A WORD OR PHRASE AFTER A WORD IN THE QUERY
                           3 DELETE A WORD OR PHRASE FROM THE QUERY
                           4 REPLACE A WORD OR PHRASE IN THE QUERY
                         SELECT EXACTLY ONE ITEM BY NUMBER
                  U 007 4

```
                    S 008   ENTER WORD OR PHRASE TO BE REPLACED; (OR JUST HIT
                            'SEND' TO SKIP THIS REQUEST AND CONTINUE)
                    U 008   37


word replacement    S 009   ENTER WORD OR PHRASE TO REPLACE 37; (OR JUST HIT
                            'SEND' TO SKIP THIS REQUEST AND CONTINUE)
                    U 009   P37


                    S 010   ANY OTHER CHANGE?
                    U 010   NO


query type          S 011   WHAT KIND OF RESPONSE TO YOUR QUERY ARE YOU EXPECTING?
resolution                      1   A LIST OF ITEMS OF INFORMATION TO BE PRINTED
                                    FROM THE DATA BASE
                                2   A YES/NO OR TRUE/FALSE ANSWER
                                3   A COUNT OF ITEMS FROM THE DATA BASE
                            SELECT EXACTLY ONE ITEM BY NUMBER
                    U 011   1


focus resolu-       S 012   ON WHICH OF THE FOLLOWING ITEMS DO YOU WANT INFORMATION
tion                        PRINTED?
                                1   SUPPLIERS
                                2   SHIPMENTS
                                3   PROJECTS
                                4   PARTS
                                5   NONE OF THE ABOVE
                            SELECT ONE OR MORE ITEMS BY NUMBER
                    U 012   1


attribute           S 013   WHICH OF THE FOLLOWING ITEMS OF INFORMATION ON SUPPLIERS
resolution                  DO YOU WANT PRINTED?
                                1   SUPPLIER NUMBER
                                2   SUPPLIER NAME
                                3   SUPPLIER LOCATION
                                4   SUPPLIER RATING
                                5   NONE OF THE ABOVE
                            SELECT ONE OR MORE ITEMS BY NUMBER
                    U 013   1,2,3,4


                    NOTE    THIS IS WHAT THE SYSTEM UNDERSTANDS YOUR QUERY TO BE:

                            PRINT THE SERIAL NUMBER, NAME, LOCATION AND RATING OF
                            EVERY SUPPLIER NOT RATED EXCELLENT AND NOT LOCATED IN
                            DETROIT WHO SENT A SHIPMENT OF PART NUMBER P37 .

                    S 014   IS THE SYSTEM'S UNDERSTANDING
                                1   CORRECT AND COMPLETE
                                2   NOT YET COMPLETE
                                3   INCORRECT
                            SELECT EXACTLY ONE ITEM BY NUMBER
                    U 014   2


                    S 015   DOES THE INTERPRETATION FAIL TO MENTION SOMETHING YOU
                            WANT PRINTED?
                    U 015   NO


                    S 016   DOES THE INTERPRETATION FAIL TO MENTION ANY SPECIFICA-
                            TION(S) ON SUPPLIERS, PROJECTS, PARTS OR SHIPMENTS ?
                    U 016   YES


                    S 017   WHAT INFORMATION DO YOU WANT TO SPECIFY FOR (OR ADD TO)
                            YOUR QUERY?
                                1   SUPPLIER(S)   (E.G. ONE NAMED ACME, ETC.)
                                2   PART(S)       (E.G. ONE WITH QUANTITY ON HAND 10,
                                                  ETC.)
                                3   PROJECT(S)    (E.G. ONE LOCATED IN HOUSTON, ETC.)
                                4   SHIPMENT(S)   (E.G. ONE SENT ON JUNE 23,1976, ETC.)
                                5   NONE OF THE ABOVE
                            SELECT ONE OR MORE ITEMS BY NUMBER
                    U 017   4
```

```
             S 018   WHICH PARTICULAR ITEM(S) OF THE FOLLOWING INFORMATION
                     ON SHIPMENTS DO YOU WANT TO SPECIFY?
                         1   SERIAL NUMBER OF PARTS SHIPPED
                         2   SERIAL NUMBER OF SUPPLIERS MAKING SHIPMENT
                         3   SERIAL NUMBER OF PROJECTS RECEIVING SHIPMENT
                         4   QUANTITY SHIPPED
                         5   DATE SHIPPED
                         6   NONE OF THE ABOVE
                     SELECT ONE OR MORE ITEMS BY NUMBER
             U 018   5

             S 019   PLEASE ENTER HERE THE DATE OF SHIPMENT YOU WISH TO SPECIFY:
variant input   U 019   AUG75
syntax for dates

             NOTE    THIS IS WHAT THE SYSTEM UNDERSTANDS YOUR QUERY TO BE:

                     PRINT THE SERIAL NUMBER, NAME, LOCATION AND RATING OF
                     EVERY SUPPLIER NOT RATED EXCELLENT AND NOT LOCATED IN
                     DETROIT WHO, DURING AUGUST 1975, SENT A SHIPMENT OF
                     PART NUMBER P37.

             S 020   IS THE SYSTEM'S UNDERSTANDING
                         1   CORRECT AND COMPLETE
                         2   NOT YET COMPLETE
                         3   INCORRECT
                     SELECT EXACTLY ONE ITEM BY NUMBER
             U 020   1


             * ***   NO OBJECTS IN THE DATABASE QUALIFY AS AN ANSWER TO
                     YOUR QUERY
```

United States, and shipments of parts from the suppliers to the projects.

The corresponding four relations are:

PROJECT (<u>JNO</u> JNAME JLOC)

PART (<u>PNO</u> PNAME QOH QOO PTYPE)

SUPPLIER (<u>SNO</u> SNAME SLOC RATE)

SHIP (<u>SNO PNO JNO DATE</u> QSHIP)

For a given project, JNO denotes its unique serial number, JNAME its

name (also unique), JLOC the city in which it is located (a project is

located in exactly one city, but a given city may be the location of one

or more projects). For a given kind of part, PNO denotes its unique

serial number, PNAME its not necessarily unique name, QOH the quantity on

hand, QOO the quantity on order, and PTYPE a broad classification of part

type (not discussed further here, because the dialog examples do not make

use of it). For a given supplier, SNO denotes the unique serial number,

SNAME the not necessarily unique name, SLOC the city in which the supplier

is located (a supplier is located in exactly one city, but a city may be

Example C

```
S 001   PLEASE TYPE IN YOUR QUERY:
U 001   HOW MANY WHITNEY SHIPMENTS HAVE A SHIPDATE 6/10/1975


S 002   IS 6/10/1975 INTENDED TO BE A DATE? (YES OR NO)
U 002   YES


S 003   WE ARE TRYING TO INTERPRET 6/10/1975 AS A DATE.
        WHICH OF THE FOLLOWING DATES DO YOU INTEND:
                    1   JUNE 10
                    2   OCTOBER 6
                    3   NONE OF THE ABOVE
        SELECT ONE ITEM OR NONE BY NUMBER
U 003   1


S 004   IS THE WORD 'WHITNEY' CORRECTLY TYPED? (YES OR NO)
U 004   YES


S 005   IS 'WHITNEY' THE NAME OF A PART? (YES OR NO)
U 005   NO
```

```
S 006   THE WORD 'WHITNEY' IS UNFAMILIAR.  IS IT ONE OF THE
        FOLLOWING:
                    1   SUPPLIER NAME       5   PROJECT LOCATION
                    2   SUPPLIER LOCATION   6   PART NAME
                    3   SUPPLIER RATING     7   PART TYPE
                    4   PROJECT NAME        8   NONE OF THE ABOVE
        SELECT BY NUMBER THE CLOSEST CATALOG ITEM
U 006   1


NOTE    THE SYSTEM HAS 2 WAYS TO INTERPRET YOUR QUERY. PLEASE
        INDICATE IF ANY OF THEM IS WHAT YOU INTENDED.
```

```
        1   COUNT THE NUMBER OF SUPPLIERS NAMED WHITNEY WHO, ON
            JUNE 10, 1975, SENT A SHIPMENT .

        2   COUNT THE NUMBER OF SHIPMENTS SENT ON JUNE 10, 1975 BY
            A SUPPLIER NAMED WHITNEY .

S 007   WHICH OF THE INTERPRETATIONS IS CORRECT:
                    1   FIRST
                    2   SECOND
                    3   NONE OF THE ABOVE
        SELECT EXACTLY ONE ITEM BY NUMBER
U 007   2


* ***   THERE IS NO SHIPMENT IN THE DATABASE SATISFYING YOUR QUERY.
```


Example D

```
S 001   PLEASE TYPE IN YOUR QUERY:
U 001   ARE THERE ANY SUPPLIERS SHIPPING TO BOTSON


S 002   IS THE WORD 'BOTSON' INTENDED TO BE: BOSTON? (YES OR NO)
U 002   YES


NOTE    SHIPPING TO BOSTON ?
        WE DO NOT HAVE PROJECTS WITH LOCATION BOSTON BUT WE DO
        HAVE PROJECTS WITH LOCATION BAKERSFIELD FRESNO
        LOS-ANGELES MONTEREY OAKLAND SACRAMENTO SAN-DIEGO
        SAN-FRANCISCO SAN-JOSE STOCKTON. IN ADDITION, WE HAVE
        SUPPLIERS WITH LOCATION BOSTON


S 003   DO YOU WISH TO CHANGE YOUR QUERY? (YES OR NO)
U 003   <HELP>
```

```
S 004   WOULD YOU LIKE
              1   INFORMATION ON THE DATABASE
              2   HELP WITH THE KEYBOARD
              3   TO MAKE CHANGE(S) IN YOUR QUERY
              4   TO ENTER A NEW QUERY AND RESTART
              5   TO RESUME ACTION ON YOUR QUERY
              6   TO END THE SESSION ALTOGETHER
        SELECT EXACTLY ONE ITEM BY NUMBER
U 004   3


S 005   DO YOU WISH TO
              1   INSERT A WORD OR PHRASE BEFORE A WORD IN THE QUERY
              2   INSERT A WORD OR PHRASE AFTER A WORD IN THE QUERY
              3   DELETE A WORD OR PHRASE FROM THE QUERY
              4   REPLACE A WORD OR PHRASE IN THE QUERY
        SELECT EXACTLY ONE ITEM BY NUMBER
U 005   4


S 006   ENTER WORD OR PHRASE TO BE REPLACED; (OR JUST HIT 'SEND'
        TO SKIP THIS REQUEST AND CONTINUE)
U 006   TO


S 007   ENTER WORD OR PHRASE TO REPLACE TO; (OR JUST HIT 'SEND'
        TO SKIP THIS REQUEST AND CONTINUE)
U 007   FROM


S 008   ANY OTHER CHANGE?
U 008   NO


NOTE    THE SYSTEM HAS 2 WAYS TO INTERPRET YOUR QUERY. PLEASE
        INDICATE IF ANY OF THEM IS WHAT YOU INTENDED.

     1  IS THERE ANY SUPPLIER LOCATED IN BOSTON WHO SENT A
        SHIPMENT ? .

     2  IS THERE ANY SHIPMENT FROM A SUPPLIER LOCATED IN BOSTON ? .

S 009   WHICH OF THE INTERPRETATIONS IS CORRECT:
              1   FIRST
              2   SECOND
              3   NONE OF THE ABOVE
        SELECT EXACTLY ONE ITEM BY NUMBER
U 009   1


* ***   YES.  THERE IS EXACTLY 1 SUPPLIER IN THE DATABASE
        SATISFYING YOUR QUERY.
S 010   DO YOU WANT IT LISTED?
U 010   YES
```

SUPPLIER SERIAL	SUPPLIER NAME	SUPPLIER LOCATION	SUPPLIER RATING
S18	ATLANTIC	BOSTON	POOR

the location of one or more suppliers), and RATE denotes the supplier

rating (admissible values are EXCELLENT, GOOD, FAIR, and POOR). For each

completed shipment, SNO denotes the supplier sending the shipment, PNO

denotes the kind of part being shipped (only one kind per shipment), JNO

denotes the project receiving the shipment, DATE denotes the date shipped

from the supplier, and QSHIP denotes the quantity of parts of the
specified kind in the shipment. As usual, the primary key of each
relation is underlined.

3.2. Formatted Screen Display

Fig. 2 shows how the display screen is divided into four viewports:
the query, history, input, and message viewports. The first two of these
are dynamically variable in size.

The query viewport at the top of the screen contains a copy of the
current state of the user's query. This state reflects the changes (e.g.,
editing, spelling correction, rephrasing) the user or the system has made
either to the user's original query or to an incomplete system rephrasing.
The query viewport may also contain a statement of the system's present
understanding of the user's intent.

Below the query viewport is the history viewport, which is a window
to an online record (history) of the session up to and including the most
recent interaction. The history may be scrolled vertically in either
direction.

Below the history viewport is the input viewport, which receives user
input from the keyboard. Finally, below the input viewport is the message
viewport, in which the system places messages to the user such as SCROLL
FORWARD FOR MORE.

3.3. Dialog Examples

The examples shown below are transcripts of actual interactions with
Version 1, omitting repetition of the query viewport. Some explanatory
comments have been inserted in the left margin. The system labels its
questions S and the user's responses U together with a 3-digit serial
number. Besides posing questions to the user, the system provides him

with information that does not require a response. Such pieces of advice
are prefixed by the word NOTE.

Example A exhibits a user query, which the analyzer was able to
analyze without resorting to clarification dialog. Note, incidentally,
that the input consists of two sentences.

The generator tells the user what it understands his query to mean by
constructing a precise English sentence from the formal query computed by
the analyzer, and then asks for the user's approval (giving him two
disapproval options in case he is dissatisfied). The user approves, and
the retriever therefore proceeds to extract the requested information from
the data base. Note that the user failed to say specifically what
information he wanted displayed about the pertinent projects. The
analyzer accordingly took the project name from a table of defaults.

Immediately after retrieval of the data, the system poses a question
(S003) that is intended solely as a psychological stimulus to the user --
subsequent system behavior is only trivially affected by the user's
answer. The aim of this stimulus is to encourage the user to employ,
wherever possible, very terse elliptical references to his previous query
in order to amplify or modify it, rather than ponderously repeating much
of it again. U003 is an excellent example of this. Since in this case
the user is amplifying the target list of attributes to be displayed, we
call this target ellipsis.

The user makes a keyboard error in entering the word LOCATION. Since
the word LOCATIO which he entered is close to just one word LOCATION in
the lexicon, the analyzer asks him if this is what he intended (S004) and
he replies YES (U004). The final output now includes the location as well
as the name of the pertinent projects. Stimulus S006 again induces the
user to employ ellipsis, but this time it is not an amplification of the
target list. Instead, it is a modification of the qualification and is
therefore called qualification ellipsis. Version 1 allows only one new

condition clause to be introduced or one existing condition to be altered

in qualification ellipsis. In the present example, one existing condition

clause involving DATE is modified from FEBRUARY 1975 to whatever precise

date or date interval will satisfy the user in place of RECENTLY.

S007 is an attempt by the analyzer to resolve the meaning of RECENTLY

in this particular query (the user's intended meanings for such fuzzy

words could change from query to query). Incidentally, the system's

restatement specifies JULY 1977, because this session took place in that

month and the user selected option 4 in response U007.

Following the user's approval (U008) of the system's understanding,

the retriever finds there are no projects satisfying the specified

conditions. Where possible without exploring too many subconditions of

the specified condition, the retriever attempts to provide an explanation

of such an empty result. In this case, it finds that there is no shipment

of any kind whatsoever in July 1977 or after. Such advice to the user

will often relieve him of the burden of asking many closely related

queries to pin down the cause of an exceptional answer from the data base.

In Example B the query U001 is not a complete English sentence. In

addition, it contains a value error, and, as we shall see, represents only

a small part of the user's total intent -- possibly because of the user's

inability to express his entire intent in a single utterance. The

interaction S002-U002 shows that the user intended 37 to be a part serial

number. In the immediately following NOTE, the analyzer informs the user

of this error. Accordingly, he calls for the helper to provide

information about what kinds of data are available concerning parts. He

then uses the query editor to change 37 to P37 (S007-U010) The analyzer

produces a formal query which is incomplete, and the menu driver acquires

the missing information (S011-U013). By now the system's version of the

query is quite complicated, but still does not satisfy the user

(S014-U014). He proceeds to request a further condition (S016-U019) and forgets to type a blank between AUG and 75 (U019). Finally (U020), he accepts the system's version, and we see how the system has helped the user to advance step-by-step from the original incomplete and erroneous input to a rather complicated, but unambiguous, error-free query. This is an example of incremental query formulation, which we believe is vital to successful support of casual users.

In Example C the ambiguities in query U001 center on the phrase WHITNEY SHIPMENTS and the date 6/10/75. WHITNEY SHIPMENTS could mean amongst other things shipments from a supplier named WHITNEY, shipments of a part named WHITNEY, or shipments to a project named WHITNEY. The query formulation front end deliberately does not have the knowledge that WHITNEY is a supplier name. In fact, the word WHITNEY, like many other data base values, does not appear in its lexicon at all.

To accommodate large data bases it would be unfair to assume that all alphabetic data base values could be stored in the front end. Thus, those attributes with few distinct alphabetic values have a list of all these values stored in the front end, and such attributes are called <u>cataloged</u> <u>attributes</u>. The remaining alphabetic-valued attributes have only their most frequently used values stored in the front end, and are called <u>cached</u> <u>attributes</u>. The word WHITNEY is an example of a non-cached value of the cached attribute SNAME.

The date 6/10/75 could mean June 10 (American style) or 6 October (European style). The at least 7-fold ambiguity in WHITNEY SHIPMENTS together with the independent 2-fold ambiguity in the date yield a 14-fold ambiguity in the overall query. By discussing these ambiguities with the user separately from one another, the analyzer keeps their resolution down to an additive, rather than a multiplicative, scale.

The interaction S006-U006 illustrates association dialog, which is applied by the analyzer to each unfamiliar word after it has unsuccessfully tried to induce its semantic category from context and from

simple questions to the user (such as S005). The attributes (and
associated relation names) listed as options in S006 are those having
values which consist of letters only (no digits).

Two restatements in English are offered to the user, because of the
system's inability in this query to precisely determine the focus of the
COUNT request. These restatements represent two logically distinct
queries.

Example D (refer to preceding page) illustrates the kind of dialog
that arises when a user's query involves a false presupposition about the
value of an attribute (project location JLOC) that happens to be cataloged
(i.e., all of its distinct values are recorded in the lexicon). In the
NOTE immediately prior to S003, the system not only tells the user that
his presupposition is wrong, but provides some positive guidance to enable
him to correct his query (which he immediately proceeds to do).
Incidentally, this NOTE is computed by the system from the knowledge base,
using an algorithm that is independent of the domain of discourse. Other
notes and questions from the analyzer are similarly synthesized -- and
this is, of course, is extremely important in making it possible to adapt
this system to support very different data bases.

In the note immediately preceding S009, the system provides two
rephrasings of the user's query that are logically equivalent, but not
psychologically equivalent. To see the difference, note that 1 focuses on
suppliers as the principal object, while 2 focuses on shipments; then
consider the referent of THEM if the user were to say LIST THEM.
Whichever option is selected (1 or 2), the same DEDUCE query is
interpreted by the RETRIEVER. The generator of Version 1 provides
multiple paraphrases that are logically equivalent whenever the query is
of the EXIST type and two or more distinct relations are involved. If
only one paraphrase were emitted in such cases, a casual user might have

one of the other paraphrases in mind as his intended query, not realize
the logical equivalence of the two, and mistakenly reject the system's
paraphrase.

Departing from the examples A through D, we now describe the system's
behavior in two important special cases. An interesting situation arises
when the menu driver receives no information at all from the analyzer, and
this can happen, but should be a very rare event. In such a case, the
menu driver first determines the type of query the user has in mind. It
then seeks the principal topics of the query. The sample data base has so
few topics that they can be directly identified with the four base
relations. In a data base with more topics, it might be necessary to use
two or more steps of interrogation to find out which base relations are
involved. In any event the menu driver does not assume that the user's
response is complete. For each base relation, the menu driver probes
depth-first which attributes are relevant and what values and comparators,
if any, are to be associated with these attributes.

When a user learns that the data base contains information about a
certain topic (e.g., projects), he may incorrectly guess that the data
base contains information about a closely related topic (e.g., managership
of projects). The user may then enter a query that is outside the domain
of discourse supported by the data base (e.g., WHO ARE THE MANAGERS OF
MONTEREY PROJECTS?). Such a query is said to contain a <u>semantic</u>
<u>overshoot</u>. The analyzer can handle some of the more frequently occurring
semantic overshoots. To do this, its knowledge base has to be broader in
coverage than the data base.

In such a case the system first informs the user that it does not have
information on the unsupported topic. It then invokes the HELP component
(without the user pressing the HELP button) and thus offers the user (in
S002) a variety of options for his subsequent interaction.

3.4. Summary of Types of Dialog

Version 1 of the RENDEZVOUS system supports six major types of dialog:

1) clarification dialog from the analyzer

     spelling and typographical errors

     ambiguity

     inconsistency with catalog

     omitted detail

     fuzzy value

     association with catalog

     semantic overshoot

2) menu-driven dialog from the menu driver

     query type

     focus

     relation

     attribute

     value

     comparator

3) verification dialog from the generator

     single rephrasing

     multiple rephrasing

4) editing dialog from the editor

     insertion

     deletion

     replacement

5) output dialog from the retriever

     how much to be output if answer is voluminous

     need for listing if count or exist query

     emptiness reason

6) continuation dialog from the analyzer

     target ellipsis

     qualification ellipsis

4. EXPERIMENTAL OBSERVATIONS

The informal experiments with RENDEZVOUS involved giving subjects a
sequence of simple problems to solve (see APPENDIX). Each subject
mentally translated each problem into one or more queries or query
fragments expressed in English of his choosing, and entered them into
RENDEZVOUS. The subject was encouraged to comment on the system's
behavior. As of August 1977 more than 30 such experiments had been
performed.

4.1. Start of Session

Prior to their sessions most of the subjects were not familiar with
the data base. However, we found that a superficial, one-screen tutorial
on its contents was enough to get them started on the problems. Most
subjects, but not all, seemed to prefer this short introduction and the
subsequent exposure to additional information as they formulated their
queries, rather than try to absorb a lengthy and detailed tutorial first.
An important factor in the user's confidence in forging ahead is the
availability via the HELP button of various kinds of help (outlined to the
user immediately after sign-on).

4.2. User Errors in English Query Input

The four most common types of error in the English queries entered by
subjects were: 1) typographical; 2) omission of items from the query
altogether; 3) inserting items in the target list that should have been in
the qualification; and 4) inserting items in the qualification that should
have been in the target list. Failing to enter a blank between
consecutive words accounted for a significant number of the typographical
errors. The spelling corrector usually caught these: for example, it
asked: IS GREATERTHAN INTENDED TO BE GREATER THAN? While the spelling and

typographical errors were often due to carelessness, the other types of errors appeared to be due to conceptual difficulties. The more complicated the query the more likely such errors were to occur. Surprisingly however, two subjects independently made an error of type 3) with a single relation, single condition-clause query, and both subjects did not realize the error until it was clearly revealed by the column headings displayed with the retrieved data. Note, however, that output column headings provide no protection against erroneous values or comparators in the qualification part of a query.

4.3. User Errors in Answering System Questions

There appeared to be four common causes for the user giving incorrect responses to system questions: 1) carelessness in reading the displayed question; 2) genuine misunderstanding of the question; 3) accidental error in entering a correctly conceived response; 4) anticipating the next question and answering it instead of the present one.

A small minority of users accounted for the errors of type 1), and we can only assume that their attention was somehow distracted. Some of the type 2) misunderstandings were due to the confusion between target list and qualification as mentioned in a different context in Section 4.2, while others were due to a confusion between instance and type (does part serial number identify an individual part or a type of part?).

When a subject made an error of type 3) and the system was unable to detect it, the subject often discovered it for himself one or two interactions later, and wanted to change his previous response. For this purpose the Version 1 HELP component should have supported (but did not) an additional option to go back to a previous response, change it, and resume query formulation activity from that point. Subjects often temporarily dug themselves into deeper trouble whether they were trying to

recover from a known blunder or trying to press on after unwittingly
misleading the system. The paraphrase generated by the system from the
combination of the user's English query input and all his subsequent
responses to system questioning almost always put a halt to the 'digging
in deeper' effect.

Although scrolling was provided to enable users to look back at their
past interactions with the system, it was not used extensively in the
experiments. When it was used, subjects tended to scroll back at most one
screen (i.e., one history viewport full of information).

4.4. User Misunderstandings of System's Paraphrase

In the tests conducted so far there have been very few cases of
misunderstanding of the system's paraphrase. The first subject to try the
integrated system misinterpreted the paraphrase PRINT THE NAME OF EVERY
SUPPLIER as referring to every supplier in Los Angeles. Her stated reason
was that earlier in the dialog the system had mentioned LOS ANGELES in a
question to her, and she thought that context had been retained thereafter
in the dialog. After the following two steps were taken, this kind of
error did not recur (although there is no way to guarantee it will never
recur):

1) the advice displayed at sign-on time was expanded to include the
   warning

   BE VERY CAREFUL NOT TO ACCEPT THE SYSTEM'S VERSION OF YOUR QUERY
   UNLESS YOU ARE REALLY SATISFIED THAT IT CAPTURES YOUR INTENT
   EXPLICITLY -- YOUR WHOLE INTENT AND NOTHING BUT YOUR INTENT;

2) the generator was modified slightly to add the phrase IN THE ENTIRE
   DATA BASE whenever the formal query is of the FIND type and has no
   qualification (i.e., has a target list only).

Testing prior to system integration showed that the paraphrase FIND
THE SERIAL NUMBERS OF PARTS WITH A QUANTITY ON HAND OF 50 could be
reasonably interpreted as meaning 50 or more, although the formal query

specified equality only. The generator was accordingly modified to output the phrase EXACTLY <integer> whenever the pertinent attribute is integer-valued and the comparator is equality. A similar change should have been made in the generator for every string-valued attribute whose set of values is naturally ordered (the only such attribute in the sample data base is supplier rating).

4.5. Getting Lost in a Maze of Menus

Prior to system integration some components were hooked up in pairs for testing purposes. One such hook-up was of the menu driver and generator (this was before the menu driver was equipped with its present feedback features). When using the menu driver without the analyzer, the subject is burdened with a long and tedious interrogation, and in these circumstances it is easy for him to lose track of what information he has supplied to the system. Accordingly, he feels uneasy about 1) how much the system knows and 2) where it is leading him. To overcome the first of these two difficulties we added to the query viewport a summary of all the information gleaned by the system through menu-driven interrogation. More needs to be done about the second problem.

The length and tedium of menu-driven interrogation can be cut down by allowing the user to employ more sophisticated responses than the mere selection of prescribed options by number. Although Version 1 does allow this to some degree, Version 2 must allow the user even more scope.

ACKNOWLEDGMENT

The two permanent staff members who worked with the author on Version 1 were J-M. Cadiou, whose principal contribution was the generator, and C. L. Chang, whose principal contributions were the menu driver, the missing join algorithm, and the DEDUCE language. Others associated with the Version 1 project on a temporary basis were N. Roussopolous and R. S. Arnold (both of the University of Texas), whose principal contributions were the retriever and the display support; and D. V. Ribbens (University of Liege, Belgium), who developed an interface package to link the analyzer with the menu driver. L. A. Zadeh (U.C. Berkeley) provided consulting help.

REFERENCES

1. E. F. Codd, "Seven Steps to Rendezvous with the Casual User", Proc. IFIP TC-2 Working Conference on Data Base Management Systems, Cargese, Corsica, April 1-5, 1974, in J. W. Klimbie and K. I. Koffeman (eds.), "Data Base Management", North-Holland 1974.
2. E. F. Codd, R. S. Arnold, J-M. Cadiou, C. L. Chang, N. Roussopoulos, "RENDEZVOUS Version 1: An Experimental English-Language Query Formulation System for Casual Users of Relational Data Bases", IBM Research Report RJ2144, San Jose, California, January 26, 1978.
3. C. L. Chang, "DEDUCE -- A Deductive Query Language for Relational Data Bases", in C. H. Chen (ed.), "Pattern Recognition and Artificial Intelligence", Academic Press, New York 1976.
4. C. L. Chang, "Finding Missing Joins for Incomplete Queries on Relational Data Bases", IBM Research Report RJ2145, San Jose, California, February 21, 1978.
5. D. L. Waltz, "An English Language Question Answering System for a Large Relational Data Base", to be published in Comm. ACM 1978.
6. G. G. Hendrix, "The LIFER Manual", Technical Note 138, Stanford Research Institute, Menlo Park, Calif., 1977.
7. J. Mylopoulos, A. Borgida, P. Cohen, N. Roussopoulos, J. Tsotsos, H. Wong, "TORUS: A Step towards Bridging the Gap between Data Bases and the Casual User", Information Systems, vol 2, no 2, pp 71-77, 1976.
8. J. F. Burger, A. Leal, A. Shoshani, "Semantic Based Parsing and a Natural Language Interface for Interactive Data Management", Proc. 13th Annual Meeting of the Association for Computer Linguistics, Boston, Oct-Nov 1975.
9. R. Simmons, J. Slocum, "Generating English Discourse from Semantic Networks", Comm. ACM, vol 15, no 10, October 1972, pp 891-905.
10. J. Slocum, "Speech Generation from Semantic Nets", Proc. 13th Annual Meeting of the Association for Computational Linguistics, Boston, Massachusetts, October 30 - November 1, 1975.
11. N. Goldman, "Computer Generation of Natural Language from a Deep Conceptual Base", A.I.Memo 247, Artificial Intelligence Laboratory, Stanford University, January 1974.

12. A. Herskovits, "The Generation of French from a Semantic
    Representation", A.I.Memo 212, Artificial Intelligence Laboratory,
    Stanford University, August 1973.
13. G. Heidorn, "Natural Language Inputs to a Simulation Programming
    System," Technical Report NPS-55HD72101A, Naval Postgraduate School,
    Monterey, California, October 1972.

APPENDIX: Problems used in Experiments

The following problems were the principal ones used in experiments
with RENDEZVOUS Version 1. The subjects were explicitly encouraged to use
their own words and phrasing, and they did. For each problem different
subjects adopted widely different modes of expression when they entered
queries into the system. This was in part due to the intentionally
verbose style in which the problems were expressed.

1. A State Senator wants the State of California to make as much use as
    possible of suppliers in Los Angeles. He has requested a list of the
    names of all such suppliers we have on record. Obtain this list from
    the system.
2. Our inventory is getting too large and the trouble appears to be due
    to those parts for which the quantity on hand is larger than 50.
    Obtain the serial numbers and quantities on order for these parts.
3. Get information on each shipment of pipes made before June 1976. The
    specific information needed is the part serial number, the project
    serial number, the date shipped, and the quantity shipped.
4. A colleague claims that pumps were shipped to only one city during
    February 1976. To which projects and which cities were pumps actually
    sent in this month?
5. By separately finding the number of suppliers rated fair (or even
    worse than that) and the number of projects in San Diego, determine
    whether there are more of one than the other.
6. It is said that there are very few suppliers with an excellent rating
    in Detroit. Just how many are there?
7. How many parts are there in the following state: the quantity on hand
    is less than 10 and the quantity on order is less than 25?
8. The auditors are trying to determine whether there is any case on
    record of a shipment originating in San Jose involving a quantity
    shipped in excess of 100. Use the system to obtain this information.

DATABASES: IMPROVING USABILITY AND RESPONSIVENESS

DESIGN ASPECTS OF THE
QUERY-BY-EXAMPLE DATA BASE MANAGEMENT LANGUAGE

Moshé M. Zloof

IBM T.J. Watson Research Center
Yorktown Heights, NY

Since the introduction of the relational model in 1970, various high level data base languages have been introduced to support this model. Many have gone through extensive behavioral tests with encouraging results, showing that non-programmers can indeed learn and use them with relatively short periods of instruction time.

One such language is Query-By-Example: a data base language which has been implemented and put in actual use for varied applications. Initial feedback from non-programmer users reinforces the results of the behavioral test.

In this paper we give our reasons for believing that Query-By-Example is easy to use, and point out some general considerations in designing a data base language.

I. INTRODUCTION

As information systems get more complex, there is need for adequate formal data base models and formal languages to support these models. Though originally successfuly, 'record-at-a-time' technology is no longer sufficient for all users, and the need to perform complex operations on the data base becomes essential. Furthermore, as computers get cheaper and more available, more small businesses are automating their manual data base operations, and one can predict that computers will soon infiltrate such domains of our lives as office, school, and home. Therefore, in order to address the non-programmer community, high level, flexible, user-friendly languages are becoming an important requirement. Recently, many such languages have emerged; they range from informal natural English and formal structured English to formal two-dimensional and formal graphical language.

One such language is Query-By-Example (1,2,3,4,5,6) which, provides the user with facilities to query, update, define and control the data base. Various psychological tests conducted on the initial language (7) have shown that it required less than 3 hours of instruction for non-programmers to be able to pose fairly complicated queries, but these queries normally required the user to know first order predicate calculus. Later, the language was implemented (8) and is currently being used (in our labatories) by non-programmers for a wide variety of applications--including expense accounts, budgeting, and accounting.

In this paper, we first briefly classify the community of potential users of a data base language and try to correlate various languages with the different classes of users; second, we classify various existing relational languages, with emphasis on what (we think) constitutes a good set of design requirements to achieve a user friendly language; finally, we will show to what extent

Query-By-Example satisfies those requirements.

II. THE RELATIONAL MODEL

The introduction of the relational model (9,10) in the early 1970's triggered the design of powerful yet easy to use relational languages. We believe this to be due to the fact that the basic data type of this model (a 'relation') can easily be mapped into the user's mental frame. In addition, this model contains such well-known, important features as:

1. A high degree of data independence;

2. It operates on one set (relation) at a time rather than on one record at a time;

3. It provides an environment in which it is easy to create and modify the data base; and

4. It allows the user dynamically to embed integrity and authority statements (independent of the underlying structure of the data base) in the system.

However, although our subsequent discussions primarily address relational languages, many of the same arguments can address other languages supporting hierarchical, network and other models.

III. LANGUAGE AND USER CATEGORIZATION

In this section we attempt to show that there is no <u>one</u> language which satisfies the need of the entire spectrum of potential users, but rather classes of languages suitable to classes of users. We start by dividing the potential user community into three fuzzy categories:

1. Casual users;

2. Non-programmer professionals;

3. Application programmers.

The "casual user" according to Codd's definition (11) is

"one whose interactions with the system are irregular in time and not motivated by his job or social role. Such a user cannot be expected to be knowledgeable about computers, programming, logic or relations".

A non-programmer professional, on the other hand, is a person motivated by the job and familiar with the particular application. One can expect such a user to learn an easy-to-use formal language and be familiar with the concepts normally required by a relational model. In this category one can include secretaries, clerks, engineers, analysts, etc.

The third category refers to the well-known conventional computer application programmer, who is familiar with one or several programming languages.

To address the class of casual users, Codd and others justifiably argue that

"the only way to entice such a user to interact with a computerized data base is to permit him free use of his native tongue".

To achieve this rather ambitious goal, Codd proposed the RENDEZVOUS System, which has seven steps, including the selection of a high level logic internal target, clarification dialogue, and restatement of user's query. (See Codd's paper, this conference.)

The question now arises: If very powerful natural language interface systems, such as RENDEZVOUS, will eventually evolve, are formal and easy-to-use languages necessary, or are they necessary only for the interim, until the natural language systems becomes an operational reality? The answer to this question, in our opinion, is that formal high level languages will always be required. We give the following reasons to support our view:

1. A casual user (by definition) is a user who does not have the knowledge of the structure of the underlying data base model. Thus the casual user can, at most, query the data base, and perhaps perform simple modification operations, but such a user certainly cannot define relations, views, integrity and authority constraints, system catalogs, reports, etc.

2. A formal high level language will always be required as an intermediate step which is used to restate the query into a formal statement and to clarify the user's intent.

3. Formal high level languages address a different class of users, namely the category of the special professional and programmer professional, who is

prepared to devote some time to learning a formal language, thus saving many unnecessary interactions with the computer.

4.   A high level data base language can be embedded into a host classical programming language (such as PL/1 or COBOL), or it can be extended to cover application programs (as in the case of the SBA--System for Business Automation [12,13]--a superset of Query-By-Example).

We conclude that although natural languages are most suitable for casual users, formal high level languages are suitable for the non-programmer professional, and they serve as an aid to the professional programmer by the possibility of embedding them into classical programming language.

IV. FORMAL HIGH LEVEL LANGUAGES

Having established that formal high level languages are a necessity, regardless of whether or not natural languages are successfully implemented, let us now classify them into various categories. Essentially there are two major classes of relational languages:

1.   Relational algebra-based languages; and

2.   Relational calculus-based languages.

Sub-classifications of the above are:

A.   Linear;

B.   Two-dimensional;

C.   Graphical.

Examples of some existing languages, most of which are partially implemented and partially in use are:

PRTV (14)--linear, based on relational algebra;

ALPHA (15)--linear, based on relational caculus;

SQL2 SQUARE   (16,17)--linear, based on a   mixture of
        relational calculus and algebra;

QUEL (18)--linear, based on relational calculus;

Query-By-Example (1-6)--linear and two-dimensional based on
        relational calculus;

Cupid (19)--Graphical, based on relational algebra; and

FORAL (20)--Graphical, based on the binary relation model.

A.   Relational Algebra vs.

Relational Calculus Languages

Although both classes of languages are considered to be high level (in the sense that both operate on sets of records rather than a record at a time, thus eliminating DO-loops), the relational algebra languages are still procedural in nature, because the user must specify a sequence of algebraic operations resulting in various intermediate temporary relations.

One may be seduced into assuming that by specifying a sequence of algebraic operations, the user has a better control of the way a transaction is processed, resulting in a better performance than the relational calculus approach.

Unfortunately, this is not generally the case. Two reasons account for this: first, the user's specified sequence of operations may not generally be the optimal sequence, thus a special optimizer will be required to map a user specified sequence into a more optimal one (indeed, sometimes the order is data dependent and depends on the numbers in the query rather than the form); second, and more important, it has been shown (8,21) that processing a transaction that follows the relational algebra operations (i.e., creating intermediate temporary relations along the way), can sometimes be very inefficient and require substantial storage space, since intermediate temporary relations may be an order of magnitude larger than the source and target relations.

B.   User-Friendly and Ease-of-Use

It is only recently, when the use of computers has infiltrated the non-programmer community, that the words "ease of use", "user friendly" and "human factors" were added to the lexicon of computer sciences terminology. The reasons these considerations did not receive earlier attention are twofold: first the use of computers was limited to the professional programmers; and second, since computers were relatively expensive, slow, and limited in memory and other storage devices, language designers were (maybe justifiably) mainly concerned with performance and implementation considerations. Today, on the other hand, the ease of use aspect of the language is receiving attention, because a non-programmer user must find it easy to learn and use, or it will be neglected, no matter how fast, efficient, and powerful the system is.

The question now arises: what is ease-of-use and how can one define and quantify it? Ease-of-use and user-friendly are fuzzy variables--far from being rigorously defined. While it is relatively easy, for example, to measure and compare the speed of two machines, it is quite difficult to define ease-of-use, or say that one language is twice as user-friendly as another; the terms are subjective and depend on the user's taste, background, environment, training, etc. Recently (7,22,23) researchers have tried to measure different languages in terms of average time required to formulate a set of queries, percentage of correct queries, confidence ratings, classification of errors, etc.

Since Query-By-Example was found to be highly user-friendly (7), and because it is being accepted by the non-programmer community, we shall try to give our considerations when designing a language.

C. Language Design Considerations

We first provide a set of human factor considerations that we found important in designing any language. These resulted partly from psychological studies and partly due to feedback from the user community. In our opinion, the extent to which a language satisfies these requirements will determine the degree of user-friendliness of that language.

1. Minimum concepts required to get started:

   A non-programmer cannot be expected to become familiar with a thick user manual in order to start using the language. Thus for simple operations the user should need to learn very little.

2. Minimum syntax:

   The language syntax must be simple and yet cover a variety of complex transactions. It is assumed that a user will not necessarily use the system continuously and if the language syntax and constructs are not straightforward, may not be able to retain its concepts for long.

3. Consistency:

   The language operators must be consistent throughout the various phrase structures. Operators must not change semantics in different contexts.

4. Flexibility:

   A high level language must have the flexibility to capture the user's thought process, thus providing many degrees of freedom in formulating a transaction.

5. Not sensitive:

   A small change in the query (such as adding another condition) should result in only a small change in the query language expression: it must not require the rewriting of the query with a new and different structure.

6. Easy to extend and modify:

   Dynamic modification of the data base by means of creating views and snapshots at any point in time provide the user with flexibility in reorganizing the data base.

7. Minimum exception rules:

   Too many exceptions to the rules imply bad language design and will require the user to be quite familiar with these rules (with longer training time).

8. Easy detection of errors:

   The language syntax and phrase structure should be such that they minimize the possibility of an error; if, on the other hand, the user formulates an erroneous transaction, a simple and clear error message should be given by the system.

9. Unified language:

   To minimize syntax change for new concepts, the same query syntax should be used for modification, definition, and control of the data base.

V.   DESIGN ASPECTS OF QUERY-BY-EXAMPLE

Here we hope to show how the novel two-dimensional programming approach of Query-By-Example covers the design

requirements just given in the previous section. At this
point, we shall assume that the reader is familiar with most
aspects of the Query-By-Example language (1-6). For
example, we shall adopt a sample data base consisting of the
following two tables:

> EMP (NAME, SAL, MGR, DEPT) and

> SALES (DEPT, ITEM, QUANT)

A. The Query-By-Example Two-Dimensional Approach

Early high-level languages were linear string type
languages, with limited power. Non-programmers could cope
with them relatively easily since they address a class of
very simple queries such as

GET NAMES SUCH THAT SAL IS GREATER THAN 10000

After the introduction of the relational model, more
powerful languages emerged. In fact most of the languages
listed in Section IV were shown to be at least relationally
complete, i.e., they support all the relational algebra
operators, or their equivalents. However, to be able to
express powerful operations, a non-programmer was required
to be familiar with mathematical concepts such as
existensial and universal qualtifiers, set theory and set
operations such as UNION, INTERSECTION, JOIN, CONJUNCTION,
DISJUNCTION, PROJECTION, etc.

Since we started with the premise that we want to appeal to a class of users who should not need to cope with these mathematical concepts, it is necessary (as far as possible) to hide these concepts "under the covers" without reducing the expressive power of the language; this is how Query-By-Example came about.

By "programming" within two-dimensional skeletons of tables, using the simple concept of 'Example Element' (variable), 'Constant Element' and the operator P. (standing for "print"), the user can formulate complicated transactions covering the equivalent of all relational algebra operators without needing to be familiar with set, relational calculus and other mathematical concepts. We now give examples of queries, mofidications, creation, and control of the data base in order to elaborate on the unique features of the Query-By-Example approach.

VI.   QUERIES

Consider the query: Find the names and salaries of all the employees who earn more than 10000 and work in the TOY Department. This query will be expressed in Query-By-Example as follows:

EMP	NAME	SAL	MGR	DEPT
	P.	P.>10000		TOY

In relational algebra, this query is equivalent to SELECTION
on DEPT and SALES and PROJECTION on NAME and SAL. As a
second example, we take a more complicated query: List the
names and salaries of all the employees who earn more than
LEWIS and work in a department that sells more than 5 pens
and less than 6 pencils. The formulation of this query
requires both relations, and is as follows:

EMP	NAME	SAL	MGR	DEPT
	P.	P.>S1		D1
	LEWIS	S1		

SALES	DEPT	ITEM	QUANT
	D1	PEN	>5
	D1	PENCIL	<6

In this example, S1, D1 are variables--'Example Elements'.
In relational algebra, this query would require SELECTION,
JOIN, INTERSECTION, CONJUNCTION and PROJECTION operators.

If the user wishes to obtain an output consisting of
data collected from several base tables (tables containing
the actual data), he maps example elements from these base
tables to a new user created output table. For example, the
construction of an output table containing the names and
departments of each employee with the corresponding items
sold by these departments is achieved by the following
formulation:

EMP	NAME	SAL	MGR	DEPT
	N			D

SALES	DEPT	ITEM	QUANT.
	D	I	

NAME	DEPT	ITEM
P.N	P.D	P.I

Example elements N, D, I are mapped from the original base tables EMP, SALES to a newly created output; i.e., the user constructs the output in the manner he wishes to see it presented. An example of how a query is actually formulated through the system with its answer set is found in the Appendix. For further examples of queries see (1).

Let us now briefly elaborate on what is achieved by this approach in contrast to conventional linear string languages.

1. The Query-By-Example fundamental object: a relational skeleton, nicely corresponds to the model objects of base relation, thus capturing the simplicity and symmetry of the relational model (seen by the user as tables).

2. The syntax is kept at a minimum, because by entering constants and variables in skeletons, the user saves:

   (a) unnecessary qualifications of every entry (such as EMP DEPT = TOY),

   (b) having to remember various phrase constructs, and

   (c) unnecessary additional syntax such as parenthesis,

colons, commas, etc.

3.   Most of the mathematical concepts are hidden from the user. For example, entering a variable $\underline{X}$ under the DEPT column implies $\exists \underline{X} \in$ DEPT; and entering two constants (or variables) in the same row implies a conjunction.

4.   The user enjoys the flexibility of formulating a query in any sequence desired, thus easily capturing the thought process.

5.   The use of linking example elements enables the user to decouple the thought process in much the same way that he would in order to express a couple of algebraic equations with several unknonws, each formulated separately with common variables associating them.

6.   Exception rules are kept at a minimum, because the user is free to specify any entry under any column and in any row as long as it conforms to the local syntax.

7.   Syntactical errors are kept at a minimum because the syntax is minimal. Further, if an error does occur, the system can detect the spatial location of that error i.e., in what table, what column, and what row the error occurs, keeping error messages simpler than those in conventional language.

VII. MODIFICATIONS, DEFINITION AND CONTROL

Like other languages, Query-By-Example started as a

query language, but evolved to a complete data base management language with facilities to create, modify, and control the data base. In order to keep these operations as easy to express as the query operations themselves, an attempt has been made to continue using the same syntax and semantics used for queries to accomplish these operations.

A. Modifications

To modify the data base only three essential operators are introduced: I., D., and U. (standing for "Insert", "Delete", and "Update", respectively). With the same query syntax and the above three operators, the user can express complicated modifications against the data base. For example, deleting Jones's tuple from a table is accomplished by entering D. against that tuple as follows:

EMP	NAME	SAL	MGR	DEPT
D.	JONES			

Here it is assumed that the NAME column is a key, the entry JONES therefore uniquely identifies the tuple to be deleted.

Updating a group of tuples is achieved by means of a query expression. For example, if we wish to replace manager ADAMS by LEWIS in all relevent employee files, we state:

EMP	NAME	SAL	MGR	DEPT
<u>N</u>			ADAMS	
<u>N</u>			U. LEWIS	

This is termed a 'query depedent update', since the system has first to query the data base to find all the employees under the manager named Adams and then update to the manager named Lewis.

The point to be made here is that with the introduction of very little syntax the user has the query expressive power to modify the data base. Furthermore, since an output of a query is itself a relation (which in turn is a language object), the user can directly edit that output by plaing D., I., or U. against the tuples to be modified. In contrast, when using a linear language to edit an output relation, the user must identify the tuples to be modified and then write new linear programs to accomplish these modifications.

B.   Table Creation

To interactively create tables, the user mimics the way he would create tables manually, that is to say starting from a blank skeleton of a table, inserting the table name and the column headings. Here, however, the user must use system row key words such as TYPE, KEY, DOMAIN, etc. to

complete the definition of a table. The definition of the
EMP table, for example, will be done as follows:

I.EMP	I.	NAME	SAL	MGR	DEPT
TYPE	I.	CHAR	NUM	CHAR	CHAR
KEY	I.	K			
DOMAIN	I.	NAMES	MONEY	NAMES	DEPTS
–		–	–	–	–
–		–	–	–	–
–		–	–	–	–

Note that placing I. against the entire row is a shorthand
notation for prefixing every entry of that row with I.

After a table is created, the user has the ability to
update any of the definition specifications in the same
manner a tuple is updated. In addition to new base tables,
the user can create 'snapshot's and 'view's which are tables
whose data are mapped from already existing ones (1).

C. Control

To control the data base (the ability to state various
integrity and authority constraints), the same query
expressions are used with the additional two row keywords,
CONSTR. for integrity constraints and AUTR. for authority
constraints. For example, if we wish to bind the salaries
of all employees who work in a department selling pens, to

less than $100,000, we state it as follows:

EMP	NAME	SAL	MGR	DEPT
CONSTR.		<100000		<u>D1</u>

SALES	DEPT	ITEM	QUANT
	<u>D1</u>	PEN	

Again, the entire query expressive power is available for stating complex constraints statements.

Authority delegations are expressed in the same style. For example, if the creator (owner) of the EMP table wishes to delegate READ authority on a subset (tuples of the TOY department only) of that table to a specific user, say Henry, it will be expressed as follows:

EMP	NAME	SAL	MGR	DEPT
AUTR(P.)HENRY	<u>N</u>	<u>S</u>	<u>M</u>	TOY

The P. in the parenthesis specifies the authority level. (P., D.) will mean authority to read and delete, but not update and insert. More on authority and integrity in (6).

VIII. THE QUERY-BY-EXAMPLE SYSTEM

Query-by-Example which is a subset of the System for Business Automation (12, 13) was built by an IBM Research

group at Yorktown   (cited in the Acknowledgments)   under the
management of Peter deJong.

Due   to   user's   feedback,   certain   reordering   of   the
implementation priorities took place.   In addition, several
new facilities have been added to the language by the group.
One such   feature is the   introduction of the   "Command Box"
object.   Via the command box a user is able to:

1.   Get a hard copy output of a query or a transaction;

2.   Map a query expression or an output into a CMS file;

3.   Store and retrieve a query   or partial query (by naming
      it   and using   the   I. and   P.   commands   to store   and
      retrieve it); and

4.   Accomplish   the   execution   of   batched   and   nested
      queries.

The system   also contains   various catalogs   summarizing
the table names and their attributes, domains, table owners,
authority delegations, etc.

                    A.   Error Messages

The   Query-by-Example system   provides the   user with   a
variety of error messages.   Essentially   there are 3 classes
of such messages.

1.   Messages   detecting   syntactical   errors: since   the
      expressions are entered in   table skeletons, the system
      can   detect the   spatial location   of an   error and   an
      appropriate message   indicating the   table,   column, and

row of the error occurrence.

2. Messages detecting integrity violations: as an example, if one inserts a tuple whose key already exists or if one enters a character string in a defined numeric field, an appropriate message will follow.

3. Warning messages in cases where an expression or part of an expression is redundant are also provided by the system.

B. Experience with Users

In the past two years, several courses on Query-by-Example were offered at T. J. Watson Research Lab. A typical course consisted of four sessions of instruction time.

In the first session, the screen management facilities were introduced. The new users were taught how to get a skeleton; add columns and lines; erase columns and tables; scroll in four directions; etc. Then simple table selections were shown and exercised.

In the second session the concept of the Example Element was introduced, first by asking the subjects to retrieve the information manually and then by teaching the Example Element concept and exercising it on various queries.

Some subjects (on the average of 20 percent) found this concept difficult to grasp and usually an additional session on the topic was required. It should be noted that subjects who had difficulties linking general data bases did much better when presented with a data base that they were familiar with (i.e. a data base that they ordinarily manipulate manually).

The third session dealt with negations and aggregate operators such as COUNT, SUM, AVERAGE, etc. This was the other area in which the new users took longer to understand and use correctly.

In the fourth session, modification of the data base was taught. The subjects had little problem here, since the concepts are similar to querying the data base.

Currently (as of April 1976), the floor system has neither the facilities for interactive definition of the data base nor the facilities for expressing integrity or authority constraints. In keeping pace with the floor system, future courses will include session to cover these features.

Unfortunately, formal statistics on subject performance are not available at this point in time. However, the fact that the students who took these courses are using Query-by-Example to run their applications is a most encouraging result in itself.

ACKNOWLEDGMENTS

I am most grateful to Peter deJong, the manager of the SBA project, for introducing me to the area of relational data bases and helping me throughout the development of this work. I am also grateful to Peter deJong, Ken Niebuhr, Roy Byrd and Steve Smith for building the system and for introducing many features without which the system would not have been as flexible, rich in functions, and easy to use.

REFERENCES

1. M. M. Zloof, "Query-by-Example: a data base language", IBM Systems Journal, Vol. 16, No. 4, 1977.

2. M. M. Zloof, "Query by Example", AFIPS Conference Proceedings, National Computer Conference, 44, 431-438 (1975).

3. M. M. Zloof, "Query by Example, The Invocation and Definition of Tables and Forms", Proceedings of the International Conference on Very Large Data Bases, Boston, Massachusetts, September 22-24, 1975, pp. 1-24.

4. M. M. Zloof, Query-by-Example: Operations on the Transitive Closure, Research Report RC 5526, IBM Thomas J. Watson Research Center, Yorktown Heights, New York, 1975.

5. M. M. Zloof, "Query-by-Example: Operation on Hierarchical Data Bases", AFIPS Conference Proceedings, National Computer Conference 45, 845-853, (1976).

6. M. M. Zloof, Security and Integrity Within the Query-by-Example Data Base Management Language, IBM Research Report RC6982, IBM Thomas J. Watson Research Center, Yorktown Heights, New York, 2/8/78.

7. J. C. Thomas and J. D. Gould, "A Psychological Study of Query by Example", Proceedings of the National Computer Conference 44, 439-445 (1975).

8. K. E. Niebuhr and S. E. Smith, "Implementation of Query-by-Example on VM/370", Research Report, IBM Thomas J. Watson Research Center, Yorktown Heights, New York, in preparation.

9. E. F. Codd, "A Relational Model of Data for Large Shared Data Banks", Communications of the ACM Vol. 13, No. 6, 377-387 (1970).

10. E. F. Codd, "Further Normalization of the Data Base Relational Model", Courant Computer Science SymposiaVol. 6, Data Base Systems, Prentice-hall, Inc., New York, NY (1971).

11. "Seven Steps to Rendevous with the Casual Users", Research Report RJ 1333, IBM Thomas J. Watson Research Center, Yorktown Heights, New York, January 1974.

12. M. M. Zloof and S. P. deJong, "The system for business automation (SBA): Programming Language", Communications of the ACM Vol. 20, No. 6, 385-396 (1977).

13. S. P. deJong, M. M. Zloof, "Communication Within the System for Business Automation (SBA)", Research Report RC 6788, IBM Thomas J. Watson Research Center, Yorktown Heights, New York.

14. S. J. Todd, "The Peterlee Relational Test Vehicle--A System Overview", IBM Systems Journal, No. 4 (1976).

15. E. F. Codd, "A Data Base Sublanguage Founded on the Relational Calculus", Proceedings 1971 ACM SIGFIDET Workshop available from ACM.

16. D. D. Chamberlin, et al., "SEQUEL 2: A Unified Approach to Data Definition Manipulation and Control", IBM Journal of R&D, Vol. 20, No. 6 (1976).

17. R. F. Boyce, et al., "Specifying Queries as Relational Expressions: SQUARE", ACM SIGPLAN/SIGIR (November 1973).

18. M. R. Stonebraker, "Getting Started in INGERS--A Tutorial", Berkeley: U. of California, ERL-M518 (April 1975).

19. N. McDonald and M. R. Stonebraker, "CUPID--The Friendly Query Lanauge", Proceedings ACM Pacific Conference, San Francisco (April 1975).

20. M. Senko, "DIAM II with FORAL LP: Making Pointed Queries with Light Pen", Proceedings of the IFIP Congress 77, Toronto, Canada, 1977.

21. P. A. V. Hall, "Optimisation of a Single Relational Expression in a Relational Data Base System", IBM U.K. Scientific Center Report No. UKSC 0076 (June 1975).

22. P. Reisner, et al., "Human Factors Evaluation of Two
     Data Base Languages--SQUARE and SEQUEL", Proceedings
     NCC 44 (May 1975).

23. B. Shneiderman, B., "Improving the Human Factors Aspects
     of Database Interactions", Dept. of Information Systems
     Management, Technical Report No. 28, January 1978.

APPENDIX

In this Appendix, we show how a typical query
actually appears on the screen. Note that since we
cannot underline in the 3270 terminal, quote marks were
used to indicate Example Elements.

The following query, then, reads:

Print out the names and ages of employees over 40 who
work in a department located in Newberg.

QUERY:

EMPS	DEPNUM	NAME	AGE	DEPTNUM	SEX
		P.	P.>40	'D1'	

DEPTS	DEPTNUM	NAME	LOCATION
	'D1'		NEWBERG

Upon executing this query, we get the following output:

EMPS	NAME	AGE
	NIELSON ARNOLD D	47
	AARON HERMAN T	53
	DILL EDWARD C	45
	FISCHER WILLIAM N	47
	HANSON RALPH K	49
	JANSEN NIELS O	56
	SILBER ABRAHAM J	47
	TWIDDLE GILBERT D	46
	UHLE GEORGE S	48
	WALTERS WILLIAM D	48
	DAVIDSON JOHN L	48
	DISTLER MICHAEL H	43
	QUART WILLIS B	53
	DE_WITT HAROLD D	53

14 OUTPUT RECORDS

DATABASES: IMPROVING USABILITY AND RESPONSIVENESS

MINISEQUEL

Relational Data Management System[1]

Nancy D. Anderson[2]
Walter A. Burkhard

Computer Science Division
Department of Applied Physics and
Information Science
University of California at San Diego
La Jolla, California

ABSTRACT

MINISEQUEL is a data base management system that provides the casual user with a high-level relational database system suitable for the truly minicomputer environment. The paper contains an overall description of the system including the relational data system and query language, the data storage system, and the required hardware system environment. The entire system will be implemented in standard PASCAL. The system design centers around interpreter-based portability techniques thus facilitating moves to new environments. Currently, the system is being implemented and the design evaluated.

---

[1]This work supported in part by NOSC contract N66001-77-C-0198 and NCR PO #35.
[2]Present address: Orincon Corporation, 3366 North Torrey Pines Court, La Jolla, California 92037.

1. INTRODUCTION

Data base management systems are created for the benefit of the end user. Codd [1] estimates by the mid 1990s that the home/casual user of data base management systems will be the dominant factor in the total utilization of data base resources. If data base systems are to become everyday tools of non-professionals, the needs and desires of the casual user must be accommodated. The current barriers to meeting the requirements of casual users are (1) the cost of the associated hardware and software and (2) the necessity of skilled applications programmers to act as middlemen.

MINISEQUEL is a relational data base system which is designed to overcome both problems and to provide a useful tool for the potential casual data base system user. It runs within a truly minicomputer environment comprised of a cpu with memory, floppy disk drives, and a crt terminal; this hardware configuration is commercially available for approximately $8,000 [2]. It has been conjectured that individual units may cost as little as $3,000 by the mid 1980s. All data base transactions are conducted in an interactive command-response mode using SEQUEL[3] command statements. MINISEQUEL provides the essential data definition and manipulation capabilities required for a data base management facility.

Another point of interest concerning the implementation of MINISEQUEL is the use of PASCAL[4] throughout. Our system is directed toward the casual user; consequently, we will not require data definition and manipulation extensions to PASCAL such as those of Schmidt [5]. Two attractive benefits ensue from our selection of standard PASCAL as the implementation language: (1) system maintenance tasks can be carried out by technicians within the field and (2) the entire MINISEQUEL system is easily portable.

The paper is divided into four subsequent sections. In Section 2, we discuss the relational data system, including the selection of the

relational data model and the structure of the query/command language.
Section 3 contains a presentation of the data storage system, including the
rudimentary operations and access methods provided. Within Section 4 we
present a description of the P-machine hardware system architecture required to support the MINISEQUEL system. Portability aspects for the entire system are discussed as well. Finally, within Section 5, we review
the overall design and present several general question areas for which we
anticipate collecting empirical data once the MINISEQUEL system is operational.

2. THE RELATIONAL DATABASE SYSTEM

Our choice of a database model was strongly affected by the fact that
data definition would be done by untrained personnel. We felt that, in
terms of the logical view of the data, the relational model was by far the
most comprehensible to the average user. The requirement that all data be
in flat tables, with named field specifiers (column heads), unique keys,
and no multiple-valued field entries, would guarantee first normal form
without causing conceptual difficulty on the part of the user. Unlike
Codasyl DBTG systems, where relationships among data items are explicity
stated via set memberships and, as a result, the data manipulation language
must navigate among the sets, in a relational scheme the data can remain
simple in structure and the complexity can be buried in the access methods
employed by the software, which are invisible to the user. The ability of
relational systems to create new relationships among data items in response
to each new query also results in efficient use of space, as a complex network of links and pointers does not have to be maintained.

2.1 Choice of a Query Language

Having chosen a relational data model, we then chose SEQUEL, a command-
oriented query language developed by IBM for their System R database

management system [3]. We felt that a query language of this type was best
suited for MINISEQUEL, on the grounds that the English-like command structure makes it easy for an untrained user to learn the language. The sharply
limited vocabulary and syntax make it possible to interpret the language
with a relatively short, compact program, but the language is far from
primitive; in fact, its recursive nature permits the building of complex
queries by means of stepwise refinement. In this respect, SEQUEL and PASCAL
are well-matched; PASCAL is a recursive block-structured language and is
therefore well-equipped to interpret a recursive SEQUEL query. SEQUEL is
designed to operate on data in first normal form, so it is technically compatible with the database produced by MINISEQUEL's data definition facility.

The following is an example of a typical SEQUEL query and shows how
recursion is employed to specify the desired data. In this case, the user
wants to know the name and age of all managers under age 35 who manage 5
or more people. He wants the response grouped according to age. Names
and ages are kept in a relation called Employee, and Staff size is kept in
a relation called Department. The link between them is the occupation
field in Employee and the manager field in Department.

> Select Name, Age
>
> From Employee
>
> Where Age ≤ 35 and (Name = Select Manager
>
> > > From Department
> > >
> > > Where Staffsize ≥ 5)
>
> Group by Age

The Group by command is an example of one of the SEQUEL functions the
user can explicitly request to have performed on the data. Others currently implemented are count, average, sum, minimum, maximum, order by,
and unique (elimination of duplicates). These functions can be called
singly or in combination (e.g. count unique), and they can be called as
part of the tuple selection process or as a final operation on tuples

already retrieved by an otherwise completed Select command.

The Select command can stand alone as a data retrieval command or it can function as the retrieval part of an update or deletion command. There are also commands to insert data into a relation, and to create and destroy relations.

Each phase in a SEQUEL query begins with a command word, which aids greatly in interpreting the language and prompting the user. However, considerable imprecision in stating the structure of the relations being accessed is also permitted. Field names do not have to be explicitly paired with relation names or specified in any particular order. Also, the steps in which the query will be processed are often not clearly specified.

In choosing the set of SEQUEL commands to be used in the first implementation of MINISEQUEL, we tried to retain the essential data definition and manipulation features of the language. We also tried to retain SEQUEL's ability to deal with imprecision in the user's specification of the data. The first goal was realized by selecting the more straightforward and important SEQUEL commands; for example, the commands for inserting tuples consisting of new data were implemented because they are essential, but the insertion command which builds and inserts new tuples composed of fields from tuples in existing relations, was rejected as convenient but nonessential.

The second goal was realized by not tampering with the syntax of individual SEQUEL commands in the interest of simplification. Again the insertion command serves as an example; it permits the specification of the fields of a tuple to be inserted to be incomplete and not in the correct order. While a command in this form is time-consuming to interpret, the form was implemented in the interest of retaining SEQUEL's ability to serve the needs of casual and imprecise users. An important result of this approach is the enhancement of MINISEQUEL's portability; since any command that is implemented is implemented fully, a user who had learned SEQUEL elsewhere would have little trouble using this system. SEQUEL capabilities that are not implemented in MINISEQUEL at this time include updates requiring more than integer arithmetic, views, and security and integrity constraints.

2.2   Commands Interpretation

MINISEQUEL initially provides a user with a prompt corresponding to the basic query language constructs: Create, Insert, Select, Update, Delete, and Kill. The user enters one of these 6 (underlined) letters C, I, S, U, D or K to begin the associated command. The Select command is evaluated relative to a parse tree; other commands are evaluated without parse trees. We have implemented an extensive series of error messages to help the user build a syntactically correct command. The evaluation of the command is accomplished by invoking various system procedures; the high level procedures that perform this task are displayed in Figure 1. Details of each of the six commands are briefly discussed in the subsequent paragraphs.

CREATE: This command establishes the relation format as well as the access method. No space is allocated beyond that required for the schema storage.

INSERT: This command inserts single tuples into storage. The FINSRT routine is invoked to construct the record and INSRTUP is called to insert the record. The insert command allows the constituent fields to be specified in any order.

SELECT: This command serves two rudimentary purposes; (1) locate or find tuples which satisfy the user command and (2) list the desired set of tuples. The select command generates and operates upon "mark" relations. When the order by, unique, or group by clauses are specified within the command, the select procedure will use search-tree techniques to expedite the processing of the command.

UPDATE: This command invokes the <u>select</u> command to locate the required

set of tuples; the marked tuples are modified and returned to

storage via the UPDTUP routine.

DELETE: This command also calls the <u>select</u> command to locate the re-

quired tuples; the marked tuples are then overwritten with a

"deleted" symbol. Both the <u>update</u> and <u>delete</u> modules utilize

the list facility of the <u>select</u> command to display the affected

tuples to the user.

KILL: This command is the converse of the <u>create</u> command; all schema

information is removed from the system and all tuples of the

specified relation are returned to free space.

The high-level structure of the MINISEQUEL system is presented in Figure 1;

the level of detail presented within the figure is substantially greater

than the level discussed within Sections 2 or 3.

3. THE DATA STORAGE SYSTEM

In this section of the paper, we present the subsystem of the data-

base management facility which provides the various capabilities of

MINISEQUEL; we shall refer to this subsystem as the storage system or

simply as the system. The system supports operations upon single tuples

of the rudimentary relations as well as the creation, deletion, and main-

tenance of relations. The storage system employs many techniques found in

other database systems, including both relational and non-relational; in

particular, we have utilized the standard indexing and pointer strategies.

An important consideration is to outline the uses of these techniques in

the minicomputer environment. However, we have also employed recently dis-

covered trie access methods. Our approach is essentially bottom up; we be-

gin with a description of the physical storage configuration, followed by a

discussion of the nature of the relations accommodated. Next we present the rudimentary operations which accomplish the basic data transactions. Finally, the access methods utilized are presented.

Many of the design considerations represented within the ensuing discussions are based upon the small environment intended for our system; in this sense, the design is relatively unique. Essentially, we favor space-saving techniques over speed of execution; our algorithms are not ineffi-cient but we will not be able to retain copies of data in the form of vari-ous access paths from one query to the next.

The data handled by the storage system resides upon floppy disks. Physical storage space is divided into fixed size areas referred to as blocks or pages. The block is our unit of disk allocation, as well as transfer between main storage and disk. Blocks are used to store records (and indices); while a block will contain records of only one relation, a single relation typically requires many blocks to store its constituent records. To fetch all tuples of a relation, it suffices to access all blocks containing the constituent records; this is essentially a sequen-tial scan of the records of the relation.

The principal data object of the relational database system is, of course, the n-ary relation which contains n-fields or domains. The two domain types supported are integer and character; the latter is a variable length field. The physical storage and logical structures of n-tuples are identical; so a logical and physical view of the stored record data will match.

3.1 Operations

The storage system provides data manipulation facilities to create, insert, fetch, and update individual n-tuples; in particular, operators FINSRT and INSRTTUP build n-tuples and insert the n-tuple into a relation respectively, operators SELECTUP and FFTCH fetch an n-tuple and isolate the value of a particular domain, and the operator UPDTUP fetches, modifies,

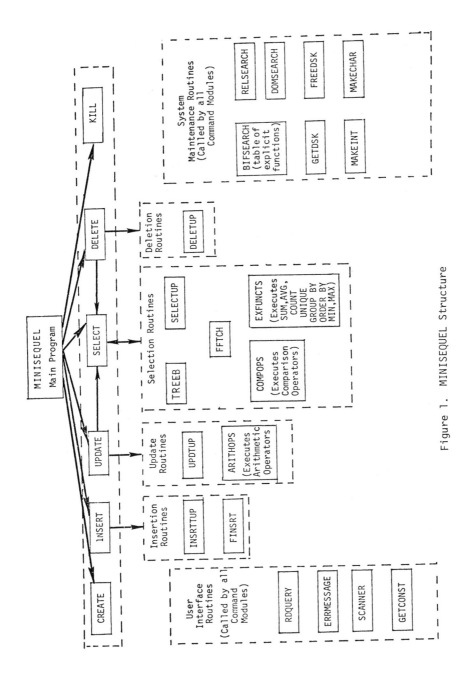

Figure 1. MINISEQUEL Structure

and then inserts a tuple. The FFTCH operation creates an ancillary "mark" relation in which records contain the block number and offset of tuples which satisfy the parameters of FFTCH. The "mark" with associated records is similar to the unary link and TID construct of System R and generally provides a partially defined ordering of the records as well as an explicit access path for the marked records.

The strict use of marks for all data manipulation routines has two advantages. One is that the amount of core space required to evaluate a query is very small; at each point in the evaluation, a mark, consisting of addresses only or of addresses paired with one data field, is the only data structure required. The other is that knowing that the result of interpreting every Select command will be contained in the same kind of data structure—a list of addresses—makes it easier to handle a query with nested Select commands.

The rudimentary operations presented perform the desired transactions upon the records within the disk storage environment. Many of these operations take advantage of PASCAL's facility for dynamic space allocation. Examples of data structures generated are a linked list of domain names not yet matched with a relation and a character array to hold a new tuple to be inserted. By allocating space for these structures only when needed and discarding them as soon as possible, the space required by the system is kept to a minimum.

All pertinent information concerning relation names, tuple format, domain size and type, access path structure, and vacant space is stored in statically maintained arrays. While the structure of these arrays is constant, the contents will vary as relations are defined and removed. The storage system provides data definition operators CREATE and KILL to define and remove relations.

3.2   Access Methods

The storage system provides for various operations upon the tuples of the constituent relations as well as the relations. Three access methods (for the tuples) are available within the system; these are sequential links, B*-trees[8], and PM-tries [9]. The first two schemes provide indexing based upon primary keys using an indexed sequential [10] organization. The PM-trie scheme provides indexing based upon secondary keys; efficient associative access paths are obtained.

The "mark" facility allows the dynamic creation of efficient access paths for subsets of the stored tuples which satisfy user queries. While it is possible to create inverted lists by this method, due to space limitation there is no facility to save marks from one query to the next unless specifically requested by the user.

4.   HARDWARE SYSTEM ARCHITECTURE

The entire MINISEQUEL system is implemented in standard PASCAL. The UCSD PASCAL project provides the language within the minicomputer environment. The hardware system required for this implementation of PASCAL consists of a crt with keyboard, two floppy disk spindles, and a cpu like an 8080, LSI-11, or 6800 with a 28K (16 bit) mainstore. A floppy disk contains approximately 500 blocks; each block consists of 512 bytes.

All PASCAL programs are compiled to run upon a 16-bit stack oriented architecture referred to as the P-machine. The hardware cpu simulates the operations of this virtual machine architecture [11]. This P-machine interpreter concept allows ease of transfer of system software among installations; in particular, it is possible to install the entire MINISEQUEL system by (1) creating the simulation for the P-machine and (2) booting from an initialized floppy disk at the site. A schematic description of the P-machine environment is presented in Figure 2.

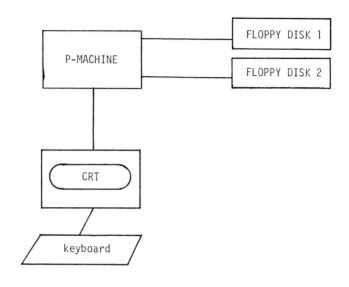

Figure 2. MINISEQUEL System Hardware Configuration

5. CONCLUSIONS AND SUMMARY

We have described the MINISEQUEL architecture, including the relational data system, the user interface, and the data storage system. One
primary guide in many decisions during the design has been to conserve
space whenever possible; a second design criteria was the desire to achieve
portability. We are extremely eager to complete our first version of the
system and commence actual use.

One set of data we anticipate gathering concerns the structure (and
size) of the data that casual users will manipulate using MINISEQUEL-like
systems. The answer to this question can have an impact upon the design
of subsequent mini-database management systems.

Another general question area for which we anticipate gathering empirical data concerns the structure of MINISEQUEL itself. Have we delin-
eated a useful database management system?' Do we have an appropriate data

definition and management language for the truly casual user? Is the particular interactive mode of transaction with MINISEQUEL effective?

We also expect to gather information concerning the efficacy of PM-trie access methods. This aspect of the project is especially exciting, since this new approach has not been used in previously implemented database management systems.

MINISEQUEL systems will be available initially in student-intensive environments. We anticipate administrative and management uses of the system when it is fully functional.

The MINISEQUEL design has included aspects of software portability to maintain a useful system over various hardware technologies and cpu architectures. While we have not adopted the database machine concept [12], we do have a rudimentary interpreter at the center of the design.

Thus, at this juncture, we have a database management system design and implementation well underway. While we have not answered all of the extremely difficult design questions which arise due to the truly mini-computer environment, we have a workable design. All indications point toward an efficient, manageable, attractive database management system for the casual user.

ACKNOWLEDGEMENT

We gratefully acknowledge assistance of Man-tak Shing in the implementation and final design stages of the MINISEQUEL project as well as the assistance of Claire Raikow in the typing and layout of the report.

REFERENCES

1. E.F. Codd, Recent investigations in relational database systems, Proc.
   of ACM Pacific 75 Conf., Boole and Babbage, Sunnyvale, 15-20.

2. Terak Corporation, Scottsdale, Arizona.

3. D.D. Chamberlin, et al., SEQUEL 2: A unified approach to data definition, manipulation, and control, IBM Journal of Research and Development, Vol. 20 (1976), 560-575.

4. K. Jensen and N. Wirth, PASCAL User Manual and Report, Second Edition,
   Springer-Verlag, New York, 1975.

5. J.W. Schmidt, Some high level language constructs for data of type relation, ACM Transactions on Database Systems, Vol. 2 (1977), 247-261.

6. M.M. Astraham et al., System R: Relational approach to database management, ACM Transactions on Database Systems, Vol. 1 (1976) 97-137.

7. UCSD (Mini-Micro Computer) PASCAL, Institute for Information Systems,
   La Jolla.

8. D.R. Bayer and E.M. McCreight, Organization and maintenance of large
   ordered indexes, Acta Informatica, Vol. 1 (1972), 173-189.

9. W.A. Burkhard, Hashing and trie algorithms for partial match retrieval,
   ACM Transactions on Database Systems, Vol. 1 (1976), 175-187.

10. S.P. Ghosh and M.E. Senko, File organization: On the selection of
    random access index points for sequential files, Journal of the
    Association for Computing Machinery, Vol. 16 (1969), 569-579.

11. P.J. Brown, Software Portability, Cambridge University Press,
    New York, 1977.

12. D.C. Tsichritzis and F.H. Lochovsky, Data Base Management Systems,
    Academic Press, New York, 1977.

Appendix A: Minisequel Syntax

Square brackets [ ] indicate optional syntatic constructs.

```
statement ::= query ;
            | dml-statement ;
            | ddl-statement ;

dml-statement ::= insertion
                | deletion
                | update

query ::= query-block-1 [ ORDER BY ord-spec-list ]

assignment ::= receiver ← query-block-1

receiver ::= table-name [ ( field-name-List ) ]

insertion ::= INSERT INTO receiver : insert-spec-list

insert-spec-List ::= ⟨ insert-spec ⟩
                   | ⟨ insert-spec ⟩ , insert-spec-list

insert-spec ::= entry-list

field-name-list ::= field-name
                  | field-name , field-name-list

deletion        ::= DELETE FROM table-name [ where-clause ]

update          ::= UPDATE table-name set-clause-list [ where-clause ]

where-clause    ::= WHERE boolean

set-clause-list ::= set-clause
                  | set-clause , set-clause-list

set-clause      ::= SET numeric-field-name = numeric-expr
                  | SET alpha-field-name = quoted-string

query-block-1   ::= select-from-clause [ WHERE boolean ]
                        [ GROUP BY field-spec-list [HAVING coolean ]]
```

```
query-block-2    ::= SELECT [ UNIQUE ] numeric-fn-value
                     FROM table-name [ variable-name ]
                     [ where boolean ] [ GROUP BY field-spec-list
                                         [ HAVING boolean ]]

query-block-3    ::= SELECT [ UNIQUE ] numeric-field-spec
                     FROM table-name [ variable-name ]
                     [ WHERE boolean ]
                        [ GROUP BY field-spec-list [ HAVING boolean ]]

query-block-4    ::= SELECT [ UNIQUE ] alpha-field-spec
                     FROM table-name [ variable-name ]
                     [ WHERE boolean ]
                            [ GROUP BY field-spec-list
                                       [ HAVING boolean ]]

table-spec-1     ::= query-block-1
                   | lit-tuple

sel-expr         ::= field-spec | numeric-fn-value

numeric-fn-value ::= built-in-fn ( [ UNIQUE ] numeric-field-spec )
                   | COUNT (*)
                   | COUNT ( [ UNIQUE ] field-spec )

field-spec       ::= alpha-field-spec
                   | numeric-field-spec

from-list        ::= table-name [ variable-name ]
                   | table-name [ variable-name ] , from-list

field-spec-list  ::= field-spec
                   | field-spec , field-spec-list

numeric-field-spec ::= numeric-field-name
                   | table-name • numeric-field-name
                   | variable-name • numeric-field-name

alpha-field-spec  ::= alpha-field-name
                   | table-name • alpha-field-name
                   | variable-name • alpha-field-name
```

```
ord-spec-list    ::= field-spec direction
                 |  field-spec , ord-spec-list

direction        ::= ASC | DESC

boolean          ::= boolean-term
                 |  boolean-term OR boolean

boolean-term     ::= boolean-factor
                 |  boolean-factor AND boolean-term

boolean-factor   ::= [ NOT ] boolean-primary

boolean-primary  ::= predicate
                 |  ( boolean )

predicate        ::= numeric-expr numeric-comp numeric-expr
                 |  alpha-expr alpha-comp alpha-expr
                 |  numeric-expr numeric-comp query-block-2
                 |  numeric-expr numeric-comp query-block-3
                 |  alpha-expr alpha-comp query-block-4
                 |  〈 field-spec-List 〉 = table-spec-1
                 |  〈 field-spec-List 〉 [ IS ] [ NOT ] IN table-spec-2
                 |  numeric-field-spec [ IS ] [ NOT ] IN table-spec-3
                 |  alpha-field-spec [ IS ] [ NOT ] IN table-spec-4
                 |  table-spec-2 Set-comp table-spec-2
                 |  table-spec-2 [ DOES NOT ] CONTAIN lit-tuple
                 |  table-spec-3 [ DOES NOT ] CONTAIN full-table-spec-3
                 |  table-spec-4 [ DOES NOT ] CONTAIN full-table-spec-4
                 |  query-block-2 numeric-comp numeric-expr
                 |  query-block-3 numeric-comp numeric-expr
                 |  query-block-4 alpha-comp alpha-expr
                 |  lit-tuple [ IS ] [ NOT ] [ IN ] table-spec-2
                 |  full-table-spec-3 [ IS ] [ NOT ] [ IN ] table-spec-3
                 |  full-table-spec-4 [ IS ] [ NOT ] [ IN ] table-spec-4

select-from-clause ::= select-clause FROM from-list

select-clause    ::= SELECT [ UNIQUE ] sel-expr-list
                 |  SELECT [ UNIQUE ] *
```

```
sel-expr-list      ::= sel-expr
                    | sel-expr , sel-expr-list

table-spec-2       ::= query-block-1
                    | [ lit-tuple-list ]

table-spec-3       ::= query-block-2
                    | [ number-list ]
                    | query-block-3

table-spec-4       ::= query-block-3
                    | [ string-list ]

full-table-spec-3 ::= table-spec-3
                    | number

full-table-spec-4 ::= table-spec-4
                    | quoted-string

set-comp           ::= numeric-comp
                    | CONTAIN
                    | DOES NOT CONTAIN
                    | [ IS ] IN
                    | [ IS ] NOT IN

lit-tuple-list     ::= lit-tuple
                    | lit-tuple , lit-tuple-list

lit-tuple          ::= ⟨ entry-list ⟩

entry-list         ::= entry
                    | entry , entry-list

entry              ::= quoted-string
                    | number

number-list        ::= number
                    | number , number-list

string-list        ::= quoted-string
                    | quoted-string , string-list
```

```
alpha-expr            ::= alpha-field-spec
                        | quote-string

numeric-expr          ::= arith-term
                        | arith-term add-op numeric-expr

arith-term            ::= arith-factor
                        | arith-factor mult-op arith-term

arith-factor          ::= [ add-op ] arith-primary

arith-primary         ::= numeric-field-spec
                        | build-in-fn ( [ UNIQUE ] numeric-field-spec )
                        | ( numeric-expr )
                        | COUNT ( [ UNIQUE ] field-spec )
                        | number


numeric-comp          ::= =  |  <>  |  >  |  >=  |  <=

alpha-comp            ::= =  |  <>

add-op                ::= +  |  -

mult-op               ::= ×  |  /

built-in-fn           ::= AVG  |  MAX  |  MIN  |  SUM

table-name            ::= identifier

field-name            ::= alpha-field-name
                        | numeric-field-name

alpha-field-name    ::= identifier

numeric-field-name  ::= identifier

number                ::= integer
                        | integer number

ddl-statement         ::= create-table
                        | kill-table

create-table          ::= CREATE TABLE table-name :
                              field-defn-List
```

```
field defn-list      ::= field-defn
                       | field-defn , field-defn-list

field-defn           ::= alpha-field-name ( alpha-type ( length ))
                       | numeric-field-name ( numeric-type ( length ))

alpha type           ::= C

numeric-type         ::= I

length               ::= 1 | 2 | ••• | 15

kill-table           ::= KILL TABLE table-name

integer              ::= 0 | 1 | ••• | 9

quoted-string        ::= `string´

string               ::= alphabet | alphabet string
                       | integer | integer string

identifier           ::= alphabet
                       | alphabet string

alphabet             ::= a | b | ••• | z
```

DATABASES: IMPROVING USABILITY AND RESPONSIVENESS

A STUDY OF THREE DATABASE QUERY LANGUAGES

David Greenblatt
Jerry Waxman

Department of Computer Sciences
Queens College
Flushing, New York

ABSTRACT: Three different database "query" languages were taught to non-programming undergraduate students. The languages, Query By Example, a Structured English Query Language, and an algebra-oriented language are all based on Codd's relational database organization - - yet the languages differ in critical aspects such as English - likeness and declarative vs. procedural problem specification. Students were given equal training in each of the three languages, after which they were given an exam of twenty questions. All the exams were graded for accuracy and time it took to complete each question. In the variables measured, results indicate Zloof's Query By Example superior.

INTRODUCTION

As more non-programming individuals are interfacing with computer database systems, it is necessary to develop languages that can be learned, understood and applied with as little effort as possible. This need has generated much research in the development of particular database query languages.

Copyright © 1978 by Academic Press, Inc.
All rights of reproduction in any form reserved.
ISBN 0-12-642150-1

We chose three candidate query languages to examine. Though all based on the relational organization promoted by Codd[1], they vary in English-likeness and procedural vs. declarative query formulation.

Our goal was primarily to determine if any of the three languages chosen had significantly better learning and application capabilities over the others when applied to a moderately non-programming sample of subjects. The variables of time, accuracy and subject confidence as related to question complexity were measured.

As a secondary goal, we attempted to verify the results of an earlier experiment by Thomas and Gould[2] that was conducted on the Query By Example language. Their work pointed out many of the qualities of Query By Example. Our experiments were conducted in the same manner as theirs -- testing the ability of subjects to grasp and use a query language. Yet, their comparison of Query By Example with other experiments was not rigorous -- "Of course, these comparisons are only approximate because the separate experiments differed in several ways, e.g., training techniques, subject populations, test questions, stringency of scoring errors".[2] By using all three languages in our experiment, we assured a controlled testing environment.

SUBJECTS

Each query language was presented to a different, random group of undergraduate students. By chance only, each group had a majority of male subjects, with the mean number of males in each group varying between 52.9% for the algebraic language subjects and 71.4% for the Query By Example group. The mean ages of the groups varied between 19.3 for Query By Example and 24.8 for SEQUEL. Academically, the three groups were relatively capable -- mean high school averages varied between 82.8/100 and 90.8/100, while college grade point averages (GPA) varied from a mean

of 2.9/4 to a mean of 3.4/4. Though previous computer training was

pretty much a negligible factor in our sample, the mean number of college

computer courses previously taken varied between 1.0 courses for the

Query By Example subjects and 3.5 courses for the algebraic language

subjects. Table I contains the subject statistics particular to each

of the three groups.

It is most remarkable that despite having the smallest mean number

of previous computer courses, the Query By Example group scored far better

than the other two groups.

DESIGN AND PROCEDURE

Each of the three groups received training on the same 25 examples.

They were then given an exam of 19 questions. The students in the Query

By Example group were additionally given a small re-training period and

subsequently, a second group of 20 questions. This procedure simulated

that of Thomas and Gould.

During the exam, no questions were permitted. The students were

given a list of operators and abbreviations unique to the language they

were learning. On each question, the students were required not only to

interpret the questions into the proper form of their query language, but

to write the time the entire question took, and how confident they were

about their answers.

The confident ratings offered a choice of very sure, fairly sure,

50-50 chance, fairly sure incorrect and very sure incorrect. When

grading, very sure was given a value of one, fairly sure a two, and so

on, through the value five for very sure incorrect.

To demonstrate the use of the three query languages, we will use the four sample questions and the sample database in Table II.

QUERY BY EXAMPLE LANGUAGE

This language is described extensively in current publications[3], and other software has been constructed upon it[4]. To use Query By Example, one fills in a table with either variable example items (which are under-lined) or constant example items (not underlined). To depict the entries to be printed, a P. is placed next to the variable example in the column. Linking tables is accomplished by use of common, linking, example items.

In Table III, the Query By Example solutions to the four sample questions of Table II are listed. In question one, 'ANDERS' is a con-stant and is therefore not underlined. To get the information contained in the other columns (corresponding to 'ANDERS'), we place the entry P. next to underlined examples in every column. Example two illustrates the use of "greater than" and "less than" operators upon constant example items. Example three requires the common linking variable Y to join the two tables. The fourth example demonstrates use of the SUM.ALL operator.

STRUCTURED ENGLISH QUERY LANGUAGE - SEQUEL

SEQUEL is discussed by its authors elsewhere [5,6]. The subjects were given the English keywords SELECT - FROM - WHERE and the operators >, <, MAX, MIN, COUNT, $\geqslant, \leqslant, \neq$. The response booklets given to the subjects had places to enter the SEQUEL interpretations of the queries with respective times and confidence ratings.

In Table IV, the SEQUEL interpretations of the four sample questions are given. The first example requires a simple SELECT-FROM-WHERE to get the entries of other columns, given requirements on a particular column. Conversely the second example gets the information in a single column given "anded" restrictions on other columns. The third example provides

for linking of two tables, necessitating the use of two SELECT-FROM-WHERE
clauses. Finally, the fourth example makes use of the SUM operator to
sum a column.

As in the other languages, the subjects were instructed that duplicates would be removed (from the output) by the system and that the
system would respond with 'NONE' if there were no entries satisfying the
given requirements.

ALGEBRAIC LANGUAGE

Though based on the Projection, Join and Division   operations
discussed in many texts, [1,7,9] the algebraic language required minor
extensions of our own for the use of special operators such as SUM, COUNT,
MAX and MIN. The response booklet was the same as that used for SEQUEL --
a place for the responses, time entries and confidence ratings.

In Table V, the sample questions are interpreted using our algebraic
language. The interpretation of sample question one requires a table
with column NAME containing only the entry 'ANDERS'. In the training
period, the subjects were taught the procedure for creating "constant"
tables. This table is then joined with the Employee table and the result
is projected over the necessary columns. In question two, three tables
are constructed and joined with the Employee table. This result is then
projected over 'NAME'. Question three has two "joined" tables. In
question four, the SUM operator is applied to the entire result, which
alone would have been a column of salaries.

TRAINING

Rather than restrict each group to a set amount of training time,
we required that each group be taught 25 examples in one of the three
query languages. The most rapid training time was one hour and 35 minutes

for Query By Example, while SEQUEL took one hour and forty minutes and the algebraic language took two hours and five minutes. For the second group of questions that were given to the Query By Example group, there was 25 minutes of training on seven examples directly after the first exam. These seven examples contained interpretations of English queries using "all" and "every", features not found on the first exam.

Throughout training, the students would attempt the examples on their own. The session's leader would frequently review each student's answer with the student. We felt that this feedback and interaction should aid in student comprehension.

TASK

The exams were much the same as those used by Thomas and Gould in their experiment. For Query By Example, twenty questions were given, but for SEQUEL and the algebraic language one question requiring a feature unique to Query By Example was omitted. The four questions in Table II are taken from the exam. The complexity of the questions can basically be determined by the number of linking variables and tables required, conjunctive and disjunctive constructions and the number of operators involved.

All of the subjects were instructed to write the time before they read the English question as 'TIME BEGIN'. Then they were to interpret the question into the particular language they had learned. Afterwards, they were told to put a confidence marking next to the rating best suiting their answer. The choices were "very sure correct", "fairly sure correct", "50-50 chance", "fairly sure incorrect", and "very sure incorrect". Finally, the subjects were instructed to write the time again as 'TIME END'.

ERROR ANALYSES

All of the exams were graded by one person familiar with the languages as they were taught. The marking for each query was for exact output, no output, wrong output and superfluous output.

RESULTS
OVERALL

Query By Example required the least training time of one hour and 35 minutes. Furthermore, Query By Example had the largest proportion of correct queries, 0.75. It also required the smallest mean time per query, .9 minutes. Finally the subjects of Query By Example were the most confident in their answers, with a confidence rating of 1.6. It is worthwhile to point out that the Query By Example group had less college computer training than the other two groups. An overall results comparison can be found in Table VI.

Statistically, we found no significant difference in mean exam time and mean correct queries among the three languages. A close examination of the individual test scores suggests that this lack of significance is due to high standard deviations in Sequel and the algebraic language for the two variables. For the mean exam time, Sequel had a standard deviation of 15.12 while that of the algebraic language scores was 14.47. Likewise, for the mean correct queries, Sequel had a standard deviation of 18.40 and the algebraic language had a standard deviation of 19.64.

With respect to the mean confidence per query, we found no significant difference between Sequel and the algebraic language $(\underline{t}(36)=\emptyset.\emptyset,p<.001)$. Yet, Query By Example was significantly superior to Sequel $(\underline{t}(36)=4.33,p<.\emptyset\emptyset1)$ and to the algebraic language $(\underline{t}(36)=4.\emptyset8,p<.\emptyset\emptyset1)$. Likewise, for the mean time per query, Query By Example proved significantly superior to Sequel $(\underline{t}(36)=6.49,p<.\emptyset\emptyset1)$ and to the algebraic language $(\underline{t}(36)=5.\emptyset6,p<.\emptyset\emptyset1)$.

INDIVIDUAL DIFFERENCES

Like Thomas and Gould previously found in Query By Example, subject sex did not relate to grade of confidence -- in any of our languages. The mean proportion correct per question varied significantly for SEQUEL and the algebraic language -- .42 to 1.00 for SEQUEL and .15 to .94 for the algebraic language. Query By Example had a range of .52 to .89 with 71% of the questions varying from .79 to only .89 correct. The only constant relationship we found in our languages was a confidence to grade relation. Our results for this relation are shown in Table VII. The table shows, almost without exception, that in queries where user confidence increased, the per cent of correct queries was also higher. We therefore support the earlier assertions of Thomas and Gould concerning this relationship.

PROBLEMS

Subjects had considerable difficulty cross-linking in one table for queries like, "Who is younger than Anders' manager?" In one question where two restrictions required cross-linking twice in one table, the proportion correct was 21.6% less than the exam mean for the algebraic language, and 46.6% less than the exam mean for Query By Example. Thomas and Gould had their second lowest proportion correct for this question. Serious analyses should be done to develop language simplifications for queries of this sort.

ERROR TYPES

There were significant errors in the use of universal quantification in the second exam given to the Query By Example subjects. We propose that one reasonable cause of this problem is the somewhat ambiguous nature of the English language in queries like, "Print any departments that sell every item that some company makes". Only careful attention determines that the qualification is on the company and not on the depart-

Another common error was the attempt to put operators on non-numeric fields. For example, the subjects had been carefully instructed that the "ITEM" column contained the names of items, not the number of items. Yet, quite often numeric operators were applied to the column. Frequency of this error could probably be substantially reduced by more descriptive column labels such as "ITEM-NAME" rather than "ITEM".

DISCUSSION
COMPARATIVE DATA

Clearly, our results substantiated the previous work of Thomas and Gould depicting some superiority of Query By Example as a database query language. In our experiment, Query By Example had the highest proportion correct, the highest mean confidence ratings, and took less than one-half the mean time per question than our closest competitive language. We must point out that the Query By Example group had a higher, overall high school average and was proportionately dominated by males.

Though our SEQUEL results were quite similar to Reisner's pilot data[8] (in mean proportion correct), we gave only one hour and forty minutes training time versus twelve academic hours. Reisner does point out that a "programming sample" could probably train for SEQUEL in about two hours. It would be worthwhile to more carefully examine the relation of extended initial training periods to mean proportion correct.

ERROR PREDICTION

Thomas and Gould previously noted the interesting subject confidence to correctness ratio. As we substantiate their findings, even for SEQUEL and the algebraic language, (see Table VII), it is logical to use feedback from the system to clarify queries given with low confidence. When the system recognizes a low confidence rating, it could rephrase the query, and respond, "Your query is equivalent to ..... Is that what you want?" The user could then respond "yes" or reconstruct his query.

Though confidence ratings seem to be good error predictors, our results seem to show that the number of tables involved is not a decisive error predictor. As a particular case in point, one exam question linking all four tables had a .85 proportion correct for Query By Example, a remarkable 1.00 for SEQUEL and .77 for the algebraic language. These proportions exceeded the total mean proportion correct for each language. We feel that once a subject has learned a particular languages linking facility, reasonable increases in the number of tables minimally increase the chance of error. Similarly, the number of columns and rows can, for the main part, be discounted as serious error predictors.

CONCLUSION

Our results showed Query By Example superior to SEQUEL and the algebraic language in learning and application ease. The authors surmise, as did Thomas and Gould, that the explicity tabular organization of Query By Example aids in query formulation -- particularly where cross-referencing of columns and/or tables is required. Further research should be done to determine and evaluate the factors directly responsible for Query By Example's superiority.

As a secondary notion, the idea of enhancing Query By Example with English or English-like commands should be considered. It is possible, that in some tables crowded with operators, underlined variables and constants, these new commands could aid the user to organize the query properly.

REFERENCES

1. Codd, E.F. A Relational Model of Data for Large Shared Data Bases
   Comm. ACM, Vol. 13, No. 6 (June]970), pp. 377-387.
2. Thomas, J.C. and Gould, J.D. A Psychological Study of Query by
   Example, Research Report RC 5124, IBM T.J. Watson Research Center,
   Yorktown Heights, N.Y., November 1974. Also AFIPS Proceedings,
   Vol. 44, 1975, pp. 439-445.
3. Zloof, Moshe M. Query By Example, Research Report RC 49]7, IBM
   T.J. Watson Research Center, Yorktown Heights, N.Y., July 1974.
   Also, AFIPS Proceedings, Vol. 44, 1975, pp. 431-438.
4. Zloof, Moshe M. de Jong, S.P. The System for Business Automation
   (SBA): Programming Language, Research Report RC 5302, IBM
   T.J. Watson Research Center, Yorktown Heights, N.Y., March 1975.
   Also Comm. ACM, Vol. 20, No. 6, (June 1977) pp. 385-396.
5. Chamberlin, D.D. and Boyce, R.F. SEQUEL: A Structured English Query
   Language, PROC. 1974 ACM Sigfidet Workshop, Ann Arbor, Michigan,
   April 1974, pp. 249-264.
6. Astrahan, M.M. Chamberlin, D.D. Implementation of a Structured
   English Query Language, Comm. ACM, Vol. 18, No. 10 (October
   1975), pp. 580-588.
7. Date, C.J. An Introduction to Database Systems, Reading, Addison-
   Wesley Publishing Company, 1975.
8. Reisner, P. Boyce, R.F. and Chamberlin, D.D. Human Factors Evaluation
   of Two Data Base Query Languages -- Square and Sequel, AFIPS
   Proceedings, Vol. 44, 1975, pp. 447-452.
9. Codd, E.F. Relational Completeness of Data Base Sublanguages,
   Courant Computer Science Symposia, Vol. 6, Data Base Systems,
   Prentice-Hall, New York, May 1971.

TABLE I. Subject Information

	Query By Example	Sequel	Algebraic Language
# Subjects Participating	8	17	13
Mean Age	19.3	24.8	20.9
Mean High School Average	90.8	82.8	87.4
Mean College GPA (Students with over 32 credits. A=4.0)	3.3	3.4	2.9
Mean # Previous College Computer Courses	1.0	1.9	3.5
Percent Male	71.4	52.9	53.9

TABLE II. A. Sample Database

Employee Table	(Name, Salary, Age, Manager, Department)
Supply Table	(Company, Item, # Received)
Sales Table	(Department, Item, # Sold)
Supplier Table	(Company, Location, Size, President)

TABLE II. B. Sample Queries

1) Print Anders' Salary, Age, Manager and Department.
2) Print the names of Employees whose salaries are less than
       $12,000, are over 28 years old, and are managed by White.
3) What are the names of people that work in Department that have
       sold more than 50 of a single item?
4) Total up the amount of salaries paid out annually to people under
       40 in all departments but the Toy department.

TABLE III. Use of Query By Example

Employee Table

	Name	Salary	Age	Manager	Department
1)	Anders	P. 13000	P. 37	P. Smith	P. X
2)	P. X	< 12000	>28	White	
3)	P. X				Y
4)		P.SUM.ALL 13000	<40		≠ Toys

Sales Table

	Department	Item	# Sold
3)	Y		>50

TABLE IV. Use of A Structured English Query Language
                         (SEQUEL)

1) Select Salary, Age, Manager, Department
   From   Employee
   Where   Name = 'Anders'

2) Select Name
   From   Employee
   Where   Salary < 12000
   And   Age >28
   And   Manager = 'White'

3) Select Name
   From   Employee
   Where   Department =

        Select   Department
        From   Sales
        Where   # Sold > 50

4) Select Sum (Salary)
   From   Employee
   Where   Age < 40
   And   Department ≠ 'Toys'

TABLE V. Use of the Algebraic Language

1) A (Name = 'Anders')
    (A [Name = Name] Employee)   [Salary, Age, Manager, Department]

2) A (Salary = 12000)
    B (Age = 28)
    C (Manager = 'White')
    (((Employee [Salary < Salary] A) [Age > Age] B)
        [Manager = Manager] C) [Name]

3) A (# Sold = 50)
    ((Sales [# Sold > # Sold] A) [Department = Department] Employee)
        [Name]

4) A (Age = 40)
    B (Department = 'Toys')
    Sum (((Employee [Age < Age] A) [Department ≠ Department] B)
        [Salary])

TABLE VI. Overall Results

	Query By Example	Sequel	Algebraic Language
Training Time (hours:minutes)	1:35	1:40	2:05
Mean Total Exam Time (minutes)	23.3	53.9	63.3
Mean Correct Queries (%)	75.2	72.8	67.7
Mean Time/Query (minutes)	.9	2.5	3.0
Mean Confidence/Query (1 to 5)	1.6	1.9	1.9

TABLE VII. Confidence to Correctness Ratio
            % of Total Queries Correct

	Query By Example	Sequel	Algebraic Language
Queries with Subject Confidence of:			
Very Sure	87	89	87
Fairly Sure	67	70	66
50-50 Chance	33	48	43
Fairly Sure Incorrect	0	57	25
Very Sure Incorrect	0	33	33

The table presents the ratio of correct responses to total
responses for each confidence group of the languages considered.

APPENDIX A

These are the example queries that were reviewed with each of the
group. The first set of examples was studied by all three groups, while
EXAMPLES II were only done by the Query By Example group.

EXAMPLES I

Use of P. ,————————————, variables and constants.

1) Print all employees.
2) Print all of our workers who are managed by Johnson.
3) Which department is managed by Lee?
4) Get me all the information we have for our employee Nixon.
5) List the names, salaries and managers of the employees who work
     in the Toy department.

Use of $<, \leqslant, >, \geqslant, -, =, \neq$

6) Our company payroll is too big ... Perhaps we should force a few
     of our personnel to retire ... Find out who is over 55 years old
     and makes more than 40000 dollars a year.
7) Print the names of all employees except those managed by Miller.
8) Print any items and companies where the number received of the item
     has been less than 100.

Use of MAX., MIN., SUM.ALL, COUNT.ALL, COUNT.ALL D.

9) What is the name of our highest paid employee?
10) What is the total of all salaries paid yearly to the Sports
        department?
11) How many (different) managers do we have working for us?

Use of Linking Variables

12) Get me the departments which have items that have been shipped
        by companies located in Alaska.
13) Give the names of employees that work in departments selling
        hairbrushes.
14) Lee is one of our good managers...Give me the names of the
        presidents of companies that ship to Lee's department.
15) Which managers control the sale of IBM products?

Linking in one table

16) Which employees make more than their managers?
17) Who in our company is older than Smith's manager?
18) Who has the same manager as Johnson?

Use of and , or

19) Which company supplies hairbrushes and underwear to us?
20) Which departments sell hairbrushes and underwear?
21) Which companies supply either hairbrushes or underwear?
22) Which departments sell items made by IBM or Burroughs?
23) Are baseballs and bats supplied to us by one company?

Use of constant letters of names, etc.

24) Find all employees with names beginning with the letter E.
25) Which managers have names ending in SON?

EXAMPLES II

Use of All, ALL _____

1) Which department gets all of its items from GM?
2) Which department gets all of GM's products?
3) Which companies supply every items to Smith's department?
4) Which companies produce every item that some department sells?

Misc. items

5) Which departments are sold out of items?
6) Are there any foremen with at most high school educations working
        for us in LA?
7) Give me a list of our young accountants...that is those under 30, with
        more than 3 dependents who have been working for us at least 2
        years; also carpenters who have been working no more than 3 years
        for us and have at least a high school diploma.

APPENDIX B

These are the two sets of exam questions given. They were used previously by Thomas and Gould. All three groups received the first set (except question 11 which was only for the Query By Example group), while only the Query By Example group received the second set.

FIRST SET

1) Find out who is the oldest person who works in the sports department
2) What are the names of people that work in departments that have sold more than 50 of a single item?
3) Who else works in the same department as Riley?
4) Anders is about 35, I think. His salary...I'm not sure...Perhaps $14,000. Anders' manager is getting older every day. Print the names of everyone younger than Anders' manager.
5) Total up the amount of salaries paid out annually to people under 40 in all departments but the toy department.
6) List people who work in departments that sell at least one item supplied by a company located in Massachusetts.
7) Print the names of employees whose salary is less than $12,000, are over 28 years old, and are managed by White.
8) Print out any companies that supply both stoves and chairs.
9) Print the names of companies located in Massachusetts, New York, or Texas.
10) Print the names of employees whose salary is over $8000, are managed by Lee, are over 25, and work in the Toys department.
11) What are the names of employees in departments that start with the letter 't'?
12) The roads between here and Mass. are blocked because of a trucker's strike. Any of the Massachusetts companies won't be getting their shipments through for a while. So, any of their items that we sell won't get replaced. You'd better print me out a list of everyone who works in a department that sells any item supplied by a Massachusetts company so I can let them know.
13) Print the names of anyone who makes more than Anders' manager and is younger than Smith's manager.
14) Anders told me that his manager is worried that younger men are being promoted ahead of him. Find out who is younger than Ander's manager.
15) I'm thinking about a raise for someone from White's group. I want only older people who are underpaid. For starters, find the people who work for White, are over 28, and make less than $12,000.
16) List the items sold by the Toy department.
17) Count up and tell me how many departments there are in this organization.
18) What items from ACME do Lee's department sell?
19) Print Anders' salary, age, manager's name and department.
20) Print the names of companies that supply either chairs or stoves.

SECOND SET

21) What items from UNI are Jones's department sold out to?
22) Print out any departments that sell every item that some company makes.
23) Massachusetts and New York are locations. The toy department is
    nearly sold out of trucks-13. Better print out the people
    working in a department such that that department gets any
    items from a company if the company is around Boston--anywhere
    in Massachusetts.
24) Print out the names of companies that supply either beds or tables.
25) Print the names of anyone who works in a department that gets all
    its items from a single company.
26) Print the names of company presidents whose companies supply every
    item to the department Jones works in.
27) Print out any companies that supply both tables and pistols.
28) Get the total number of dependents of the single women employees in
    NYC who are over 50 years old and have worked for us for at
    least 20 years; also get the total number of dependents of all
    women, working for us as secretaries, who are over 50 years
    old, have worked for us for at least 20 years, and are located
    in L.A.
29) The accounting people need to know how many married women over 30,
    with no dependents, work in Dept. 300; and how many single
    employees who have at most a Junior College degree have worked
    for us for more than 5 years and are employed in St. Louis,
    Dept. 400.
30) Do we have many NYC programmers who are college graduates, and over
    30 years of age, but have no dependents?
31) How many nurses work for us, how many maintenance men work for us,
    and how many secretaries work for us?
32) What are the names of the salesmen that work for us?
33) Are there many married people with at least 4 dependents, who have
    worked for us for at least 6 years?
34) Find all the single employees who work in KC, make over $80,000,
    have at most a bachelor's degree, and are under 30; and all
    the secretaries in Dept. 20 who work in San Francisco, have
    3 dependents and have worked for us for 5 years; and all the
    women programmers working in Jersey City, hired in 1971, who
    have at most a high school diploma.
35) We need to know the names of the single women, who are at least 64
    years old, who work for us; and the names of the men who hold
    the position of supervisor and worked for the company for at
    least 30 years.
36) I think there must be about 30 people managed by White, who makes
    $12,000. So...list the people over 28 who are managed by White.
    Of course, I'm only talking about those who make less than
    $12,000.
37) Print Smith's salary, age, manager's name and department.
38) Print the departments whose entire line of items is supplied by a
    single company.
39) Find out whether any departments sell every item that is supplied
    to our company.
40) List the names of employees who are younger than Anders' manager.

These are samples of the Answer booklets used.

STUDENT NUMBER _____

AGE _____

COLLEGE GRADE POINT AVERAGE _____ on _____ CREDITS

COLLEGE COMPUTER COURSES _____

OTHER COMPUTER TRAINING _____

APPROXIMATE OVERALL HIGH SCHOOL AVERAGE _____

SEX _____

Work as quickly as you can without making errors.
For each problem write the time before you begin reading the English question,
    write the answer,
    write your confidence rating,
    and record the time again.

You will have about 1/2 hour to do these 20 questions.
No questions will be permitted after we begin.

The following are symbols you may need. You may refer back to them if you need.

< , ∨ , > , ∧, = , ≠ , [ ], MWX MIN, SUM, COUNT, COUNT D, ()

(Exam Cover Sheet)

TIME BEGIN _____
VERY SURE ___
FAIRLY SURE ___
50-50 CHANCE ___
FAIRLY SURE INCORRECT ___
VERY SURE INCORRECT ___

TIME END _____

TIME BEGIN _____
VERY SURE ___
FAIRLY SURE ___
50-50 CHANCE ___
FAIR SURE INCORRECT ___
VERY SURE INCORRECT ___

TIME END _____

TIME BEGIN _____
VERY SURE ___
FAIRLY SURE ___
50-50 CHANCE ___
FAIRLY SURE INCORRECT ___
VERY SURE INCORRECT ___

TIME END _____

TIME BEGIN _____
VERY SURE ___
FAIRLY SURE ___
50-50 CHANCE ___
FAIRLY SURE INCORRECT ___
VERY SURE INCORRECT ___

TIME END _____

(Exam for Sequel and Algebraic Language)

(First Exam for Query By Example)   TIME BEGIN _____

EMPLOYEE FILE

NAME	SALARY	AGE	MANAGER	DEPARTMENT

SUPPLY FILE

COMPANY	ITEM	# REC'D

COMPANY	LOCATION	SIZE	PRESIDENT

S
U
P
P
LIER-FILE

SALES FILE

DEPARTMENT	ITEM	# SOLD

_____ VERY SURE
_____ FAIRLY SURE
_____ 50-50 CHANCE
_____ FAIRLY SURE INCORRECT
_____ VERY SURE INCORRECT
TIME END _____

TIME BEGIN _____

EMPLOYEE FILE

NAME	PROF.	LOC.	SAL.	AGE	DEP.	MARD.	DEPT.	HIRED	DEG.	SEX	MAN.

SUPPLY FILE

COMPANY	ITEM	# REC'D

COMPANY	LOCATION	SIZE	PRESIDENT

S
U
P
P
LIER-FILE   (Second exam for Query By Example)

SALES FILE

DEPARTMENT	ITEM	# SOLD

_____ VERY SURE
_____ FAIRLY SURE
_____ 50-50 CHANCE
_____ FAIRLY SURE INCORRECT
_____ VERY SURE INCORRECT
TIME END _____

THE EXTENDED RELATIONAL ALGEBRA,
A BASIS FOR QUERY LANGUAGES

T.H. Merrett[1]

School of Computer Science
McGill University
Montreal, Quebec

We introduce a new monadic operator into the relational algebra, the QT-selector, and show that, together
with the Cartesian product, it includes and generalizes
the known operations of the relational algebra (apart
from μ-join). A modification of the QT-selector gives
the QT-expression, which we consider as an alternative
to first-order predicate calculus. Assuming the most
unsophisticated representation of relations, we give a
one-pass algorithm to implement the most important
special case, the linear QT-expression, and we discuss
extension of the algorithm to the general QT-expression.
We give a classification of database queries and show
that only the simplest formulations of the extended relational algebra have been exemplified in the database
literature. Our aim is to extend the usability of databases by extending the range of operations that can be
performed on them.

Key Words and Phrases: database access, relational
model, relational algebra, query languages, query
implementation, predicate logic, quantifiers.

CR Categories: 3.74, 4.33, 4.34, 5.21

---

[1]Supported by grant NRC-A4365, National Research Council
of Canada.

0. INTRODUCTION

The proposals made in this paper have four motivations.
First, human factors studies, such as Reisner (1975), of query
languages and the general trend of database languages
(Merrett 1977b) suggest that the predicate calculus is difficult for most people to acquire and that a more transparent
way of expressing quantified assertions or requests is
needed. Second, pace the classical logicians (Ross 1949), the
quantifiers, all and some, are not adequate for modern data
processing. Third, we perceived an efficient way of examin-
ing single relations to satisfy quantified assertions or requests, which could easily be extended to multiple relations
by using the relational algebra (Codd 1972). Fourth, we found
that the relational algebra itself, which has grown since its
original proposing (Codd 1970), can be reduced to one binary
and one unary operator - the Cartesian product and the QT-
selector, which is described below.

This paper starts with the latter consideration - the
problem of generalizing the relational algebra. The relational algebra of Codd (1972) consists of two monadic operations,
Cartesian product, division and a family of six θ-joins. In
addition, Merrett (1977b) proposes two more θ-joins and a new
family of six μ-joins. It is important to find some underlying principles since this proliferation of algebraic operations suggests that many of them are somewhat ad hoc and have
been proposed to meet specific practical problems. To improve
database usability we must be able to define new operations
when we encounter problems that require them. This requires
a generalization of the relational algebra. This paper shows

that the QT-expression provides such a generalization: we

propose it for use in conjunction with the more familiar

operations that it extends.   We also show how QT-expressions

can perform most of the functions of the first-order predi-

cate calculus, and more besides, and we demonstrate its effec-

tiveness, in the context of an algebraic programming language,

in formulating queries.   These applications, together with

the fast implementation algorithm which we give, establish

QT-expressions as a practical means for extending the us-

ability of a relational database.

We begin by establishing notation and terminology.   A

domain is a set whose elements are atomic, that is, not fur-

ther divisible, and are called values.   One or more domains

may be considered, but any value belongs to one and only one

domain.   An m-ary relation is a subset of the extended

Cartesian product (Codd 1972) of m domains, not necessarily

distinct.   It is important to distinguish the various occur-

rences in a relation of a given domain, and we say that the

m-ary relation is defined over m distinct attributes, by

which we mean names that are given to the occurrences of

domains in the relation in order to distinguish them.   The

introduction of the term, attribute, enables us to loosen the

definition of the extended Cartesian product to allow the

domains to occur in any order in the relation, since each

domain-occurrence is named uniquely as an attribute.   So far

our terminology is familiar to most relational database ini-

tiates.   We now introduce the idea of the attribute-set, which

is the set of values in a given relation corresponding to a

given attribute.   An attribute-set is a subset of some domain.

Any value belongs to one or more attribute-sets.

We write $R(D_1,D_2,...,D_m)$ or $R(A_1,A_2,...,A_m)$ to describe an m-ary relation R in terms of its domains, D_i , or its attributes, A_i , i=1,...,m . The formal difference between the two is that $D_i=D_j$ is permitted for i≠j ; but $A_i=A_j$ only if i=j . In this paper, relations will be described in terms of attributes, but we also need the concept of a domain.

We will also write R(A,B,...) where A,B,... are sets of attributes, $A = \{A_{i_1},A_{i_2},...,A_{i_k}\}$, $B = \{A_{j_1},A_{j_2},...,A_{j_\ell}\}$, etc. We will refer to a tuple, r , an element of R ; to the $\underline{A_i}$-component, $r[A_i]$, of r , which is a value; and to the A-component or B-component of r , defined $r[A] = \{r[A_{i_1}],r[A_{i_2}],...,r[A_{i_k}]\}$ and $r[B] = \{r[A_{j_1}],r[A_{j_2}], ...,r[A_{i_\ell}]\}$, respectively. Formal definitions of these concepts can be found in the literature. The sets, A,B,..., of attributes should not be confused with attribute-sets, defined earlier. We call them   attribute-groups   for   distinction.

We may need to compare components of tuples on A and B, which we can do if k=ℓ and if $r[A_{i_p}]$ θ $r[B_{j_p}]$ is defined (true or false) for p = 1,...,k and θ is a comparison operator such as = , < , ≥ , etc. We define

$$r[A] \; \theta \; s[B] = r[A_{i_1}] \; \theta \; s[B_{j_1}] \; \wedge \; r[A_{i_2}] \; \theta \; s[B_{j_2}] \; \wedge \cdots$$

$$\wedge \; r[A_{i_k}] \; \theta \; s[B_{j_k}]$$

for tuples r and s (which may be the same). If $r[A] \; \theta \; s[B]$ is defined, we call A and B comparable.

In the next section, we unite the unary operations, restrict and project, into a single, more general, operation, the T-selector.   We also discuss   the natural and theta

joins and show   that the T-selector combined with the Carte-

sian product generalizes these.   Then we consider quantifiers,

which are necessary to include relational division in the

formalism.   This leads us to the QT-selector and the QT-join.

In section 3 we show how the QT-selector can be specialized

to serve in place of the predicate calculus and give illustra-

tions from logic textbooks.   Section 4, on implementation,

reassures us that all these extensions of the relational

algebra and predicate calculus are not mere pipe-dreams: it

gives a one-pass algorithm for the single-relation QT-expres-

sion and discusses efficient implementations of multiple-rela-

tion expressions.   Finally, we use the features of the extend-

ed relational algebra to classify queries and we give some

examples.

1.   EXTENDING THE RELATIONAL ALGEBRA

The relational algebra contains two monadic operations,

project (Codd 1970) and restrict   (Codd 1972).   The pro-

jection of $R(A,\bar{A})$ on A is defined

$$R[A] = \{r[A] : r\varepsilon R\} \quad . \tag{1-1}$$

The θ-restriction of $R(A,B,C)$ on A and B (where C may

be empty) is

$$R[A\theta B] = \{r : r\varepsilon R \wedge (r[A] \, \theta \, r[B])\} \quad . \tag{1-2}$$

This can be extended to the notion of selection of R   on T ,

$$R[T] = \{r : r\varepsilon R \wedge r[T]\} \tag{1-3}$$

where T is <u>any</u> logical condition that can be defined on a
single tuple and the notation r[T] slightly extends the
component notation: r[T] is true if T is true for r and
false otherwise. T is called a <u>tuple-predicate</u>. We would
write T as AθB and r[T] = r[A] θ r[B] if we wished to
specialize selection to θ-restriction.

There is advantage (and often no loss in performance over
projection) in combining projection and selection. We call
the result the <u>T-selector</u>

$$A \underline{if} \ T \ \underline{in} \ R = \{r[A] : r\epsilon R \ \bigwedge \ r[T]\} \tag{1-4}$$

for which we use a slightly altered notation. This expression is a monadic operation of the relational algebra,
creating a new relation from an old.

As a notational convenience, if T is true for every
tuple in R , we will omit "<u>if</u> T" in (1-4), and if A is all
the attributes of R , we will omit "A" in (1-4). Thus
projection is

$$A \underline{in} \ R \tag{1-5}$$

and selection is

$$\underline{if} \ T \ \underline{in} \ R \tag{1-6}$$

Combining the T-selector with the Cartesian product
generalizes most of the dyadic operations on relations defined in Codd (1970), Codd (1972) and Merrett (1977a). We
define the <u>T-join</u> of R and S ,

$$A \underline{if} \ T \ \underline{in} \ (R \times S) \tag{1-7}$$

where A is a group of attributes drawn from those of R or
S or both. It is straightforward to show that joins such as
the natural join are special cases. For example, the θ-join
of R(A,$\bar{A}$) on A with S(B,$\bar{B}$) on B is, for comparable A
and B ,

$$R[A\theta B]S = A, \bar{A}, B, \bar{B}, \underline{if} \; A\theta B \; \underline{in} \; (R \times S)$$

$$= \underline{if} \; A\theta B \; \underline{in} \; (R \times S) \; . \qquad\qquad (1-8)$$

The natural join of R(A,$\bar{A}$) on A with S(B,$\bar{B}$) on B is
a projection of a special case of the θ-join

$$R[A*B]S = A, \bar{A}, \bar{B} \; \underline{if} \; A=B \; \underline{in} \; (R \times S). \qquad\qquad (1-9)$$

The maybe join (Codd 1975) may be written

$$R[A?B]S = \underline{if} \; A=\phi \; \mathbf{V} \; B=\phi \; \underline{in} \; (R \times S) \qquad\qquad (1-10)$$

where ϕ is the null value.

   This leaves us with μ-join (Merrett 1977a,b) and with
division, which was introduced (Codd 1972) to provide an
algebraic counterpart to the universal quantifier of predicate
calculus. We now extend the T-selector to include quantifiers.

2.   QUANTIFIERS

   A proposal to introduce quantifiers into the relational
algebra may seem, at first sight, a strange one. Quantifiers
are what distinguish predicate calculus from propositional
logic (Boolean algebra) and seem to be the essence of a
"calculus"-like rather than an algebraic approach. This is
not true. It is in fact a historical accident that one

branch of logic should be thought of as an algebra and the other called a calculus, since there is no fundamental distinction between the two words. But we can, for interest, compare predicate calculus with The (infinitesimal) Calculus, which, as a branch of Analysis, admits of a much more fundamental and time-honoured distinction from Algebra. A characteristic feature of integral calculus is the use of dummy or bound variables, which are used to range over the real line: x in $\int f(x)dx$. This feature also appears in predicate calculus, as x in $\forall x \ Mx \rightarrow Ax$, only it is less clear what x "ranges over". Specifying the range of x is exceedingly important when computation is involved. It is also important conceptually, and inadequacies of the predicate calculus in this respect lead to the rather contorted formulation $\forall x \ Mx \rightarrow Ax$ for "every man is an animal" (Suppes 1957). Since x ranges over not only all men but some other entities (unspecified) as well, we must first restrict its range to men before going on to the assertion about animals. Thus, we must use implication rather than some more obvious logical structure in $Mx \rightarrow Ax$. This problem becomes worse in more complicated phrases, especially involving the universal quantifier, and accounts, we believe, for much of the difficulty of using predicate calculus.

    This is an attempt to say why many people find predicate calculus a difficult formalism in which to express assertions or queries: in a phrase, bound variables. The reader may disagree with the reasoning, but it seems evident that bound variables cause trouble. Formalists of integral and differential calculus have shown that they are unnecessary, and we now propose an algebraic alternative to predicate calculus which also avoids them. It will be an interesting and important empirical test to see how the following proposal fares in comparison with predicate-calculus based approaches.

Our view of quantifiers is that they specify quantities, and furthermore, quantities of something. This point of view leads us to two ideas about quantified expressions. The first generalizes the classical quantifiers, all and some, into quantifiers with practical value in a world that usually wants to know precisely how much. The second eliminates the troublesome bound variables. Together they make the implementation of quantifier logic on relations not harder but easier, as we shall see in section 4.

Our basic concern in quantified expressions will not be "all" and "some" but in "the number of" and "the proportion of". A practical database application is more likely to be concerned about customers with three or more accounts than about customers with some accounts, or more interested in products accounting for at least 20% of the sales than in products accounting for all of the sales. We define the quantifier symbols, "#" and "." , to symbolize "the number of" and "the proportion of", respectively. Of these, # is the more fundamental since . suffers from ambiguities that must be resolved in any particular application.

We allow a quantifier to use any arbitrary predicate applied to # , the number of, to . , the proportion of, or to both. "All of" and "some of" are special cases, ".=1" and "$\#{\geq}1$" . "Three or more of" is "$\#{\geq}3$" and "at least 20%

of" is ".${\geq}.2$" . "Most of" would be ".${>}.5$" and "an odd number

of" could be expressed "mod($\#$,2) = 1".

We answer the questions, "the number of what?", "the

proportion of what?", "most of what?", etc. by: the

attribute-set. A quantifier is defined as a quantifier pre-

dicate followed by an attribute-group. A quantifier pre-

dicate is any Boolean-valued expression containing one or

both of the symbols "#" or ".": we call it a predicate

rather than a proposition because the quantifier symbols

serve only to mark locations which, on evaluation, will be

filled by actual quantities. For example, if some relation

contained the attribute, MEN , we would express "all men" by

(.=1)MEN . Quantifying an attribute-group, as opposed to a

single attribute, is a simple extension.

This enables us to define the linear QT-selector as

A if QT in R where QT in R is a logical condition called

a linear QT-predicate on $R(A,B_1,\ldots,B_k,C)$, where

$A,B_1,\ldots,B_k,C$ are attribute-groups:

$$QT = QT_1$$
$$QT_j = Q_j\{^{\#}_{\,.}\}\ B_j,\ QT_{j+1}\quad j=1,\ldots,k \qquad\qquad (2\text{-}1)$$
$$QT_{k+1} = T\ \underline{in}\ R$$

where $Q_j\{^{\#}_{\,.}\}$ is a quantifier predicate using one or both of

the quantifier symbols. The meaning of the linear QT-pre-

dicate can be defined in terms of projection and equivalence

reduction (Merrett 1977a) as follows. The value of QT_j is

the Boolean value of $Q_j\{^{s_j}_{s_j/\#_j}\}$ where $\#_j$ is the cardinality* of the attribute-set B_j in R where S_j is the equivalence reduction over R_{j+1} :

$$S_j = + \underline{of} \ (\underline{if} \ QT_{j+1} \ \underline{then} \ 1 \ \underline{else} \ 0) \ \underline{by} \qquad (2\text{-}2)$$

$$(A,B_1,\ldots,B_{j-1}) \qquad\qquad j = 1,\ldots,k$$

and where R_j is the "projection" which creates Q_j :

$$R_j = R_{j+1}[A,B_1,\ldots,B_{j-1},Q_j] \qquad j = 1,\ldots,k+1 \qquad (2\text{-}3)$$

$$R_{k+2} = R \ .$$

To illustrate these definitions, we analyze the QT-selector,

$$u,v \ \underline{if} \ (\#\geq 1)w, \ (\#>2)x, \ y = z \ \underline{in} \ EG \qquad (2\text{-}4)$$

for relation $EG(u,v,w,x,y,z)$. A is $\{u,v\}$, B_1 is w , B_2 is x , T is $y=z$. We have the interpretations of QT_j in (2-1), R_j in (2-3) and S_j in (2-2) as shown in Table 2.1. This will create a relation, on attributes u

TABLE 2.1   Expansion of QT-selector (2-4)

j	QT_j	S_j	Q_j	R_j
4				EG
3	$y=z \ \underline{in} \ EG$		$y=z$	$EG[u,v,w,x,Q_3]$
2	$(\#>2)x, \ QT_3$	$+ \ \underline{of} \ (\underline{if} \ y=z$ $\underline{then} \ 1 \ \underline{else} \ 0)$ $\underline{by} \ (u,v,w)$	$S_2>2$	$R_3[u,v,w,Q_2]$
1	$(\#\geq 1)w, \ QT_2$	$+ \ \underline{of} \ (\underline{if} \ S_2>2$ $\underline{then} \ 1 \ \underline{else} \ 0)$ $\underline{by} \ (u,v)$	$S_1 \geq 1$	$R_2[u,v,Q_1]$

* We adopt the convention that if $\#_j=0$, $Q_j(S_j/\#_j)$ is $\underline{true}$.

and   v , consisting of those tuples of R_2 for which Q_1 is
true. R_2 in turn was created by selecting tuples of R_3
for which Q_2 is true. Q_1 is generated by comparing the
count, S_1 , with the value 1 specified in the outermost
quantifier. This count, for each different value of the
attribute-group {u,v,w} , is found by equivalence reduction.
This process can be followed, backwards, to the original
relation, R_4=EG .

The general definition, in Merrett (1977a), of equivalence reduction is not of concern here. It suffices to say
that + of (if cond then 1 else 0) by D counts all tuples,
for each value of attribute-group D , for which the condition, cond , is true. Applying (2-4) to the example relations of Table 2.2 will reveal the effect of this and of the
other constructs of Table 2.1. The final result is a relation on (u,v) containing the single tuple, (A,1). A QT-
selector using the proportionate quantifier symbol which
would give the same result when applied to EG in Table 2.2
is

     u,v if (#≥1)w, (.=1)x, y=z in EG

since there are only three different values in the attribute-
set, x .

The implementation algorithm in section 4 gives a slightly more powerful interpretation, by retaining whole tuples
of R at each stage, instead of projection components, so
that more data is available to each quantifier predicate.

TABLE 2.2   Example of EG , with Derived Relations

R_4=EG	R_3=EG[u,v,w,x,Q_3]

R_4 ($\underline{u}$ $\underline{v}$ $\underline{w}$ $\underline{x}$ $\underline{y}$ $\underline{z}$)	R_3 ($\underline{u}$ $\underline{v}$ $\underline{w}$ $\underline{x}$ $\underline{y=z}$)	$\underline{S_2}$
A 1 X Y α α	A 1 X Y true ⎫	1
A 1 X Y α β	A 1 X Y false ⎭	
A 1 Y X β β	A 1 Y X true ⎫	
A 1 Y Y α α	A 1 Y Y true ⎬	3
A 1 Y Y β β	A 1 Y Z true ⎭	
A 1 Y Z α α	A 1 Z X true ⎫	
A 1 Z X α α	A 1 Z Y false ⎬	2
A 1 Z X β β	A 1 Z Z true ⎭	
A 1 Z Y α β	A 2 X X false	0
A 1 Z Z α α	B 1 Y X true	1
A 2 X X α β		
B 1 Y X β β		

R_2=R_3[u,v,w,Q_2]	R_1=R_2[u,v,Q_1]

R_2 ($\underline{u}$ $\underline{v}$ $\underline{w}$ $\underline{S_2>2}$)	$\underline{S_1}$	R_1 ($\underline{u}$ $\underline{v}$ $\underline{S_1\geq1}$)
A 1 X false ⎫		A 1 true
A 1 Y true ⎬ 1		A 2 false
A 1 Z false ⎭		B 1 false
A 2 X false	0	
B 1 Y false	0	

From the linear QT-selector and the Cartesian product, we have the linear <u>QT-join</u> of R and S ,

   A <u>if</u> QT <u>in</u> (R × S)

We can now examine division. The <u>division</u> of R(A,$\bar{A}$) on A by S(B,$\bar{B}$) on B is defined, for comparable A and B ,

$$R[A \div B]S = \{r[\bar{A}] : r \epsilon R \wedge S[B] \subseteq \{r'[A] : r'[A] \frown r[\bar{A}] \epsilon R\}\}. \tag{2-5}$$

Using the definition of set inclusion, we may write this

$$R[A \div B]S = \{r[\bar{A}] : r\epsilon R \wedge \forall x(x\epsilon S[B] \to x \frown r[\bar{A}]\epsilon R)\}$$

$$= \{r[\bar{A}] : r\epsilon(R \times S) \wedge \forall x(x\epsilon(R \times S)[B] \to$$

$$x \frown r[\bar{A}]\epsilon(R \times S)[A,\bar{A}])\} \qquad (2-6)$$

We show the equivalence of this to the QT-join

$$\bar{A} \underline{if}(.=1)B, \ A=B \ \underline{in} \ (R \times S) \ , \qquad (2-7)$$

which, after applying the definitions of linear QT-join and linear QT-selector, is

$$\{r[\bar{A}] : r\epsilon(R \times S) \wedge (\#_B = + \ \underline{of} \ (\underline{if} \ A=B \ \underline{then} \ 1 \ \underline{else} \ 0)$$

$$\underline{by} \ \bar{A})\} \qquad (2-8)$$

where $\#_B$ is the total number of different values of the attribute-set of B in $R \times S$ and hence in S and where the summation is evaluated on $(R \times S) [\bar{A},B,A=B]$. Values of $\bar{A}$ are only selected in (2-8) such that for each value, the number of different values of B for which A=B in the tuple is equal to the number of different values of B in $R \times S$. This is equivalent to saying that values of $\bar{A}$ are selected such that for all values of B in $R \times S$, these values concatenated with the value of $\bar{A}$ form a tuple of $(R \times S) [A,\bar{A}]$. Thus (2-8) and (2-6) are equivalent.

Some variants of division that this formulation gives rise to are "not all division",

$$\bar{A} \ \underline{if} \ (.<1) \ B, \ A=B \ \underline{in} \ (R \times S) \qquad (2-9)$$

and "most division",

$\qquad$ $\bar{A}$ _if_ (.>5) B, A=B _in_ (R × S) .   (2-10)

A useful alternative to division is "converse division",

$\qquad$ $\bar{A}$ _if_ (.=1) A, A=B _in_ (R × S) .

The problem with the universal quantifier and its generalization involving the "proportion of" quantifier symbol is
that the proportion is _relative_. For this reason it would be
incorrect to specify division as

$\qquad$ R[A÷B]S = $\bar{A}$ _if_ (.=1) B _in_ R[A=B]S :

the value of $\#_B$ might be wrongly given. In using the QT-
join to _express_ assertions or queries this is perhaps the
trickiest point. (If we know $\#_B$ in advance, division can be
implemented using the equi-join or even the natural join.)
This problem does not arise for the existential quantifier or
its generalization.

It is evident from this discussion that the linear QT-
join is a powerful extension of the dyadic operations of the
relational algebra.

3. QT LOGIC

Quantifiers give the QT-selector a logical capability
that can be compared with first-order predicate calculus. We
make this comparison in this section. Using the QT-predicate, which has a scalar Boolean value, we give some examples
from a textbook of elementary logic, which also serve to
illustrate the notions developed so far in the paper. Then

we mention some limitations of QT logic as defined so far.

We introduce a variant of the linear QT-selector, the
linear QT-counter, # A if QT in R , which simply gives the
cardinality of the corresponding QT-selector, the relation
A if QT in R . This quantity could be obtained by using
simple reduction from the domain algebra (Merrett 1977a,b),
but it is useful enough and easy enough to implement that it
warrants a separate structure. Similarly, .A if QT in R
gives the proportion of A in R that satisfy QT . Other
quantities such as sum, average, etc, which can also be obtained with the domain algebra, are not provided as QT-expressions.

We allow a mixture of QT-counter and QT-selector, with
form A_1, # A_2 if QT in R , which gives the attribute-group
A_1 and, for each value of A_1 , the number of distinct
values of attribute-group A_2 in tuples with this value of
A_1 . This mixture, together with linear QT-selectors, QT-
predicates and QT-counters, form the set of linear QT-expressions.

Using the linear QT-predicate defined in the last section, we will formulate some of the exercises of Lambek (1976),
chapter XI. The exercises are formulated in terms of the
sets poets, hippies, rich people and Maoists, eg. "all poets
are hippies", "all rich people hate all Maoists", "some rich
people hate only Maoists who hate some hippies." Since set
membership is the same as possessing a property*, we express
these sets as the Boolean-valued attributes p , h , r , m ,
respectively, in the relation P (for people) with key n

---

* Cantor's axiom for sets. cf Suppes (1957)

(for name): P(n,h,p,r,m) . We also use relation H (for

hates) between individuals, H(n1,n2) , with attributes

appropriately renamed.

(a) All poets are hippies   (.=1)n, p→h in P

                                or (#=#n if p in P)n, p∧h in P

                                   <<all poets,also hippies in P>>

(b) Some poets are Maoists   (#≥1)n, p ∧ m in P

(c) No poets are rich   (#=0)n, p ∧ r in P

(d) Only poets are hippies   (.=1)n, h→p in P

(e) Nixon is rich   n='Nixon' ∧ r in P

(g) Not all rich people are   (.<1)n, r→m in P
     Maoists

(i) No poet is both rich and   (#=0)n, p ∧ r ∧ h in P
     a hippie

(n) All Maoists hate Nixon   (#=#n if m in P)n1, n2='Nixon'

                                    ∧ m in P[n*n1]H

(o) All rich people hate all   (#=#n if r in P)n1,
     Maoists
                                    (#=#n if m in P)n2 in

                                    (H[n1*n](n if r in P))

                                    [n2*n](n if m in P)

                                    <<all rich people, all Maoists

                                    in hate (rich people,Maoists)>>

Further examples are given, and explained, in Merrett (1977c).

     It is certain that the range of quantifiers provided by

QT logic far exceeds that of the predicate calculus. Not

only are quantifiers such as "no" and "not all" much easier

to handle, but also quantifiers constructed from arbitrary

quantifier-predicates, such as "at least 3 of", "at most 16

of", "between 3 and 16 of", "an odd number of", etc., can be

expressed.

4. IMPLEMENTATION

The secret of efficient implementation of QT-expressions
lies in the fact that all projections and equivalence reductions in equations (2-2) and (2-3) are controlled by the
same attributes, $A, B_1, \ldots, B_{j-1}$, at level j . If the relation is sorted lexicographically on $A, B_1, \ldots, B_k$, then
linear processing of the relation will be needed to evaluate
the QT-expression. The only exception is that if an attribute occurs both in A and in some B_j , some back-tracking
will be needed to obtain all values of the attribute which
have been selected in a QT-selector. The amount of back-
tracking depends on how near the beginning of A the attribute occurs, and on the number of values of succeeding attributes in A for which the quantifier-predicate of this attribute is satisfied. If we disallow such repetition (for the
discussion of this section) and restrict attention to linear
QT-expressions without nesting, we can give a one-pass
algorithm. We feel justified in excluding the cost of sorting because, even for the pure representation of relations
(Date 1971), sorting may on occasions be unnecessary, and
because, in forthcoming work, we propose representations in
which sorting is almost never necessary for this operation.

For the restricted case, A <u>if</u> $Q_1 B_1, \ldots, Q_k B_k, T$ <u>in</u> R ,
here is the one-pass algorithm, with R assumed sorted
lexicographically on $A, B_1, \ldots, B_k$. QT_{k+1} is initially false
and S_j is initially 0, $j = 0, \ldots, k$.

<u>For</u> each tuple

    <u>Comment</u> "control break" is the position of the first

        attribute group, counting left to right with

        A at position 0 , at which the tuple

        differs from the previous tuple. The first

        tuple is assumed identical with its "pre-

        decessor" and the "last tuple" is an imaginary

        successor to the actual final tuple, giving

        a control break of -1 .

    <u>If</u> control break $\geq$ k , do logical or of QT_{k+1} with

        tuple-predicate

    <u>else</u> add, to S_k , 1 if QT_{k+1} else 0

        <u>if</u> control break = k , $QT_{k+1} \leftarrow$ tuple predicate

        <u>else</u> <u>for</u> each attribute-group, j $\leftarrow$ k-1 <u>by</u> -1 <u>to</u>

            max (0, control break)

            $QT_{j+1} \leftarrow$ quantifier-predicate$_{j+1}$

            add, to S_j , 1 if QT_{j+1} else 0

        <u>if</u> control break $\leq$ 0 , add tuple to QT-selector

                  or, if last tuple, assign

                  value to QT-predicate

                  from QT_0 or to

                  QT-counter from S_0

        <u>if</u> not last tuple, $QT_{k+1} \leftarrow$ tuple predicate

                  $S_j \leftarrow 0$ for j $\leftarrow$ max (0, con-

                  trol break) +1 <u>to</u> k

<u>end</u> for each tuple   (4-1)

The reader should apply this algorithm to QT-selector
(2-4), using the relation EG in Table 2.2.

For a general QT-expression, all relations must be sorted
lexicographically at the beginning, but since no further
sorting is necessary for the μ-joins, the whole can be implemented by pipelining tuple-by-tuple into a hierarchy of
multi-way merges. The operation is still linear in cost. In
algorithm (4-1), we allow the whole tuple to be accessible
at all levels, in case a quantifier-predicate needs to use a
value from the tuple. It may be desirable in the general
case to reduce the width of the merged tuples by suitable
projections in the pipelines.

5. QUERIES

Based on the features of the extended relational algebra –
conventional relational operators, domain algebra and QT-expressions – a classification of queries may be made. This is
really a classification of formulations of queries in the
relational algebra rather than of the queries themselves.
However, it gives a reasonable subjective indication of how
difficult it is to formulate the query.

We make the classification along six dimensions, to each
of which we attribute two to four values. The values indicate
subjective complexity, which increases with the value. The
dimensions themselves have some correlation with subjective
difficulty, and we present them in order of decreasing difficulty. There is some arbitrariness here, of course, exaggerated by an attempt to keep the number of dimensions and the
number of values in each as small as possible.

TABLE 5.1. Classification of Query Formulations.

ID	Property	Values			
		0	1	2	3
1	linear vs general QT-expr	linear	general	—	—
2	simple vs compound attrib-groups	simple	compound	—	—
3	domain algebra	none	scalar,reduc.	equiv,fcn,par	QT-expr. in
4	nesting of QT-expressions	none	in relation	in quantifier	in tuple-pred.
5	quantifiers	none	#	., both	—
6	conventional relational alg.	none	any join	division	Cart. product

Table 5.1 outlines the properties and values of dimensions, D , 1 to 6. In D2 , we refer to the possibility of
compound attribute-groups appearing not only after quantifiers
but as the control of joins, equivalence reductions, or other
operations that are used explicitly in formulating the query:
in any of these cases, a query needing compound attribute-
groups seems much more difficult to grasp than one involving
groups of only one attribute. D3 uses the domain algebra
categories (Merrett 1977a,b) of scalar, reduction, equivalence reduction, functional mapping and partial functional
mapping. Value 3 is given if the domain algebra statement
itself contains a QT-expression. The rest of Table 5.1 is
straightforward.

According to this classification, the exercises in section
3 fare as follows

000000	e
000010	b,c,i
000020	a,d,g
000210	a,n
000211	o

In a study, we used the extended relational algebra to
formulate 187 different queries including all those published
in the following papers: Codd (1971), Bracchi et al (1972),
Boyce et al (1973), Chamberlin et al (1974), Copeland and Su
(1974), Rothnie (1974), Held et al (1975), Rothnie (1975),
Zloof (1975), Astrahan and Chamberlin (1975), Pirotte (1976),

Lacroix and Pirotte (1977a), Pirotte and Wodon (1977),
Prenner (1977), Lacroix and Pirotte (1977b). Their distribution according to our classification is shown in Table 5.2.
Some queries had more than one formulation, thus occupying
more than one slot in the classification. Difficulty increases roughly from the bottom left to the top right corner
of this representation. It was apparent during the exercise
that simple queries could be written down as simple transla-
tions from English into QT logic notation but that complex
queries had to be thought of procedurally before they could
be formulated. Each query was formulated in a single expression with the support of at most two domain algebra statements, statements to rename relations and attributes and, a
couple of times, two or three statements to create a working
relation when additional data was needed. The only queries
we did not handle properly were two involving quota retrieval
in Codd (1971) and Pirotte and Wodon (1977): these require
the subalgebra facilities of Aldat (Merrett 1977b) and needed
more programming than we wished to use.

We now give examples of queries and their formulations
from a few of the categories. It is interesting to begin
with an example from Rothnie (1974) and Rothnie (1975), which
are papers discussing implementation. We see how, in Aldat,
the programmer can follow simple guidelines to control efficiency. These are: select and project at the lowest possible level of the expression and use dyadic operations according to the following categories of decreasing preferability -
μ-join, division, θ-join (θ = <, ≤, ≥, >), Cartesian
product.

TABLE 5.2   Distribution of Some Published Database Queries

	-0-00-	1-	2-	10-	1-	2-	20-	1-	2-	30-	1-	2-	-1-00-	1-	2-	10-	1-	2-	20-	1-	2-	30-	1-	2-
1-3--3																								
2																								
1																								
0																								
1-2--3																								
2																								
1																								
0																								
1-1--3																								
2																								
1																								
0																								
1-0--3																								
2																								
1			1	2																				
0																								
0-3--3																								
2																								
1																								
0				1																				
0-2--3														3										
2				1																				
1		1		5	6																			
0	10	2		1																				
0-1--3				2																				
2																								
1	1			6																				
0	11			1																				
0-0--3			2	2		4																		
2	2			6	1																			
1	10	4	2	27	7	6	2			3	1		1			1								
0	41	9	7							6														

Q1. (Rothnie 1974, #4; R1(A1,A2,A3,A4,A5);

                                    classific . 010101)

            RANGE R1 T1

            RANGE R1 T2 SOME

            GET W1 T1.all attributes:

            T1.A3<3 AND (T1.A2=T2.A1 AND T2.A4<5)

            OR (T1.A3=T2.A1 AND T2.A4>395)

In formulating this with a QT-expression, we adopt the following, informal, renaming convention to eliminate conflicts
among attribute names: a relation and all its attributes may
be renamed by adding a suffix character (such as ' or a
digit) to the relation name and to all the attribute names.
In the following examples, we rename this way implicitly,
since no confusion should arise.

    A1,A2,A3,A4,A5 in ((if A3<3 in R1)[A2*A1']

    (A1' if A4'<5 in R1')[(A1,A2,A3,A4,A5)∪(A1,A2,A3,A4,A5)]

    R1[A3*A1'](A1' if A4'>395 in R1'))

Here, natural joins of R1 with itself suffice to give the
equality conditions T1.A2=T2.A1 , T1.A3=T2.A1 . It is
appropriate to think of the natural join as a case of QT-join
specialized for efficiency. From this point of view, our
formulation of Q1 is possibly nearly optimal. Since our
efficiency guidelines are so simple, it would be an easy
matter to include them in an automatic translator, and possibly to tune them to the actual relation. This approach,
of using relational algebra in conjunction with single-relation query operations seems first to have been used in
Bracchi et al (1973).

We now give ten examples from Boyce et al 1973, Zloof
1975, Pirotte 1976 and Lacroix and Pirotte 1977a, without
further explanation, to illustrate a variety of queries and
their formulations. The reader should bear in mind that
QT-selectors are not proposed for a direct query language
but as a new algebraic operation in the programming language,
Aldat. We use operations, such as division and natural join,
which have already in this paper been derived from QT-selectors because we feel this would be appropriate in a programming language, both for familiarity and for efficiency.

Q2. (Boyce et al 1973, Q5; EMP(NAME,SAL,MGR); classific.
     000001) Find the names of employees who make more than
     their manager.
     NAME if SAL>SAL1 in EMP [MGR*NAME1] EMP1

Q3. (Zloof 1975, Q10; SALES (DEPT,ITEM), SUPPLY (SUPPLIER,
     ITEM); classific. 000102) Find the department(s) that
     sells all the items supplied by Parker.
     DEPT in SALES [ITEM÷ITEM](ITEM if SUPPLIER = 'PARKER'
     in SUPPLY)

Q4. (Pirotte 1976, Q11; EMP (NAME,SAL); classific. 000103)
     List the name of the employees whose salary is greater
     than the salary of ANDERSON.
     NAME if SAL>SAL1 in EMP×(SAL1 if NAME1= 'ANDERSON' in
     EMP1)

Q5. (Zloof 1975, Q12; SALES (DEPT,ITEM), SUPPLY (SUPPLIER,
ITEM); classific. 000123) Find the department(s) which
sells only all the items supplied by Parker.

DEPT if (.=1) ITEM , (.=1) ITEM1, ITEM = ITEM1 in SALES×
(ITEM1 if SUPPLIER1 = 'PARKER' in SUPPLY1)

Q6. (Lacroix and Pirotte 1977a, E8; SALES (DEPT,ITEM),
SUPPLY (COMP,DEPT,ITEM); classific. 002111) List every
department selling all the items which are supplied to
it.

let ITDEP be equiv + of 1 by DEPT

DEPT if (#=ITDEP) ITEM in SALES1 [DEPT1*DEPT] (DEPT,
ITDEP in (DEPT, ITEM in SUPPLY))

Q7. (Pirotte 1976, E24; USEDUNDER (CONF,COMP), CONFVAL
(CONF,VALUE); classific. 002001) For each company,
give each configuration that it uses together with the
next larger value that it also uses.

let NEXVAL be equiv min of (if VALUE1>VALUE then VALUE1
else empty) by COMP

COMP, CONF, CONF1 if VALUE1=NEXVAL in (USEDUNDER
[CONF*CONF] CONFVAL)   [COMP*COMP1] (USEDUNDER1
[CONF1*CONF1] CONFVAL1)

Q8. (Pirotte 1976, E23; USEDUNDER (CONF,COMP), CONFVAL
(CONF,VALUE), CPUCONF(CONF,CPU); classific. 002111)
List the cpu model of each configuration which has the
largest value among configurations of some company.

let CMVAL be equiv max of VALUE by COMP

CPU in CPUCONF [CONF*CONF](CONF if (#≥1)COMP,VAL=CMVAL in
USEDUNDER [CONF*CONF] CONFVAL)

Q9. (Lacroix and Pirotte 1977a, E9; SALES (DEPT,ITEM),
     SUPPLY (COMP,DEPT,ITEM), LOC(DEPT,FLOOR) <u>classific</u>.
     010001) List each department that sells items supplied
     to departments located at the same floor.
     DEPT1 <u>if</u> DEPT1≠DEPT2 <u>in</u> (SALES1[DEPT1*DEPT1] LOC1)
     [(ITEM1,FLOOR1)*(ITEM2,FLOOR2)] (SUPPLY[DEPT2*DEPT2]LOC2)

Q10. (Pirotte 1976, E18, USEDUNDER(CONF,COMP), IMPLUNDER
     (CONF,LANG,SYS); <u>classific</u>. 100021) List companies
     which use at least one configuration, except those
     companies which have FORTRAN implemented on all their
     configurations.
     COMP <u>if</u> (#≥1) CONF <u>in</u> USEDUNDER ∧ (.<1) CONF,
     LANG='FORTRAN' <u>in</u> USEDUNDER [CONF*CONF] IMPLUNDER

Q11. (Pirotte 1976, E11; IMPLUNDER (CONF,LANG,SYS);
     <u>classific</u>. 012113) List configurations where all the
     pairs language-system available together on the con-
     figuration are such that the language is available
     under system S and the system supports language L .
     <u>let</u> INCONF <u>be</u> <u>equiv</u> + <u>of</u> 1 <u>by</u> CONF
     CONF <u>if</u> (#=INCONF)(LANG,SYS), LANG=LANG1 ∧ SYS=SYS1
     <u>in</u> (CONF,INCONF, LANG, SYS <u>in</u> IMPLUNDER)×(LANG1 <u>if</u>
     SYS1='S' <u>in</u> IMPLUNDER1)×(SYS1 <u>if</u> LANG1='L' <u>in</u> IMPLUNDER1)

REFERENCES

Astrahan, M.M., and Chamberlin, D.D. (1975). Implementation of a structured English query language. CACM 18,10, 580-7.

Boyce, R.F., Chamberlin, D.D. King, W.F., and Hammer, M.M. (1973). Specifying queries as relational expressions: SQUARE. IBM Research Laboratory, San Jose, RJ 1291.

Bracchi, G., Fedeli, A., and Paolini, P. (1972). A language for a relational data base management system. Proc. Sixth Annual Princeton Conf. on Info. Sci. and Syst., 84-92.

Chamberlin, D.D., and Boyce R.F. (1974). SEQUEL: a structured English query language. ACM SIGMOD Workshop on Data Description, Access and Control (Ann Arbor, Mich.), 249-64.

Codd, E.F. (1970). A relational model of data for large shared data banks. Comm ACM 13, 6, 377-87.

Codd, E.F. (1971). A data base sublanguage founded on the relational calculus. ACM SIGFIDET Workshop Data Description, Access and Control. (San Diego, Calif.), 35-68.

Codd, E.F. (1972). Relational completeness of data base sublanguages. In R. Rustin, ed., Database Systems. Prentice-Hall, Englewood Cliffs, N.J.

Codd, E.F. (1975). Understanding relations (Installment #7). FDT 7, 3-4, 23-28.

Copeland, G.P., and Su, S.Y.W. (1974). A high level data sublanguage for a content-addressed segment-sequential memory. ACM SIGMOD Workshop on Data Description, Access and Control (Ann Arbor, Mich.), 265-76.

Date, C.J. and Hopewell, P. (1971). Storage structures and physical data independence. Proc. ACM SIGFIDET Workshop Data Description, Access and Control (San Diego, Calif.), 139-68.

Held, G.H., Stonebraker, M.R. and Wong, E. (1975). INGRES - A relational data base system. Proc. AFIPS National Computer Conf. (Anaheim, Calif.), 409-16.

Lacroix, M., and Pirotte, A. (1977a). ILL: an English structured query language for relational data bases. In G.M. Nijssen, ed., Architecture and Models in Data Base Management Systems (Working Conference organized by IFIP Technical Committee 2, Nice, Jan 1977) North Holland, Amsterdam, 237-60.

Lacroix, M. and Pirotte, A. (1977b). Domain-oriented relational languages. Proc. Third Internat. Conf. on Very Large Data Bases. (Tokyo).

Lambek, J. (1972). Mathematical Logic. McGill (revised 1976).

Merrett, T.H. (1977a). Relations as programming language elements. Info. Processing Lett. 6, 1, 29-33.

Merrett, T.H. (1977b). Aldat - augmenting the relational algebra for programmers. Technical Report SOCS-78.1, McGill.

Merrett, T.H. (1977c). The extended relational algebra, a basis for query languages (a preliminary version of the present paper, giving additional details). Technical Report SOCS-78.2, McGill.

Pirotte, A. (1976). Explicit description of entities and their manipulation in languages for the relational data base model. Thèse de doctorat en Sciences Appliquées, Université Libre de Bruxelles. M.B.L.E. Research Laboratory Report R336.

Pirotte A., and Wodon, M. (1977). A comprehensive formal query language for a relational data base: FQL. RAIRO Informatique/Computer Science, 11, 2, 165-83.

Prenner, C.J. (1977). A uniform notation for expressing queries. Electronics Research Laboratory, University of California, Berkeley, Memorandum No. UCB/ERL M77/60.

Reisner, P., Boyce, R.F., and Chamberlin, D.D. (1975). Human factors evaluation of two data base query languages - Square and Sequel. Proc. AFIPS National Computer Conf. (Anaheim, Calif.), 439-46.

Ross, W.D. (1949). Aristotle's Prior and Posterior Analytics. A Revised Text with Introduction and Commentary. Oxford U.P.

Rothnie, J.B. (1974). An approach to implementing a relational data management system. ACM SIGMOD Workshop on Data Description, Access and Control (Ann Arbor, Mich.), 277-94.

Rothnie, J.B. (1975). Evaluating inter-entry retrieval expressions in a relational data base management system. Proc. AFIPS National Computer Conf. (Anaheim, Calif.) 417-24.

Suppes, P. (1957). Introduction to Logic. Van Nostrand, Princeton.

Zloof, M.M. (1975). Query by example. Proc. AFIPS National Computer Conf. 44 (Anaheim, Calif.), 431-8.

Simplifying Design and Implementation

DATABASES: IMPROVING USABILITY AND RESPONSIVENESS

AN IMPLEMENTATION OF FORAL USING IDMS

Daniel Goldschmidt
Allen Reiter

Department of Computer Science
Technion - Israel Institute of Technology
Haifa, Israel

FORAL is a non-procedural data specification and manipulation language based on binary associations. IDMS is a commercial database management system based on a "network" model and belonging to the CODASYL DBTG
group of languages. We describe an implementation of a subset of the
FORAL query language over existing IDMS databases. The mappings from
FORAL to IDMS data types cause some problems and require trading off language power and user convenience against efficiency of execution; this
tradeoff is left to the database asministrator. The data structures and
algorithms used in query translation and execution are also described.

Key words: Binary associations, database, data management, network model,
query language, searching
Computing Reviews categories: 4.33, 3.74.

1. INTRODUCTION

We describe an implementation of a "binary associations" query language (FORAL) over a database management system which belongs to the
"network" family (IDMS).

One of the strengths of FORAL is its use of context for conciseness
in the query specification and for semantic integrity checking. Its world
is composed of entities and facts. FORAL does not distinguish between one
to many, many to one and many to many relations, nor do reflexive relations
merit any special treatment.

IDMS on the other hand has a record/field orientation in its data
representations, and requires special treatment of many to many and

reflexive relations. This necessitates special treatment in setting up
file schema and also results in some restrictions on the end user of FORAL.
The reason why one would choose to implement FORAL using such a seem-
ingly unsuitable vehicle as IDMS is simple: expediency and availability.
In his original papers describing FORAL (references [2],[3],[4], and [5])
Senko describes a data management system DIAM suitable for implementation.
However, there are no known implementations of DIAM, and to such an
implementation was outside the scope of the project. At the same time, it
seemed to us that the many interesting features of FORAL merited attempting
a direct implementation over a commonly used DBMS.

Another reason for using IDMS for the implementation was the existence
of several databases which would be candidates for using the language for
on-line queries. These databases are being maintained via conventional
COBOL-plus-IDMS programs; had we chosen a different vehicle for FORAL and
still wanted to use it to search these databases, two different copies of
the same database (with all the ensuing problems) would have to be maintained. (The alternative - conversion of the entire system - was not even
contemplated.)

Sections 2 and 3 of the paper summarize the salient characteristics of
FORAL and IDMS. Section 4 deals with the problem of mapping FORAL
structures onto IDMS, and the resulting language restrictions. Some
technical details pertinent to our construction of the FORAL query executor
are described in Section 5, and illustrated by example in Section 6.

2. AN OVERVIEW OF THE FORAL LANGUAGE

FORAL is a language for user interaction with computer stored databases.
As that, it has been designed to be easily understood by non-programmer
users. User transactions are written in terms of real world things and
their attributes rathen than in term of fields, records, files, etc.

FORAL is less procedural than most computer languages, the user
specifying the information needed, and not how to get it. Special emphasis
has been placed in the construction of a set of English-like rules for ease
of use and understanding.

To state FORAL queries, a user refers to a base structure similar to
the DIAM ([3]) type diagram, although he may be working over a different
kind of data base system. This diagram is a graphical representation of
the information (corresponding to the DIAM II Infological level) present
in the database.

This diagram is constructed using two types of building blocks:

1) Entity sets, which are sets of entities from the real world.

2) Fact sets, which provide a way for describing entities.

Since most entities cannot be stored in a computing system, "storable entities" are used to stand for them. For example, we cannot store an "employee entity" in a computing system, but we can use a storable entity such as "234". In this case, "234" is an Identifier Value representing one specific employee. We could also have a department represented by "234", so that the value "234" would be a member of two entity sets, say EMP-NO for employees and DEPT-NO for departments.

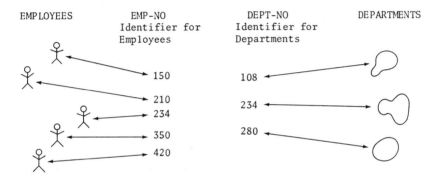

Figure 1. Two Identifiers with their
Identifier Values

In Fig. 1 we have four entity sets. The entities of two of the sets, EMP-NO and DEPT-NO can be stored in a computer and used to identify themselves. They can also be used to identify the entities of other sets, in this case employees and departments.

A Fact Set connects two entity sets, and indicates that the members of one of the entity sets describe in some way members of the other entity set. Fact Sets go in both directions.

For example, the Fact Set

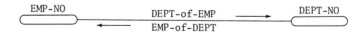

relates the Entity Sets EMP-NO and DEPT-NO. The names above and below the line are called attribute names, and distinguish the two directions of the relationship.

A basic fact is represented by the association of Identifier Values for two entities.

For example,

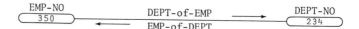

If our context is centered on "EMP-NO,350", then we can get a particular
attribute value of this employee by following the association line named
"DEPT-of-EMP" to the value "234" to the other end. This tells us that the
entity EMP-NO "350" has an attribute named "DEPT-of-EMP" with the attribute
value "234".

The converse is also true. If our context is at "DEPT-No,234", we can
get a value of the departments attribute called EMP-of-DEPT by following
the association line. This tells us the employee number of one of the
employees of this department. Note that in this representation there is
no difference between one to many, many to many, or many to one relationships.

Context was mentioned earlier. It plays a very important role in
FORAL, making the statement of queries simpler and more English-like, and
assuring a greater semantic integrity. For example, you can ask for the
attribute DEPT-of-EMP only if the context is at EMP-NO. If only one Fact
Set connects two Entity Sets, context enables us to use the target entity
set name instead of the attribute name, thus making the sentence more
readable in many cases.

A FORAL query specifies a tree[*] over the network defined by the DIAM
diagram (the "world"). The tree hierarchy is similar to the hierarchy
imposed by the context, only connected nodes can be present. The FORAL
query language is very concise, permitting the equivalent of a complete
computer program to be stated in one sentence.

The query tree is specified using a very small set of operators. We
will explain their use by stating queries over the database shown by the
DIAM diagram of Figure 2.

Some of the arrows emanating from the "ovals" have "*" on them.
These indicates the Preferred Identifier for the Entity Set in the oval.
For example, the preferred identifier for EMPLOYEES is EMP-NO. When

---

[*] A FORAL query may "loop back" on itself, with the same entity appearing
several times in different roles. Its representation is however always
a tree, with different nodes corresponding to each role of the entity.
See example below in Section 2.5.

EMPLOYEES is addressed, the corresponding value of EMP-NO will be printed out.

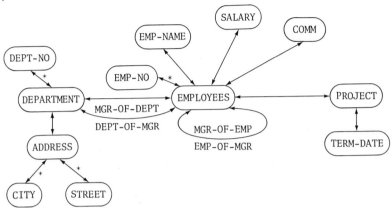

<u>Figure 2</u> Sample DIAM diagram

2.1 <u>Initial Context</u> At first, we state the "initial entity set in context":

EMPLOYEES

this is the whole query, a list of the EMP-NO for all the EMPLOYEES in the database will be printed.

<u>Printing Direct Attributes of the Context</u>

(a) EMPLOYEES print EMP-NAME, SALARY.

The output will be a three column list, with the EMP-NO, EMP-NAME and SALARY of each EMPLOYEE.

(b) DEPARTMENT print EMPLOYEES.

This will produce a two column output, giving for each DEPARTMENT its DEPT-NO and the EMP-NO of each one of its EMPLOYEES

120	341
	820
	905
250	410
	509
	⋮

2.2 <u>Printing Indirect Attributes of the Context</u>

Indirect attributes of an Entity Set are given by entity sets not immediately adjacent to the oval representing it. To specify them, the "of" phrase is used. The whole path is defined, by stating the names of

the attributes from the desired attribute to the context, linked by the
word "of".

For example, the names of the employees of a department are an indirect
attribute of the department. In FORAL we write:

a) DEPARTMENT print EMP-NAME of EMPLOYEE of DEPARTMENT

We will get two columns as in the previous query, but instead of the
employee numbers will appear now the EMP-NAME's.

b) EMPLOYEES print

SALARY, CITY of ADDRESS of DEP-MGR of EMPLOYEES, EMP-NAME

We will get four column output, containing the employee id., salary,
city of the department they manage, and their name.

2.3 Moving the Context. The context is moved from one entity set to
another (which is connected to it by a fact set) by means of the "for"
phrase. The new entity set is then the entity set in context.

a) DEPARTMENT for EMPLOYEE

print EMP-NAME, SALARY

This will produce a four column output, listing all the DEPARTMENTS
(actually DEPT-NO) and for each one, all its EMP-NO, together with the
EMP-NAME and SALARY each EMPLOYEE. The context can be moved further
by subsequent uses of the "for" phrase.

2.4 Qualifying Entity Set Members. The user can specify which values of
and entity set or attribute are to be selected for processing by means of
the "where qualifies".

a) EMPLOYEES (where SALARY gt 30) print EMP-NAME

The output will consist of two columns, listing the EMP-NO and EMP-
NAME of those EMPLOYEES whose salary is greater than 30. The "where"
clause has its own context, which can be moved in the usual way be
means of the "for" phrase. It can contain any number of test relations,
connected by "and", "or". These relations can involve constants, direct
attributes, indirect attributes (by means of "of" phrases) and also
functions on the attributes.

b) For each employee whose department is in Atlanta, print his name and
the number and street of his department:

EMPLOYEE (where CITY of ADDRESS of DEPARTMENT of

EMPLOYEE eq "Atlanta" print EMP-NAME

for DEPARTMENT print STREET

c) Print all the employees with department number greater than 200 and
located in New York:

EMPLOYEES (where for DEPARTMENT, DEPT-NO gt   200 and
CITY of ADDRESS of DEPARTMENT eq "New-York"

2.5 Multigraph Queries. When an entity set name which was in context at
a higher level appears again as the target of a "for" phrase, the context
jumps back to the previous context (thus effectively returning to the
previous point in the tree). If, instead, we want to keep going "down"
in the tree (the members of the new entity set are subordinate to our
current context), we follow the entity set name with a "called" phrase.

a) EMPLOYEES
        for DEPARTMENT
            (where DEPT-N) gt 250)
            print ADDRESS
        for EMPLOYEES
            for PROJECT print TERM-DATE

b) EMPLOYEES
        for DEPARTMENT
            (where DEPT-NO gt 250)
            print ADDRESS
        for EMPLOYEES called
            EMP_WITH_DEPT_NO_GT_250
        for PROJECT print TERM-DATE

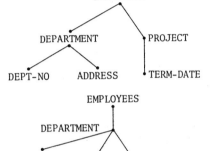

Looking at the resulting trees it is easy to understand the difference
between boty queries.

FORAL has many other interesting features not dealt with here. These
include: the FORAL Input Language, designed to maintain the data base, the
file specification part of the output language, which specifies from which
file the information is to be extracted (if it is not the central data
base) and whether the results should be outputed or stored in a temporary
file for further processing, the "footnote" option, which enables the user
to state parts of his query at a later time, the "all" option, which
specifies that all the direct attributes of the entity in context are to be
printed (instead of listing each one of the attributes), various functions
such as arithmetic operators, count, etc. (Most of these features were
omitted from our implementation.)

3. AN OVERVIEW OF IDMS

A complete description of IDMS can be found in Ref. [6]; we give here
a brief overview sufficient for our purposes.

<u>Schema</u>. The IDMS "world" is described in a data base schema. The schema
is built using two types of blocks: records and sets. There can be any
number of record types, each one composed by a number of fields. Every
occurrence of a record type contains information in its fields.

The structure of the data base is given by its sets. A set always has
a record type as its owner, and one or more record types as its members.
A record can be part of many sets, thus permitting the specification of a
network.

If a record type is the owner of a set, every one of its occurrences
is the start of a chain which links all the member records which are sub-
ordinated to this owner record occurrence.

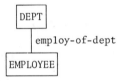

The set employ-of-dept has as its owner the record DEPT, and as its
member, the record EMPLOYEE. A particular instance of this set could be:

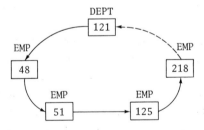

There are some restrictions on the schema structure. For example, a record
type cannot be the owner and a member of the same set; a member record
occurrence can appear at most once in one set occurrence (i.e. the
employee-125 record cannot be part of the set employ-of-dept for depart-
ment-121 and for another department).

If such constructs are required in a data base, a "dummy" record-type
may be used, and the set is split into two sets.

For example, if in a manufacturing data base we want to represent the
relationship between assemblies and the parts of which they are composed,

we would like to have

composed-of

Instead we have to define

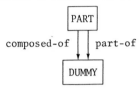

composed-of part-of

To find which parts compose a given part, we traverse the instances of the composed-of set and for every DUMMY record we reach, we ask for its owner instance in the part-of set.

Retrieval Functions. IDMS supplies a number of data base functions which permit accessing records in the data base, either following sets or sequentially by order of appearance in storage. Retrieval can also be on the basis of a supplied key.

The functions relevant for us are:

OBTAIN NEXT RECORD (recordname) SET (setname)
    to retrieve the member records of a given set occurrence

OBTAIN OWNER SET (setname)
    to retrieve the owner record of the current occurrence of the named set.

OBTAIN CALC RECORD (recordname)
    to retrieve the record using its key.

OBTAIN NEXT RECORD (recordname) AREA (areaname)
    to retrieve the records of a given type in the sequence of appearance in the data base.

These functions are invoked from programs written in a host language.

Our task is to write a general-purpose FORAL query processor which generates the requisite sequence of calls to IDMS functions.

4. A MAPPING OF FORAL STRUCTURES ONTO IDMS STRUCTURES

There are a number of substantial differences between the data base structures used by FORAL and those used by IDMS.

First, FORAL has only entities and relations; IDMS has records, fields and sets. While relations may roughly correspond to sets, we have to decide whether entities are to be mapped onto records or onto fields, or what; this decision has important implications on usage and performance.

Second, as mentioned earlier, FORAL allows many-to-many and reflexive

relations, and their internal handling is of no interest to the user. In
the diagram presented to the end user, such relations are not distinguish-
able from one-to-many and many-to-one relations. In IDMS, however, the
representation of such relations necessarily involves adding new record
types and new sets; without some naming conventions or additional information in the file schema, the user would have to provide specifications
which are not part of the FORAL language.

Since FORAL relations are represented by IDMS sets, and since sets
link records, not fields, it is clear that if we map entities onto fields
we will lose some of the power of FORAL, since we will not be able to
represent relations between these entities and others. Actually, the
situation is somewhat better than that: we can make use of the implicit
connection between a record type and the fields which it contains to
represent a FORAL relation between the entity corresponding to a field
and the entity corresponding to a record. (Such relations are sometimes
called properties in other systems.) We can similarly relate two fields
in the same record type to one another. Nevertheless, a FORAL entity
mapped onto an IDMS field in one record type cannot be explicitly related
to an entity mapped onto a different record type or onto a field in a
different record type.

On the other hand, we could choose to map FORAL entities only onto
records; this would give us the full power of FORAL since every relation
can now be represented by an IDMS set (or two sets, for many-to-many and
reflexive relations). Each record would contain one field (to store the
value), but the field name would have no semantic significance. This
solution, while ideal in theory, is not feasible for a number of reasons.
First, the storage overhead (in the form of pointers for representing all
of the necessary connections) would be formidable. Second, even the most
trivial retrieval operation would take an inordinate amount of time, for
to collect what we normally would think of as a record would now require
separate calls for collecting all its fields which may be dispersed
throughout the storage medium. Finally, we set out to build a query language which would also work with existing file schemata for some real data
bases; not unnaturally, these contained a number of different fields per
record type, and we wished to allow a user access to these; in fact, we
did not want a user to be concerned with the specifics of our mapping.

We compromised by allowing either mapping: an entity can correspond
either to a record type or to a field type. The data base administrator
(when setting up the file schema initially) can trade off retrieval power
versus efficiency. Once a schema is set up, the user is not concerned

with this mapping, except for one important restriction: we do not allow
the FORAL <u>context</u> to be left at an entity corresponding to a field.

Assuming that we start with an existing IDMS data base, we have no
difficulty executing a FORAL query over it (assuming that every record
type indeed can be interpreted as an entity). If, however, we start with
a FORAL world view and want to define an IDMS schema for it, we need to
know how to map many-to-many and reflexive relations. Specifically, we
need some naming convention or external definitions so that the "dummy"
record types which are necessarily introduced in IDMS are transparent to
the user.

We chose the latter possibility, i.e. in addition to the standard IDMS
schema we utilize a stored schema which translates a FORAL relation and its
inverse into an IDMS set or an IDMS dummy record and two connecting sets.
Thus, the FORAL diagram

is represented in IDMS thus:

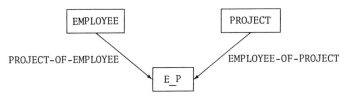

and an additional file schema tells the system that the FORAL "ALL projects
of an employee" in IDMS is executed as "Run through the PROJECT_OF_EMPLOYEE
set and for each E_P record find its owner in the EMPLOYEE_OF_PROJECT set".

Similarly, the FORAL diagram

has the IDMS equivalent

Note that in this example, without naming conventions or some explicit
externally-provided information the system would have no way of knowing
which IDMS set corresponds to the FORAL "MANAGER_OF" relation and which
to its inverse.

Not allowing the FORAL context to rest on a "field" entity does not

seem to be much of a restriction in normal usage; the user would not want
to remain on such a "dead-end" entity in any case. Entities represented
by fields are related automatically to the entity represented by the record;
although this relation does not have an explicit IDMS name, we use the
field name to stand for the relation (in effect, we name the relation, not
the entity). An important consequence of this is that we now allow what
are in effect two different FORAL entities to have the same name as in the
following FORAL diagram:

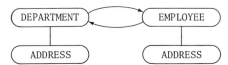

(The ADDRESSes are fields in the corresponding record types.) From the
user's point of view, the appropriate FORAL diagram is actually

where the entity implied by the lower oval (represented by the value of
ADDRESS) is unnamed and not explicitly accessible.

     IDMS has one other "implicit" way of representing a logical relation
between two record types: if record type A is stored using a key
("LOCATION MODE IS CALC"), and record type B has a field whose value
domain ranges over the keys of A, then a occurrence of B defines one or
more specific occurrences of A. Such n-m relations are part of the
normal semantics of an IDMS data base. Note, however, that this relation
is one-way: given an occurrence of A, there is no way to find the corresponding B's, short of scanning all of them.

     We decided to allow such relations to be explicit in FORAL schema.
Such relations can only be traversed in one direction, however, since we
did not want a user inadvertently to execute very time-consuming searches.

5.   IMPLEMENTATION OF FORAL IN IDMS

     The general query processor schematic is shown in Fig. 3. The program
can be divided into two well defined phases: Translation and execution.
     The translator nucleus is a standard top down parser, which calls a
scanner to obtain the next symbol and (when making a reduction) calls
semantic routines which build the execution tree. (A reader not familiar

with compiler-writing is referred e.g. to the excellent book by Gries [7].) The FORAL schema is used in this phase in order to complete information supplied in the query and to perform semantic correctness checking.

The execution phase consists of calls to IDMS to retrieve relevant records; it is driven entirely by the "execution tree" produced by Phase 1. Once a record is brought into core, its effect on the query status is evaluated and all of its relevant information extracted. When appropriate, results are displayed to the user by the PRINT routine.

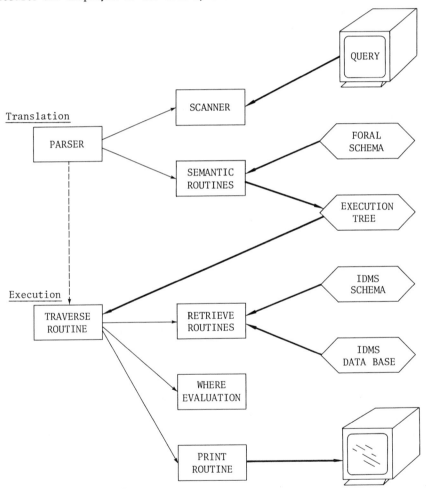

Figure 3: General Program Layout

We now describe the phases in more detail.

5.1 <u>Translation</u>. Our translator is driven by a reduced BNF description of FORAL (see Appendix. A BNF description of the complete FORAL Output Language appears in reference [8]). Not all of the FORAL features are implemented, but enough to provide the nucleus of a working system and to test FORAL feasibility in a real environment.

The input to the translator is the FORAL query, and its output is a tree representation of it called an "execution tree", containing further information which is taken from the FORAL schema.

<u>The Execution Tree</u>. A glance of the trees in Section 2.5 will give the reader insight into the kind of data structures which are required for the internal representation of the query.

We build a tree in which each node (a "record descriptor" node) corresponds to a record type to be visited along a certain access path when the query is executing. Each time a "for" clause occurs, we have a branch emanating from the "context" node. The information present in each node is: the record name, the set name which leads to it, its role in the set (owner or member), a second name if the "called" option was used (see 2.5), and pointers to two auxiliary data structures: a "print chain", listing in this record to be displayed, and (if a "where" clause was present) a "where tree" used to test whether the retrieved record occurrence meets the qualification criteria specified.

The FORAL schema is used to augment the information present in the input query when the execution tree is being built; when going from one node to another the query only lists the target entity name or relation name; the schema provides the missing record or set name, the preferred identifier, and the set direction. The semantic correctness of the query in terms of consistency with the schema is also tested.

The <u>print chain</u> contains a link for every field listed in the print specification as well as for the preferred identifier. If the field is a direct attribute (i.e. an IDMS field in the current record) the link points to a field descriptor. If, however, the field is an indirect attribute (if "of" phrases are present, i.e. fields of related records are implied) the link starts a chain of record descriptor nodes (structured as above) which indicates the records and sets to be traversed in getting to the desired field value.

The <u>where tree</u> consists of a "decision table" which describes the logical structure of the query (AND - OR connectives and parentheses) and a chain of relations to be tested. In the simplest case, an entry in this chain consists of a direct attribute, relational operator, and constant value; the corresponding field in the record occurrence is tested against the constant. If an indirect attribute is specified, a chain of record descriptor nodes leads to the field occurrence to be tested. If however an embedded "for" phrase occurs in the "where" clause (leading to an iterated search), the entry contains a link to another "where" tree, a subtree of the present one.

The decision table is used for optimal query execution: while the predicate is being evaluated the facts known so far are recorded in a table, and parts of the query which no longer affect the value of the predicate are skipped. In this way unnecessary comparisons are avoided. (Note that when an indirect attribute value is involved, this can save a great deal of time in accessing other records.) The data structure and associated algorithms for this are described in [9].

5.2 Query Execution. The second phase consists of "executing" the execution tree. At the heart of this is a depth-first recursive tree traversal routine shown schematically in Figure 4. For each node reached in the execution tree, the corresponding IDMS record is retrieved. If the record qualifies for further processing, its "print chain" is displayed and its subtree in the execution tree is traversed. In both cases, the next record in the current set is retrieved, and the process repeated until the set is exhausted; the process then continues with its father, etc.

```
Print-Verify (node)
        do while (not-end-of-record)
        Validate (node)
        if OK then print (node)
                Print-Verify (son)
        end
        Print-Verify (brother)
end Print-Verify
```

Figure 4: Outline of the recursive tree
traversal routine.

The record retrieval is performed using standard IDMS routines, selected according to the corresponding execution tree node information. For the root node, if the corresponding IDMS record has CALC location and keys are provided in the query (in the"where"clause), direct (CALC) retrieval is performed; otherwise, the file is searched sequentially, the first time

using OBTAIN FIRST RECORD (recordname) in AREA, and afterwards OBTAIN NEXT
RECORD (recordname) in AREA. For the other nodes, a loop of OBTAIN NEXT
RECORD (recordname) SET (setname) is used, or OBTAIN OWNER SET (setname),
depending on the set's direction, as stated in the execution-tree node.

The "Validate node" routine in Figure 4 works similarly. It receives
as its parameters a current context (in the form of a given record occurrence) and a "where tree" which refers to attributes of this record or to
related record occurrences; it must evaluate the predicate expression
represented by the "where tree" and return a value TRUE or FALSE. If an
entry in this tree refers to a direct attribute, it is evaluated directly;
if it involves an indirect attribute, all possible related records are
tried until a TRUE value is received or until the possibilities are exhausted (in which case the value is FALSE); if the entry refers to an
embedded "where tree", the routine calls itself recursively to evaluate
the entry for all possibilities. As soon as one evaluation of TRUE is
obtained, traversal is terminated, and evaluation continues with the next
entry. This action differs from that of the PRINT-VERIFY routine, which
visits every qualifying node. (See also reference [10] where a similar
mechanism is described.)

6. A QUERY EXAMPLE

Consider the following query: "For each department located in New
York, print the names and numbers of the employees with salary greater than
1000 who earned over 500 in commission". In FORAL, this is expressed   as
follows:

```
DEPARTMENT (where CITY of ADDRESS of DEPARTMENT
                 EQ 'NEW YORK')
         for EMPLOYEE (where SALARY GT 1000
                         and COMM GT 500)
             print NAME, COMM
```

The execution-tree for this query is shown in Figure 5.

The first node contains only the record name, DEPARTMENT. All the
DEPARTMENT records will be retrieved sequentially. For each one, the
where clause has to be evaluated. It consists of only one comparison, but
one of the arguments is an indirect attribute. The owner in the set
ADDR-OF-DEPT is retrieved, and the CITY field is compared to 'NEW YORK'.
If there is no match, this DEPARTMENT record does not qualify and the next
one is retrieved.

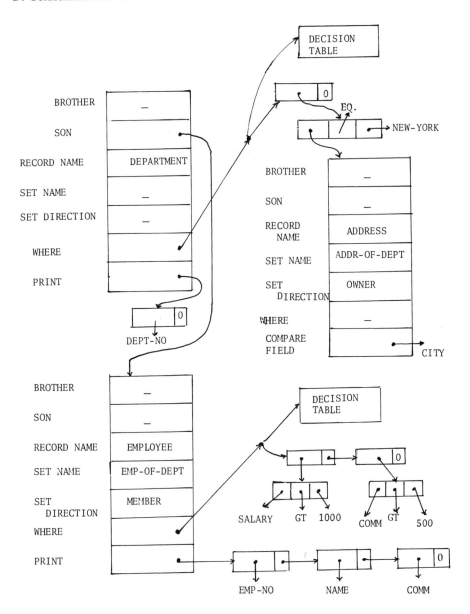

Figure 5. Execution tree example

If the DEPARTMENT qualifies for further processing, its DEPT-NO field (preferred identifier) is printed and the traversal continues with the son node.

At this node the record name is EMPLOYEE, the setname is EMP-OF-DEPT and the set direction is MEMBER, so we retrieve the employees of this department using OBTAIN NEXT EMPLOYEE RECORD WITHIN EMP-OF-DEPT SET. For each retrieved record, we test its where-clause. The SALARY field is compared with 1000 and if it is greater, then COMM is compared with 500. The Boolean expression is evaluated by means of the related decision table. If the record qualifies, its EMP-NO, NAME and COMM fields are printed.

In any case, we then proceed with the next record (we again issue OBTAIN NEXT EMPLOYEE RECORD WITHIN EMP-OF-DEPT SET). When the end of the set is reached, we go back to the first node, and retrieve the next DEPARTMENT record.

7. SUMMARY

We have described one particular implementation of FORAL. The major interest in the implementation lies in the fact that the data structures and data manipulation language belonged to an entirely different class, with a different underlying data model. We want briefly to summarize our experience in this respect, for it is also relevant to implementations of high-level query languages.

1. The major problem is in mapping the basic data types from one system onto the other. No totally satisfactory solution should in general be expected; the sacrifices are on the one hand language power reduction and restrictions on the user and on the other hand efficiency (or even feasibility) of execution. By requiring an extra level of data description (in the form of a FORAL schema) we have in effect passed the decision on the tradeoffs to the data base administrator when designing a new data base; this we believe is the proper approach. This also enabled us to use FORAL with existing data bases.

2. No particular difficulties with performance were encountered. Whatever inherent shortcomings there may be in IDMS, these were not exaggerated by adding a FORAL "front end" to the system. Conversely, there is no a priori reason to believe that any other general-purpose DBMS (or even DIAM) would perform better as a base for FORAL.

3. The data manipulation language of a network systems such as IDMS is well-suited to executing the tree-traversal operations inherent in hierarchical query structures.

Our implementation of a subset of FORAL (only the query language stripped of functions and other features) took about one half man-year of effort, and consists of 1500 PL/I statements. This is, of course, an order-of-magnitude less effort than a full "from scratch" FORAL implementation, and suggest the following as a general implementation strategy: "If you want to try out a new language, look around for the <u>easiest</u> way to implement it. One can always improve the implementation base later, if this is indicated".

REFERENCES

[1] CODASYL Data Base Task Group, April 1971, Report.
[2] Senko, M.E. "An Introduction to FORAL for Users, Version 2", Parts I
       &II, Basic Information Structure and Basic Query Concepts, Work-
       ing Paper (IBM Research, Yorktown Heights, N.Y.), 1975.
[3] Senko, M.E. "FORAL II and DIAM II; Information Structure and Query-
       Maintenance Language". Unpublished.
[4] Senko, M.E., Altman, E.B., Astrahan, M.M. and Fehder, P.L. "Data
       Structures and Accessing in Data Base Systems", IBM Sys. J., 12,
       pp. 30-93, 1973.
[5] Senko, M.E. "DIAM II with FORAL LP: Making Jointed Queries with
       a Light Pen", Research Report (IBM Research, Yorktown Heights,
       N.Y.), 1976.
[6] "IDMS Data Definition Language and Data Manipulation Language User
       Guides, Release 3.1". Cullinane Corp., Wellesley, Mass., 1975.
[7] Gries, D. Compiler Construction for Digital Computers, Wiley, 1971.
[8] Fidrich, Ilona, "A BNF Syntax for the Query Language FORAL with a
       Discussion of Possible Modification". Internal Report, Theoret-
       ical Laboratory, Institute for Coordination of Computer
       Techniques, Budapest, Hungary, 1977.
[9] Gudes, E. and Reiter, A., "On Evaluating Boolean Expressions",
       Software - Practice and Experience, Vol. 3, pp. 345-350, 1973.
[10] Reiter, A., Clute, A., and Tenenbaum, J.M. "Representation and
       Execution of Queries over large Tree-Structured Data Bases".
       Information Processing '71, North-Holland, pp. 460-472, 1972.

APPENDIX

A BNF Specification of our FORAL Subset

Underlined tokens are terminals and are not further defined.

`<Query>::=<entity set print clause>[<for attrib. print clause>]`

`<entity set print clause>::=<initial context indicator>[<print clause>]`

`<initial context indicator>::=<initial entity set specif>[(<where qualifier>)]`

`<initial entity set specif>::=<entity set name>|system`

`<print clause>::=PRINT field specif.>{,<field specif,>}_o^n`

```
<field specif.>::=<field spec>|<renamer> | ALL
<field spec>::=<field name>[<chain specif.>]
<chain specif>::=OF<relation spec><chain specif>|OF<name in context>
<relation sepc>::=<inverse attribute name>[(<where qualifier>)]
<renamer>::=CALLED<name for output>
<for attrib. print clause>::=<removed context indicator>|<print clause>]
<removed context indicator>::=<context remover>
                        [(<where qualifier>)[<removed contect indicator>]]
<context remover>::=FOR<context specif>
<context specif>::=<attribute name>[<called phrase>]
<called phrase>::=CALLED<new name>
<where qualifier>::=WHERE<condition>
<condition>::={<condition on the attrib>}[<log.oper condition>]
             {<logical term>      }
<log.oper>::= ,|AND|OR
<condition on the attrib>::=[<removed context indicator>,]<relation>
<relation>::=<field spec><incomplete relation>
<incomplete relation>::=<relation symbol>{<field spec>|<element spec>}
<relation symbol>::=EQ|NE|LT|LE|GT|GE
<logical term>::=(<condition>)
<element spec>::=<constant>[,<element spec>]
```

Semantics of some of the tokens are as follows:

fieldname: a field of the record in context

inverse attribute name: relation leaving from the subcontext at the right, can be recordname or a set name

name in context: the context of the print specification

constant: a number or a string enclosed in quotes

CALLED<new name>: indicates the context goes down the tree and not back to the previous occurrence of this entity as the entity in context.

DATABASES: IMPROVING USABILITY AND RESPONSIVENESS

DESIGN & PERFORMANCE TOOLS
FOR
IMPROVING DATABASE USABILITY & RESPONSIVENESS

James P. Fry
Toby J. Teorey

Database Systems Research Group
Graduate School of Business Administration
The University of Michigan
Ann Arbor, Michigan

The technology of database management systems has evolved to the point of general acceptance and wide application. This fact is documented in numerous surveys and the availability of several textbooks dealing with this topic. Although a great deal of attention has been focused on the selection and acquisition of these systems, little has been reported on how to apply these capabilities to the solution of real-life problems. Today the main problem facing the database administrator is not whether to use these database management systems, but how to use them effectively. In order to address this problem, it is generally agreed that the database administrator needs design tools at each step in the life-cycle to perform his function effectively. Using a framework of the data-based development and operation cycle various tools are surveyed which are currently being developed in the research environment. It is our contention that database usability and responsiveness can be greatly improved through the development and application of these tools to database application implementation. A database design and implementation laboratory is proposed as a means of developing these tools.

1.0 INTRODUCTION

Database management systems (DBMS) technology has evolved to the point of acceptance and wide application [U9], a fact which is documented by the numerous surveys [WU1,2,3,U4] and the availability of several textbooks [e.g., T3,9,10] dealing

151

exclusively with this topic. Although a great deal of attention has been focused on the selection and acquisition of
DBMS [A6] little has been reported on the actual utilization
of these systems. Aside from the introduction of the database administration function [A1,2,4,5,7] little attention
has been given towards the effective application of these
systems to existing problems. Thus the major problem facing
the database administrator is not whether to use this technology, but how to use it effectively [F10,DL25]. This
problem can be summarized by a number of issues that arise
through the life-cycle of an application:

i)   What are and how can user requirements be expressed?

ii) How can these requirements be translated into an
     effective design?

iii) When should and how can the design be adapted to new
     and/or changing requirements?

1.1 Data-based Development & Operation Cycle

The information system life-cycle is presented from the
viewpoint of the designer/user rather than from the customary
viewpoint of the software system implementor. It will
consequently be denoted as the data-based development and
operation cycle. The reader should note that this viewpoint
disregards two important steps--selection of system hardware
and software--which are beyond the scope of this paper. We
assume that a database management system has been selected
and we take the perspective of developing applications which
utilize the technology. Figure 1-1 indicates the importance
of the database administrator to the basic steps of the data-
based development and operation cycle. These steps are:

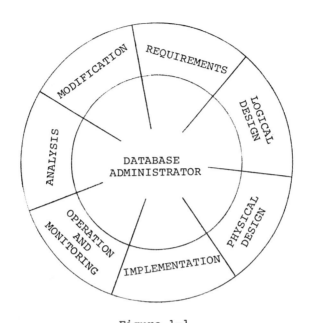

Figure 1-1

Data-based Development and Operation Cycle

1. Requirements Formulation and Analysis

2. Logical Design and Analysis

3. Physical Design and Evaluation

4. Implementation

5. Operation and Monitoring

6. Analysis

7. Modification and Adaptation

We further make the observation that these steps can be organized into two phases--development and operation. The development phase consists of steps 1-4 and the operation phase steps 5-7. To provide a framework for surveying database administration tools in Section 1.3 and reviewing the current research in Section 2.0, each step will be discussed in terms of its task and objective.

It is generally agreed in order to address this problem the database administrator needs several tools throughout the various phases of the data-based development and operation cycle to perform his function effectively. Currently under research and development are a number of these tools. It is our contention that database responsiveness and usability can be improved by applying these tools to the development and operation of database applications. Towards this thesis we present the data-based development and operation cycle and use it as a basis in Section 2.0 for surveying current tools being developed for database administration. We conclude this paper by analyzing the major issues in the development of design tools.

1.1.1 Application Development Phase. Requirements Formulation and Analysis is the first step in the application development phase. This step is probably the most ill-defined, difficult, and time-consuming of the entire process. It is, however, the most important because the majority of subsequent design decisions are based on this step and it consequently has a cascading effect on the other steps of the application development phase. The major tasks are collecting information content and processing requirements from all of the identified and potential users of the database. It also analyzes requirements to ensure consistency of user objectives and minimizes redundancy of information.

Logical Design, Step two in the application development phase, has two components--database and programs. Logical database design addresses the design and implementation of an information structure from consolidation and specification of user information requirements. The result of the logical

design step is a database definition or schema, usually
expressed in a data definition language. If the data definition includes physical parameters (e.g., CODASYL areas, page
sizes, etc.), selection of appropriate characteristic values
are deferred until the physical design step. The program
design component addresses the development of structured
programs using the host language and the data manipulation
language of the DBMS. The output is a functional specification of the program modules or a set of representative ad-hoc
queries to the database.

Physical Design consists of two components as did logical
design. Physical database design involves the selection of
the storage class and the fine tuning of its implementation
such as the specification of block size and device allocation.
The result of the physical database design is a complete,
implementable design. For example, in a CODASYL/DBTG system,
the storage class could be a Pointer Array and the fine
tuning would result in the selection of a page size and
buffer discipline. The program component addresses the
development of the structured data manipulation language
programs for the given logical database design. The output
is a set of implementable algorithms.

Implementation is the fourth step in the application
development phase. Implementation concerns the creation of
programs and databases based on the results of the logical
and physical design steps, and the loading of the database
with data. The actual database loading task is an often
overlooked but costly problem. The existing data must be
translated from its current form (logical structure and
physical format) to the new form resulting from a successful

database design. If the data were already processable by the
DBMS, the process would be either a restructuring or reformatting [R1]; otherwise, it would be database creation [WU1].
Application program development is highly dependent on the
host language selected and the existing logical structure,
and to a lesser extent, on the physical structure. The objective of this component is to develop reliable and efficient database access programs to satisfy user processing
requirements.

Briefly, we have reviewed the four steps of the application development phase. It is important to realize that an
incorrect analysis/decision in the development phase will
lead to an improper implementation and ultimately lead to
a non-responsive application system. Furthermore, compared
to the operation phase, many more design and performance
tools are available which are less expensive to operate.
This will be discussed in detail in Section 2.0.

1.1.2 Database Operation Phase. Although only three
steps in length, the operation phase is the most visible to
the user and the interaction of the steps important to the
maintainer. As indicated in Figure 1-2, in contrast to
the sequential iterative nature of the development phase, the
operation phase is a closed loop continuous cycle.

Operation and Monitoring, the first step of the operation
phase, entails the logging of the actual system operation.
The logging task will provide the data about the validity of
the user requirements and identify critical system performance areas.

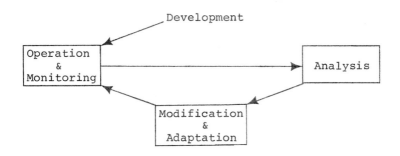

Figure 1-2

Operation and Adaptation Phase

Analysis, the second step of the operation phase, receives the data from the monitoring steps and performs the analysis to indicate whether the existing system should be timed or subsequent redesign of the implementation is necessary.

Modification and Adaptation, the third step, addresses the changes in the design and tuning (to the various degrees of freedom provided) the implementation which results from new requirements, inputs from the monitoring phase, and by analysis of user satisfaction with the current design. The objective is to optimize performance within the existing system by reorganizing the database and/or changing the programs.

Database reorganization is a broad term used to describe any change in the logical or physical structure of the database. Changes range from inversion of a relationship (restructuring) to the tuning of the storage structure (reformatting).

Finally, <u>program adaptation</u> refers to the process of modifying application programs, when necessary, to provide correct results from restructured databases. Typically, this problem results from lack of logical data independence [U9], and the modifications include new sequences of data manipulation operations to traverse a new logical structure and changing variables to count logical records if blocking factors are changed.

1.2 Database Administration Tools

Associated with each step in the data-based development and operation cycle, tools and aids have been developed to assist the database administrator. As indicated in Figure 1-3, these tools range from documentation mechanisms to sophisticated design methodologies. Of the tools necessary for the management of the database, the most important are the requirements formulation and the database design methodology. The design of the database pervades the whole data processing activity from the satisfaction of the user requirements to the performance of the application.

At the center of the application development phase is the catalogue function. Resulting from the requirements formulation and analysis step is a set of validated data and processing requirements which serve as input to the remaining steps of this phase. While there does not exist any "off-the-shelf" packages specifically for documenting processing requirements, there are several software packages for data requirements called Data Dictionaries/Directories. The Data Dictionary/ Directory (DD/D) function provides the centralized management of the data about the database. Its processing function is to store and retrieve this data, e.g., narrative data defini-

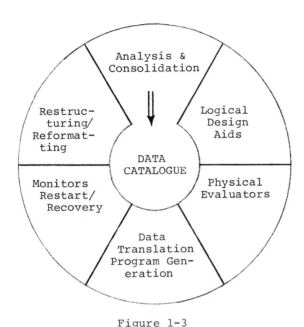

Figure 1-3

Database Administration Tools

tions, and to provide reports for the database administrator.
It also generates encoded stored-data definitions for the
database management system. Over the past years a number of
DD/D packages have become available in the market place.
Although no one DD/D package provides all of these functions
and some packages are being extended to include program
(process) inventory, the following are considered basic
functions [DD2].

  1. Storage of Data Definitions - the storing of symbolic
     and encoded data definitions for multiple databases,
     both machine processable and not.

  2. Interrogation of Data Definition - the preparation
     of reports of data items definitions and relation-
     ships for both the database administrator and the
     user.

Table 1

Data Dictionary/Directory Features
Excerpt from DD3

	LEXICON ARTHUR ANDERSON & CO.	DATA DICTIONARY CINCOM SYSTEMS	DB/DC DATA DICTIONARY IBM
Cost	Approximately $9,000–$18,000 (Lease)	Approximately $11,500 (Purchase)	$523/month for 12 months (Perpetual Lease)
System	IBM S360/370, System 3	IBM S360/370	IBM S360/370
Input Form	Free-form DDL	Fixed-form initially; keyword oriented maintenance	Display Forms DBMS DDL Free-form command
Output -Form	Hard copy & Microform	Hard copy	Hard copy
-Interface	IDMS, IMS, TOTAL	TOTAL, SOCRATES via conversion utility	IMS
-Special	DD & RD Dictionary Maintenance Report DBMS-generation description	---	Interactive Display Forms
-Program Data Areas	COBOL, PL/1, ALC	NONE	COBOL, PL/1, ALC
Access/Pro-cessing	Cross Reference KWIC/KWOC AD HOC	Cross Reference --- AD HOC	--- --- via GIS

160

Table 1 (continued)

	DATA MANAGER MSP CORP.	DATA CATALOGUE Synergetics Corp.	UCC 10 University Computing Company
Cost	$9,900-up (Purchase)	Approximately $15,000	Approximately $17,000
System	IBM 360/370	IBM S360/370	IBM S360/370
Input Form	Free-form DDL	Fixed-form DDL Free-form DDL	Fixed-form Display (3270) menu
Output -Form	Hard copy & Microform	Hard copy & Microform	Hard copy
-Interface	ADABAS, IDMS IMS, MARK IV, S2000 TOTAL	IMS, MARK IV, TOTAL	IMS
-Special	Display source file Test file generation systems documentation	Update transactions from user program	Program profiles, Record layouts, 3270 Message Control Block, Master Terminal Operator Report
-Program Data Areas	COBOL, PL/1, ALC	COBOL, PL/1, ALC	COBOL, PL/1, ALC
Access/Pro- cessing	Cross Reference KWIC/KWOC AD HOC	Cross Reference KWIC/KWOC AD HOC	Cross Reference KWIC/KWOC ---

161

3. Generation of Database Quality Procedures - the
   creation of input validation programs, program test
   data, and sample output programs from the data
   definitions.

4. Perform Security and Integrity Functions - the
   control of the access to the DD/D and the preserva-
   tion of the definitions as to the standards and con-
   versions of the corporation.

5. Maintain Statistics on Utilization - the recording
   and storage for each element in the database of a
   profile of its usage and the programs that use it.

6. Processing of Definition - the generation of encoded
   data definition for database management systems
   (e.g., DBD and PSB for IMS), the re-definition of
   existing elements, and the addition of new elements.

Table 1 summarizes some of the DD/D packages capabilities and
should not be considered complete; for a more detailed profile see [DD3]. The remainder of the database administration
tools and aids will be covered in the next two sections.

2.0 DESIGN AND PERFORMANCE TOOLS FOR
THE DATABASE ADMINISTRATOR

Following the data-based development and operation cycle
presented in Section 1.1, we present the design and performance tools available to the database administrator at each
step in the cycle. A brief description of the tool is
provided to denote its application to the application development phase. The next section discusses the tools available to
the database administrator in the database operation phase.

2.1   Requirements Formulation and Analysis

The preparation of the inputs to a database design process is a complex technical and administrative task dealing
with all aspects of information required--the various types,
large volumes, the appropriate sources, its representation,
and manipulation.

A conceptual breakthrough in understanding user database
requirements and their role in the design process was made
through the identification of two perspectives--Information
Structure (ISP) and the Usage Perspective (UP) [DL23]. The
salient contribution of this effort is the decomposition of
user requirements into those which contribute to the design
of the information structure and to those which contribute to
the application processing of the information structure.

The collection of the requirements for these two perspectives is a complex task requiring input from the entire
organization and therefore needs to be aided through the use
of a formal mechanism for specification and control. Several
collection mechanisms and information analysis aids are in
prototype use, including PSL, CADIS, CASCADE, and CADES [RL1,
2,3]. These collection mechanisms are all similar in that
they provide formats for specification of both ISP and UP
type information and perform basic consistency checking.

2.2   Database Design

In this section we review the database design strategies
by first reviewing the general design methodologies and then
the specific design approaches.

2.2.1 <u>General Design Methodologies</u>. Most practitioners
would agree that there are two separate phases to the design
process; the design of a logical structure which is processable by the DBMS and describes the user's view of the data;
and the selection of a physical structure such as indexed
sequential, or direct access method (if such an option is
available within a DBMS). Other than the logical/physical
delineation, the overall structure of the design process is
not well-defined. Novak and Fry define four basic components
which are necessary to achieve a database design methodology
[DL26]:

   i)   A structured design process that consists of a
        series of steps where one alternative among many
        is chosen.

  ii)   Design techniques to perform the enumeration re-
        quired in i) and evaluation criteria to select an
        alternative at each step.

 iii)   Information requirements for input to the design
        process as a whole and to each step.

  iv)   Descriptive mechanism to represent the information
        input and the results at each design step.

With respect to a structured design process, most researchers have identified two fundamental phases in logical
design--information structure design phase (ISD) and the
information structure implementation phase (ISI) [M6,7,8,
DL24].

Information Structure Design

The Information structure design phase is concerned with
the synthesis and description of the diverse user's information requirements into a preliminary database design. The
result of this phase is a representation of the information
in terms of an Entity Diagram.

The focal point of the Entity Diagram is entities which
represent or model a specific information aggregate specified
in the requirements. Entities are described by attributes
which contain the detailed information about the entity and
one or more of these attributes serve as an identifier to
distinguish between different entity instances. Relationships between entities depict the functional aspects of the
information represented by the entities.

Various approaches abound to forming well structured
Entity Diagrams with the only commonality among these
approaches being the four basic design decisions (or steps)
[DL26]:

  i)   Selection of entities

 ii)   Selection of entity attributes

iii)   Identification of key-attributes for entities

 iv)   Selection of relationships between entities

While commonality exists in these steps to create an information structure, no agreement exists as to the order in which
these steps are to be performed.

Smith and Smith's approach to developing a design strategy employs the notion of abstraction [DL29,30]. Two types of
abstraction are considered: generalization transforms similar objects into higher level objects, and aggregation com-
bines low level objects into aggregates. In their first

paper [DL29], the aggregation abstraction is developed using the Codd type relation as the design component. The strategy is to develop a hierarchy of relations by aggregation into higher level objects or decomposition into lower level objects. In their second paper [DL30] the abstraction generalization is developed and generalization hierarchy is introduced. This design strategy, an extension of their previous work, is based on the intersection of aggregation and generalization hierarchies. As an extension of this strategy into the information structure implementation phase, they also discuss the mapping of the generalization/abstraction hierarchies into DBTG and relational schemas.

Other decomposition methods utilizing relations include the work of Aurdal [WDL1] and Bernstein [DL27]. However, these methods begin with fully specified relations. Aurdal's decomposition algorithm is based on functional dependencies to decompose the large, unnormalized "entity" relations into smaller, normalized "entity" relations and "relationship" relations. A "relationship" relation consists of foreign keys. Bernstein, on the other hand, in his Ph.D. dissertation developed an algorithm for synthesizing 3NF relations based on nonredundant functional dependencies.

While the Entity-Relationship approach proposed by Chen [M10,13] fits nicely into the ISD and ISI framework, its primary contribution is that of a descriptive mechanism. The E-R diagrams express entities and relationships by rectangles and triangles or diamond-shaped boxes respectively. The attributes of the entity and relationships are indicated by arrows from the rectangles or diamond-shaped boxes.

Information Structure Implementation

Given an Entity Diagram as a representation of the content and structure of the information structure design, the
implementation of this design is addressed next. The primary
objective of the information structure implementation is to
take the Entity Diagram and the processing requirements as
input and create a DBMS processable schema for output. Although the placement of the dividing line between ISD and ISI
is open to some debate, as is the relationship of logical to
physical design, the distinction is important to developing
a methodology.

Viewing the ISI strictly from processing perspective
yields a number of techniques that perform generic data
aggregation without regard to an information structure, i.e.,
the records formed may have no natural meaning. Included
in this category are Sheppard's data using matrix [DL8],
Hoffer's clustering algorithm [DL14], Belford's clustering
algorithm [DL15] and IBM's Data Base Design Aid [DL11,12].

Sheppard pioneered in this area with the introduction of
the Item-use Matrix. The matrix is a cross listing indicating which items are used with which processes (applications).
By analyzing how frequently an item is used by the application
and how many other items are used within each application,
particular patterns of usage emerge. Based on these patterns
items are identified which are strong candidates for entity
keys, as well as items that are clearly attributes. In this
method there is no clear distinction between records and
entities; they are assumed to be similar.

The clustering methods of Hoffer and Belford view data requirements as a collection of unrelated data items and employ knowledge of the processes' usage of data items to cluster items into records. These record types will be efficient for the known processes by having items that are used together frequently in the same record type, thus minimizing extra accesses for a given application request. This method does not attempt to identify entities, as does the Sheppard method.

Physical Database Design Aid

Physical database design has advanced through several stages of development, to a point where several analytical aids are available as evaluation mechanisms. The principal origin of these works can be traced to the formal model for list oriented data structures developed by Hsiao and Harary [M5]. This model views the file as a collection of records organized on linked lists. A directory is used to model the access to the records by indicating the record key values, number of records containing these keys, the number of lists each key is on, and a pointer to each list. Based on this model Martin was the first to derive a set of cost equations for measuring the various organizations such as multilist, cellular multilist and inverted list [DE12]. Using a simulation approach Cardenas [DP30] built a system to aid in the selection of various file structures which was based on a set of user requirements and a given set of cost equations for each file structure. Other simulation models which measured specific access methods were developed by Senko and his colleagues at IBM [DP5,10,14].

Severance, recognizing that the Hsiao-Harary model only addressed list type record sequencing, extended the model to include a broader class of structures. He introduced a two parameter (each two-valued) model to describe physical record accessing mecnanisms--data direct, data indirect, pointer sequential, and address sequential. Given the characterization of the database and a series of cost equations, Severance developed a semi-heuristic search mechanism to identify the optimal design [DP23].

In a major theoretical breakthrough, Yao [DE3,4,8] formulated an analytical approach to modeling file (storage) structures in which a single model and cost function could be used to characterize most file organization alternatives. Sequential, indexed sequential, direct access, multilist, and inverted organizations could all be defined in terms of the basic parameters of this general model.

The theoretical work of Yao was extended and implemented to characterize existing file organizations in operational environments. A software package entitled the File Design Analyzer (FDA) [DE6,7] was developed to evaluate well-known file organizations in terms of I/O processing time and secondary storage space required to service a set of user applications. Examples of FDA extensions are the modeling of batched transactions and multi-access interference due to shared secondary storage. The program provided the means for gaining insight regarding the optimal choice of storage structure parameters by allowing the analyst to conduct on-line sensitivity analysis. Validation was accomplished on a Honeywell 635 system under stand-alone conditions.

2.2.2 Specific Design Methodologies. The specific
design methodologies fall into two broad categories--those
which are reported in the published literature and those
which are not. They are specific in the sense that they are
based upon and aimed towards a specific database management
system. We focus our attention on those which have been
documented and comment on those which are not.

CODASYL/DBTG Design Strategies

It is interesting to note that by far the majority of
the documented design strategies are directed towards the
CODASYL/DBTG approach. Resulting from the initial work of
the CODASYL Database Task Group [S1,2] and extended by the
Data Description Language Committee [S5] CODASYL/DBTG is a
specification for a common host language database management
system. Several vendors, both hardware and software, have
implemented systems [V12,13,15,30], with varying levels of
conformance to the specification. As evidenced by the
surveys and number of users, these systems are becoming widely
used [WU1,2,3] and although there are many database management systems available today [U5,9] CODASYL/DBTG approach
appears to be the only candidate suitable for standardization
[F10]. With the proven technology of CODASYL/DBTG dating back
to 1964, the research has recently been directed to the
effective use of this technology.

While there have been some efforts directed toward the
design of DBTG databases [U5,DL7] the scope of this research
has been quite broad. More recently, however, there have been
some important research contributions to the logical and
physical design of DBTG databases.

Methodologies for the design of DBTG (logical) data
structures have been proposed by Gerritsen [DL21], Bubenko
et al [DL24], Bachman [DL1], Mitoma [DL18,19], and Berelian
[DL28]. While the main objectives of these research efforts
are similar, they differ substantially in their approach to
modeling the system. Recently the work of Mitoma was extended
by Berelian [DL28] to allow a larger set of implementation
alternatives for database relations, extend the objective
function to page faults, and include security constraints
in addition to storage and feasibility constraints. Bachman
[DL9] considers the effects of alternative techniques for the
implementation of DBTG sets on database system performance.

Although several results have been obtained in logical
database design, this is not true for the physical design of
DBTG databases. The closest effort to date has been the
development of an operational network database evaluator by
Teorey and Oberlander [DE13]. The Database Design Evaluator
employs purely analytical techniques to evaluate Integrated
Data Store (I-D-S) (a precursor development to DBTG) physical
databases in terms of resource utilization and total response
time for a wide range of user applications. In addition to
the network database design of I-D-S, the Database Design
Evaluator evaluates sequential and indexed sequential databases in terms of the major components of response time for
user transactions or queries: CPU time, I/O processing time,
and queuing time for CPU and I/O resources. The operational
software package considers various levels of interference
from other processes in the computer system so that a realistic assessment of total system delays is possible. Analytical techniques include combinatorial analysis and exponen-

tial queuing network analysis. The various algorithms used
vary in complexity, but none is worse than polynomial complexity. Examples of new areas of model development are
buffering and physical clustering into DBTG-like "areas".

The undocumented database design strategies are the
result of several years of database practice and experience
by particular database designers. Over a period of time
these practitioners have developed design strategies for
design databases for particular vendor systems. These
strategies attempt to translate the user's requirements into
the best implementation based on the specific capabilities
and implementation tradeoffs of particular DBMSs. An interactive dialogue is used by the designer to map the users
information and processing requirements into an effective
database for the particular DBMS.

While these strategies undoubtably result in good database designs, the actual strategy lies with the designer,
and since it has not been documented, this strategy is not
duplicatable.

In summary, there are a number of database design techniques and these are fairly independent and non-integrated
(Figure 2-1). Some are general in that they are applicable
to any system; others are specifically related to a particular DBMS. Methods of evaluating design alternatives in
logical design are non-existent and their development in the
physical design area has begun very recently, thus allowing
only on-line testing to determine the quality of the design.

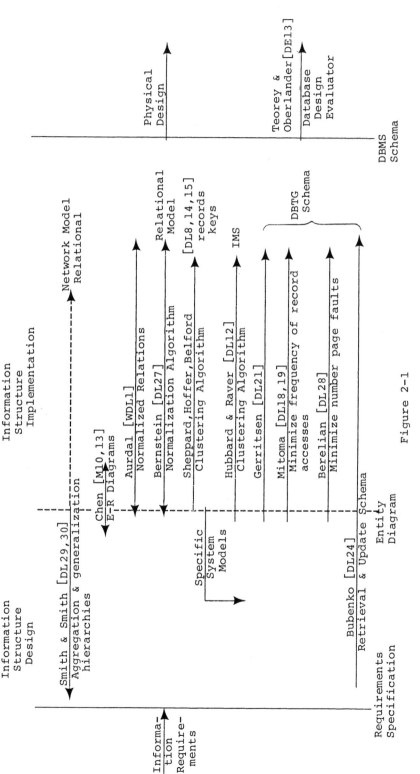

Figure 2-1

Database Design and Evaluation Techniques

3.0 DATABASE OPERATION PHASE

In this section we review the design and development
tools that are available to the database administrator in
the operation phase of the data-based development and operation
cycle. As in the previous section, we follow the steps set
forth in Section 1.1.2.

3.1 Monitoring and Operation

Probably the most important tool in this step is system
monitors because they either validate or refute and feedback
into the requirement formulation and analysis phase.

A monitoring package is needed for applications to
collect the statistics on the utilization of the databases
access paths. Some preliminary work has been performed at
the University of Michigan in which these programs are
procedures augmented with special DML procedures to collect
the necessary statistics. In a similar approach, Belford
[DL15] at the University of Illinois, proposed a monitoring
mechanism based on well known statistical gathering procedures. In this preliminary study algorithms were investigated to collect statistics on data usage patterns exhibited
by the application programs. They are currently developing
tests and simulations to evaluate and determine the effects
of various parameter choices on the efficiency of the
algorithm.

In one of the few reported implementations of a DBMS
performance monitor, Krinos [GG1] reports on the implementation of a monitor in the United Aircraft Information Management System (UAIMS). Using both the DBMS and the operating
system software monitoring facilities, the activity of both

DBMS and non-DBMS applications for a period of one year and found that DBMS applications required more interactive cycle time for both user turnaround, think time, and also for system response time. Another conclusion the report came to is the DBMS applications were far more compute bound. Oliver and Joyce [Z7] report on their experience with monitoring REGIS, the Relational General Information System. In contrast to the development of statistics on access path utilization at Michigan, their performance monitor collected data about utilization of the REGIS command language. It was used to measure performance improvements over the operation of REGIS and also to predict system performance.

3.2 Analysis and Modification

Data Modification

Based on the inputs from the Monitoring phase or a change in the basic requirements, it is often necessary to modify the database structure logically or physically. Depending on the degree of data independence, such a modification may require that the application program be adapted to the modified database structure. Essentially, two types of transformations are available to adapt the database design [R1]: i) Restructuring: the transformation on the logical and structure of the database, e.g., the inversion of a database relationship, and ii) Reformatting: the transformation to physical structure of the database, e.g., changing blocking factors, page sizes, or reallocation of data across physical devices. These two types of transformations represent the two ends of a data reorganization spectrum. Consequently, most data reorganization operations cannot be classified as purely logical or physical.

The reformatting transformation should be applied because
they are the easiest to perform and require the least amount
of data independence. As an aid to selecting which transformation to perform, the Database Design Evaluator (DBDE) by
Teorey and Oberlander [DE13] can be inexpensively run and
used to evaluate a number of candidate storage organizations
simply by varying storage parameters. In this database design
methodology DBDE would be used to identify the parameters most
sensitive to the database performance so they could be varied
accordingly.

The restructuring transformation requires a greater degree
of data independence and are, in general, more complex. In
formulating restructuring operations for several hierarchical
databases, three levels of abstraction are necessary to define restructuring types (Navathe and Fry [R6]). These
restructuring types form the basis for restructuring languages
and several have been proposed: CONVERT by IBM Research [R2],
APSL by the University of Michigan [R9], and CDTL by System
Development Corporation [R3]. Using this restructuring formulation Lewis and Fry [UR2] survey and compare these languages. Unfortunately, a complete restructuring function
does not exist within current database management systems.
Although some offer capabilities in this area, a comprehensive
restructuring function is only available through data translation [DT6,10,12,13,15].

Determining when to perform a database reorganization is
another important issue in the modification phase. Optimal
or near-optimal data reorganization points can be determined
on the basis of minimal total cost. Total cost is defined in
this context as a weighted function of secondary storage space

and the file access time for a given set of activities over
a specified time interval t. Storage space is computed as
the space to house the entire file including intermediate
data such as pointers, directories, etc. File access time
for the user application includes the retrieval, modification,
insertion and deletion of records; modification and insertion
of keyword values at an intermediate access path level; and
query type retrieval.

In an earlier study, the optimum reorganization points
solution by Shneiderman [RA1] assumed a linear cost function,
linear file growth rate and known database lifetime T, and a
closed form solution for the optimal fixed-length reorganization interval t_s was determined. For a linear file growth
rate and linearly increasing reorganization cost, t_s was
found to be approximately proportional to $T^{\frac{1}{2}}$. As $T \to \infty$, t_s
becomes undefined. More recent results by Yao, Das, and
Teorey [RA2] relax some of Shneiderman's constraints and
provide an approximate solution for the infinite time horizon.

Program Adaptation

Little research has been performed in this area with the
exception of some preliminary work [PT8,9,11] however; the
CODASYL System Committee has formed the Database Program
Conversion Task Group to study this problem.

4.0 CONCLUSIONS/DIRECTIONS

We have surveyed the design and performance tools available to the database administrator using the designers'/
users' view of the information system life-cycle. It is our
thesis that database usability and responsiveness could be
greatly improved by providing tools for the database administrator at each phase of the data-based development and
operation cycle. Moreover, with concentration on the design
and performance tools for the first four steps,   (the development phase) greater benefits would be accrued. The following
reasons are cited.   First, there are more tools available
in the development phase and their application of the results
is easier because the implementation has not started. Second,
the mistakes and errors in the development phase are propa-
gated to the operation phase which results in poor database
usability and responsiveness.

4.1 Significant Issues

Several major issues remain. Probably the single most
important issue is the assurance of consistency and integrity
throughout the major steps in the data-based development and
operation cycle. With a wide number and diverse implementations of these tools, the database administrator who desires
to combine these computer aided design tools into an overall
methodology is faced with an overwhelming array of problems.
First, the software packages must be acquired, which involves
the usual problems of importing and installing foreign code
in a new computing environment. Since most of the tools

focus on a specific phase of the design process, the next problem is the integration of two or more software tools to form a design sequence.

The second issue is related to the status of the design tools. Since most of the tools are available in a research laboratory, they need to be upgraded into an operational status and integrated into a design methodology for a database designer to use. A myriad of new problems arises when one considers how a designer will use the tools. Many design tools will use the similar input parameters but at a different level of aggregation. To maintain consistency the designer must use the same values for each case. In the overall design process the designer will almost certainly choose to use each tool several times to obtain different trial values of the design parameters. These considerations create the giant bookkeeping problem of maintaining and properly coordinating the inputs and outputs of the software tools.

The third and final issue is the lack of design tools for the hierarchical and network databases in the logical design step of the data-based development cycle. While several design tools have been developed for the physical design step, comparatively few have been researched or developed for logical design.

4.2 Database Designer's Workbench

To address these issues it is suggested that a facility
be developed similar to those that have been designed in
other professions (e.g., the Engineers' Laboratory or the
Craftsmen's Workbench).

The primary goal of the Designer's Workbench is to
develop and implement strategies to allow autonomously
developed computer based design aids and problem specification methodologies to be integrated into a comprehensive,
coordinated design system. The resulting system should
provide a convenient, user-friendly environment in which a
database designer can work. Moreover, it should provide a
comfortable work-reducing framework in which a researcher
can develop and experiment with new design tools.

The following are set forth as objectives of the Database Designer's Workbench [UE3].

   1. Data Integration - One of the primary integration
       functions of the Designer's Workbench is the develop-
       ment of a composite Development Database, which
       incorporates the input and the output parameter
       values of the various design tools.

   2. Design iteration - While at present the typical
       design process does not involve significant design
       tool iteration, the availability of computer design
       aids may be expected to substantially change this
       situation. Trial designs will become the common
       methodology. The Designer's Workbench must facili-
       tate this mode of operation.

3. Design Audit - The system should keep a historical record of each operation the user performs, and provide the capability for the user to enter annotations on design progress (e.g., reasons for performing new trials). This would serve to document the design and would provide a valuable mechanism for studying the design process itself.

4. Design Tool Execution Control - In order to keep proper records on design activity and properly coordinate the parameter values used by various design tools, the Designer's Workbench should initiate execution of the design tools. Therefore, it must provide the user appropriate commands to control the design process.

5. User-oriented - The Designer's Workbench should be user-friendly and support varying degrees of verbosity in order that both beginners and experts may use the system comfortably. The mechanisms for achieving desired activities should be straightforward as far as the user is concerned. Complexities should be absorbed into Workbench software.

6. Extensibility - Finally, to accommodate rapidly changing state-of-the-art database design methodologies and technologies, the Designer's Workbench must be able to incorporate new design tools as they become available. It should also maintain upward compatibility with all design processes in progress when a new design tool is installed.

The implementation of the Database Designer's Workbench
began in August 1976, under contract with the government and
the PSL and FDA packages mentioned in Section 2.0 have been
integrated and are operational in laboratory environment
[UE5,16].   Other packages [DP34,36,UE2] are being integrated
during 1977/78.

BIBLIOGRAPHY

Excerpts from "Database Research and Systems Bibliography", Database Systems Research Group Technical Report
76 DB 3.

(A)   DATA ADMINISTRATION

A1   Guide International, "The Data Base Administrator,"
      Nov. 1972.
A2   Canning, R. G., "The Data Administrator Function,"
      EDP Analyzer, 10,11 (Nov. 1972).
A4   Lyon, J. K., "Data Base Administrator," Wiley Inter-
      science Series, New York, 1976.
A5   Winkler, A., et al., "The Data Administrator's Hand-
      book," United States Air Force Academy unclassi-
      fied report USAFA-TR-76-1, National Technical
      Information Service, Springfield, Va., Jan. 1976.
A6   CODASYL Systems Committee Report, "Selection and
      Acquisition of Data Base Management Systems," ACM,
      New York, March 1976.
A7   Database Administration Working Group, "B.C.S./CODASYL
      DDLC," Report, June 1975.

(DD)   DATA DICTIONARY

DD2   Canning, R. G., "The Data Dictionary/Directory Func-
      tion," EDP Analyzer, 12,10(1974).
DD3   Leong-Hong, B., and Marion, B., "Technical Profile of
      Seven Data Element Dictionary/Directory System,"
      NBS Special Publication 500-3, U.S. Department of
      Commerce, Feb. 1977.

(DE) DATABASE DESIGN EVALUATION

DE3   Yao, S. B., "Evaluation and Optimization of File
      Organizations through Analytic Modeling," Ph.D.
      dissertation, The University of Michigan, Ann
      Arbor, 1974.
DE4   Yao, S. B., and Merten, A. G., "Selection of File
      Organization Using an Analytical Model" Proceed-
      ings of the First International Conference on
      Very Large Databases, ACM, N.Y., 1975, pp. 255-67.
DE6   Teorey, T. J., and Das, K.S., "Application of an
      Analytical Model to Evaluate Storage Structures,"
      Proceedings of the International ACM-SIGMOD
      Conference on Management of Data, ACM, N.Y., 1976,
      pp. 9-20.
DE8   Yao, S. B., "An Attribute Based Model for Database
      Access Cost Analysis," ACM Transactions on Data-
      base Systems, 2,1(1977):45-67.
DE12 Martin, L. D., "A Model for File Structure Determina-
      tion for Large On-Line Data Files," Proceedings of
      File 68 International Seminar File Organization,
      1968, pp. 793-834.

DE13   Teorey, T. J., and Oberlander, L. B., "Network Data-
       base Evaluation Analytical Modeling," Proceedings
       of the 1978 National Computer Conference, 47,
       AFIPS Press, Montvale, N.J., 1978.
DE15   Hulten, C., and Soderlund, L., "A Simulation Model
       for Performance Analysis of Large Shared Data
       Bases," Proc. 1977 International Conference on
       Very Large Data Bases, Tokyo, Oct. 6-8, 1977.

                    (DL) LOGICAL DATABASE DESIGN

DL1   Bachman, C. W., "Data Structure Diagrams," Data Base,
       1,2(1969):4-10.
DL7   Curtice, R. M., "Data Base Design Using a CODASYL
       System," Proceedings of the 1974 National Computer
       Conference, 43, ACM, N.Y., pp. 473-80.
DL8   Sheppard, D. L., "Data Base: A Business Approach to
       System Design," Cincom Systems, Inc., Cincinnati,
       Ohio, Aug. 1974.
DL9   Bachman, C. W., "Implementation Techniques for Data
       Structure Sets," Data Base Management Systems, ed.
       by D. A. Jardine, North-Holland, Amsterdam, 1974.
DL10   Senko, M. E., "Information Systems: Records, Relations,
       Sets, Entities and Things," Information Systems,
       1,1(1975):3-13.
DL11   IBM, Data Base Design Aid - A Designer's Guide, Program
       Number 5748-XX4, GH20-1627-0.
DL12   Hubbard, G., and Raver, N., "Automating Logical File
       Design," Proceedings of the First International
       Conference on Very Large Data Bases, ACM, N.Y.,
       1975, pp. 227-53.
DL14   Hoffer, J. A., "A Clustering Approach to the Generation
       of Subfiles for the Design of a Computer Data Base,"
       Ph.D. dissertation, Cornell University, Ithaca,
       1975.
DL15   Belford, G., "Dynamic Data Clustering and Partitioning,"
       Research in Data Management and Resource Sharing
       Preliminary Research Study Report, University of
       Illinois at Urbana-Champaign, Urbana, May 1975.
DL18   Mitoma, M. F., and Irani, K. B., "Automatic Data Base
       Schema Design," Proceedings of the First Interna-
       tional Conference on Very Large Data Bases, ACM,
       N.Y., 1975, pp. 286-321.
DL19   Mitoma, M. F., "Optimal Data Base Schema Design,"
       Ph.D. dissertation, The University of Michigan,
       Ann Arbor, 1975.
DL21   Gerritsen, R., "A Preliminary System for the Design of
       DBTG Data Structures," Comm. ACM, 18,10(1975):557-67.
DL23   Kahn, B. K., "A Method for Describing the Information
       Required by the Data Base Design Process," Pro-
       ceedings of the International ACM-SIGMOD Conference
       on Management of Data, ACM, N.Y., 1976, pp. 53-64.
DL24   Bubenko, J., Berild, S., Lindencrona-Ohlin, E., and
       Nachmens, S., "From Information Requirements to
       DBTG Data Structures," Proceedings of the ACM-
       SIGMOD/SIGPLAN Conference on Data: Abstraction,
       Definition and Structure, ACM, N.Y., 1976, pp. 73-85.

DL25 Fry, J. P., and Kahn, B. K., "A Stepwise Approach to Database Design," Proceedings of the ACM Southeast Regional Conference, ACM, N.Y., 1976, pp. 34-43.

DL26 Novak, D., and Fry, J., "The State of the Art of Logical Database Design," Proceedings of the Fifth Texas Conference on Computing Systems, IEEE, Long Beach, 1976, pp. 30-39.

DL27 Bernstein, P. A., "Synthesizing Third Normal Form Relations from Functional Dependencies," ACM Transactions on Database Systems, 1,4(1976): 277-298.

DL28 Berelian, E., "A Methodology for Data Base Design in a Paging Environment," Ph.D. dissertation, The University of Michigan, Ann Arbor, 1977.

DL29 Smith, J. M., and Smith, D. C. P., "Database Abstractions: Aggregation and Generalization," ACM Transactions on Database Systems, 2,2(1977): 105-33.

DL30 Smith, J. M., and Smith, D. C. P., "Database Abstractions: Aggregation," Communications of the ACM, 20,6(1977):405-13.

(DP) PHYSICAL DATABASE DESIGN

DP5 Senko, et al., File Design Handbook, Final Report, Contract Report AF 30602-69-C-0100, Nov. 1969.

DP10 Lum, V. Y., Ling, H., and Senko, M. E., "Analysis of a Complex Data Management Access Method by Simulation Modeling," Proceedings of the AFIPS 1970 FJCC, 37, AFIPS Press, Montvale, N.J., 1970, pp. 211-22.

DP14 Wang, C. P., and Lum, V., "Quantitative Evaluation of Design Trade-offs in File Systems," Proceedings of the Symposium on Information Storage and Retrieval, College Park, Md., 1971, pp. 155-62.

DP23 Severance, D. G., "Some Generalized Modeling Structures for Use in Design of File Organization," Ph.D. dissertation, The University of Michigan, Ann Arbor, 1972.

DP30 Cardenas, A. F., "Analysis and Performance of Inverted Data Base Structures," Comm. ACM, 13,5(1975): 253-64.

DP34 Eisner, M. J., and Severance, D. G., "Mathematical Techniques for Efficient Record Segmentation in Large Shared Databases," Journal of the ACM, 23,4(1976):619-35.

DP35 March, S., and Severance, D., "The Determination of Efficient Record Segmentations and Blocking Factors for Shared Files," ACM Transactions on Database Systems, 2,3(1977):279-96.

DP36 March, S., and Severance, D., "The Determination of Efficient Record Segmentations and Blocking Factors for Shared Files," ACM Transactions on Database Systems, 2,1(1977):27-44.

DP39 Hammer, M., "Self-adaptive Automatic Data Base Design," Proc. 1977 National Computer Conference, 46, AFIPS Press, pp. 123-29.

(DT)   DATA TRANSLATION

DT6   Rameriz, J. A., Rin, N. A., and Prywes, N. S.,
       "Automatic Conversion of Data Conversion Programs
       Using a Data Description Language," Proceedings
       of the 1974 ACM SIGFIDET Workshop on Data Descrip-
       tion, Access and Control, ACM, N.Y., 1974, pp.
       207-25.
DT10   Bakkom, D. E., and Behymer, J. A., "Implementation of
       a Prototype Generalized File Translator," Pro-
       ceedings of the 1975 ACM-SIGMOD International
       Conference on Management of Data, ed. by W. F.
       King, ACM, N.Y., 1975, pp. 99-110.
DT11   Navathe, S. B., and Merten, A. G., "Investigations
       into the Application of the Relation Model of
       Data to Data Translation," Proceedings of the
       1975 ACM-SIGMOD International Conference on
       Management of Data, ed. by W. F. King, ACM,
       N.Y., 1975, pp. 123-38.
DT12   Birss, E. W., and Fry, J. P., "Generalized Software
       for Translating Data," Proceedings of the 1976
       National Computer Conference, 45, AFIPS Press,
       Montvale, N.J., 1976, pp. 889-99.
DT13   Lum, V. Y., Shu, N. C., and Housel, B. C., "A General
       Methodology for Data Conversion and Restructuring,"
       IBM R&D J., 20(1976):483-97.
DT15   Swartwout, D. E., Deppe, M. E., and Fry, J. P.,
       "Operational Software for Restructuring Network
       Databases," Proceedings of the 1977 National
       Computer Conference, 46, AFIPS Press, Montvale,
       N.J., 1977, pp. 499-508.

(F)   FUTURE

F10   ACM/NBS, "Data Base Directions: The Next Steps,"
       Proceedings of the Workshop of the National Bureau
       of Standards and the Association for Computing
       Machinery, NBS Special Publication 451, U.S.
       Dept. of Commerce, Washington, D. C., 1976.

(GG)   GENERAL

GG1   Krinos, J. D., "Interaction Statistics from a Database
       Management System," Proceedings of the 1973
       National Computer Conference, 42, AFIPS Press,
       Montvale, N.J., 1973, pp. 283-90.

(M)   MODELS-THEORY

M5   Hsiao, D., and Harary, F., "A Formal System for Infor-
       mation Retrieval from Files," Communications of
       the ACM, 13,2(1970):67-73.
M6   Sundgren, B., "An Infological Approach to Databases,"
       Ph.D. dissertation, University of Stockholm,
       Sweden, 1973.
M7   Langefors, B., "Theoretical Aspects of Information
       Systems for Management," Proceedings of the IFIP
       Congress, North Holland, Amsterdam, 1974, pp. 937-45.

M8   ANSI/X3/SPARC/Study Group - Data Base Systems,
      "Interim Report," ACM-SIGMOD Newsletter: fdt,
      7,2 (Dec. 1975).
M10   Chen, P., "The Entity-Relationship Model - Towards a
      Unified View of Data," Transactions on Database
      Systems, 1,1(1976):9-36.
M13   Chen, P., "The Entity-Relationship Model - A Basis
      for the Enterprise View of Data," Proceedings of
      the AFIPS Conference 46, AFIPS, Montvale, N.J.,
      1977, pp. 77-84.

                    (PT) PROGRAM TRANSLATION

PT8   Honeywell Information Systems, "Functional Specifica-
      tions Task 609 Database Interface Package,"
      Defense Communication Agency Contract DCA 100-73-
      C-055.
PT9   Kintzer, E., "Translating Database Procedures,"
      Proceedings of the 1975 ACM National Conference,
      ACM, N.Y., pp. 359-62.
PT11 Dale, A. G., and Dale, N. B., "Schema and Occurrence
      Structure Transformation in Hierarchical Systems,"
      Proceedings of the 1976 ACM-SIGMOD International
      Conference on Management of Data, ACM, N.Y.,
      pp. 157-68.

                    (R) RESTRUCTURING

R1   Fry, J. P., and Jeris, D., "Towards a Formulation of
      Data Reorganization," Proceedings of the 1974 ACM-
      SIGMOD Workshop on Data Description, Access and
      Control, ed. by R. Rustin, ACM, N.Y., pp. 83-100.
R2   Shu, N. C., Housel, B. C., and Lum, V. Y., "CONVERT:
      A High-Level Translation Definition Language for
      Data Conversion," Comm. ACM, 18,10(1975):557-67.
R3   Shoshani, A., "A Logical-Level Approach to Data Base
      Conversion," Proceedings of the 1975 ACM-SIGMOD
      International Conference on Management of Data,
      ACM, N.Y., pp. 112-122.
R6   Navathe, S. B., and Fry, J. P., "Restructuring for
      Large Data Bases: Three Levels of Abstraction,"
      ACM Transactions on Database Systems, 1,2, ACM,
      N.Y., 1976, pp. 138-58.
R9   Swartwout, D., "An Access Path Specification Language
      for Restructuring Network Databases," Proceedings
      of the 1977 SIGMOD Conference, ACM, N.Y., pp.
      88-101.

                    (RA) REORGANIZATION

RA1   Shneiderman, B., "Optimum Data Base Reorganization
      Points," Comm. ACM, 16,6(1973):363-65.
RA2   Yao, S. B., Das, K. S., and Teorey, T. J., "A Dynamic
      Data Base Reorganization Algorithm," ACM Trans-
      actions on Database, 1,2(1976):159-174.

(RL)   REQUIREMENTS LANGUAGES

RL1   Strunz, H., "Systems for Systems Development (A Review
       of the Current State of the Art)," Approaches to
       System Design, ed. by Boot, 1973, pp. 53-62.
RL2   Krohn, M., "Use of the Computer as a Systems Documen-
       tation and Design Aid," Approaches to Systems
       Design, ed. by Boot, 1973, pp. 105-11.
RL3   Teichroew, D., and Hershey, E. A., "PSL/PSA: A
       Computer Aided Technique for Structured Documenta-
       tion and Analysis of Information Processing
       Systems," IEEE Transactions on Software Engineering,
       SE-3,1, 1977, pp. 41-48.

(S)   SPECIFICATIONS

S1   CODASYL Data Base Task Group, October 1969 Report,
       ACM, N.Y., 1969. (Superceded by 1971 DBTG Report,
       currently out of print).
S2   CODASYL Data Base Task Group, April 1971 Report, ACM,
       N.Y., 1971.
S5   CODASYL Data Description Language Committee, CODASYL
       Data Description Language Journal of Development,
       June 1973, NBS Handbook 113, ACM, N.Y., 1974.

(T)   TEXT

T3   Cagan, C., Data Management Systems, Melville, Los
       Angeles, 1973.
T9   Martin, J., Principles of Data-Base Management,
       Prentice-Hall, Englewood Cliffs, N.J., 1975.
T10   Date, C. J., An Introduction to Database Systems,
       Addison-Wesley, Reading, Mass., 1975.

(U)   SURVEY

U4   GUIDE International, "Comparison of Data Base Manage-
       ment Systems," Smith, Bucklin, & Associates,
       Chicago, Ill., Oct. 1971.
U5   Taylor, R., and Frank, R., "CODASYL Data-Base Manage-
       ment Systems," Computing Surveys, 8,1(March 1976):
       67-104.
U9   Fry, J. P., and Sibley, E. A., "Evolution of Database
       Management Systems," Computing Surveys, 8,1(March
       1976):1-42.

(UE)   UM DATABASE DESIGN EVALUATION

UE2   Teorey, T.J., et al., "The Database Design Evaluator,"
       Working Paper 77 DE 7.2, Data Translation Project,
       The University of Michigan, Ann Arbor, 1977.
UE5   Wilens, M. N., and Volz, R. A., "Interactive Database
       Design Laboratory - Design Concepts Manual,"
       Working Paper 77 DE 5.2, Database Systems Research
       Group, The University of Michigan, Ann Arbor,
       December, 1977.
UE16   Volz, R. A., Wilens, M. E., and Fry, J. P., "Toward
       an Interactive Database Design Laboratory,"
       Technical Report 77 DE 9, Database Systems Research
       Group, The University of Michigan, Ann Arbor, 1977.

(UR)   UM RESTRUCTURING

UR2   Lewis, K., and Fry, J., "A Comparison of Three Trans-
lation Definition Languages," Working Paper DT 5.1,
Data Translation Project, The University of
Michigan, Ann Arbor, 1975.

(V)   VENDOR SYSTEM

V12   Cullinane Corporation, "Integrated Database Management
System Program and Reference," Cullinane Corporation, Boston, Mass.

V13   DECSYSTEM 10, "Data Base Management System Programmer
Procedures Manual," DEC-10-APPMA-B-D, 2d ed.,
Digital Equipment Corporation, Maynard, Mass.

V15   Honeywell Information Systems, I-D-S/II Related Publications, Honeywell Information Systems, Waltham,
Mass.

I-D-S/II Programmer Reference Manual	DE09
I-D-S/II Data Base Administration Guide	DE10
Interactive I-D-S/II Reference Manual	DE11
UFAS (United File Access System)	DC89
I/O Supervisor	DD82
File Management Supervisor	DD45

V30   Sperry Univac, "Univac 1100 Series, Data Management
System (DMS 1100) Schema Definition, Data Admin-
istrator Reference," Sperry Rand Corporation, Blue
Bell, Pa., 1972, 1973.

(WDL)   LOGICAL DATABASE DESIGN

WDL1   Aurdal, E., "A Multi-Level Procedure for Design of
File Organizations," CASCADE Working Paper 36,
University of Trondheim, Norway, June 1975.

(WU)   SURVEY

WU1   Fry, et al., "Data Management Systems Survey," Report
MTP 329, MITRE Corporation, Bedford, Mass.,
1969, (AD 684 907).

WU2   Minker, J., "Generalized Data Management Systems -
Some Perspectives," Technical Report, Computer
Science Center, University of Maryland, College
Park, Md., Dec. 1969.

WU3   Koehr, et al., "Data Management Systems Catalogue,"
Technical Report MTP 139 MITRE Corporation,
Bedford, Mass., 1973.

(Z)   RELATIONAL SYSTEM

Z7   Oliver, N. N., and Joyce, J. D., "Performance Monitor
for a Relational Information System," Proceedings
of the 1974 ACM Conference, 1974, pp. 329-33.

Data Quality, Integrity, and Security

AN AUTHORIZATION MECHANISM FOR A DATA-BASE

Arditi Joel

Zukovsky Eli

Computer Center

Weizmann Institute of Science

Rehovot, ISRAEL

A multiuser data base system must permit users to selectively share data while retaining the ability to restrict data accesses. There must be a mechanism permitting information to be accessed only by properly authorized users. Further, relation creation and destruction are dynamic processes, as are granting, checking and revoking of authorization.

In it's most general form the authorization schema is a directed graph of granted privileges originating from the relation creator.

The Weizmann Institute DB1 system has an authorization mechanism that gives an efficient and "natural" representation for the dynamic authorization mechanism by reducing that general graph to an directed tree of granted privileges.

I. INTRODUCTION

A multiuser database system must permit users to selectively share data while retaining the ability to restrict data access. There must be a mechanism permitting information to be accessed only by properly authorized users.

There are two extremes in the implementations of Authorization Mechanisms for Database Systems (see 1,2):

(a) DBA mechanism - Only a central "data base

administrator" has the power to create and destroy
shared relations and to specify access control for
them.

(b) Dynamic **authorization** mechanism - No central DBA and
also:

    * Any data base user may be authorized to create a new
relation and to perform actions upon it.

    * The relation creator may grant various privileges on
that relation to various users.

    * Any user who has granted a privilege may
subsequently revoke it.

In current implementations that uses the dynamic approach
(see 6), the information on authorization in a system is kept
in system relations of the following structure:

SYSAUTH<USER, RELATION, ACCESS, GRANT OPTION, GRANTOR>

SYSAUTH<USER, VIEW, ACCESS, GRANT OPTION, GRANTOR>

The task of the DBA that uses an authorization mechanism
in which only the DBA can grant authorization to access
information, may be very difficult. In the following real
example we shall see a case in which it is impossible to apply
the DBA approach.

A big bank has control over several smaller banks one of
which operates in another country. Some of the banks has their
own DP specialists. All those banks may have different
management policies. The owning bank decided that all the
banks will share a common database. Since every bank manager
has the authority to specify the rules upon which
authorization to access information will be given in his bank,
it seems unlikely that the DBA of the owning bank will manage
the authorization mechanism for all the banks. This is
especially true for the bank that is located in another
country. In our opinion it is more logical that those banks
who have their own DP specialists will manage their own
authorization mechanism.

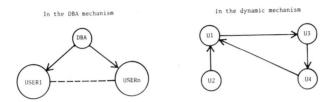

In the DBA mechanism   In the dynamic mechanism

FIGURE 1. A chain of grantors and grantees.

On the other hand an organization that uses the dynamic approach may face several problems:

* "parralel transfer" - In the example of the bank, branch managers have the GRANT option. In the dynamic approach one branch manager can grant his rights to other branch managers. Such action may give managers that agree to cooperate undesired advantages from the viewpoint of their superiors.

* "private applications" - In the dynamic mechanism the creator of a relation is the only one that can grant authorization to access this relation.

In the bank example this enables a branch manager who has private resources of financial information, to add this information to the database and to exploit it for his own benefit without the knowledge of his superiors. This example lead us to the conclusion that in such organizations every information that is known to an employee must be known also to his superior.

A database system that adopts the dynamic approach must check every request at run time because in general authorization can be defined in terms of views (5), and views are in general value dependent. Checking authorization at run time may be a waste for that part of the authorization schema which is not value dependent.

Large enterprises generally have hierarchic structure. Strict rules define how rights of upper level management can be transfered to the lower levels of the enterprise. The right

to access information is also bound to these rules. Although
we may find non hierarchical components within these
enterprises, they do not affect the general hierarchical
pattern of their structure.

In view of the chracteristics of the hierarchical
structure, there are improvements that can be made to the
system relations that describe authorization. These
improvements will reduce the amount of data that must be kept
for the description of the authorization schema of a
Data-base.

The approach that was developed for the Weizmann Institute
DB1 system follows the management rules of an hierarchic
enterprise model in order to solve the problems raised by the
dynamic approach. It exploits characteristics of hierarchical
structures to achieve a better efficiency in regard to system
information.

In the DB1 system, authorization is given at the
data-schema level. This means that authorization over a
relation is not value dependent. Value dependent authorization
is regarded as a PRIVACY act by the system.

For example:

All the managers in store departmetns are authorized to
access the PERSONNEL relation. The authorization act of the
DB1 allows each manager to access any PERSONNEL relation. Only
a PRIVACY act can restrict a manager to access only relations
of employees that he manages.

In the DB1 system PRIVACY acts are handled by the
Triggered Operations Mechanism of the system (see next
chapter). Whenever the manager accesses a PERSONAL relation a
triggered operation is invoked to check that the user
accessing the relations is indeed the manager of the employee.
If the check fails the relation is not transfered to the user.
This triggered operation is created automatically whenever an
instance of the PRIVACY relation (see chapter VI) is inserted
to the data base.

Since a description of the DB1 system is not yet
published, the next chapter will give a brief survey of it.

II. THE DB1 SYSTEM

The DB1 system (7) is an operational database system that gives a unique solution to the problem of writing complex update programs, in a shared database environment. The general structure of the DB1 system is given in figure 2.

The Internal Schema. The internal schema of the DB1 database is a graph. The nodes are called segments. Each segment is a tuple of fields. The segments are connected among themselves by links. In the physical implementation of the graph there are two types of links: physical links and logical links. The physical links and the segments create a forest in the database graph.

The DB1 system contain several subsystems. The most important ones are the Universal Transaction Proccessor (UTP) and the DBPL1 language (8).

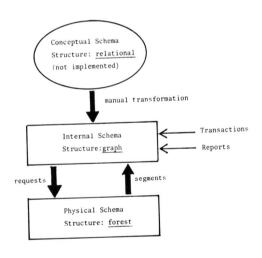

FIGURE 2. The DB1 general structure.

The Universal Transaction Proccessor (UTP). The UTP proccesses transaction that are sent by the end user to the database. The standard structure of a transaction (which is an input line) is as follows:

<transaction#><operation><field 1>......<fieldN>

The main possible operations are: Insert, Change, Delete, List a segment and List all segments.

Transactions are described to the system by filling the form given in figure 3. A filled line in a form can be punched or entered from an online terminal.

All the updated transactions in the DB1 system are proccessed by the UTP. Concurrency control, checkpoints, restarts, error handling and checking of update authorization are done only by the UTP.

A major part of the UTP is the Triggered Operations Mechanism (TOM). Triggered operations are invoked whenever the segments to which they are attached are being updated. Using TOM the system can perform consistency checks, compute values for fields, maintain logical links and maintain controlled data redundency. Triggered operations are defined by the database designer. Their definition is declarative and it is done through a special form.

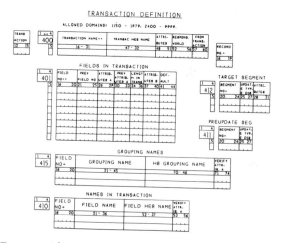

FIGURE 3. Transaction definition form.

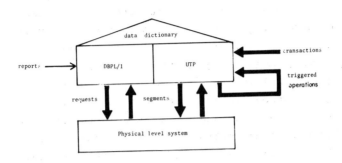

FIGURE 4. The main componnents of the DB1 system.

The DBPL1 language. The DBPL1 is an extension of PL1. The
language is used to access the database in order to create
reports. The user who writes programs in DBPL1 refers (in the
present implementation) to the internal schema. A DBPL1
command defines a group of segment instances that correspond
to a qualification given by the user. DBPL1 handles
automatically the looping through their group.

The Conceptual Schema. We tend to choose relations for the
representation of the conceptual schema. In the present
implementation of the DB1 system the user refers to the
internal schema.

Relations are used only by designers for their planning.
The description of the authorization mechanism that follows
will be also in terms of relations.

III. BASIC PRINCIPLES

In the tree structure model of an enterprise all the nodes
of the same type that have the same parent are authorized to

access the same information (remember that the authorization
concept relates only to the data schema level). A model for a
large enterprise is an hierarchic tree that at each level have
several type of nodes. Each node represents a job in the
enterprise and similar jobs form nodes of the same type. Equal
jobs are similar jobs that have also the same privacy acts on
the information they are authorized to access.
Several management rules exist in the model:

* Every employee reports only to his direct superior.
* If a manager is granted the right to define the jobs of
the employees he manages, no one in the enterprise can
change this definition without his approval.
* Every change in job definitions is made known to the
employee only through his direct superior.
* Employees that have similar jobs and the same manager
have similar job definition.

These rules are reflected in the model for the management
of information in an enterprise that is described in this
paper.

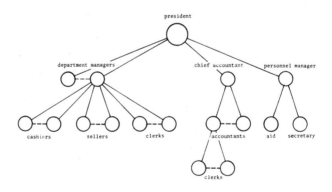

FIGURE 5. An organizational structure of an enterprise.

In an enterprise, it is very likely that many users are authorized to access the same information (remember that our authorization schema is value independent). Examples:

(1) The managers of store departments may access the PERSONNEL relation and the SALES relation with the same access options and with the same grant options.

(2) All clerks that have similar jobs in an office may be authorized to access the same information.

Attaching authorization to a user in the case of similar jobs will cause the creation of many instances of the SYSAUTH relation that differ only in the USER attribute and this results in a waste of data-base volume. Further, addition of a job to a set of similar jobs in the organization means addition of instances of the AUTH relation that differ from existing instances only by the USER attribute. When a user leaves his job all these instances must be deleted. When a user changes his job within the organization the existing instances must be deleted and a new set of instances must be defined. As a conclusion it seems worthwide to gather all the common information of the similar jobs into one entity. This entity is called WORLD.

definition 1: a WORLD W is a set of information units W(I) (relation aggregates, relations, attributes), with the access options defined for them, that are granted to a group of users W(U).

definition 2: A world B is included in a world A if every information unit I in B is included in A. A has at least the same rights to manipulate I as B.

Any user that wants to access information must do it through a world. The entrance to a world is allowed only when the user identifies himself by the proper password.

In the DB1 system every user that is authorized to access information through his world can be authorized to grant other users (through their worlds) any part of his world's rights. For simplicity we shall refer to the world as a grantor rather than to a user that is included in this world.

IV. THE MODEL

Our authorization mechanism uses several system relations.
These relations define the WORLD, include information units
within it and identify the users that belong to it. The
following relation defines a world in the data base:

WORLD <WORLD#, WORLD-NAME, GRANTOR#>

The GRANTOR is a world known to the system.

The authorization to access a relation is defined by the
following relations:

INFO-1 <WORLD#, RELATION NAME, ACCESS, GRANT>

The authorization mechanism also refers to attributes
within relations in another system relation:

INFO-2 <WORLD#, RELATION NAME, ATTRIBUTE NAME, ACCESS, GRANT>

In the DB1 system relations that contain data on the same
subject are aggregated and get a common title. It is possible
to authorize access to all the relations within such an
aggregate.

INFO-3 <WORLD#, AGGREGATE NAME, ACCESS, GRANT>

For example the following relations may be aggregated in the
MANPOWER aggregate:

EMPLOYEE <EMPLOYEE#, SEX, BIRTH-DATE, NAME>
SALARY <EMPLOYEE#, YEAR, MONTH, SALARY>
CHILDS <EMPLOYEE#, CHILD NAME>

The INFO-3 relation reduces in many cases the amount of
input to system information on authorization. Aggregates are
not defined especially for the authorization mechanism, they
are information units were already defined in the system for
other purposes.

The access options are: READ, INSERT, CHANGE, DELETE and
FORBIDDEN. The FORBIDDEN option enables the grantor to exclude
attributes from an authorized relation. For example:

A world named 'clerks' is given authorization to read all
the information gathered in the 'manpower' aggregate except

the 'salary' attribute. If only inclusion was allowed
authorization would have been defined by the following
relations:

    INFO-1<'clerks','employee','read','no grant'>

    INFO-1<'clerks','childs','read','no grant'>

    INFO-2<'clerks','salary','year','read','no grant'>

    INFO-2<'clerks','salary','month','read','no grant'>

Using the FORBIDDEN access option authorization can be
defined by a smaller number of relations:

    INFO-3<'clerks','manpower','read','no grant>

    INFO-2<'clerks','salary','salary','forbidden','no grant>

The GRANT OPTION may be:

    1) GRANT - The world can grant some or all of the rights
to access information units it has to other worlds.
These worlds must be defined by the granting world and
must be included in it.

    2) NO GRANT - This is the default grant option for an
information unit.

The world has no right to grant authorization to access
this information unit to other worlds.

A. User Authentication

A user is defined by the following relation:

    USER <USER#, USER-NAME, PASSWORD, WORLD#>

A user can be restricted to use specific terminals. The
restriction is done using the following relation:

    TERMINAL <USER#, TERMINAL ADDRESS>

When a user wants to access the data-base he supplies the
following parameters:

    USER-NAME PASSWORD

The system identifies the user, check the password and
then determine the world to which the user belongs.

B. World Decomposition

An important component in the authorization mechanism is the following relation which enables the inclusion of one world within the other:

INCLUDED WORLD <WORLD#, INCLUDED-WORLD#>

where INCLUDED-WORLD# is a WORLD# in the WORLD relation. A world can be included in more than one including world.

The advantage of this relation can be shown by the following example:

Let A and B be worlds in some information system that have the same authorization, over a part of the information authorized to them. Denote this common part by C.

Let A' and B' be A and B, respectively, without C. Now let us define world C' that contains only C. Let's also define the relation instance.

INCLUDED WORLD {<A'#,C'#>, <B'#,C'#>}

The definition of the authorization to access data which is common both to A and B, is done only once in C', therefore the amount of meta-data in the system is reduced.

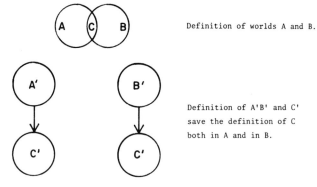

Definition of worlds A and B.

Definition of A'B' and C'
save the definition of C
both in A and in B.

FIGURE 6. Reducing meta data in world definition.

The process shown by the example and figure 6 is called
"world decomposition".

C. Granting Authorization in the Mechanism

An important rule in the DB1 system is that a world can
have only one GRANTOR. This rule reflects the management rule
that a job definition can be done only by one manager. This
approach does not affect the generality of the mechanism,
because if there are two grantors G1 and G2 that want to grant
authorization to a world A on relations R (G1) and R (G2)
respectively, then we can always find a third grantor that can
grant both R (G1) and R (G2) to A. The DBA can always be this
third grantor.

Adopting this approach means that in our system figure 1
will have the shape of an hierarchical tree.

Any WORLD that has the GRANT option over at least one
information unit, can be a GRANTOR in the system. Any GRANTOR
is authorized to insert instances of the WORLD relation. The
GRANTOR can read, change and delete only WORLDS that he has
created.

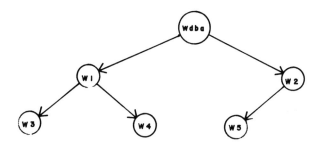

FIGURE 7. Chains of grantors and grantees in the DB1
system.

Instances of the relations INFO-1, INFO-2 and INFO-3 can
be created or manipulated only by the GRANTOR of the related
world. The rights to access the information unit and the grant
option that are given by the GRANTOR must be no more than the
rights the GRANTOR himself have. A value for the world
attribute in the USER relation can be inserted only by the
grantor of the related world. The USER relation itself which
is the key to the control on the authorization mechanism can
be created only by the DBA. These rules prevents "parralel
transfer".

Every WORLD that has users attached to it (except for the
WORLD of the DBA) must be included in it's GRANTOR world. The
DBA is the grantor of himself. As a result a world that
appears in some USER relation must be contained directly or
indirectly in the world of the DBA. This assection is checked
by the system and it ensures that no user of the data base
will be able to access data that is not authorized to the DBA.
Only authorized users can create or delete relations. The
creator of a relation does not have automatically the right to
access the instances of the relation or to grant the
authorization to access the instances to other users ("private
applications" are not possible). In this way the authorization
mechanism is both dynamic and it maintains the central role of
the DBA in the information system.

Let A be a world and B be a world. The relation
INCLUDED-WORLD <A#,B#> is true only if:
  * It is created by the world G which is the GRANTOR of B.
  * G is the GRANTOR of A or G=A.
  * A# > B#

The first two rules ensure that every world will have only one
GRANTOR. It reflects the management rule that job definition
can be done only by one superior manager. The third rule
ensures a tree structure for the schema of world inclusion in
the system.

The tree in figure 7 seems now to be more realistic for
enterprises that have an hierarchical organizational
structure. It may sometime be less convenient, but surely it

is more "controlled" because it prevents "parralel transfer" and "private applications". It is less subject to errors because the need to maintain the authorization for users that have similar jobs is reduced.

As it can be seen in figure **8** all the worlds that are created by the same world (e.g. the DBA) form a sub-forest in the grantor-grantees tree. This sub-forest is called the grantor forest (e.g., MANAGERS PERSONNEL and SALES form the grantor forest of the DBA.)

definition 3: All the worlds that were defined as included in world A by it's GRANTOR (including A itself) are called the grantee-tree of A. Example: PERSONNEL and MANAGERS form the grantee tree of PERSONNEL. The grantee tree of A contain all the information units that were authorized to A.

For each world W the system checks that there are no conflicts between a INFO-1, INFO-2 and INFO-3 relation in his grantor forest and the matching relations in his grantee tree.

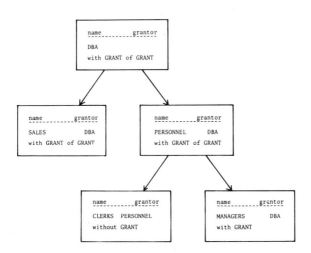

FIGURE 8. Worlds hierarchy in the DB1 system.

D. Authorization Revocation

Special attention has been given in the DB1 system to deletion and change operations in order to prevent a loss of system information due to some misuse of the authorization mechanism.

When the GRANT option is replaced by the NO GRANT option in an information unit I in a world W, then all the occurrances of I in the grantor forest of W are deleted.

If the accessing option over a relation that is included in a world A with the grant option is changed, then this change is carried on through all the grantor forest of A.

If an instance of INFO-1 INFO-2 or INFO-3 in world A is deleted, it is also checked that the same instance is not included in the grantee tree of A. If this check fails, it means that the delete operation does nothing that changes the authorization of A. In such a case, the system does not accept the operation.

A WORLD relation can be deleted only if no user is attached to it and there is no INCLUDED WORLD relation that contains this world as the included world. The second part of the rule ensures that no world will lose information due to some deletion of an INCLUDED-WORLD that does not take into account all it's including worlds.

V. THE IMPLEMENTATION

The DB1 schema uses records, segments and fields instead of aggregates, relations and attributes. Every definition of meta data in the system is done by meta transactions that are handled by the UTP in the same way as user transactions.

In each transaction that appear in the form in figure 9, the operation type is filled in column 5.

The WORLD transaction corresponds to the WORLD relation. The grantor is added automatically by the UTP according to the world that was declared by the active user when he had entered the system.

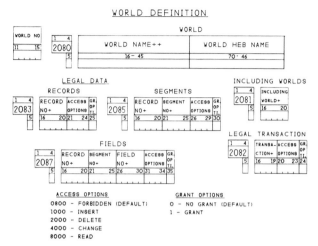

FIGURE 9. World definition form.

The transactions grouped under the LEGAL DATA title correspond to the INFO-3 INFO-2 and INFO-1 relations.

The INCLUDING WORLD transaction is used to define the INCLUDED WORLD relation. The choise of this transaction is a matter of convenience in the implementation. As it can be seen in the form, it is possible in the implementation to give authorization to a transaction rather than to the information units it accesses. The system can allow it because transaction definition is kept as meta data in the system.

User Authentication. User authentication and privacy are defined by the meta transactions shown in figure 10.

The transactions correspond to the relations that were defined in the model for user authentication and privacy (see in the next chapter). The PASSWORD transaction enables the designer to give several passwords to the user.

SECURITY - USERS RECOGNITION

DB USERS

USER-ID								

	USER NO++	USER NAME++	USER HEB NAME	WORLD NO	ATTRI- BUTES
2140	16 19	20 - 45	65 - 46	66 70	71 74

ALLOWED TERMINAL				PASSWORDS	
	SEQ NO+	TERMINAL ID+		SEQ NO+	PASSWORD+
2141	16 17	18 - 25	2142	16 17	18 - 37

PRIVACY

	RECORD NO+	SEGME- NT NO+	FIELD NO+	PRIVATE VALUES		
				LOW VALUE++	PREV LOW VAL.	HIGH VALUE
2146	16 20	21 25	26 30	31 - 40	41 - 50	51 - 60

FIGURE 10. User definition form.

VI. FURTHER ISSUES

A. Privacy Acts

By using INFO-1 INFO-2 and INFO-3 relations a world can receive authorization to access any relation that is defined in the data-base. The authorization act in the DB1 system is value independent, value dependent authorization is a privacy act in the system.

The common privacy demand is to restrict a user who wants to access a relation to those instances in which the value of a certain attribute fails to be within the boundaries of a specific domain. This type of privacy acts are described by the following relation:

PRIVACY<USER#,RELATION,ATTRIBURE,PRIVATE VALUE,HIGH VALUE>

The 'attribute' is an attribute included in the 'relation'. 'Private value' and 'high value' are used to establish the domain of values that are allowed to the user. If only a discrete value is allowed 'high value' can be

omitted. The PRIVACY relation can be used to describe several
allowed domains or several discrete values.

Whenever a new instance of the PRIVACY relation create a
new value for the tuple ('user#','relation','attribute'), a
special triggered operation is created automatically by the
system (the user doesn't write any routines). Whenever the
relation 'relation' is accessed that triggered operation is
invoked and it checks that the value of the attribute is
within the domain described by the PRIVACY relation. The
privacy act succeeds if the check succeeds.

For example: In the PERSONNEL relation

   PERSONNEL<EMPLOYEE#, NAME, SEX, DEPARTMENT, MANAGER>

we want to ensure that department managers will be able to
access only the relations of their employees. For the manager
of department 48 (code) the following relation will be
defined:

   PRIVACY<'user#', 'personnel', 'department', 48>

On every access to the PERSONNEL relation by the manager
of department 48 the employee department will be compared with
the value 48. Only on equal values the system will transfer
the relation to the manager of department 48.

A user who wants to define complex privacy acts that can't
be expressed by mean of the PRIVACY relation, must define a
special purpose triggered operation.

B. Authorization in DBPL1 Programs

In the DB1 system all update transactions are handled by
the UTP that checks that the user sending a transaction is so
authorized. Reports are written using the DBPL1 language.

At compilation time the DBPL1 compiler checks that the
program accesses only authorized relations.

The checking of authorization at compilation time is
possible due to the distinction between AUTHORIZATION acts and
PRIVACY acts, which must be checked at run time. The ability
to check whatever possible at compilation time saves CPU time.
The DBPL1 can produce the code is needed to invoke privacy
acts at run time.

<u>Statistical Programs</u>. It is possible (especially for
statistical programs) that a world will be able to get
authorization to use a program although not all the relations
the program accesses are authorized to it. Two features are
being implemented in the DB1 system that will be usefull for
the solution of the case:

* All programs that access the database (they are all
written in DBPL1) are documented in the database itself.
The documentation includes descriptions and
cross-references to the information units the program
accesses.

* All these programs are run by a special monitor. This
monitor is the only program in the system that can access
the library in which the object modules are kept. This
ensures protection against attempts to temper with object
modules.

To solve the problem of statistical programs the following
relation is added to program documentation:

PROG-AUTH<WORLD#, PROGRAM NAME>

At any activation of a program the user must identify
himself and must give his password.

A grantor can create a PROG-AUTH relation only if he is
authorized to read all the information units accessed by the
program.

The monitor checks that the user who activates a program
is authorized to do it. The DBPL1 compiler does not perform
any authorization checks for programs that appear in the
PROG-AUTH relation.

VII. SUMMARY

The authorization mechanism of the DB1 system solves
several problems such as "parralel transfer" and "private
application" that are encountered in the general dynamic
mechanism. It is simpler and more realistic than the general

dynamic mechanism. It is also more economical in terms of meta data volume and in it's maintenance because authorization is defined only once for a set of users that have authorization schemas. It is based on the assumption that the needs of a real organization generally have a certain structure while for extreme cases there is always a solution. Special safeguards were established to prevent disasters in the authorization mechanism as a result of misuse.

ACKNOWLEDGMENTS

The authors wish to express their thanks to Professor A.Reiter, Professor E.Shamir, J.Finkel, E.Raban for their helpful criticism, to Z.Messinai for his valueable comments and many fruitful discussions on the subject of security, to S.Timor for his suggestions at the design and implementation stages.

REFERENCES

1. GRIFFITHS, P.P. AND WADE, B.W. An authorization mechanism for a relational Data-base system ACM Trans. on Data-base systems 1,3 (September 1976), 242-255.

2. STONEBRAKER, M., WONG, E., KREPS, P., and HELD, G. The Design and Implementation of INGRES ACM TRANS. on Data-base systems 1,3 (September 1976), 189-222.

3. MINSKY, N. Intentional Resolution of Privacy Protection in Data-base systems. Comm. ACM 19,3 (March 1976), 148-159.

4. KAM, J.B., ULLMAN, J.D. A model of statistical Data-bases and their Security. ACM Trans. on Database systems 2,1 (March 1977), 1-10.

5. CHAMBERLIN, D.D., GRAY, J.N., and TRAIGER, I.L. Views, authorization, and locking in a relational database system. Proc. AFIPS 1975 NCC, VOL 44, AFIPS Press, Montvale, N.J., 425-430.

6. M.M Astrahan and al. System R: Relational Approach to Database Management. ACM Trans. on Data-base systems 1,2 (June 1976) pp. 97-137.

7. Messinai, Z., Arditi, J., Timor, S. The DB1 system (paper in preparation)

8. Raban, E. The DBPL1 language M.Sc. thesis Weizmann Inst. 1978.

DATABASES: IMPROVING USABILITY AND RESPONSIVENESS

TYPE CONCEPTS FOR DATABASE DEFINITION

Joachim W. Schmidt

Institut für Informatik
Universität Hamburg
Hamburg, W. Germany

Several facilities for type definition are outlined and applied to database definition. A declarative method given by the data structure relation/23/ is compared with a procedural method given by the capsule mechanism class/2/. Comparison is done mainly with respect to type representation and constraint definition.
The mapping of relational databases to user programs by means of classes is sketched by an example.

I. INTRODUCTION:

HIGH LEVEL PROGRAMMING LANGUAGES AND HIGH LEVEL DATA MODELS

In most high level approaches to data manipulation and data storage the concept of data type plays a central role. Although this concept has been refined several times, types have always served as tools for at least two purposes:

- for generating instances of value - carrying devices (variables);
- for specifying certain constraints to be maintained while operating on variables.

The user of a type need not care about the unnecessary details of either the representation of a variable by some storage structure or the supervision of the constraints by some controlling procedures.

215

Type concepts differ mainly in the extent to which a
language allows a user to shape the tools given by types so
as to meet his specific needs. While older programming languages offer merely a fixed set of built-in types (e.g.
integer, real, character), constrained by prescribed operations, newer languages allow types to be defined by stating
the necessary details of representation and constraints:

- About one decade ago, programming languages were developed which offer some built-in facilities for type
  definition, commonly called data structures /18/, /25/.
  New types may be defined by applying data structures
  (e.g. record, array, set) to types already defined
  (i.e., declarative type definition). Operations on
  variables of user-defined types are mainly restricted
  to accessing components and to the operations already
  defined for the standard type components.
- Languages developed in the last few years offer additionally a very general algorithmic facility for type
  definition (i.e., procedural type definition) /13/,
  /15/. Capsule /11/ or information hiding /20/ mechanisms (e.g. class, module, cluster, form) are provided
  so that types can be defined by both the necessary details for type representation and the consistency constraints to be maintained for variables of that type.

Furthermore, since capsule mechanisms may be applied
repeatedly, types may be mapped, step by step, from higher,
user - oriented levels to lower levels, ending with the
built-in language constructs. At every level, the view of the
data may be abstracted from the details which are not necessary for the data usage - details with regard to data representation, data constraints, data access etc..

The term high level data model is used to denote a user-
oriented view of the value - containing devices of a database (see e.g. /8/). In the relational model, for example,
data are presented to the user structured as sets of n-tuples,
constrained by a tuple-identifying key and by a set of operations /5/. Data models may, of course, be more complicated
(see /16/).

High level data models have, as Janus[1] does, two faces:
one face is looking at the requirements of an individual user,
such as appropriateness, adaptability, representation inde-
pendency of the data view; the other one is facing system
requirements, such as overall database consistency or runtime
efficiency and storage utilization.

To achieve these diverging demands, there has always been
some kind of multi-level approach to database systems.
Currently, the database administrator supports the system
with extra information at different levels: on the appropriateness of a specific user view, on integrity constraints,
on access paths. However, the different levels and their requirements were not well defined, nor were the requirements
for the mapping facilities between the levels. Information is
passed in some inconsistent and unstructured way from the
database administrator to the database system. The necessity
of a clean level structure and of some flexible mapping mechanisms is now widely accepted /19/.

Some conclusions drawn from the above discussion are:

- High level data models require powerful and well controlled mapping facilities in order to support multi-
  level database systems.
- High level programming languages offer mapping facilities and a methodology for programming multi-level
  structured systems.

It is the main purpose of this paper to investigate to
what extent type definition facilities of high level programming languages meet some of the needs of high level data
models. To be concrete and in correspondence with our previous
investigations, the concepts are designed in close agreement

---

[1]Janus: an ancient Italian deity, regarded as having doors
and entrances under his protection; represented
with a face on the front and another on the back
of his head. (The Shorter Oxford English Dictionary on Historical Principles, Oxford University
Press, 1973).

with the developments starting with standard Pascal /25/.

Section II. briefly reviews the declarative type definition facility introduced into Pascal by the data structure
relation /23/. Advantages and disadvantages of this data
structure are treated in section III.. A procedural type definition method as given in Concurrent Pascal /2/ by the concept of a class will be investigated in section IV.. The
interfacing of databases, defined by classes with user programs will be outlined in section V. by an example.

A number of general issues concerned with data type definition and data base definition are treated in /22/. The
approach in this paper is more pragmatic and consists of
applying particular programming language concepts to specific
problems in database definition.

II. SOME HIGH LEVEL CONSTRUCTS FOR DATA

STRUCTURED AS RELATIONS

In /23/, we introduced into Pascal a new declarative type
definition facility. We will review briefly the data structure
relation and the operations defined for relation variables.

A. Type Definition and Variable Declaration

By means of the data structure relation, a user may define
relation types and thereafter declare relation variables. The
declaration of a relation variable, rel, looks like:

> $type$ $rectype=record$ $field1:type1;...fieldk:typek;...end;$
> $reltype=relation<fieldk>$ of $rectype;$
> var $rel:reltype;$

While defining the type $reltype$, the field identifier $fieldk$
is distinguished. $<fieldk>$ denotes the key of that type, that
is, a particular value for $fieldk$ may occur at most once among
the tuples of a variable of type $reltype$.

A relational database, represented by a collection of
relations, may be declared as a variable by means of the data
structure database. A database variable is used as a formal
parameter in the program heading in order to connect a relational database as an external variable to a user program:

Example:

```
program dbuser(dbrel);
type ...
        rectype1=record...    ;
        reltype1=relation...    ;
        ...
var    dbrel=database rel1:reltype1;rel2:...;...end;
        ...
begin
        with dbrel do
        begin                     {access to the components
        ...                        of an external database to
        end                        be bound to dbrel at runtime}
end.
```

B. Altering and Reading Operations

The value of a relation variable may be altered by insertion, deletion, replacement, or assignment of tuples. The
modified target relation and the modifying source relation
have to be of the same type.

The statement $rel1:+rel2;$ inserts into the target relation
$rel1$ copies of those tuples of the source relation $rel2$ whose
key values do not already occur in some tuple of $rel1$.

The statement $rel1:-rel2;$ deletes from $rel1$ those tuples
also contained in $rel2$.

The statement $rel1:\&rel2;$ replaces in $rel1$ those tuples
whose key values occur in tuples of $rel2$ by a copy of the
corresponding tuple in $rel2$.

The statement $rel1:=rel2;$ assigns to $rel1$ the value of
$rel2$.

An anonymous 1-tuple relation may be constructed out of a record variable by means of the elementary relation constructor [<record variable>]. A relation constructed in this way is type-compatible with every relation variable whose type is based on the type of the record variable. The empty relation is denoted by [].

For reading a relation tuple by tuple, two standard procedures *low(rel)*, *next(rel)* and a Boolean function *aor(rel)* (all of relation) are defined. Furthermore, a buffer variable *rel↑* is implicitly declared for each relation variable. By the procedure call *low(rel)*, the tuple of the relation *rel* with the lowest key value is assigned to the buffer variable *rel↑*. By *next(rel)*, the tuple with the next highest key value is assigned to *rel↑*. If such a tuple does not exist the function call *aor(rel)* returns the value true and *rel↑* will be undefined.

Tuple-at-a-time access to a relation may also be gained by the control structure

foreach rec in rel do <statement>;

The implicitly declared record variable, *rec* (control record variable), is of that record type used in the type definition of the relation, *rel* (range relation variable). The order of tuple access is defined by the system.

C. Predicates over Relations

For the purpose of testing conditions for relation variables, expressions of the propositional logic, usually given in high level programming languages, are extended to predicates.

The quantifier some may be used to test for a tuple that satisfies a certain logical expression. If such a tuple exists in the relation *rel*, the predicate

some rec in rel(<logical expression>);

is true, otherwise, it is false.

The predicate

all rec *in* rel(*<logical expression>*);

is true if the logical expression is satisfied by all tuples
in the relation *rel*, otherwise, it is false. Logical expressions contain terms consisting of components of the control variable, program variables or constants, connected by
the relation operators =, <, >, ≠, ≤, and ≥. Terms may be
connected by the logical operators <u>and</u>, <u>or</u>. Since logical
expressions may also contain quantifiers, predicates may be
nested.

D. A General Relation Constructor

Predicates may be used to generalize the concept of the
elementary relation constructor introduced in section II.B.
The relation constructor

[*each* rec *in* rel:*<logical expression>*]

constructs an anonymous relation containing those tuples of
the range relation, *rel*, that satisfy the logical expression.
Constructed relations may, for example, be assigned to some
result relation. The most general form of the relation constructor is

[*each* (...;reci.fieldk;recj.fieldl;...)
  for ...reci,recj,...*in* ...reli, relj,...:*<logical*
                                       expression>]

The tuples of the constructed relation are assembled from the
components of the control record variables ... reci,recj,....
The correspondence between control record variables and range
relation variables is implied by their positions in the respective lists. For more details of these constructs see /23/.

III. DATABASE DEFINITION BY A DATA STRUCTURE RELATION

The data structure <u>relation</u> is claimed to be suitable for
defining relational databases. According to earlier remarks,
relation types should support at least two goals: the creation
of relation variables and the maintenance of constraints by
specifying only the necessary details. In this section we will
analyse to what extent representation and constraints of a
relation variable may be determined by the user.

A. Representation of Relations

A relation variable is represented by components (tuples)
of some user-defined type. The number of tuples may vary at
runtime. Elementary access to the tuples is given in two
ways: ordered by increasing key values through the standard
access functions *low(rel)* and *next(rel)* and in a system-de-
fined order by the control structure <u>foreach</u>.
The data structure <u>record</u> is used to define the type of
the tuples. Tuples are represented by a fixed number of components (fields) defined by scalar types or by a type string
of user-defined length (i.e. <u>packed</u> <u>array</u> [1..n] <u>of</u> char).
Arguments for restricting field types mainly to scalar types
are due to the relational model as defined by /5/ ('flat'
records, first normal form). Admitting some structured types
(<u>record</u>, <u>array</u>, Pascal-<u>set</u>) at least for non-key fields
should increase the expressive power of the relational model
to some extent.
While these representations seem to meet the requirements
of a wide variety of applications, they also show some severe
shortcomings. Since relations may hold a large number of
tuples, efficient tuple access may require a representation
(e.g., by a secondary index), based on the expected usage of
the data. At present, this additional information is given by
the database administrator, outside the data structure <u>rela-
tion</u>. Also data may be shared by several users not all interested or authorized to have the same view of the data. Therefore, there should be a facility to influence the represen-

tation, for example, by specifying the components to be shared by relation variables of different types.

B. Constraining Relational Databases

The consistency constraints one would like to have maintained for the data in a relational database may be divided into three categories:

(1) attribute constraints: to be checked on the basis of the fields of a tuple;

(2) intra-relation constraints: to be checked on the basis of the tuples of a relation;

(3) inter-relation constraints: to be checked in the basis of the relations of a database.

In the following sections, we will analyze to what extent constraints of the different categories can be maintained by means of types and type checking.

1. Attribute Constraints. Pascal offers a wide variety of possibilities for attribute type definition. In addition to the standard scalar types integer, real, char, and Boolean, the user may define its own scalar types by enumerating the identifiers which denote the values, e.g.,

type *daytype=(mon, tues, wed, thur, fri, sat, sun);*
    statustype=(student, technician, instructor, professor,
        emeritus);

Subrange types may also be used for attribute types. They are declarable on any other already defined scalar type - called its associated scalar type, e.g.,

type *tdaytype=mon..fri;*
    ttimetype=815..1800;
    estatustype=technician..professor;

For attribute definition there is also a need for a string
type of user-defined length, e.g.,

> *type* *enametype=*<u>*packed*</u> *<u>array</u>[1..20] <u>of</u> char;*

The formation process of a value is strictly supervised in
Pascal. This is done mainly by imposing rules on the types of
operation results and on the types of the operands involved.
Thus, for the value of every expression the type is defined
and may be checked before assigning it to a variable.

<u>Example:</u>

> *<u>type</u> daytype=(mon,tues,wed,thur,fri,sat,sun);*
> *tdaytype=mon..fri;*
> *ttimetype=815..1800;*
> *trectype=<u>record</u> tenr,tcnr:integer;ttime:ttimetype;*
>   *tday:tdaytype;...<u>end</u>;*
>
> *<u>var</u> trec:trectype;*
>
> *<u>begin</u>*
>   ...
> *trec.tcnr:=trec.tenr;*
> *trec.tenr:=trec.tcnr+trec.ttime;*
> *<u>if</u> trec.tenr=trec.ttime <u>then</u> ... ;*
> *trec.tday:=trec.ttime;*   *{type error}*
> *trec.ttime:=1900;*   *{type error}*
> *trec.tday:=sat*   *{type error}*
> *<u>end</u>.*

The last three statements are rejected by the compiler because
of a type error.

In Pascal, "a data type defines the set of values a variable may assume" (/12/ p. 12). Hence, two types defining the
same set of values will be regarded as identical types. Therefore, extra type definition for the fields *tenr* and *tcnr*, e.g.,

> *<u>type</u> enrtype=integer;*
> *cnrtype=integer;*

will not effect the last program with respect to type compatibility.

However, if the variable *trec* is interpreted as a lecture
announcement to be entered into a timetable, *tenr* as the
employee number of the lecturer, and *tcnr* as the course number, then also the first three statements in the last example
should not be accepted.

A straightforward approach for attacking those problems
by type definition and checking is discussed in the following
section.

a. Interpreted types. The user may define interpreted
types by means of a data structure interpretation[1] and by
the attribute types treated in section III.B.1. - called
its associated uninterpreted type. Interpreted types are
denoted by a '∂' in front of the associated uninterpreted
type; the associated uninterpreted types have to be identified
by a type identifier.

type *trectype=record* *tenr:* ∂*enrtype; tcnr:* ∂*cnrtype;...end;*

For variables of interpreted types the assignment opera-
tion and the relational operations =, <, >, $\neq$, $\leq$, $\geq$ are defined. Both operands have to be of the same interpreted type
i.e., to be declared by the same type identifier. Suppose the
fields *tenr* and *tcnr* in the last example are of the interpreted types ∂*enrtype* and ∂*cnrtype*, then also the first three
statements would not be accepted because of type error.

b. Deinterpretation. Occasionally, say for computing new
values from interpreted variables and for assigning the results, the strict type checking for interpreted variables may
be relaxed. This can be done by an operation called deinterpretation and denoted by a '∂' behind an interpreted variable.
Deinterpretation references the uninterpreted value of an
interpreted variable.

---

[1]to interpret: to show the meaning of; to construe in a
             particular way, as a part of a play
             [Websters Handy College Dictionary, New
             American Library, 1972].

Example:

type *enrtype=integer;*
     cnrtype=integer;
     . . .
     trectype=record *tenr:∂enrtype;tcnr:∂cnrtype;...end;*
var   *trec:trectype;*
begin

     . . .
     trec.tenr∂:=trec.tcnr.;
     trec.tcnr∂:=17;
     *trec.tcnr∂:=trec.tcnr∂*trec.tenr∂*
end.

The constraints introduced by interpretation are thus bypassed
by deinterpretation.

It should be noted that most of the constraints expressed
by the domain constraint language of Hammer and McLeod /9/
can be maintained by type definition and type checking. In
terms of /9/ our approach is more state transition oriented,
while their approach is based more on state snapshot evaluation (i.e., on exception definition and handling).

   2. Intra-relational Constraints. Databases are used to
store descriptions of both "real world" entities and associations among entities. A single relation variable is capable
of holding every description based on the same set of attributes. In general, a subset of these attributes - a key - is
sufficient to identify an individual entity. Constraining
key values to be unique within a relation, (i.e., maintaining
a functional dependency of the tuple attributes on the key
values) has consequences for the definition of the insertion
operation. By the statement

   rel1:+rel2;

only those copies of tuples from *rel2* which have key values
not already present in *rel1* are inserted into *rel1*.

The user has some facility for monitoring an insertion operation: a standard predicate, *allsource*, is defined that becomes true iff all tuples of the source relation, *rel2*, have been inserted into the target relation, *rel1*. A second standard predicate, *sometarget*, becomes true iff at least one tuple has been inserted into the target relation. These predicates are correspondingly set by deletion, replacement, and assignment operations. The maintenance of additional functional dependencies would be straightforward, though expensive at run-time.

However, there are many constraints not expressible by functional dependencies and hence not expressible by the data structure <u>relation</u>. For example, the constraint that the number of employees having the status of an instructor may not exceed that of the professors can not be expressed by relations.

3. <u>Inter-relational Constraints.</u> Relational variables can hold descriptions of both entities and associations among entities. While constraints for entities may be checked on the basis of a single relation, more than one relation is involved when associations are constrained. Examples of the following kind, causing severe inter-relational inconsistencies, cannot be avoided by means of the data structure <u>relation</u>.

<u>Example</u>:

In a relational database, *dbrel*, two relations, *erel* and *trel*, describing employees and a timetable, are associated by the fact that an employee announces a lecture. The employee may be identified by an employee number, the announcement may be described by an entry in the timetable containing the lecturer's employee number:

```
program dbuser(dbrel);
type enrtype=integer;
    ...
    erectype=record enr:∂enrtype;...end;
    ereltype=relation<enr> of erectype;
    trectype=record tenr:∂enrtype;...end;
    treltype=relation<tenr,...> of trectype;
    ...
var  dbrel:database erel:ereltype;trel:treltype;...end;
     erec:erectype;
     trec:trectype;
begin
     with dbrel do
     begin
         erec.enr∂:=7;          {initialization of
         ...                     employee record}
         erel:+[erec];
         trec.tenr∂:=7;         {initialization of
         ...                     timetable record}
         trel:+[trec];
         erel:-[erec]
     end
end.
```

An employee record is initialized and inserted into *erel*. Then
an associated tuple, describing a lecture announcement by this
employee, is inserted into *trel*. Finally, the associated tuple
in *erel* is deleted, leaving the database inconsistent. A lecture is announced by a non-existing lecturer.

Hammer and McLeod introduced an extra relation constraint
language /9/ for constraints not expressible by attribute
specification. In the following section, we will analyze to
what extent the introduction of the class concept will meet
our needs for data base definition.

IV. CLASSES FOR DATABASE DEFINITION

Defining databases declaratively by the data structure
relation, has some shortcomings. To overcome them there are
at least two solutions: extend substantially the declarative
type definition or introduce a procedural type definition
facility.

Extending declarative definition is mainly done by methods
derived from Floyd's assertional /6/ and Hoare's axiomatic
/10/ approach to program specification. Examples applying
those techniques to data specification may be found in /7/,
/26/. Declarative definition methods for relational databases
have been developed by /9/, /17/.

This paper is concerned mainly with a programming language
approach to database definition. Hence, procedural type definition will be preferred as provided by languages with a
capsule mechanism. To be concrete, we will apply the class
concept as given in Concurrent Pascal /2/.

In addition to local variables and a statement body for
initialization, a class consists mainly of two characterizing
sets:

- a set of exported properties (variables, functions,
  procedures defined by class entries): properties defined
  inside the class and accessible from outisde, defining
  the behavior of that class;
- a set of imported properties (access rights defined by
  class parameters): properties defined outside the class
  and accessible from inside, defining the environment
  for that class.

As in section III., we will treat representational and
consistency aspects separately.

A. Representation of Classes

The value of a class variable may be represented by the
internal (local) variables of the defining class and possibly
by external variables for which access rights are stated ex-

plicitly in the class parameters. Consequently, defining a
type (e.g., *emptype*) by a class could be done in different
ways:

Solution 1: Representation by local relation variables

type emptype=class(<access rights>);
    var erel:ereltype;
    ...   {*function and procedure entries*}
begin
    ...   {*class initialization*}
end;

Declaring *erel* by

var entry erel:ereltype;

would allow all system components with access to a variable of
type *emptype* to read its local variable *erel*.

Solution 2: Representation by external relation variables

type emptype=class(var erel:ereltype;...);
    ...   {*function and procedure entries*}
begin
    ...   {*class initialization*}
end;

This solution has the advantage that we can define several
sets of class types which access the same set of external relation variables. In data base terminology, this means that
different views can be defined on the same set of relations.
Although this solution is not in exact agreement with Concurrent Pascal which requires the external variables to be of
some class type, we will use it for the forthcoming examples.

Solution 3: Representation by external class variables

type emptype=class(eclass:eclasstype;...);
    ...   {*function and procedure entries*}
begin
    ...   {*class initialization*}
end;

The type of the external class variable may be defined by

    type e*classtype*=c*lass*(*<access rights>*);
       var ...   *{local variables}*
        ...   *{function and procedure entries}*
    begin
        ...   *{class initialization}*
    end;

This solution will show its superiority as soon as there are
means for internally representing e*classtype* more efficiently
than the standard representation of e*reltype*. A substantial
contribution towards this end could be the introduction of
particular key types that enable a direct mapping of relations
into direct access files /24/.

B. Classes for Database Constraints

The value of a class variable may be altered and accessed
only through the entries in the defining class. The requirements for constraining the altering operation differ significantly from the needs for the widely unrestricted querying
of a database. Therefore, these aspects will be treated separately.

1. Database Alteration. The example in section III.3.
demonstrates how, due to the weak restrictions imposed on
altering operations, the relations of a database may become
inconsistent. If types are specified procedurally, the altering operations may be defined by class entries that would
enforce additional constraints.

Provided that there exists a database formed by three
relation variables: e*rel* for employees, c*rel* for courses, and
t*rel* for a timetable associating lecturing employees and their
courses, then the definition of corresponding class types may
look like this:

Example:

```
type employeestype=class(var erel:ereltype;trel:treltype);
    var entry status:record inserted,deleted,
                                        updated:boolean end;
    ...
    procedure entry insert(erec:erectype);
    begin
       erel:+[erec];
       status.inserted:=sometarget
    end;
    procedure entry delete (enr:enrtype);
    begin
       if some trec in trel(trec.tenr=enr)
       then status.deleted:=false
       else begin
                erel:-[each erec in erel:erec.enr=enr];
                status.deleted:=sometarget
           end
    end;
    procedure entry update(...);
    begin
       ...
    end;
begin
    ...                         {class initialization}
end;
type timetabletype=class(var trel:treltype;erel:ereltype;
                                        crel:creltype);
    var entry status:record inserted,deleted,updated:
                                        boolean end;
    ...
    procedure entry insert(trec:trectype);
    begin
       if some erec in erel(erec.enr=trec.tenr) and
          some crec in crel(crec.cnr=trec.tcnr)
       then begin
                trel:+[trec];
                status.inserted:=sometarget
           end;
```

```
        else status.inserted:=false
    end;
    procedure entry delete(...);
    begin ...end;
    procedure entry update(...);
    begin ...end;
begin
    ...                        {class initialization}
end;
type coursestype=class(var crel:creltype;trel:treltype);
    var entry status:record inserted,deleted,updated:
                                    boolean end;

    ...
    procedure entry insert(...);
    begin ...end;
    procedure entry delete(...);
    begin ...end;
    procedure entry update(...);
    begin ...end;
begin
    ...                        {class initialization}
end;
```

If we declare the following variables

```
var   emp:employeestype;
      tim:timetabletype;
      cour:coursestype;
```

then *emp* has access to the relation variables *erel* (read and
write) and *trel* (read only); *tim* has access to *trel* (read and
write), *erel* (read only), and *crel* (read only); *cour* has
access to *crel* (read and write) and *trel* (read only). Strictly
speaking, the access refers to the actual parameters, given
to the class variable by some initializing statement (see
example section V.B.).

The insertion of a record into the class variable, *tim*,
is now controlled by the procedure entry *insert* defined by
the classtype *timetabletype*. The procedure *insert* prevents
a record from being inserted if the employee number in its

field *tenr* is not equal to the employee number in field *enr*
of some tuple in the relation *erel*. Correspondingly, no entry
in the class variable *emp* can be deleted if associated tuples
in the relation *trel* exist. Inter-relational constraints,
and others, can thus be handled. For example, the intra-
relational constraint mentioned in section III.B.2. that
the number of the employeed instructors may not exceed that
of the employeed professors would result in the following
insert entry for *employeestype:*

> *procedure entry insert(erec:erectype);*
> *begin*
>   *if erec.estatus∂≠ instructor or*
>   *size([each rec in erel:rec.estatus∂= instructor])+1≤*
>   *size([each rec in erel:rec.estatus∂= professor])*
>   *then begin*
>   *erel:+[erec];*
>   *status.inserted:=sometarget*
>   *end;*
>   *else status.inserted:=false*
> *end;*

The consistency constraints considered so far can be defined
in advance for all users of a data base. The queries a user
may ask a database can, however, not be anticipated; therefore, they are not implementable by predefined procedure
entries.

   2. Querying a Database. The arguments for constraining
data extraction from a database seem to be less clear than
those for constraining data insertion. Data security, data
semantics, consistency of constraints for data insertion and
extraction are some of the related problems.
   The only restrictions for data base querying, imposed by
the constructs introduced so far, are those of a query
language based on first order predicate calculus. In this
section, we do not intend to leave this frame; instead we
will show how the query facility given by the general relation
constructor interacts with a database, defined by classes.

This interaction may take place via an additional function
entry *value* in the class definitions which returns a relational snapshot of the value of a class variable.

Example:

type *employeestype*=*class(var:erel:ereltype;trel:treltype);*
> *var* *entry* *status:...;*
> *function* *entry* *value:ereltype;*
> *begin*
>> *value:=erel;*
> *end;*
> ...   {*procedure entries see example*
>   *section* IV.B.1.}
> *begin*
> ...   {*class initialization*}
> *end;*

Allowing functions to have values of a structured type, such
as the relation-valued function entry *value*, is again a
generalization of Concurrent Pascal. Now, the general relation
constructor may be applied as introduced in section II.D.,
instead of referencing relation variables calling relation-
valued functions.

Value entries may be more complex, e.g., when constructing
a new relation by restricting or combining others. Querying
a database can be further constrained by defining relations
by interpreted types and by disallowing deinterpretation
within the constructor.

V. INTERFACING DATABASES WITH USER PROGRAMS: AN EXAMPLE

In this section, a (concurrent) program will be sketched
consisting of the types, variables, and statements that define
a database example and that are necessary to interface and
run a (sequential) user program.

Interfacing a user program is mainly done by a process
variable that has, in addition to local variables, access
rights to the database, and by interface procedures. Access

rights may be restricted by interface procedures before they
are passed to user programs via the construct *program* and via
a compiler-generated prefix.

A. Database Definition: Relations and Classes

As in our previous example, a relational database will be
defined by the components *erel, trel,* and *crel.*

```
type enrtype=integer;
    ...
    erectype=record enr:∂enrtype;...end;
    ereltype=relation<enr> of erectype;
    ...
    trectype=record tenr:∂enrtype;tcnr:...;...end;
    treltype=relation<tenr,tcnr,...> of trectype;
    ...
    crectype=record cnr:...;...end;
    creltype=relation<cnr> of crectype;
    dbreltype=database erel:ereltype;trel:treltype;
                                        crel:creltype end;
    statustype=record inserted,deleted,updated:boolean
                                                    end;
```

Next, the three class types *employeestype, timetabletype,*
and *coursestype* will be defined which access the relational
database. The type *dbclasstype* essentially represents the
constrained view of the database to be presented to the user:

```
type employeestype=class(var erel:ereltype;trel:treltype);
    var entry status:statustype;
    function entry value:ereltype;
    begin ...end;
    procedure entry insert(erec:erectype);
    begin ...end;
    procedure entry delete(enr:enrtype);
    begin ...end;
    procedure entry update(...);
    begin ...end;
```

```
begin
       ...                    {class initialization}
end;

type  timetabletype=class(var  trel:treltype;erel:ereltype;
                                   crel:creltype);
       var entry status:statustype;
       function entry value:treltype;
       begin ...end;
       procedure entry insert(trec:trectype);
       begin ...end;
       procedure entry delete(...);
       begin ...end;
       procedure entry update(...);
       begin ...end;
begin
       ...                    {class initialization}
end;

type  coursestype=class(var  crel:creltype;trel:treltype);
       var entry status:statustype;
       function entry value:creltype;
       begin ...end;
       procedure entry insert(crec:crectype);
       begin ...end;
       procedure entry delete(...);
       begin ...end;
       procedure entry update(...);
       begin ...end;
begin
       ...                    {class initialization}
end;

type  dbclasstype=database  emp:employeestype;
                             tim:timetabletype;
                             cour:coursestype end;
```

B. Interface Definition: Processes and Interface Procedures

Now, the system component *userprocesstype* can be defined which is a <u>process</u> type that has access to the components of the database defined by *dbclasstype*. The access rights may be restricted further by so called interface procedures before they are given to user programs via the construct <u>program</u>. The statement part of *userprocesstype* provides for loading and starting user programs.

<u>type</u> *userprocesstype=*<u>process</u>*(emp:employeestype;*
                                         tim:timetabletype;
                                         cour:coursestype);
  <u>var</u> *code:...*   *{storage space for user*
                                         program dbuser1}
                                         {interface procedures}
  <u>function</u> <u>entry</u> *estatus:statustype;*
  <u>begin</u> *estatus:=emp.status* <u>end</u>*;*

  <u>function</u> <u>entry</u> *tstatus:statustype;*
  <u>begin</u> *tstatus:=tim.status* <u>end</u>*;*

  <u>function</u> <u>entry</u> *cstatus:statustype*
  <u>begin</u> *cstatus:=cour.status* <u>end</u>*;*

  <u>function</u> <u>entry</u> *employees:ereltype;*
  <u>begin</u> *employees:=emp.value* <u>end</u>*;*

  <u>function</u> <u>entry</u> *timetable:treltype;*
  <u>begin</u> *timetable:=tim.value* <u>end</u>*;*

  <u>function</u> <u>entry</u> *courses:creltype;*
  <u>begin</u> *courses:=cour.value* <u>end</u>*;*

  <u>procecure</u> <u>entry</u> *insertemployee(erec:erectype);*
  <u>begin</u> *emp.insert(erec)* <u>end</u>*;*

  <u>procedure</u> <u>entry</u> *deleteemployee(enr:enrtype);*
  <u>begin</u> *...end;*

```
procedure entry updateemployee(...);
begin ...end;

procedure entry inserttimetable(trec:trectype);
begin tim.insert(trec) end;

procedure entry deletetimetable(...);
begin ...end;

procedure entry updatetimetable(...);
begin ...end;

procedure entry insertcourse(crec:crectype);
begin cour.insert(crec) end;

procedure entry deletecourse(...);
begin ...end;

procedure entry updatecourse(...);
begin ...end;

program dbuser(...);
entry estatus,tstatus,cstatus,
      employees,timetable,courses,
      insertemployee,deleteemployee,updateemployee,
      inserttimetable,deletetimetable,updatetimetable,
      insertcourse,deletecourse,updatecourse;
begin
   ...              {process initialization: loading
   dbuser(...;code);   and starting of the user program
   ...                  dbuser1}
end;
```

Now, variables of the defined types may be declared and
initialized:

```
var dbrel:dbreltype;
    dbclass:dbclasstype;
    userprocess:userprocesstype;
begin                    {statement body of the (concurrent)
    with dbrel,dbclass do      program:initialization}
```

```
begin
    init emp(erel,trel),tim(trel,erel,crel),cour(crel,
         trel),userprocess(emp,tim,cour)
    end
end.
```

This is the end of the (concurrent) program defining the
database.

C. Prefix and User Program

The front end of the interface between a database and its
user is represented by a compiler-generated prefix to (sequential) user programs. The prefix consists of the headings of
the interface procedures and the types of their parameters:

```
type enrtype=integer;        {prefix to user program}
     ...
     erectype=record enr:∂enrtype;...end;
     ereltype=relation<enr> of erectype;
     ...
     trectype=record tenr:∂enrtype;tcnr:...;...end;
     treltype=relation<tenr,tcnr,...> of trectype
     ...
     crectype=record cnr:...;...end;
     creltype=relation<cnr> of crectype;
     statustype=record inserted,deleted,updated:boolean
                                                    end

     function estatus:statustype;
     function tstatus:statustype;
     function cstatus:statustype;
     function employees:ereltype;
     function timetable:treltype;
     function courses:creltype;
     procedure insertemployee(erec:erectype);
     procedure deleteemployee(enr:enrtype);
     procedure updateemployee(...);
```

```
procedure  inserttimetable(trec:trectype);
procedure  deletetimetable(...);
procedure  updatetimetable(...);
procedure  insertcourse(crec:crectype);
procedure  deletecourse(...);
procedure  updatecourse(...);
```

For the following user program, *dbuser1*, the prefix plays essentially the same role as the external database variable *dbrel* does for the program *dbuser* in section III.B.3. The main difference is that the database may be altered only by calling the corresponding procedures which maintain the database constraints.

```
program dbuser1(...);            {user program}
var erec:erectype;
    trec:trectype;
    ...

begin
    erec.enrϑ:=7;                 {initialization of
    ...                            employee record}
    insertemployee(erec);
    trec.tenrϑ:=7;                {initialization of
    ...                            timetable record}
    inserttimetable(trec);
    ...;
    deleteemployee(erec.enr)
    ...;
end;
```

In this example, the employee record containing the employee number 7 will not be deleted because there exists an associated timetable record.

An interpretation of the whole program in terms of the currently discussed multi-level structure for databases /1/ will be done elsewhere. Also, the definition of several user processes and the synchronization of parallel access to databases will be treated later.

VI. CONCLUDING REMARKS

The programming language Concurrent Pascal was designed
to serve as a "programming language for structured programming of computer operating systems". Operating systems and
user programs are related by the fact that "an operating
system should be in complete control of resource allocation
and input/output. But a user program must be able to call
the operating system and ask to perform these functions"
(see /3/ pp. 1,4). Our current investigation is concerned
with to what extent the introduction of relational constructs
allows replacing the term "operation system" by "database
system" in the statement above.

Differing requirements for type definition in high level
programming languages and high level data models result to a
great extent from the complexity of databases. A "real world"
organization to be modelled by a database may consist of a
very large number of entities (of hundred of types) and many
of them may be associated (by dozens of relationships). "Does
the database really model the organization accurately? Are
all significant interrelationships accounted for? Is the
database adequately protected against a faulty program or a
faulty hardware device? Can the database structure logically
evolve as the organizational requirements change?" (see /14/,
p. 384)

Extended declarative specification methods certainly may
have advantages over procedural methods as far as rigor and
conciseness of database definition are concerned. Declarative definition may facilitate formal methods for proving
the completeness and the consistency of constraints /4/. On
the other hand, procedural definition methods are more flexible and may, for the present, be more appropriate for in-
vestigating the mapping requirements of a multi-level database architecture /21/. Our approach, using declarative
language constructs (e.g., the relation constructor) within
procedural type definition, may show some of the advantages
of both approaches.

ACKNOWLEDGMENTS[1]

The author is grateful to M. Brodie, H. Fischer and
D. Tsichritzis for their comments on earlier versions of
this paper.

REFERENCES

/1/   ANSI/X3/SPARC Study Group on Data Management Systems.
       Interim Report. ACM FDT 7, 2(1975).
/2/   Brinch Hansen, P. The Programming Language Concurrent
       Pascal. IEEE Transactions on Software Engineering 1,
       2 (June 1975), pp. 199-207.
/3/   Brinch Hansen, P. Job Control in Concurrent Pascal.
       Information Science Report, California Institute
       of Technology (March 1975).
/4/   Brodie, M.L., and Tsichritzis, D. Data Base Constraints.
       In Tsichritzis, D. (Editor). A Panaché of DBMS
       Ideas. University of Toronto, Technical Report
       CSRG-78 (Feb. 1977), pp. 19-37.
/5/   Codd, E.F. A Relational Model of Data for Large Shared
       Data Banks. Comm. ACM 13, 6 (June 1970), pp. 377-387.
/6/   Floyd, R.W. Assigning Meanings to Programs. Proceedings
       of the Symposium in Applied Mathematics Vol. XIX,
       American Mathematical Society (1967), pp. 19-32.
/7/   Guttag, J.W. The Specification and Application to Pro-
       gramming of Abstract Data Types. University of
       Toronto, Technical Report CSRG-59 (Sept. 1975).
/8/   Hammer, M.M. Data Abstraction for Data Bases. Proceed-
       ings of Reference /22/, pp. 58-59.
/9/   Hammer, M.M., and McLeod, D.J. Semantic Integrity in a
       Relational Data Base System. Proceedings of the
       International Conference on Very Large Data Bases,
       Framingham, MA. (Sept. 1975), pp. 25-47.
/10/   Hoare, C.A.R. An Axiomatic Basis for Computer Program-
       ming. Comm. ACM 12, 10 (Oct. 1969), pp. 576-580.
/11/   Horning, J.J. Some Desirable Properties of Data Ab-
       straction Facilities. Proceedings of Reference
       /22/, pp. 60-62.
/12/   Jensen, K., and Wirth, N. PASCAL User Manual and Report,
       2nd Edition, Springer-Verlag (1976).
/13/   Lampson, B.W., Horning, J.J., London, R.L., Mitchell,
       J.G., and Popek, G.L. Report on the Programming
       Language EUCLID. SIGPLAN Notices 12, 2 (Feb. 1977).
/14/   Ledgard, H.F., and Taylor, R.W. Two Views of Data
       Abstraction. Comm. ACM 20, 6 (June 1977), pp. 382-384.

---

[1]This work was supported in part by Deutsche Forschungs-
gemeinschaft, Bad Godesberg.

/15/　Liskov, B. A Note on CLU. Computation Structure Group,
　　　　Memo 112, Massachusetts Institute of Technology,
　　　　Project MAC (Nov. 1974).

/16/　McGee, W.C. On User Criteria for Data Model Evaluation.
　　　　ACM Transactions on Database Systems 1, 4 (Dec.
　　　　1976), pp. 370-384.

/17/　McLeod, D.J. High Level Domain Definition in a Rela-
　　　　tional Data Base System. Proceedings of Reference
　　　　/22/, pp. 47-57.

/18/　Naur, P. (Editor). Revised Report on the Algorithmic
　　　　Language ALGOL 60. Comm. ACM 15, 1 (Jan. 1963),
　　　　pp. 1-17.

/19/　Nijssen, G.M. (Editor). Modelling in Data Base Manage-
　　　　ment Systems. North Holland Publishing Company
　　　　(1976).

/20/　Parnas, D.L. On the Criteria to be Used in Decomposing
　　　　Systems into Modules. Comm. ACM 15, 12 (Dec. 1972),
　　　　pp. 1053-1058.

/21/　Pelegatti, G., Paolini, P., and Bracchi, G. Models,
　　　　Views, and Mappings in Multilevel Database Repre-
　　　　sentations. To be published in Information Systems.

/22/　SIGPLAN/SIGMOD. Conference on Data: Abstraction, De-
　　　　finition, and Structure. Salt Lake City, Utah
　　　　(March 1976).

/23/　Schmidt, J.W. Some High Level Language Constructs for
　　　　Data of Type Relation. ACM Transactions on Database
　　　　Systems 2, 3 (September 1977), pp. 247-261.

/24/　Schmidt, J.W. On the Implementation of Relations: A Key
　　　　to Efficiency. University of Toronto, Technical
　　　　Report CSRG-89 (January 1978).

/25/　Wirth, N. The Programming Language PASCAL. Acta Informa-
　　　　tica 1,1 (May 1971), pp. 35-63.

/26/　Zilles, S.N. Data Algebra: A Specification Technique
　　　　for Data Structures. Ph.D. Thesis, Massachusetts
　　　　Institute of Technology, Project MAC (1975).

DATABASES: IMPROVING USABILITY AND RESPONSIVENESS

DATABASE CONSISTENCY AND INTEGRITY
IN A MULTI-USER ENVIRONMENT

Michael F. Challis[1]

Departamento de Informática
Pontifícia Universidade Católica do Rio de Janeiro
Rio de Janeiro
Brasil

1. INTRODUCTION

In this paper we propose a solution to the twin problems of data base consistency and integrity that is based on a particular "storage" model: briefly, an extra block-to-block mapping is inserted between the "logical" data base and the physical data file that contains it, thus providing a simple means of economically representing several similar "instances" of one data base at the same time. The basic technique has been used by the author to provide integrity in a single-user environment for the JACKDAW data base package ([2], [3]) and has also recently been reported independently by Lorie ([9]).

Section 2 introduces the problems of consistency and integrity, and briefly discusses conventional solutions such as "logging" and "roll-back" features. Section 3 describes the model on which the technique is based, and Section 4 explains its use in a single-user environment. We show how a user may design his applications programs to ensure whatever degree of consistency he requires, and how he may test new applications programs safely on a "live" data base without compromising its integrity.

Sections 5 and 6 extend the technique for use in a multi-user environment. In Section 5, the concept of "indivisibility"

---

[1]Partially supported by the Brazilian government agencies FINEP and CNPq.

is carefully examined, and a user primitive $indivis(t)$ is
suggested which allows a process P to attempt to execute a
transaction t without interference from other concurrent
processes, and in such a way that any effects of t appear to
occur at a single moment from the point of view of those other
processes. In the case where conflict between processes is
unlikely, such an attempt will normally be successful, and we
believe it to be a useful alternative to, say, the use of
semaphores or record "locks". Other facilities for testing sets
of co-operating processes on live data bases, and for accessing
"snap-shots" of data bases from which consistent reports can be
taken are also suggested. Section 6 develops an implementation
of these features to show that the cost involved is not high
provided that the various instances concurrently represented
are not too divergent.

2. CONSISTENCY AND INTEGRITY

    In this section, we define the properties of consistency
and integrity as applied to data base systems; for a more
detailed discussion of these concepts, references [10] (see
sections 2.5 and 2.6) and [5] (chapter 24) should be consulted.
    A data base is said to be $consistent$ at a particular
moment if all the semantic constraints governing allowable
relationships between records, values of fields, etc. are
satisfied. Some examples may help to illustrate this concept:
a) A new record with a particular key is to be added to a
    data base. The data base is not consistent until both the
    new entry has been added, and the index for the key field
    has been updated.
b) A record is to be deleted. The data base is not consistent
    until all references to that record have also been removed
    (such references include entries in indexes as well as
    pointers from other records).
c) A travel agent is booking a holiday. The data base is not
    consistent until the outward flight, hotel and return
    flight have all been reserved.

The simplest way to ensure consistency is to arrange that
any sequence of interdependent updates is *indivisible*: that is,
no other process (including a read-only process) may have
access to the data base until the sequence is completed.

In a single-user environment this is easy to achieve,
provided we have perfect hardware and software; for then each
run of an applications program is indivisible, and so we need
only make sure that each program leaves the data base consistent before terminating.

But hardware and software are never perfect, and so there
is always the possibility that any program may be interrupted
at an arbitrary moment, thus leaving the data base in an
arbitrary and possibly inconsistent state. (For example, the
program may simply run out of time.) Considerations such as
these lead to the concept of integrity: a data base system is
said to have *integrity* if, after an arbitrary halt, the data
base may be recovered to some consistent version.

One common way to provide data base integrity is by means
of logging, check-point and roll-back facilities (see [16] for
example). Every change to the data base is recorded on a
separate logging file, and, at appropriate moments, each
application program writes a "check-point" record to the log
to note that the data base is consistent. When restarting after
a failure, the system uses the information recorded on the log
to "roll-back" the data base to a consistent state. This paper
describes a different solution to the problem which does not
require logging and roll-back facilities; further advantages
of this solution are the provision of extra facilities, such
as the ability to test new programs safely on a live data base.

3.   THE BASIC DATA BASE MODEL

Before proceeding to details of the solution adopted, we
describe the "physical" (or "storage") model of the data base
upon which the solution depends.

We suppose that the data base is composed of a sequence of
data blocks, all of the same size, which are referenced by

sequence number. Any physical pointers within the data base
(between records for example) are represented by "block number/
offset" pairs, and so the unit of access is the block which is
referenced by sequence number. This is, of course, a representation of the data base at a very low level. The interface
to the user will be in terms of records and fields, and is
unlikely to include any references to physical locations. It
should also be understood that the correspondence between
physical blocks and logical records is not necessarily one-to-
one.

In order to develop a solution to the integrity problem we
insert an extra mapping between this model of the data base
and the "data file" itself on disc. The data file, too, is
composed of a sequence of fixed size blocks, but each block of
the data base is not necessarily associated with the corresponding block in the data file. For the remainder of this
paper we will use the word *logical* to refer to aspects of the
data base model and *physical* to refer to aspects of the data
file; thus the data base is modelled as a sequence of *logical*
blocks which are mapped onto the *physical blocks* of the data
file. The one-to-one mapping which defines this correspondence
is called the LP *mapping*.

e.g. A logical data base of four blocks might be represented
in a physical data file of six blocks as follows:

0	1	2	3	4	5
L_0	L_2		L_3	L_1	

The LP mapping is:

$LP(0) = 0$; $LP(1) = 4$; $LP(2) = 1$; $LP(3) = 3$

We say that physical blocks 2 and 5 are *spare*.

We see that a logical data base is defined by a physical data
file together with an LP mapping. In particular, one data file
may represent more than one data base, and it is this possibility that provides the key to the integrity technique presented in this paper.

The technique may be extended in an obvious manner to the
case where a logical data base is represented on several data
files with different block sizes; this covers several well-
known commercial data base systems such as ADABAS ([14]) and
TOTAL ([15]).

4.   THE SINGLE-USER ENVIRONMENT

4.1   The Integrity Technique

This section briefly describes the technique used to ensure integrity in a single-user environment. As mentioned in Section 1, this technique was independently proposed by Lorie, and the reader is referred to [9] for a more complete presentation.

For the sake of argument, we suppose that the LP mapping defining the logical data base is held in a physical block specially reserved for this purpose, called the *root block*. Then the data file is self-defining in the sense that a particular instance of the logical data base is defined by the contents of the root block; we call this the *disc instance*.

Each indivisible section of a program is executed in the following steps:

i) Initialisation. The LP mapping describing the disc instance is copied into core; we call the data base defined by the core LP mapping the *current instance*.

ii) Updating. Whenever a logical block is updated for the first time within this section, a new spare physical block is allocated to it, and the LP mapping in core is appropriately updated. A note of the number of the physical block previously allocated is added to a list of "pending" blocks. (Such pending blocks belong to the disc instance but not to the current instance.)

iii) Flushing. At the end of the section, the modified LP mapping in core is written back to the root block, so that the current instance becomes the new disc instance. Blocks in the pending list are now no longer needed and are marked as spare.

The cycle is repeated to execute the next indivisible section, although it is not, of course, necessary to repeat step (i).

The effect is that the disc instance changes directly from one consistent state to the next; any intermediate steps are defined only by current instances in core, which are lost when a program terminates. So integrity is assured: if a program terminates unexpectedly within an indivisible section, then the instance made available when the data file is next opened will be that corresponding to the consistent state in force just prior to entering the interrupted indivisible section.

As an example, consider the following situation where the indivisible section includes two updates to logical block 1 and one to logical block 3:

The initial state is as follows (block 0 is the root block):

	0	1	2	3	4	5	6	7
DISC:	$1 \to 3$ $2 \to 1$ $3 \to 6$	L_2		L_1			L_3	

CORE: $1 \to 3$ Pending blocks: None
         $2 \to 1$
         $3 \to 6$

To update block 1, we first read physical block 3 into core and alter it; since this is the first change to this logical block within the section, we assign a new physical block before writing the altered logical block back to disc - in this example we choose physical block 2. We record the previously allocated block (number 3) in the pending list:

	0	1	2	3	4	5	6	7
DISC:	$1 \to 3$ $2 \to 1$ $3 \to 6$	L_2	L_1'	L_1			L_3	

CORE: $*1 \to 2$ Pending blocks: 3
          $2 \to 1$
          $3 \to 6$

(* An asterisk against a mapping element indicates that the logical block has been altered during the current section.)

Next, we update logical block 3 in the same way:

	0	1	2	3	4	5	6	7
DISC:	$1 \to 3$ $2 \to 1$ $3 \to 6$	L_2	L_1'	L_1	L_3'		L_3	

CORE: $*1 \to 2$ Pending blocks: 3, 6
          $2 \to 1$
         $*3 \to 4$

We now make a further alteration to logical block 1. This is not the first change, and so there is no need to assign a new physical block:

	0	1	2	3	4	5	6	7
DISC:	$1{\to}3$ $2{\to}1$ $3{\to}6$	L_2	L_1''	L_1	L_3'		L_3	

CORE: $*1{\to}2$ $2{\to}1$ $*3{\to}4$ Pending blocks: 3, 6

The section is now complete and we rewrite the modified mapping to the root block, and mark the pending blocks 3 and 6 as spare:

	0	1	2	3	4	5	6	7
DISC:	$1{\to}2$ $2{\to}1$ $3{\to}4$	L_2	L_1''		L_3'			

CORE: $1{\to}2$ $2{\to}1$ $3{\to}4$ Pending blocks: None

Note that this technique is efficient in the sense that we do not need to make extra copies (or "before-images") of logical blocks before altering them, since the original versions continue to exist until they are no longer needed. In a similar way, the recovery process is non-existent, since there is no inconsistent version of the data base to roll back.

On the debit side, the physical data file must include enough spare blocks to record new versions of all blocks updated during a single section. In the worst case, this would require the file to be twice the size of the logical data base, but in practice only a small portion of a large data base is likely to be altered indivisibly.

A different solution to the integrity problem is provided by the "differential file" concept ([13]), where records modified in a large data base are stored separately in a *changes* file instead of overwriting their originals in the *master* file. Our technique can be viewed as an extension of this in which the master and changes files are merged together.

4.2 Practical Considerations

The implementation illustrated above has been deliberately simplified for didactic purposes, and there are several improvements which may be made in practice.

a) Core buffers. Normally, there will be several core buffers available to hold copies of data blocks. Any core buffer whose contents differ from the corresponding disc block must be written back whenever a new disc instance is recorded.

b) Alternate root blocks. It is better to allocate two physical blocks which are used alternately as root blocks. In this way, the mapping defining the previous disc instance is not overwritten when the new LP mapping is written to disc at the end of a section; so if an I/O error occurs during this transfer, the previous disc instance can still be recovered.

c) Large data bases. In a data base of any size, it is unlikely that the LP mapping will fit into a single block, but it is a simple matter to extend the scheme, permanently allocating two separate sets of physical blocks to be used in turn for holding the disc instance mapping.

With large mappings it also becomes increasingly inefficient to hold the entire mapping in core and to write it back when flushing at the end of each indivisible section. The solution to this is to "page" the mapping itself, being careful to allocate new physical blocks to altered logical blocks in much the same way as new blocks are allocated to updated data blocks in the simple scheme.

4.3 User Facilities

4.3.1 Flushing and Indivisibility. We have so far assumed that $flushing$ (that is, defining a new disc instance) takes place whenever (and only when) an indivisible section is completed. We believe that it is better in practice to separate these concepts, providing the following facilities for the user:

$flush()$ - this procedure call causes a new disc instance
                   to be recorded.

$indivis(p)$ - this prevents any further flushing until
                   procedure p has been executed.

Unless a call of $indivis$ is active, the package is free to flush whenever it likes: for example, the system might choose to construct a new disc instance every 30 seconds, or after every 200 updates, or whenever the number of spare blocks

available is less than 50. In particular, the system would
probably choose to flush immediately before entering an indivisible section in order to make available as many spare blocks
as possible, and will certainly flush before closing the data
file upon the successful completion of an update run. We also
assume that each basic data base access procedure is indivisible.

The user now has available a choice of techniques for
achieving the degree of consistency that he desires.

A simple program which applies a sequence of independent
updates may choose not to use either *flush* or *indivis*; it may
safely be re-run after an error, since a second application of
the same update can do no harm. A more sophisticated version
of the same program might make regular calls to *flush*, recording on its own "log" data set the number of the last input
record processed prior to the flush, thus reducing wasted
processing time if it needs to be re-run. This log data set may,
of course, be the data base itself, and this suggests the
provision of extra procedures which make it easy for a program
to record messages about its own progress:

    recordmessage(identifier, message)

        - to associate *message* with *identifier* in the data base.

    message := readmessage(identifier)

        - to read the *message* associated with *identifier*; a

          special value is returned if no such message exists.

    message := readdelmessage(identifier)

        - to read and then delete any message associated with

          identifier.

By associating a common message identifier with a suite of
programs it is easy to ensure that all are executed in a
defined sequence: upon successful completion, each program
assigns a new value to the identifier, which will be checked
by the next program in the sequence.

The *indivis* procedure would be used by a more complex
program which applies a sequence of "transaction" updates.
Each transaction is composed of a number of dependent updates,
but is independent of other transactions. Flushing may or may
not be explicitly requested as in the previous example.

Finally, a very time-consuming series of dependent updates

can be split into smaller sections, each of which is executed
indivisibly. At the end of each section, progress is noted
using *recordmessage*, and the data base is then flushed. If this
approach is adopted, other programs must be aware of the
corresponding message identifier and should check its value
before proceeding, in case the update program had failed to
complete successfully when it was last run.

4.3.2 Testing programs. If we treat the whole of a
program as an indivisible section, and do not flush the data
base before terminating, then the data base defined by the disc
instance will remain unaltered. In other words, we are able to
test update programs on "live" data without compromising its
integrity. A similar facility is suggested in [11] in the
context of differential files. This special case is so important that a "test only" mode of opening a data base should be
provided.

5. THE MULTI-USER ENVIRONMENT

5.1 Indivisibility

In this section we examine the meaning of *indivisibility*
in a multi-user environment in some more detail, and suggest a
multi-user analogue of the *indivis* procedure defined for the
single-user case.

Suppose that we have a set of concurrent processes accessing a data base, and that one of them (say P) specifies a
transaction t that is to be executed indivisibly. One way to
do this is to halt all other processes allowing only P to
continue, but this may be needlessly inefficient; for example,
if the purpose of t is to reserve a seat on an aeroplane flight,
then only those processes accessing the same aeroplane seat
actually need to be halted.

As t is executed, references will be made to fields and
records in the data base and decisions will be taken based on
the values found; t will then usually record these decisions
in the form of alterations to the data base.

We can think of the information upon which t bases its
decisions as its *requirement*, and the alterations that it makes
may be called its *effect*. We can represent a requirement as the
union of a sequence of conditions on the records, fields,
relationships etc. that are represented in the data base:

e.g.   (record X exists) & (field Y of record X = 25) &

(record A points to record B) & ...

and an effect may be represented as a sequence of updates:

e.g.   (create record Y) & (field Z of record Y := 24) & ...

We may now state more precisely those conditions under which
a process P' may be allowed to execute concurrently with P
whilst t is active:

i) P' must not alter the validity of t's requirement, for
such alterations may invalidate t's decisions.

ii) P' must not access records or fields that take part in
t's effect; if it does, it may itself take erroneous
decisions based on an inconsistent view of the data
base.

Note that a transaction's requirement may require that a
particular record does <u>not</u> exist, and that in this case
condition (i) above means that P' must not create that record.
Such records are called *phantom* records, and the concept of
predicate locking has been described to handle such cases
(see [7]). A predicate lock for a transaction t essentially
defines a logical area of the data base to which other processes must be denied access (or given restricted access)
whilst t is active. The notions of requirement and effect may
be viewed in the same way: the effect defines the logical area
which must be denied completely to other processes, and the
requirement defines a "read-only" area.

One way to ensure that conditions (i) and (ii) above are
complied with is to use the *critical section* concept (see [6]).
Those sections of each process that might violate either
condition are designated as mutually exclusive critical sections, and semaphores are used to guarantee that at most one
process is executing within a critical section at any particular moment. The difficulty here lies in attributing suitable
semantics to each semaphore that is to be used, and in ensuring
that all processes (including those to be written in the

future) obey the rules that have been chosen.

A simple allocation of semaphores will often result in
unnecessary sequencing: for example, if the seat reservation
transaction is guarded by a semaphore S, then two instances of
this transaction will never execute concurrently even if they
are for different flights. This suggests the provision of
certain "standard" semaphores by the data base system itself,
such as one or more "access" semaphores associated with each
record. Commonly two are provided: the system uses one to
sequence all accesses to the record, and the other to sequence
update accesses only. These semaphores may be accessed by a
user process through *lock* and *unlock* primitives, which allow
a process P to gain *exclusive* access to a record R (no other
processes may access R) or *shared* access (other processes may
read R).

As with semaphores, the general use of locks introduces the
possibility of "deadlock", where two or more processes become
mutually blocked, each one attempting to lock some part of the
data base that has already been locked by one of the others
(see [4] for a general discussion). When this occurs, one or
more of the processes must be "backed-out" in order to allow
others to continue.

The problem of locking a phantom record may be solved
(albeit clumsily) by exclusively locking all records of the
appropriate type, and so a common generalisation of record
locking is to provide locking facilities of a coarser "granularity" controlling access to certain sets of records such as:
- all records referenced by record R
- all records of type T
- all records in the data base

In [8], a protocol based on such a hierarchy of lockable
objects is presented. Any process wishing, for example, to lock
a record within this protocol must first place an "intention"
lock on all higher level objects in the hierarchy. This makes
it easy for the system to determine whether a particular
request is compatible with other requests already granted, and
simplifies the detection and resolution of deadlocks.

Here we suggest a different technique which requires only
that transactions are marked as indivisible by use of the

indivis procedure:

$$b := indivis(t)$$

At time T_0 when this call is made, a copy I_0' is made of the current instance I_0 of the data base. The transaction t is then applied to the copy I_0' to produce a new instance I_1' at time T_1; in the meantime, other processes operating on the current instance I_0 have produced a possibly modified instance I_1:

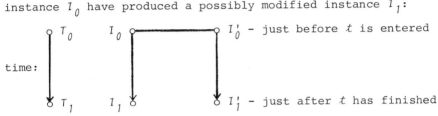

time:

T_0 I_0 I_0' - just before t is entered

T_1 I_1 I_1' - just after t has finished

During execution of t we keep a note $R(t)$ of those records and fields (and their values) read by t from the initial instance I_0': it is clear that $R(t)$ will include t's requirement. We also keep a note of any alterations made by t in $E(t)$, which thereby represents t's effect.

At time T_1 we examine I_1 to see if items mentioned in $R(t)$ and $E(t)$ have remained unaltered since time T_0. If so, we may safely apply the alterations $E(t)$ to I_1, the effect being as if t had, indeed, been executed indivisibly at time T_1; we say that the call of *indivis* has been successful, and return a result of *true*. If not, the call is unsuccessful, and a result of *false* is returned. (A special case arises if $E(t)$ is empty; in this case, t has no effect and so its execution is "invisible" to the other processes. So we may suppose that it was indivisibly executed at time T_0 and return a result of *true*.)

In the proposed realisation of *indivis* (see section 6.2) the data base is copied by copying the LP mapping, and the sets $R(t)$ and $E(t)$ are represented as lists of those logical blocks referenced and updated by t. A new physical block is allocated whenever a logical block is updated, and so it is easy to determine whether $R(t)$ and $E(t)$ remain unaltered in I_1, and, if so, to apply $E(t)$ to I_1: we simply alter the LP mapping for I_1 to reflect the changes made. Note that phantoms are accounted for, since the block in which a phantom might appear will be recorded in $R(t)$ when t examines the data base to see if the record exists. These considerations show that it is indeed possible to implement *indivis* in an efficient manner.

Choosing the block as the unit of representation for requirement and effect means that certain transactions which could logically execute concurrently will be prevented from so doing. (For example, two transactions which update separate records which happen to lie in the same block.) The importance of this will clearly depend on the size of the block and the distribution of transactions, but a recent paper ([12]) suggests that a large "granule" size is often more efficient than a small one when the locking overhead (as in this case) is less.

How does _indivis_ compare with a more conventional approach using locks? We saw above that transactions competing for locks may enter deadlocks which can only be resolved by backing out one or more of the processes; such a situation may be further complicated by the fact that another transaction may already have taken a decision based on values recorded by the transactions to be backed out, and so should itself also be backed out. To avoid this "snowball" effect it is usual to insist that a transaction exclusively locks those records that it updates, only releasing them upon termination. Such precautions are not necessary with _indivis_, since the essence of the technique is the concurrent existence of separate instances of the data base. If we suppose for the moment that all processing is by means of indivisible transactions, then a "deadlock" corresponds to the existence of "incompatible" instances; it is "resolved" when the first transaction to complete incorporates its corresponding instance into the current instance, and the other processes are "backed out" when they complete unsuccessfully and their corresponding instances are abandoned.

Another advantage of _indivis_ is that the programmer is no longer responsible for specifying the area of the data base to which a transaction is "sensitive"; this area is instead determined dynamically by the system in the sets $R(t)$ and $E(t)$. So the programmer is protected from mistaken assumptions about process interactions, and is less likely to corrupt the data base; on the other hand, undisciplined use of _indivis_ may result in much wasted processing time if many calls are made before a transaction succeeds.

It is clear that _indivis_ is most appropriate in circumstances where conflict is unlikely. A suitable candidate might

be the seat reservation system where many copies of the reservation process are executing concurrently. Each reservation is
recorded indivisibly, and will only fail if another concurrent
reservation for the same seat completes first.

In a system where conflicts are common, explicit sequencing
(using semaphores or locks) is indicated. For example, suppose
a data base contains details of tickets for a show which are to
be allocated sequentially. If several processes are concurrently
processing ticket applications, it is clear that the critical
sections in which a ticket is allocated are always mutually
exclusive, and it is never sensible to attempt to execute two
such sections concurrently. In this case, the constraint is
simple and the system designer may use a single semaphore to
force sequential ticket allocation.

It is interesting to relate *indivis* to the facilities
offered by System R ([1]), where a user may associate a particular "level of consistency" with each transaction t as
follows:

   level 3 - t is indivisible.
   level 2 - changes made by a concurrent transaction t'
               are only made available to t when t'
               terminates.
   level 1 - t sees changes made by concurrent transactions
               as they happen.

An additional constraint applied to all levels is that any data
altered by one transaction will not be altered by any other
until the first has completed. (This makes it possible to "back
out" one transaction when a deadlock occurs without undoing the
effects of any other.)

indivis corresponds to a level 3 transaction, except that
it might fail. (In System R, locks are applied to enforce the
various consistency levels, and all transactions will eventually complete: transactions backed-out from deadlocks are
repeated as necessary.) Processes accessing the current
instance are more like level 2 transactions in that they only
see changes made by successful *indivis* transactions, but
(unlike System R transactions) they may (and will) freely
interact with each other. There is no equivalent to the level 1
transaction (which in System R may even see changes that are
later "undone").

5.2   Integrity

As in the single-user environment, all basic calls to the
data base system are indivisible, and the procedures *flush*,
recordmessage, *readmessage* and *readdelmessage* are provided
with identical definitions. (Note that calls of *recordmessage*
and *readdelmessage* may be used as *V* and *P* operations on a
binary semaphore because they are indivisible.)

The *indivis* procedure defined in the last section may also
be used simply as a consistency aid: if a process terminates
unexpectedly in the middle of an indivisible section, then we
can be sure that no part of the effect of that section has
been incorporated into the current instance of the data base,
and hence cannot possibly appear in the disc instance.

As before, individual processes may make calls of *flush*
to guarantee that the disc instance will at least reflect
progress up to a certain point, and/or may record progress
using *recordmessage*.

5.3   Testing Programs

One possibility is to define a procedure *test(p)* which
applies *p* to a copy of the current instance; when *p* terminates,
the copy is thrown away. (*test* is similar to *indivis* except
that no attempt is made to incorporate the modified copy into
the current instance upon completion.) This however, allows us
to test only single processes, and so we suggest a more powerful facility which allows the user to create and access
secondary versions of the data base. Each such secondary
version starts life as a copy of the current instance of the
primary version, and is then modified independently by the set
of processes under test. Secondary versions differ from the
primary version in that there are no disc instances associated
with them: in other words, a secondary version is lost when
the last process accessing it terminates.

5.4   Read-only Access

A common problem in a multi-user environment is that of
obtaining consistent reports. For example, consider the case
of a program which generates a summary of items in stock followed by a detail report showing the location of these items by
warehouse. If stock figures are updated whilst this program is
being executed, the totals in the two reports will not tally.

This problem may be solved by specifying the entire program
as an indivisible transaction; in this way, the program will
operate on an (unchanging) copy of the current instance. Since
the transaction has no effect (in the sense of section 5.1)
the call of *indivis* will always be successful. This is such a
common requirement that we suggest a special mode of "read-
only" access in the next section.

5.5   User Facilities

This section gives a formal description of the facilities
suggested above.

When a process first requests access to the data base, it
must specify both the *version* and the *access mode* desired:

open(version, mode)

  version = 0 means that the process is a production program
    which is to access the primary (i.e. "live") version of
    the data base. This is the only version represented by
    the disc instance.

  version = n (>0) means that the process is to be tested on
    a secondary version of the data base. If version n does
    not yet exist, it is created by taking a copy of the
    current instance of the primary version.

  mode = 0 means that the process wishes to access the
    current instance of the specified version at all times.
    It is allowed to alter this instance.

  mode ≠ 0 means that the process is read-only, and is to be
    applied to a copy of the current instance of the speci-
    fied version.

The procedures for manipulating instances are:

  $flush()$ - this has no effect unless it is applied to the
  current instance of the primary version. In this case, a
  new disc instance is recorded.

  $b := indivis(p)$ - if this is applied to the current instance
  of a version, the procedure p is applied to a copy of this
  instance and an attempt is then made to incorporate the
  result into the current instance once again. The result is
  $true$ if and only if the attempt is successful. If it is
  applied to any other (read-only) instance, the effect is
  simply to execute p and return $true$.

We can represent the relationships between the various instances of a data base that exist at a particular moment as
follows:

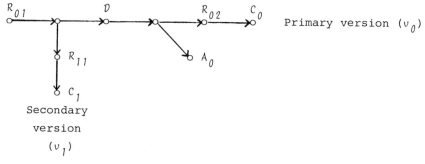

In this example there is one secondary version with two active
instances and five active instances of the primary version.
R_{01}, R_{02} and R_{11} are read-only versions, and C_0 and C_1 are the
current instances of the two versions. D represents the most
recent disc instance (created by a call of $flush$) and A_0
represents a currently active $alternative$ instance created by
a call of $indivis$ that has not yet completed.

6.   IMPLEMENTATION

     This section outlines a possible implementation stage by
stage. We first permit access to the primary version only,
showing how read-only instances and flushing can be implemented

next we show how to manage alternative instances, thus realis-
ing *indivis*. Finally we indicate how to manage secondary
versions.

6.1   Read-only access and Flushing

6.1.1   <u>Introduction.</u> At any moment, the various active
instances of the data base can be represented in order of
creation as:

where each R is a read-only instance, D corresponds to the disc
instance, and C is the current instance.

New read-only instances are created by calls of *open*, and
an existing read-only instance is released when its associated
process terminates. The current instance is created when the
first process opens the data base, and is released when the
last process terminates. The disc instance is always present:
when the data base is flushed, a new disc instance is created
and the previous one is released.

Associated with the data base is a positive integer known
as the current *epoch* which is increased by one whenever a new
instance is created. The value of this integer at the time of
creation of an instance is known as the *epoch* of that instance,
and may be used to identify it. Note that the epochs of the
active instances of a data base are not necessarily consecutive
since instances are not necessarily released in the same order
as they were created; but *epoch(I)* is always less than *epoch(J)*
for an instance I older than J.

Each instance I_k of epoch k is defined by its LP mapping
LP_k. A new current instance I_{n+1} is created by creating a new
mapping LP_{n+1} equal to LP_n. As soon as logical block ℓ of I_{n+1}
is altered for the first time, a new physical block p' is
assigned to it in LP_{n+1} so that the alteration appears only in
instance I_{n+1} and not in any preceding instances. The physical
block p previously assigned to ℓ cannot be marked as spare,
since it is still a part of I_n, and, possibly, of other
preceding instances; indeed, it can only be reused when all

instances of which it is a part have been released.

In general, a physical block p is in one of the following
states:

a)   in *current* use, if $LP_n(\ell) = p$ for some ℓ, where n is the
      epoch of the current instance.

b)   *pending*, if it is not in current use, but there exists an
      active instance with epoch k such that $LP_k(\ell) = p$ for
      some ℓ.

c)   *spare*, if it is neither current nor pending.

When a logical block of the current instance is updated for
the first time, the newly assigned physical block changes state
from spare to current, and the original block from current to
pending. Each pending block belongs to a sequence of one or
more active instances, and becomes spare when all the instances
of that sequence have been released.

We keep track of pending blocks by recording their epoch of
allocation *alloc* and epoch of release *rel*: a pending block p
becomes spare as soon as there is no active instance I such
that:

$$alloc(p) \leq epoch(I) < rel(p)$$

$alloc(p)$ is recorded in the physical block itself at the time
of allocation. At the time of release, this value is used to
determine the first instance I to which p belongs; this
instance is given by:

$$epoch(H) < alloc(p) \leq epoch(I)$$

where H is the active instance immediately prior to I.
The pair $(p, rel(p))$ is then added to a list associated with I.

In this way, a list is kept for each instance I of those
pending blocks which belong to I but not to any older instance.
When I is released, this list is scanned to see if any pending
blocks mentioned can now be made spare; this will be possible
if:

$$rel(p) \leq epoch(J)$$

where J is the active instance immediately following I.
Pairs $(p, rel(p))$ which do not satisfy this condition are
simply added to the list associated with J.

Using this technique, it is easy to keep an up-to-date list
of spare blocks available for allocation - that is, of blocks
which do not form part of any active instance. But when the

data base is flushed, we must include on disc a list of those blocks which <u>would</u> be spare if no other instances were active: for only the disc instance survives if processing terminates unexpectedly, and we will need to know which blocks are spare when we re-open the data base. This list consists of the union of the set of spare blocks and the set of pending blocks at the time when the new disc instance is made.

6.1.2 Practical Considerations.

The mappings LP_k and LP_{k-1} are likely to share many elements in common, and so a single compact representation for all LP_i can be chosen which allows us to take advantage of this. For example, when the size of the logical data base is large, it becomes necessary to page the LP mapping itself, using a further "LP to physical" mapping (LPP) as an index; in this way each LP_k is defined by LPP_k. This suggests that we keep track of LP instances using the same techniques as those described above for data base instances. For example, copying an LP mapping is reduced to making a copy of the (much smaller) LPP mapping, provided that we allocate a new physical block and alter the LPP mapping describing the current LP mapping whenever one of its blocks is updated for the first time.

Another point concerns the list of spare blocks from which physical blocks are allocated during processing. There is no need to either read this in its entirety when the data base is opened, or to write it all back each time the data base is flushed. It is sufficient to maintain two "windows" on the "front" and "back" of the list: new blocks are allocated from the front window and blocks made spare when an instance is released are added to the back window. The front window is replenished from disc whenever more blocks are needed and the back window is emptied to disc when it becomes full, or whenever the data base is flushed.

6.1.3 Dumping.

Even the disc instance will not allow us to recover the data base if it is physically damaged, and so it is prudent to take periodic "back-up" copies on tape. Our technique favours an incremental approach, whereby only those blocks altered since the last dump are copied to tape. These may be determined by comparing $alloc(p)$ with the epoch of the last dump for each block p in the data base: only those created

after the previous dump need to be copied. But such a complete
scan of the data base is likely to be unacceptable, particularly if dumping is relatively frequent, and a much better
technique is suggested in [9], where an extra bit is associated
with each element of the LP mapping to say whether that logical
block has been altered since the previous dump. This bit is
called the "cumulative shadow bit" in [9]; here we shall call
it the *dump* bit, and it is set whenever a logical block is
updated.

Whenever the incremental dump process is scheduled, a new
read-only "tape instance" T is created:

The new current instance C is represented by the mapping LP_C
which is a copy of LP_T in which all the dump bits have been
cleared.

The incremental dumper may now copy at leisure those
physical blocks of T indicated by the dump bits in LP_T; when
it has finished, the instance T is released, and any pending
blocks required only by the dumping process are automatically
made spare. (Thus there is no need for the "long term shadow
bit" of [9], whose purpose is to indicate that the corresponding block has not yet been dumped and so cannot be freed.)

6.2   Alternative Instances and *indivis*

We denote the alternative instance that is created from
instance I by a call of *indivis* by I':

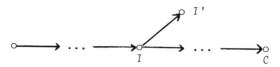

Associated with I' we keep:

   LP' - its LP mapping.

   R - the set of logical blocks which includes the informa-
           tion involved in the requirement of I'.

   E - the set of logical blocks which includes its effect.

As I' is processed, each logical block that is referenced
is added to R, and each logical block that is updated is added
to E. New physical blocks are assigned to updated logical
blocks in the usual way, so that $LP'(E)$ defines the set of
physical blocks that are *local* to I': they belong only to I'
and are not shared with any other instance. When the transaction is complete, we must determine whether we can safely
incorporate the effect of I' into the current instance C. This
will be possible provided that other processes operating on
the "main-line" instances have not altered any of the blocks
involved in the transaction's requirement or effect: in other
words, if the contents of the logical blocks described by
$R \cup E$ are the same in instance C as in instance I. This can be
easily checked by comparing the appropriate elements of the LP
mappings defining the two instances.

If incorporation is possible, the LP mapping for C is
updated by reference to E to include the local blocks of I';
if not, the local blocks are returned directly to the spare
block list.

6.3 Secondary Versions

The treatment of secondary versions is very similar to that
of the primary version; the main difference lies in the treatment of spare blocks.

Each secondary version is essentially treated as a separate
entity, with its own epochs unrelated to those of the primary
version. As logical blocks of a secondary version are updated,
new physical blocks are assigned which are *local* to that
version: they can never be shared with any other secondary
version or with the primary version. Thus a secondary instance
will be composed partly of local blocks and partly of blocks
acquired from (and probably shared with) the primary version.

The actions taken when a physical block is released depend
on its state. If it is local, it is recorded as a pending block
in a list associated with some secondary instance in the usual
way. If it is not, no action is taken since we presume that it
is still required by the primary version.

7. CONCLUSIONS

This paper has described a solution to the problems of
consistency and integrity in large data bases, and a possible
implementation has been presented. By giving some details of
this implementation we hope we have shown that the technique
is efficient provided that the various data base instances
that co-exist do not differ drastically one from the other.

The technique is based on the provision of an extra
block-to-block mapping between a logical data base and the
physical data file upon which it resides. In this way, many
similar instances of one data base may be economically
represented in the same data file by different mappings. But
only one mapping (and hence only one data base) is defined in
the data file itself: this is the so-called disc instance,
which is the only instance preserved when data base processing
terminates (whether normally or abnormally). By ensuring that
new disc instances are only created when certain consistency
constraints are satisfied, we can ensure the integrity of a
data base across unexpected system and application program
failures.

An extension of the technique is particularly useful in a
multi-user environment, and in this paper we have suggested
three facilities:

  i)   The provision of a "frozen" copy of an ever-changing data
       base (for the use of a report generator, for example).

 ii)   The provision of a copy of a live data base on which a
       new program or set of co-operating programs can be
       safely tested.

iii)   The ability to "split" a data base into separate inst-
       ances: a "main-line" instance and one or more "alter-
       native" instances. The main-line instance continues to
       be accessed by (possibly several) current processes
       whereas access to each alternative instance is restr-
       icted to the single process P that created it.

       P is free to make consistent changes to the alternative
       instance based on decisions about its contents which
       cannot be affected by the actions of other concurrent

processes. When P completes its "critical" task, an
attempt is made to combine the two instances: if this
is possible without compromising the integrity of P's
decisions and alterations, then it is done; otherwise
the alternative instance is abandoned, and P must try
again.

The technique was originally developed solely as a means
of ensuring data base integrity in a single-user environment,
and is used for this purpose in the JACKDAW data base package.
This system has been in use at the University of Cambridge
since 1973, supporting an administrative data base containing
details of Computing Service users and their resource alloc-
ations. During this period, the data base survived unscathed
all operating system and application program failures, thus
demonstrating the value of the integrity feature. Further
development of JACKDAW is now in progress at Pontifícia
Universidade Católica in Rio de Janeiro.

ACKNOWLEDGMENTS

The JACKDAW package was designed and implemented whilst the
author was employed by the Computing Service at the University
of Cambridge, England. Further work has been financially
supported by the Brazilian government agencies Financiadora de
Estudos e Projetos (FINEP) and Conselho Nacional do Desenvol-
vimento Científico e Tecnológico (CNPq).

REFERENCES

[1] Astrahan, M.M, et al. "System R: Relational approach to
     data base management" ACM Trans. Database Syst. 1, 2
     (June 1976).
[2] Challis, M.F. "The JACKDAW database package" Proc. SEAS
     Spring Technical Meeting, St. Andrews, Scotland, April
     1974.

[3] Challis, M.F. "Integrity techniques in the JACKDAW
     database package" Monografia em Ciência da Computação
     9/77, Depto de Informática, Pontifícia Universidade
     Católica, Rio de Janeiro, Brasil (1977).
[4] Coffman, E.G., Elphick, M.J. and Shoshani, A. "System
     Deadlocks" ACM Comp. Surveys 3, 2 (June 1971).
[5] Date, C.J. "An Introduction to Database Systems"
     Addison-Wesley, Reading, Mass. (Second Edition, 1977).
[6] Dijkstra, E.W. "Co-operating Sequential Processes"
     Programming languages: NATO advanced study institute.
     Editor: F. Genuys, Academic Press, London, 1968.
[7] Eswaran, K.P., Gray, J.N., Lorie, R.A. and Traiger, I.L.
     "The notions of consistency and predicate locks in a
     data base system" Comm. ACM 19, 11 (November 1976).
[8] Gray, J.N., Lorie, R.A. and Putzolu, G.R. "Granularity
     of locks in a shared data base" Proc. VLDB conference,
     Framlingham, Mass., 1975.
[9] Lorie, R.A. "Physical integrity in a large segmented
     database" ACM Trans. Database Syst. 2, 1 (March 1977).
[10] Palmer, I. "Database systems: A practical reference"
     CACI Inc. International, London, 1975.
[11] Rappaport, R.L. "File structure design to facilitate
     on-line instantaneous updating" Proc. ACM SIGMOD
     conference, 1975.
[12] Ries, D.R. and Stonebraker, M. "A study of the effects
     of locking granularity in a data base management
     system" ACM SIGMOD conference on management of data,
     Toronto, August 1977.
[13] Severance, D.G. and Lohman, G.M. "Differential files:
     their application to the maintenance of large data-
     bases" ACM Trans. Database Syst. 1, 3 (September
     1976).
[14] - "ADABAS Introductory manual" Software AG, Hilber-
     strasse 20, 61 Darmstadt, W. Germany.
[15] - "TOTAL Users manual" Cincom Systems Inc.
[16] - "IMS/360 Utilities reference manual" IBM SH20-0915.

Improving Performance

PERFORMANCE CONSIDERATION
IN RELATIONAL DATA BASE DESIGN

E. L. Lozinskii

Department of Computer Science
Hebrew University
Jerusalem,Israel

I. INTRODUCTION

It is widely accepted that the main foundation of a data base design

is a data structure which embodies the data presented in a data base and

the   relations among them. Data base design and the corresponding data

base structure have a substantial influence on the performance of the

system which uses the data base. So, in order to provide a high

efficiency of the system certain performance criteria should be taken into

consideration in the stages of data base design and updating.

Last years, after the appearance of the classical paper of E.F. Codd

(1970) the relational model has become an effective and widely adopted

tool for data base analysis, definition,description and representation

both on the logical and the physical levels.

A data base, DB, describes certain objects of the world having

certain attributes, and the relationships among them. Thus, DB is

characterized by a set of <u>domains</u>, D (corresponding to the set of

objects' attributes described by DB), and by a set of <u>functional</u>

<u>dependencies</u>, $F = \{f_i\}$ (corresponding to the relationships among the

attributes). According to the relational model a data base is a

collection of <u>relations</u>, $R = \{R_i\}$, each relation containing a set of

domains $\{D_i | D_i \in D\}$ (all the terms and concepts not defined here are

those of (Codd, 1970, 1972a, 1974)).

We shall say that a functional dependency $f_i \in F$ between subsets of domains A_i and B_i, $f_i : A_i \to B_i \mid A_i, B_i \subseteq D$, is <u>supplied</u> by a collection of relations R iff there is a relation, $R_j \in R$, that contains all the values of the domains of A_i which are mapped into B_i and all the corresponding values of the domains of B_i. In other words, if $A_i = \{A_{i1}, A_{i2}, \ldots, A_{i|A_i|}\}$, $B_i = \{B_{i1}, B_{i2}, \ldots, B_{i|B_i|}\}$ then a relation R_j supplying f_i must contain all the tuples of the form

$$(\ldots a_{i1}, a_{i2}, \ldots, a_{i|A_i|}, \ b_{i1}, b_{i2}, \ldots, b_{i|B_i|} \mid \ ^{|}a_{ij} \in A_{ij} \wedge b_{ij} \in B_{ij})$$

which satisfy f_i. As a special case A_i can belong to one of the candidate keys of R_j. A collection of relations R <u>represents</u> a DB iff all $f_i \in F$ are supplied by the relations of R. (This is a particular case of a more general representation of DB by R when the transitive closure of the set of functional dependencies supplied by R contains the transitive closure of F).

The concepts of normalization in general and third normal form (3NF) in particular are the kernel concepts of the relational data base model (Codd, 1970, 1972a). The aims of normalization formulated first in (Codd, 1970, 1972a) are summarized in (Codd, 1974) as follows:

"1. To reduce the need for restructuring the collection of relations as new types of data are introduced, and thus increase the life span of application programs;

2. To reduce the incidence of undesirable insertion, update, and deletion anomalies."

Iff R represents DB and all $R_i \in R$ are in 3NF then R gives a 3NF-representation of DB.

Among all possible representations of DB there is an optimal 3NF-representation which contains a minimal number of relations (and has additional properties (Codd, 1972a)).

II. PERFORMANCE-ORIENTED CONSTRUCTING OF RELATIONS

As was shown by many authors (Codd, 1972a, 1974; Bernstein and Beeri, 1976; Rissanen and Delobel, 1973; Wang and Wedekind, 1975) not only 3NF-representation but even optimal 3NF-representation is not unique. This fact provides an initial opportunity of taking into account certain performance criteria in the design of an efficient representation of a data base. However a strong consideration of performance criteria may lead to a conflict with 3NF-representation requiring an introduction of relations in 2NF and even in 1NF into the efficient representation of a DB. Such an introduction of relations which are not in 3NF may be expedient even though it causes problems of update and consistency anomalies (Codd, 1972a). It may not be out of place to note here that 3NF does not eliminate all the update and consistency anomalies, especially among prime attributes (Date, 1975; Bernstein and Beeri, 1976). The Boyce-Codd normal form (BCNF) introduced in (Codd, 1974) extends the requirement of full functional dependency to all domains of a relation and in that way significantly decreases update and consistency anomalies (at least tuple updates in a BCNF relation are independent).

However, as is shown by Bernstein and Beeri (1976) there are sets of functional dependencies for which no BCNF relations exist, and the problem of determining whether a given relation is in BCNF is NP-complete.

Existing methods for constructing of relations which represent a given data base are intended to produce a collection of relations in optimal 3NF, and can be summarized as follows (Wang and Wedekind, 1975; Bernstein and Beeri, 1976):

1. For a given set of functional dependencies F find a nonredundant covering H.

2. Construct a collection of relations by partitioning the covering H into subsets of functional dependencies with equivalent left sides, and by

constructing for each subset a relation which contains all the domains appearing in that subset.

It was shown (Wang and Wedekind, 1975; Lozinskii, 1977) that performance-oriented considerations can prompt further transformation of relations, and that 3NF-representation may be considered as an intermediate point for further constructing of relations in order to take into account not only a logical data structure but also certain factors which affect a data base performance and efficiency. Important factors of this kind are characteristics of jobs and updating flow (external factors), and parameters of a hardware and operating system (internal factors). These affecting factors act during a data base operation and they do not remain invariable but change mirroring the changes occurring in the system itself and in the ambient world. Thus, methods used in data base design should consider performance criteria not only at the stage of initial constructing of relations but should also contain facilities for taking into account efficiency factors when updating a data base during its evolution. These considerations lead to the following schema (fig. 1) of adaptive constructing of a collection of relations for efficient representation of a data base.

We shall consider the following model of a data base operation. A data base represented by a collection of relations R is accessed by a set of jobs (queries) Q.   Each query $Q_j \in Q$ is considered as a request for the values of a subset of domains $A_j \subseteq D$ which are related to those values of a subset of domains $B_j \subseteq D$ which satisfy given conditions. We shall denote such a query $Q_j = (A_j, B_j)$. $A_j \cup B_j$ is the set of domains specified by Q_j. Let q_j be the frequency of occurence of Q_j; $c(Q_j)$ - the cost of execution of Q_j. During the data base operation the relations $R_i \in R$ are updated. Let p_i be the frequency

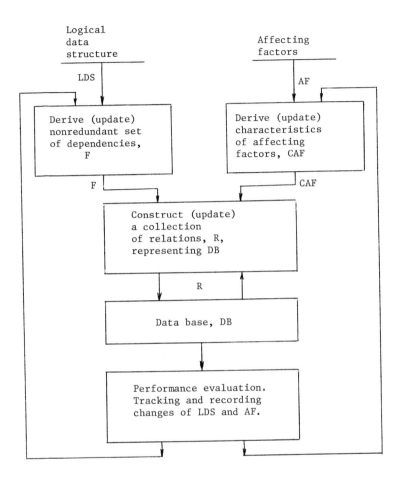

Figure 1. Adaptive constructing of relations

of updating R_i; $u(R_i)$— the average cost of updating R_i.

As the performance criterion of a data base operation we shall use the <u>total operational cost</u>, C, of queries execution and relations updating. Let $R^{(1)}$ be one of the possible representations of a data base. Then the total operational cost of this representation is as follows (the superscripts refer to the representation)

$$C^{(1)} = \sum_{Q_i \in Q} C^{(1)}(Q_i) + \sum_{R_i \in R^{(1)}} U^{(1)}(R_i), \qquad (1)$$

where $C^{(1)}(Q_i) = q_i c (Q_i)$; $U^{(1)}(R_i) = p_i u(R_i)$.

Let $R^{(1)}(Q_j)$ denote a set of relations $(R^{(1)}(Q_j) \subseteq R^{(1)})$ which must be accessed in order to execute Q_j using the $R^{(1)}$ representation of DB. We shall say that the relations belonging to $R^{(1)}(Q_j)$ are attached to Q_j in $R^{(1)}$, and the set $Z^{(1)} = \{R^{(1)}(Q_j) \mid Q_j \in Q\}$ is the attachment set of $R^{(1)}$. To all relations $R_i \in R^{(1)}$ we shall assign a usage vector $V_i^{(1)} = \{\rho_{ij} \mid j = 1,2,\ldots,|Q|\}$ such that if R_i is attached to Q_j then $\rho_{ij} = 1$, else $\rho_{ij} = 0$. A relation R_k with zero usage vector, $(\forall Q_j \in Q)(\rho_{kj} = 0)$, will be called an unused relation.

Let us consider another representation of the data base $R^{(2)}$, for which all the following abcd-conditions hold:

a) $R^{(2)}$ contains a new set of relations, $R^+(k)$ (such that $R^+(k) \cap R^{(1)} = \phi$), which is attached to a query Q_k in $R^{(2)}$, $R^+(k) \subseteq R^{(2)}(Q_k)$;

b) $R^{(2)}$ contains all the relations attached in $R^{(1)}$ to all $Q_j | j \neq k$;

c) $R^{(1)}$ and $R^{(2)}$ are θ-equivalent , i.e. $R^{(1)}$ and $R^{(2)}$ are each derivable from the other using operations of a relationally complete algebra only (Codd, 1972b);

d) $R^{(2)}$ does not contain unused relations provided that the condition c) is satisfied.

Let $R^*(k)$ denote the set of relations which belong to $R^{(1)}$ but not to $R^{(2)}$, then

$$R^{(2)} = (R^{(1)} \setminus R^*(k)) \cup R^+(k). \qquad (2)$$

The total cost of a representation $R^{(2)}$:

$$c^{(2)} = \sum_{Q_i \in Q} C^{(2)}(Q_i) + \sum_{R_i \in R^{(2)}} U^{(2)}(R_i) \qquad (3)$$

The following proposition will be helpful.

Proposition 1: Given $Q, R^{(1)}, Z^{(1)}, R^{(2)}$. If a representation $R^{(2)}$

satisfies the abcd - conditions then there exists such an attachment set

$Z^{(2)}$ in $R^{(2)}$ that for all $Q_k \in Q$

$$c^{(1)} - c^{(2)} \geq c^{(1)}(Q_k) - c^{(2)}(Q_k) + u^{(I)}(R^*(k)) - u^{(2)}(R^+(k)) \qquad (4)$$

Proof: Let us consider the following algorithm which constructs $Z^{(2)}$.

Algorithm 1:

attach $R^{(2)}(Q_k)$ to Q_k in $R^{(2)}$;

$Z^{(2)} := \{R^{(2)}(Q_k)\}$;

for all $Q_i \in Q \mid i \neq k$ do

   begin

      attach to Q_i a set of relations $\tilde{R}^{(2)}(Q_i)$ in $R^{(2)}$;

      if $c^{(2)}(Q_i) < c^{(1)}(Q_i)$ then $R^{(2)}(Q_i) = \tilde{R}^{(2)}(Q_i)$

         else $R^{(2)}(Q_i) = R^{(1)}(Q_i)$;

      $Z^{(2)} := Z^{(2)} \cup \{R^{(2)}(Q_i)\}$;

   end.

Using the attachment set $Z^{(2)}$ produced by Algorithm 1 one receives

for all $Q_i \in Q \mid i \neq k$

$$c^{(2)}(Q_i) \leq c^{(1)}(Q_i) \qquad (5)$$

because if $R^{(2)}(Q_i) = R^{(1)}(Q_i)$ then $c^{(2)}(Q_i) = c^{(1)}(Q_i)$.

From (2) follows

$$\sum_{R_i \in R^{(2)}} u^{(2)}(R_i) = \sum_{R_i \in R^{(1)}} u^{(1)}(R_i) - u^{(1)}(R^*(k)) + u^{(2)}(R^+(k)). \qquad (6)$$

So (5) and (6) imply (4). Q.E.D.

The difference $c^{(1)} - c^{(2)}$ between the total costs of represent-

ations $R^{(1)}$ and $R^{(2)}$ as a result of the introduction of $R^+(k)$ will

be called the gain of $R^+(k)$. A set of relations $R^+(k)$ will be called a

reducing set iff its gain is positive, because it allows to reduce the total cost of a representation. To each query $Q_i \in Q$ we shall assign a pair (α_i, β_i) such that if there exists a set of relations $R^+(i)$ for which

$$\Delta C = C^{(1)}(Q_i) - C^{(2)}(Q_i) + U^{(1)}(R^*(i)) - U^{(2)}(R^+(i)) > 0,$$

then $\alpha_i = \Delta C$ and $\beta_i = R^+(i)$, else $\alpha_i = 0$ and $\beta_i = \phi$.

Given $DB, Q, R^{(1)}, \{R^{(1)}(Q_j)\}_{j=1}^{|Q|}, \{v_i\}_{i=1}^{|R^{(1)}|}, C^{(1)}, \{C^{(1)}(Q_j)\}_{j=1}^{|Q|}$ we shall consider the following algorithm which reconstructs representations of DB by introduction of reducing sets.

Algorithm 2:

1. Initialize $\tilde{Q} = Q$; $\tilde{R} = R^{(1)}$; $\tilde{R}(Q_j) = R^{(1)}(Q_j)$ $|j = 1, 2, \ldots, |Q|$;
   $\tilde{C} = C^{(1)}$; $\tilde{C}(Q_j) = C^{(1)}(Q_j)$ $|j = 1, 2, \ldots, |Q|$;

2. While a condition Ω is satisfied do
   begin

2.1   for all $Q_j \in Q$ do
       begin

2.1.1   introduce a new set $R^+(j)$ attached to Q_j;

2.1.2   construct a new representation $R^{(2,j)}$
          satisfying the abcd-conditions;

2.1.3   attach $R^{(2,j)}(Q_j)$ to Q_j;

2.1.4   determine the set of unused relations $R^*(j)$;

2.1.5   compute ΔC;

2.1.6   assign (α_j, β_j) to Q_j;

2.1.7   if $\alpha_j = 0$ then $\tilde{Q}: = \tilde{Q} \setminus \{Q_j\}$;
       end;

2.2 find Q_m such that $\alpha_m = \max(\alpha_j | Q_j \in \tilde{Q})$;

2.3 $\tilde{R}:= R^{(2,m)}$;

2.4 $\tilde{R}(Q_m): = R^{(2,m)}(Q_m)$;

2.5 $\tilde{Q}: = \tilde{Q} \setminus \{Q_m\}$;

2.6 for all $Q_j \in \tilde{Q}$ attach $\tilde{R}(Q_j)$ to Q_j;

2.7 compute $\tilde{C}$, $\{\tilde{C}(Q_j) \mid Q_j \in Q\}$;

   end;

3. $R^{(2)} := \tilde{R}$; $R^{(2)}(Q_j) := \tilde{R}(Q_j) \mid j = 1,2,\ldots,|Q|$;

4. $C^{(2)} := \tilde{C}$; $C^{(2)}(Q_j) := \tilde{C}(Q_j) \mid j = 1,2,\ldots,|Q|$.

   Algorithm 2 has the following properties.

1) During an execution of step 2 the algorithm reconstructs DB

representations in such a way that the total cost of successive

representations decreases monotonously.   Indeed, all the new represent-

ations constructed at step 2.1.2 (by introduction $R^+(j)$ at step 2.1.1)

satisfy the abcd-conditions, and a query Q_m chosen at step 2.2 has a

positive α_m. Thus, Proposition 1 and the definition of α imply that

the gain of $R^+(m)$ is positive, and so the total cost of each new

representation R is less than the previous one.   Finally $C^{(2)} < C^{(1)}$.

2) The behaviour of Algorithm 2 depends upon the form of condition Ω.

If this condition is $\tilde{Q} \neq \phi$, then the algorithm stops after a finite

number of executions of step 2 (which is at most $|Q|$), because the

cardinality of $\tilde{Q}$ decreases monotonously at steps 2.1.7 and 2.5.

3) Because during an execution of step 2 the total cost decreases

(property 1), a trade-off can be achieved (under certain circumstances)

between the reduction of the total cost of the initial representation $R^{(1)}$

and the algorithm's running time, t_a, if the condition Ω is of the

form $\alpha \geq \varepsilon$ or $t_a \leq \tau$, where ε and τ are parameters controlling

the trade-off.

4) The efficiency of Algorithm 2 depends on the efficiency of its internal

steps, especially of the introduction and attachment procedures (steps

2.1.1, 2.1.3, 2.6). Step 2.1.1 introduces a new set of relations, $R^+(j)$,

intended for constructing of a new representation (step 2.1.2) with a

lower total cost. Let R^0 denote the optimal representation which

minimizes the total operational cost over the set of all possible representations of a given data base, and let $R^0(Q_j)$ stand for a set

of relations attached to Q_j in R^0. We shall call <u>the best introduction</u>

a set $\bar{R}^+(j)$ that contains those relations of $R^0(Q_j)$ which are not

included in a representation $\tilde{R}$ currently under reconstruction:

$\bar{R}^+(j) = R^0(Q_j) \setminus \tilde{R}$. The better is the proximity (from the standpoint

of the admitted criteria) between $R^+(j)$ and $\bar{R}^+(j)$ the better is the

introduction procedure. So far as neither R^0 nor $R^0(Q_j)$ are known one

may consider the gain of $R^+(j)$ as an indication of this proximity. <u>A</u>

<u>good introduction procedure</u> should be expected to form a reducing set

(positive gain) in most of the cases when such one exists. If the

introduction procedure of step 2.1.1 is not good enough in this sense

then a number of queries for which a reducing set potentially exists

will be assigned $\alpha = 0$ (step 2.1.6) and will be excluded from the

current query set $\tilde{Q}$(step 2.1.7). So, for those queries the optimal

attachment will not be approached. Using such a relatively weak intro-

duction procedure one should modify Algorithm 2 by excluding step 2.1.7

and requiring $\alpha_m > 0$ at step 2.2.

III. ATTACHMENT OF RELATIONS TO QUERIES

A given set of functional dependencies, F, can be represented by an

AND/OR graph (Nilsson, 1971) in the following way. Let $G = (V,W,E_1,E_2)$

denote an AND/OR graph, where V is a set of AND-nodes and terminal

nodes, W is a set of OR-nodes, E_1 is a set of AND-arcs (the arcs

going out of AND-nodes), E_2 is a set of OR-arcs (the arcs going out of

OR-nodes). We shall say that an AND/OR graph G <u>displays</u> a given set of

dependencies $F = \{f_i\}$ iff for each $f_i \in F$ such that $f_i : A_i \rightarrow B_i (A_i$

and B_i are sets of domains) the following holds:

(1) $V \supset \{v_j \mid D_j \in (A_i \cup B_i)\}$, v_j denotes the node displaying D_j, and

(2) $W \ni w_i$, and

(3) $E_1 \supset \{(v_k,w_i) \mid D_k \in A_i\}$, and

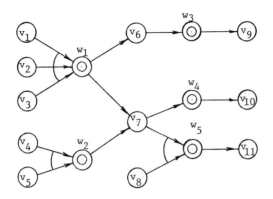

FIGURE 2. $G = (V,W,E_1,E_2)$, $V = \{v_i\}_{i=1}^{11}$, $W = \{w_i\}_{i=1}^{5}$

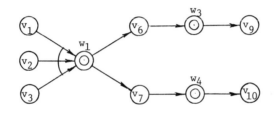

FIGURE 3. $g(S,I,T)$, $S = \{v_1,v_2,v_3\}$,

$I = \{w_1,v_6,v_7,w_3,w_4\}$, $T = \{v_9,v_{10}\}$

(4) $E_2 \supset \{(w_i,v_m) \mid D_m \in B_i\}$, and

(5) there are neither other nodes nor other arcs in G.

In words, V contains nodes corresponding to all the domains appearing

in F; for each distinct left-side set of domains A_i (of a functional

dependency f_i) there is an OR-node $w_i \in W$ which accepts incoming arcs

from all the AND-nodes corresponding to A_i and emits outgoing arcs to

all the nodes corresponding to B_i. For example, fig 2 shows an AND/OR

graph which displays the following set of dependencies:

$F = \{D_1D_2D_3 \rightarrow D_6D_7, D_4D_5 \rightarrow D_7, D_6 \rightarrow D_9, D_7 \rightarrow D_{10}, D_7D_8 \rightarrow D_{11}\}$.

The AND-arcs going to the same OR-node are linked by a bow, OR-nodes are

marked by a double circle.

We shall say that a relation R_i _answers_ a query $Q_j = (A_j, B_j)$ iff R_i contains all the tuples of the form

$(a_{j1}, a_{j2}, \ldots, a_{j|A_j|}, b_{j1}, b_{j2}, \ldots, b_{j|B_j|}, \ldots)$ which satisfy all the dependencies of F

(here $A_j = \{ A_{jk} \mid k=1,2,\ldots, |A_j| \}$, $B_j = \{ B_{jk} \mid k=1,2,\ldots, |B_j| \}$, $a_{jk} \in A_{jk}$, $b_{jk} \in B_{jk}$). This definition and the definition of "supply" (see Section I) imply the following

Proposition 2. If a set of relations U supplies all the dependencies among the domains specified by a query Q_j then U answers Q_j.

Let us consider an AND/OR graph G that displays a set of functional dependencies F over a set of domains D. We shall call _fragment_ of G a subgraph, g, of G with all the following properties:

a) g contains a set of nodes, S, called _starting nodes_, which have no incoming arcs;

b) g contains a set of nodes, T, called _terminal nodes_, which have no outgoing arcs; a set of nodes of g which are not in S and not in T is called a set of _internal nodes_, I;

c) each of the terminal nodes is reachable from each of the starting nodes, i.e. g contains a path between all pairs of nodes $(v_i, v_j \mid v_i \in S \wedge v_j \in T)$.

We shall say that a relation R_i _covers_ a fragment g iff R_i supplies all the functional dependencies among the domains displayed by the starting and terminal nodes of g. A relation R_i covers a fragment g(S,I,T) _with respect to a query_ Q_j (abbr. Q_j-_covers_) iff R_i covers g, and I contains no nodes displaying domains specified by Q_j. For example, fig. 3 shows a fragment g of the graph of fig. 2. Suppose $D(v_i) = D_i$ ($D(v_i)$ denotes the domain displayed by v_i); $Q_1 = (\{D_9\}, \{D_1, D_2, D_3\})$ (in words Q_1: "What is the value of D_9 related to given values of D_1, D_2, D_3?"); $Q_2 = (\{D_{10}\}, \{D_7\})$;

$R_1 = (\underline{D_1}, D_2, D_3, D_9, D_{10})$; $R_2 = (\underline{D_7}, D_{10})$; $R_3 = (\underline{D_1}, D_2, D_3, D_9)$ (the primary

keys of relations are underlined). Then R_1 Q_1-covers g but does not

Q_2-cover it; neither R_2 nor R_3 covers g.

A set of fragments $\gamma = \{g_i\}$ of an AND/OR graph G will be called

a fragmentation of G iff

(1) each node and each arc of G belongs to one of the fragments of γ,

and

(2) if an OR-node w_j of G belongs to a fragment $g_i \in \gamma$ then to

g_i belong all the AND-nodes v_k of G for which (v_k, w_j) belongs to

G, and

(3) ther is no node in G which is a starting or terminal node in one

of the fragments of γ and an internal node in the other one.

For example, fig. 4 shows a number of fragments of the graph G of fig.2.

Here the sets $\{g_1, g_2, g_3, g_6, g_7\}$ and $\{g_1, g_2, g_4, g_7\}$ are fragmentations of G,

but the set $\{g_2, g_5, g_6, g_7\}$ is not because $v_7 \in S_6 \wedge v_7 \in I_5$ violating

requirement (3) of the definition.

Proposition 3: If a set of relations U covers (Q_j-covers) a fragment-

ation $\gamma = \{g_i(S_i, I_i, T_i)\}$ of a fragment $g(S, I, T)$ then U covers

(Q_j-covers) g.

Proof: (We give an idea of the proof. A more rigorous proofs of the

propositions of this paper are not given here for brevity). Let us

consider two nodes $v_{i_1} \in S$ and $v_{i_n} \in T$, and a path

$L = (v_{i_1}, v_{i_2}, \ldots, v_{i_{n-1}}, v_{i_n})$. Let $g_{j_1} \in \gamma$ contain the arc (v_{i_1}, v_{i_2}),

hence $v_{i_1} \in S_{j_1}$. Let v_{i_k} be a node on the path L that belongs to

the terminal nodes of g_{j_1}, then U supplies the dependency between

$D(v_{i_1})$ and $D(v_{i_k})$. If $v_{i_k} \neq v_{i_n}$ then there exists a fragment $g_{j_2} \in \gamma$

containing $(v_{i_k}, v_{i_{k+1}})$. According to (3) $v_{i_k} \in S_{j_2}$. Let v_{i_e} be a node

of L belonging to T_{j_2}, then U supplies the dependency between $D(v_{i_k})$

and $D(v_{i_e})$, and consequently between $D(v_{i_1})$ and $D(v_{i_e})$. If $v_{i_e} \neq v_{i_n}$

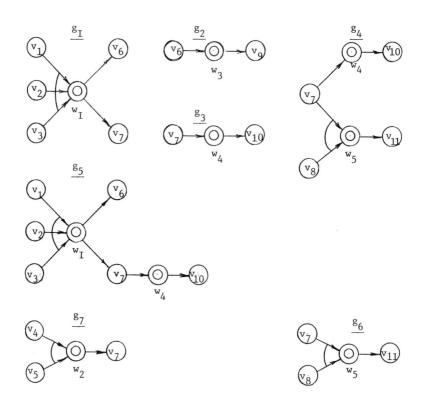

FIGURE 4. Fragments of the graph G of FIGURE 2.

we find g_{j_3} containing $(v_{i_e}, v_{i_{e+1}})$ and so on. Proceeding this way we reach a node v_{i_m} such that $v_{i_m} = v_{i_n} \land v_{i_m} \in T_{j_4}$. Hence U supplies the dependency between $D(v_{i_1})$ and $D(v_{i_n})$. Because each terminal node of g is reachable from each starting node of g we prove using the same procedure that U supplies all the dependencies between the domains displayed by S and the domains displayed by T.   Q.E.D.

The idea of attaching a set of relations $R(Q_j)$ to a query Q_j is to construct an AND/OR graph, G_j, which displays all the dependencies among the domains specified by Q_j, then to find a fragmentation of G_j Q_j-covered by a subset of R. Let a relation $R_i \in R$ supply a set of dependencies $\varphi_i \subseteq F$, and let δ_i denote a set of all domains appearing in the left-side parts of all the dependencies $f \in \varphi_i$. Given an

AND/OR graph $G = (V,W,E_1,E_2)$ displaying all the functional dependencies
of a given nonredundant set F, a set of relations R representing F,
a query $Q_j = (A_j,B_j)$, the following algorithm forms a set of relations
$R(Q_j) \subseteq R$ that supplies all the functional dependencies among the domains
specified by Q_j.

Algorithm 3:

1. Initialize $\tilde{R} := R; U := \phi$; $X := A_j \cup B_j$ (X is an ordered set of
   domains, say, alphabetically ordered).

2. Consider G as a directed graph ignoring the bows linking AND-arcs.
   Find the shortest path between each pair of nodes of G displaying the
   domains specified by Q_j (the domains of X). If there is a domain of X
   not displayed by G or there is a node of G displaying a domain of A_j
   and not reachable from all the other nodes of G displaying the domains
   of X, then assign $R(Q_j) = \phi$ and stop.

3. Construct AND/OR graph $G_j = (V_j,W_j,E_{1j},E_{2j})$ consisting of all the
   shortest paths found at step 2. Find the shortest path between each pair
   of nodes of G_j (If it was not found at step 2). Let Y be an ordered
   set of all these shortest paths.

4. While $E_{1j} \cup E_{2j} \neq \phi$ do
   begin

   4.1. Delete from X all the domains displayed by the nodes of G_j
        which have no outgoing arcs.

   4.2. Find a relation $R_i \in \tilde{R}$ for which $\delta_i \cap X \neq \phi$. So, R_i
        supplies functional dependencies left parts of which contain
        domains belonging to X.

   4.3. Find a fragment $g_i(S_i,I_i,T_i)$ of G_j which is Q_j-covered by
        the relation R_i found at step 4.2.

   4.4. Delete from $E_{1j} \cup E_{2j}$ all the arcs belonging to g_i.

   4.5. Insert T_i into X preserving the order of domains in X.

Assign $U: = U \cup \{R_i\}$; $\tilde{R}:= \tilde{R} \setminus \{R_i\}$.

end

5. Assign $R(Q_j): = U$. Stop.

An application of Proposition 3 and its proof to analysis of
Algorithm 3 leads to the following

Proposition 4: A set $R(Q_j)$ returned by Algorithm 3 is a set of relations

attached to Q_j in R.

Indeed, $R(Q_j)$ supplies all the dependencies among the domains

specified by Q_j, hence $R(Q_j)$ answers Q_j.

Let τ_3 denote a <u>measure of complexity</u> of Algorithm 3 (say, the

running time), and t_k - the complexity of step k. We shall use the

following notation: n,m- the number of nodes, arcs (respectively) of G;

n_j, m_j - the number of nodes, arcs of G_j; μ_j - the number of domains

specified by Q_j; r - the number of relations in R; ν - the maximum

number of domains contained by a relation $R_i \in R$.

Because X must be ordered

$$t_1 = O(\mu_j \log \mu_j).$$

In order to find all the shortest paths sought at step 2 one must

solve all pairs problem (Fredman, 1975; Yao et al., 1977) or μ_j times

solve single source problem (Johnson, 1977). Hence

$$t_2 = O(\min(n^2 \log n, \mu_j n^2, \mu_j(n+m) \log n)).$$

At step 3 one must solve all pairs problem for G_j, hence

$$t_3 = O(n_j^2 \log n_j).$$

Because X is ordered

$$t_{4.1} = O(n_j \log n_j),$$

and $t_{4.2} = O(r \cdot \nu \cdot \log n_j)$.

In order to find a fragment g_i Q_j-covered by R_i it is sufficien

to find all the paths in G_j between each pair of nodes displaying the

domains which appear in the dependencies supplied by R_i, and to detect
all the internal nodes of these paths which display domains specified by
Q_j. All these paths are already found at steps 2 and 3, and contained in
Y. So, one has to search at most ν^2 paths among n_j^2 ordered ones, and
at most μ_j nodes within each sought path. Hence

$$t_{4.3} = 0(\mu_j \ \nu^2 \log n_j).$$

Using search indices for E_{1j} and E_{2j},

$$t_{4.4} = 0(m_j \log m_j).$$

Because the order in X must be preserved

$$t_{4.5} = 0(\nu \ \log n_j).$$

Initially $E_{1j} \cup E_{2j}$ contains m_j arcs. Because each fragment g_i
contains at least one arc which is deleted from $E_{1j} \cup E_{2j}$ at step 4.4,
the number of executions of loop 4 is at most m_j. Hence

$$\tau_3 = 0(\max(r\nu, \ \mu_j \nu^2, m_j) \cdot m_j \log n_j). \qquad (7)$$

In most practical cases $2 \le n_j < n$, $1 \le m_j < m$, $r\nu < m, \mu_j\nu^2 < m$.
So (7) implies the following very overstated estimate

$$\tau_3 = 0(m^2 \log n).$$

Let $\bar{F}$ denote the number of all appearances of domains in all the
functional dependencies belonging to F (if F is written down as a
sequence of names (or numbers) of domains appearing in each $f_i \in$ F then
$\bar{F}$ is the length of this sequence); $|F|$ denotes the cardinality of F
(the number of functional dependencies contained by F). The definition
of an AND/OR graph $G - (V,W,E_1,E_2)$ displaying F implies
$|V| = |D|, |W| \le |F|$ because OR-nodes which have only one incoming arc
can be ignored (e.g. dotted circles in fig. 5), n $= |V| + |W| \le |D| + |F|$,
m $= |E_1| + |E_2| \le \bar{F}$. Hence

$$\tau_3 = 0(\bar{F}^2 \log (|D| + |F|)).$$

The attachment made by Algorithm 3 can be improved (at the expense of running time) by taking into account the size of relations involved in processing. Let $s(D_i)$ denote the size of domain D_i (the number of distinct values of D_i), and $s(R_j)$ denote the size of relation R_j (say, the product of the number of tuples by the number of domains contained in R_j). Then

a) Each arc (x,y) of the graph G considered by Algorithm 3 can be given a weight $s(D(x))$, and then all the shortest paths found at steps 2 and 3 should be weighted shortest paths.

b) At step 4.2 a relation R_m can be sought which has the least size $s(R_m) = \min (s(R_i) | R_i \in \tilde{R} \wedge \delta_i \cap X \neq \phi)$.

c) At step 4.2 a relation R_k can be sought for which $|\delta_k \cap X| = \max_{R_i \in \tilde{R}} (|\delta_i \cap X|)$.

IV. INTRODUCTION OF NEW RELATIONS

As stated above, the efficiency of Algorithm 2 (in term of the total cost reduction of the reconstructed representation of DB) depends on the efficiency of the procedure which introduces new relations, on the proximity between a set of new relations produced by the procedure and the best introduction. According to Proposition 3 to each fragmentation of a graph can correspond a set of relations which Q_j-covers the graph and, hence, may be attached to Q_j. It can be shown that the number of distinct fragmentations of a graph, and so the number of distinct attachments to a query can increase exponentially with a growing number of nodes. Hence, a search for the best introduction can be impractically hard and not justified by the expected decrease of total cost.

More expedient is a <u>heuristic procedure</u> which in most cases

introduces a reducing set of relations having a positive gain. In fact,
such a procedure introduces a set of relations which is only a candidate
for a reducing set, and which is accepted or rejected after checking
(at step 2.1.5 of Algorithm 2) whether its gain is positive. We present
here two possible heuristics of this kind.

$\underline{\text{H1}}$. Given $R^{(1)}(Q_i)$, let $g_j(S_j,I_j,T_j)$ denote a fragment Q_i-covered
by R_j, $j = 1,2,\ldots,\ |R^{(1)}(Q_i)|$, and let $R_k,R_e \in R^{(1)}(Q_i)$ Q_i-cover

fragments g_k and g_e such that

(1) $J = T_k \cap S_e \neq \phi$, and

(2) T_k contains no nodes displaying domains specified by Q_i. If T_k
contains no starting nodes of all the fragments Q_i-covered by $R^{(1)}(Q_i)$
except g_e, then form a fragment $\tilde{g}(\tilde{S},\tilde{I},\tilde{T})$ such that $\tilde{S} = S_k$ and $\tilde{T} = T_e$,
and include into $R^+(i)$ a relation $\tilde{R}$ which Q_i-covers $\tilde{g}$.

Fig. 5 shows the graph displaying the following set of dependencies:
$F = \{D_1 \rightarrow D_2 D_3 D_4, D_4 \rightarrow D_5 D_6, D_5 D_6 \rightarrow D_7 D_8\}$, where D_1-employee number,
D_2-employee name, D_3-department number, D_4-employee address,
D_5-distance to working place, D_6-transport used, D_7-fare, D_8-travelling
time. Let us consider a representation, $R^{(1)} = \{R_1,R_2,R_3\}$,
$R_1 = (\underline{D_1}D_2 D_3 D_4)$, $R_2 = (\underline{D_4}D_5 D_6)$, $R_3 = (\underline{D_5 D_6}D_7 D_8)$, and a query
$Q_1 = (\{D_7,D_8\},\{D_1\})$, in words, "what are the fare and travelling time of
given employees (given a list of employee numbers)?" The set attached to
Q_1 in $R^{(1)}$ is $R^{(1)}(Q_1) = \{R_1,R_2,R_3\}$. Iterative application of H1
introduces a new relation $R^+(1) = (\underline{D_1}D_7 D_8)$.

$\underline{\text{H2}}$. Given $R^{(1)}(Q_i)$, let $R_k,R_e \in R^{(1)}(Q_i)$ Q_i-cover fragments g_k
and g_e such that

(1) $J = T_k \cap S_e \neq \phi$, and

(2) each of T_k,T_e contains at least one node displaying a domain
specified by Q_i. Let K be a set of all nodes of T_k displaying domains
specified by Q_i, and let L be a set of all such nodes belonging to T_e.

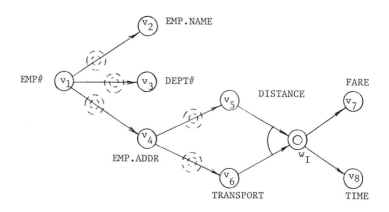

FIGURE 5. A sample graph.

If T_k contains no starting nodes of all the fragments Q_i-covered by $R^{(1)}(Q_i)$ except g_e, then include into $R^+(i)$ a relation $\tilde{R} = (D(S_k), D(K), D(L))$, where $D(S_k)$ denotes the set of all domains displayed by S_k.

For example, let us consider (with reference to fig. 5) a query $Q_2 = (\{D_4\}, \{D_3, D_7\})$, in words, "what are the addresses of those employees of a given department who pay a given fare?" The set attached to Q_2 in $R^{(1)}$ is $R^{(1)}(Q_2) = \{R_1, R_2, R_3\}$. An application of both H1 and H2 introduces $R^+(2) = (\underline{D_1} D_3 D_4 D_7)$, which is in 2NF, by the way.

Many practical data bases use non-3NF relations similar to $R^+(2)$ which are intended to answer frequent queries. For example, an inventory data base often contains a relation of the form $(\underline{P\#}, PN, P, Q, C)$, where $P\#$ stands for part number, PN-part name, P-price for a unit, Q-quantity on hand, C-total cost, and the functional dependencies defined on these domains are $\{P\# \to PN, P, Q; P, Q \to C\}$. This relation is stored in addition to a price-list relation $(\underline{P\#}, PN, P)$.

C.P. Wang and H. H. Wedekind (1975) describe a data base (for an airline reservation system) prompted by performance-oriented considerations which contains, for example, the relation (<u>route segment, date,</u>

fℓ#, equipcode, load 1, load 2), where route segment → fℓ#; fℓ#→equip-code; route segment, date → load 1, load 2.

Let us now estimate the complexity τ_2 of Algorithm 2. The complexity of both H1 and H2 is $O(r^2)$. It can be shown that the running time of all the steps of loop 2.1 is less than the running time of step 2.1.3 which is (using Algorithm 3) $O(\bar{F}^2 \log (|D| + |F|))$. The number of executions of loop 2.1 is $|\tilde{Q}| \le |Q|$. So, the running time of loop 2.1 is

$$t_{2.1} = O(|Q| \bar{F}^2 \log (|D| + |F|)).$$

The running time of Algorithm 2 is determined by that of block 2 which depends on the condition Ω, as it was stated in section 2. If the condition is of the form $\tilde{Q} \ne \phi$ then

$$\tau_2 = O(|Q|^2 \bar{F}^2 \log (|D| + |F|)).$$

V. CONCLUSION

The efficiency of a data base system depends on the extent to which performance criteria are taken into consideration in the process of its design. In this paper we show an application of performance criteria (e.g. total operational cost of jobs execution and relations updating) to relational data base design and updating (caused by changes of affecting factors, e.g. appearance of new queries) in the framework of adaptive constructing of its collection of relations.

An algorithm (Algorithm 2) is presented which reconstructs a collection of relations representing a data base in the direction of total cost reduction. Two main internal steps of Algorithm 2 are analysed: attaching of a subset of a current collection to a query, and introducing of new relations. Algorithm 3 is given that attaches relations to a query using AND/OR graphs for displaying of a given logical data structure. Two heuristics for introducing of new relations are described.

ACKNOWLEDGMENTS

The author is indebted to his anonymous referees for helpful comments on a previous draft of this paper.

REFERENCES

Bernstein, P.A. and Beeri, C. (1976). University of Toronto, Technical Report CSRG-73.

Codd, E.F. (1970). Comm. ACM 13:377.

Codd, E.F. (1972a). In "Data Base Systems, "Courant Computer Science Symp. 6 (R. Rustin, ed.) p.33. Prentice-Hall, New York.

Codd, E.F. (1972b). Ibid, p.65.

Codd, E.F. (1974). In "Proc. IFIP-74", 1017. North-Holland.

Date, C.J. (1975). "An Introduction to Database Systems". Addison-Wesley, New York.

Fredman, M.L. (1975). In "Proc. IEEE 16th Annual Symp. on Foundations of Computer Science", p.98.

Johson, D.B. (1977). J. ACM 24:1.

Lozinskii, E.L. (1977). In "Systems for Large Data Bases" (P. C. Lockeman and E. J. Neuhold, eds), p.95. North-Holland.

Nilsson, N.J. (1971). "Problem-solving Methods in Artificial Intelligence!' McGraw-Hill, New York.

Rissanen, J. and Delobel, C. (1973). IBM Research Report RJ 1220. San Jose California.

Wang, C.P. and Wedekind, H.H. (1975). IBM J. Research. and Dev. 19:71.

Yao, A.C., Avis D. M. and Rivest, R.L. (1977). In "Proc. 9th Annual ACM Symp. on Theory of Computing".

REPRESENTING DATA BASES
IN SEGMENTED NAME SPACES

Virgil Gligor[1]

Department of Computer Science
University of Maryland
College Park, Maryland

David Maier[2]

Department of Electrical Engineering
and Computer Science
Princeton University
Princeton, New Jersey

I.   INTRODUCTION

New data base systems, based on the CODASYL DBTG specifi-

cation (ACM, 1971), stress the importance of the schema and

subschema concepts and their interactions with respect to the

requirements of access control, concurrency, and data indepe-

dence (Chamberlin et al., 1975; DEC, 1976; Griffith and Wade,

1976).

In general, mechanisms implementing the schema specifica-

tions perform data base representation. Thus, data base enti-

ties are grouped in files, records, sets, etc., in such a way

that programs operating on the users' behalf need not be con-

cerned with the organization of data on physical devices.

[1]Research supported by National Aeronautics and Space
Administration under contract NAS 5-24407.
[2]Research supported by an IBM fellowship.

295

Furthermore, data base entities receive location independent
names and, as a result, the programming of the data base is
simplified substantially.

During the representation of the data base, its administrator may attempt to perform a series of space and/or access
time optimizations using the schema mechanisms (Kou, 1977;
Wong and Yao, 1975). These optimizations are designed to
take into account the requirements of all users of the data
base. By contrast, the subschema specifications refer to individual users, or groups of users, and are designed to present them with a more stylized image of the data base.

Although it is not entirely clear what a subschema should
accomplish, it is agreed that (1) from the access control
standpoint, the subschema restricts the user's and his/her
programs' view of the data base (Minsky, 1976), and (2) from
the consistency standpoint, the subschema defines what programs operating on the user's behalf may lock/unlock when
concurrent operations are allowed (Chamberlin et al., 1975;
DEC, 1976). Hence, mechanisms which implement subschema
specifications perform a mapping between the data base representation and the users' views of the data base. This is
illustrated in Figure 1.

Access control mechanisms are important for two reasons.
First, in multiuser data base systems, they enforce the
authorization specifications of the subschema which determine
what data may be released to, or modified by, each user and
his/her programs. Second, access control mechanisms help
minimize the propagation of errors and other effects of
failures which occur during the execution of data base programs. Therefore, they enforce data isolation.

In multiuser data base systems, concurrency is introduced
to improve the responsiveness and the utilization of the system. Thus, data base programs with long running times or
those which perform frequent input-output operations are
scheduled concurrently with other data base programs which may
require less running time, or which may not perform many
input-output operations. Because these programs are scheduled
concurrently, they must use locking mechanisms. Locking
mechanisms prevent concurrent programs from performing simul-
taneous updates on shared data and, therefore, help maintain
the consistency of shared data. However, the use of locking
mechanisms introduces the possibility of <u>locking conflicts</u>
which may result in the performance degradation of concurrent
programs. If the possibility of locking conflicts is not
minimized, then the concurrent operation of data base programs
may, in fact, decrease the system's utilization and responsiveness.

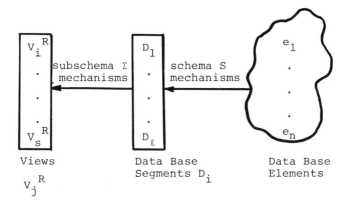

FIGURE 1. The role of a schema/subschema concepts in
           a segmented system.

In this paper we will consider only the subschema specifications designed by the data base administrator. Consequently,
all the coexistent views of the data base are known to the
data base administrator.[3] Thus, for the same user's view,
specification complexity may change from the schema to the
subschema, or vice-versa, as a function of the mechanisms
which implement these specifications, and also as a function
of the individual administrator's judgement.

We will show that, for data bases represented in segmented
name spaces - in spite of the use of sophisticated mechanisms
implementing the subschema specifications - there still
remains a polynomially complete problem in the design of the
data base representation. This problem appears when the
representation is performed in such a way that each user's
view is the best approximation of its definition. The best
approximation is shown to be necessary to meet the requirements for authorization, data isolation and minimization of
locking conflicts. The practical implications of this are also
discussed.

II.   PROBLEMS OF DATA BASE REPRESENTATION

An operating system is said to support segmented name
spaces if files can be mapped and addressed in the virtual
memory. Generally, operating systems running on hardware
which supports segmentation - such as the Honeywell MULTICS
(Organick, 1972) and the Burroughs B6700 Master Control Program (Organick, 1973) - perform the mapping of files in the

---

[3]Therefore our view concept is included in the one presented in (Chamberlin et al., 1975). However, it is independent of the nature of the data base system (i.e., relational,
hierarchical, or network).

virtual memory. However, segmented name spaces may also be
supported by systems without hardware support for segmentation
- such as TENEX (Murphy, 1972) and VM 370 (IBM, 1972).

Representing a data base in segmented name spaces has a
number of advantages. First, several mechanisms, which must
be included in the schema mechanisms, are provided already by
systems supporting segmented name spaces. For example,
facilities for locking, physical attribute specification,
back up and recovery, accounting and certain exceptional condition handling, are provided on a per segment basis in these
systems. Of course, the data manager must extend these
facilities to make them usable at the data base level. Second,
the segment becomes the common denominator for information
naming, sharing and distribution / revocation of access privileges. Third, the programming conventions which the data base
designer must make in the implementation of the schema and
subschema mechanisms are simplified considerably. Fourth, it
is generally believed that systems in which capabilities are
used to name segments - and objects of abstract types (Griffith and Wade, 1976; Jones and Wulf, 1975; Minsky, 1976) -
constitute a solid basis for implementing access control in
data base systems.

However, certain costs accrue. Most systems incur a fixed
cost for mapping any segment in the virtual memory regardless
of the segment size. In systems having paged segments, at
least two pages must be mapped for each segment (i.e., one
page for the page table and the other for the data) even
though the required segment size may be much smaller than a
page. Furthermore, the costs incurred for directory entry set-
up are the same for small segments as for large ones.

It follows that a large number of small segments is significantly more costly than a small number of large segments which also add up to the same memory size. Consequently, the representation of a (potentially large) data base in segmented name spaces would have to be restricted to a certain number of segments irregardless of their sizes.

In addition, a significant number of segment access methods are sequential rather than random. This means that, even if the segments are paged, there will be a potentially large number of pages in the virtual memory which may not be used after an initial set of sequential accesses. In this case, the use of segment buffering would be advisable. Segment buffering can be implemented as an extension of the segment mapping facilities in much the same way as the sequential file access is implemented in TENEX. Although little use will be made of the segmentation hardware, the other facilities provided on a per segment basis remain useful.

Consider a <u>data base</u> D consisting of a set of unnamed entities, $D = \{e_1, \ldots, e_n\}$. The data base administrator must design a schema S which specifies (among other things) a representation of the data base D^R as a set of K segments $\{D_\ell\}$, $\ell = 1, \ldots, K$ such that $D^R = \bigcup_{\ell=1}^{K} D_\ell$. Hence, the schema S partitions the set D into K segments. Furthermore, the data base administrator must design a subschema Σ which provides the view definitions V_i, $i = 1, \ldots, s$ and their corresponding representations in terms of the data base segments.

A <u>view definition</u> V_i is a subset of D, and is provided by an access predicate (or a combination of access predicates)

defined by the subschema Σ on D. All access predicates
under consideration will be simple predicates. The reader
should refer to (Eswaran, et al., 1976) for several examples of
simple predicates.

A view (representation) V_i^R is defined as the subset of
segments D which corresponds to the view definition V_i,
i.e., $V_i^R = \{U\ D_\ell\ |V_i \cap D_\ell \neq \Phi,\ \ell=1,\ldots,K\}$.

In the above definition we have emphasized a single function of the schema S, viz., that of partitioning the data
base into a set of segments. However, the schema S also
specifies the data organization in terms of fields, records,
and sets of data. We have assumed (tacitly) that these are
part of the data base definition D. Consequently, D (and
not D^R) appears to be the domain of the subschema Σ.

A.   Authorization and Data Isolation

Each user of a data base system along with the programs
operating on his/her behalf - called "user programs" hence-
forth - will be assigned one or a set of view definitions.
These view definitions are specified by the subschema designed
by the data base administrator using a suitable language. The
view definitions may be overlapped or disjoint depending upon
whether or not the corresponding users and user programs share
parts of the data available to them. The view definitions may
also be nested because some users may be authorized to perform
accesses on other users' data. Several examples of users with
different views of a data base were given by Stonebraker and
Wong (Stonebraker and Wong, 1974).

How should the schema S and the subschema Σ be designed in a system which supports a segmented name space? In answering this question we will assume that a number of progressively more sophisticated mechanisms are available to implement the subschema specifications.

EXAMPLE 1.   Consider a subschema Σ_1 which specifies each view definition V_i and represents it by a set of segments V_i^R after schema S is designed. Hence, each user program is presented with a set of segments such that $V_i^R \supseteq V_i$. The schema S is not refined enough to allow $V_i^R = V_i$ for all V_i ; the reason for this is the limitation of the number of data base segments to K . As mentioned above, this limitation is due to the inherent cost of each segment.   □

Most systems supporting segmented name spaces can restrict the per segment access privileges to a subset of read, write, append, etc. Providing access privileges on a per segment basis is not sufficient because the granularity of access in data base systems is often smaller than a segment. Therefore, subschema Σ_1 has the problem of authorizing more access privileges than are needed by the user programs for accessing the views defined by $\{V_i\}$ i=1,...,s. This results in the violation of one of the most fundamental design principles of access control mechanisms called the "least privilege" (or the "need to know" principle) (Jones and Wulf, 1975; Saltzer and Schroeder, 1975). The immediate implications are: (1) a user may gain access to information to which he/she is unauthorized, and (2) the effects of hardware or software failures during the execution

of a user program may propagate to other users. Hence, both

the requirements for authorization and data isolation are

compromised.

A measure of the extent to which the requirements of this

principle are violated is $\mathbb{C} = \sum_{i=1}^{S} (|v_i^R| - |v_i|)$. There-

fore, the optimization goal in the design of the data base

representation is to make $\mathbb{C} \to 0$. To decrease $\mathbb{C}$, the data

base administrator has the following non-exclusive options:

1. Redesign the schema S using K segments (perhaps)
   adjusting their sizes as needed.

2. Make use of a system which supports indirect access
   to a set of data segments through calls to the entry
   points of protected subsystems (e.g., MULTICS,
   Plessey (England, 1974), CAP (Needham, et al., 1977),
   etc.), and redesign the subschema Σ specifications
   accordingly. "A protected subsystem is a collection
   of program and data segments that is 'encapsulated' so
   that other executing programs cannot read or write
   the program and data segments. Also they cannot dis-
   rupt the intended operation of the component programs,
   but can invoke the programs by calling designated
   entry points. The encapsulated data segments are the
   protected objects." (cf. reference Saltzer and Schroeder, 1975, p. 1302)

EXAMPLE 2. Consider the same schema S. A subschema Σ_2

will represent the view definition V_i as a set of entry

points of a protected subsystem whose protected objects are

the set of segments V_i^R . The set of entry points of the protected subsystem are associated on a one to one basis with the procedures $P_i = \{P_{i_1}, \ldots, P_{i_n}\}$.

The only way by which user programs may access the data segments of the view V_i^R is by invoking some procedure $P_{ij} \in P_i$. In addition to implementing various kinds of accesses - such as Insert, Delete, Update, Retrieve, etc. - for the particular view V_i^R , these procedures also implement the access restriction $V_i \cap V_i^R$ if $|V_i^R| - |V_i| > 0$. Other procedures which have the same code - but implement access restrictions on the other view representations - will be specified by Σ_2 as entry points in other subsystems. Thus, $\mathbb{C} = 0$.   □

Unfortunately, this approach has three major drawbacks. First by performing experiments with the interface offered by the procedures P_{ij} , a user may find out how to persuade them into accessing the set $V_i^R - V_i$. Hence, the access control mechanisms implemented by P_i may be subverted. Clearly, $\mathbb{C}$ may decrease somewhat, but it does not reach zero.

Secondly, consider that the interfaces of all procedures P_{ij} for all i and j are "narrowed" by making them implement data dependent access checks. If the number of views is large, then the number of procedures implementing essentially the same kind of access - but differing in the predicate which their access check enforces - may grow very large. This may make the access control mechanism implemented by P_i impractical. Hence, redesigning the schema S as suggested by alternative (1) above is still necessary.

Third, it is known that if the data base is partitioned into protected objects and each protected subsystem encapsulates a single protected object, then n-ary operations on protected objects are precluded for $n \geq 2$ (Gligor, 1977; Needham, et al., 1977).

Finally, it should be noted the indirect access mechanism achieves similar results as the query modification mechanism proposed in Stonebraker and Wong (Stonebraker and Wong, 1974). The modification of each user query will implement the access restriction $V_i \cap V_i^R$ if $|V_i^R| - |V_i| > 0$.

The data base administrator may attempt to use a segmented system which provides more sophisticated access control mechanisms. The most important systems in this category are the ones which support the implementation of abstract data types either through capability sealing/unsealing (Gligor, 1977) or through capability amplification (Jones and Wulf, 1975). Let us assume (1) that the type operations implement the accesses mentioned above on the views V_i^R and (2) that they are implemented by the protected subsystems' programs. Furthermore, let us assume that each operation may, in fact, perform actions on more than one type as suggested by Jones and Liskov (Jones and Liskov, 1977).

EXAMPLE 3. Consider the same schema S and a new subschema Σ_3 . The subschema Σ_3 will represent each view definition V_i as (1) a capability having a type mark T_i which points to a representation segment containing capabilities for all data segments in V_i^R , and (2) a capability for a protected subsystem, whose programs implement operations on the objects representing the data base.

The only way in which a user program may access the segments of a view V_i^R is by invoking an operation - through a
call to a subsystem entry point - and presenting it with capabilities for objects of type T_i as parameters. Because
capabilities (and consequently type marks) cannot be forged,
the mechanisms which implement the subschema Σ_3 specifications can encode the access restrictions $V_i \cap V_i^R$ into the
type mark T_i whenever $|V_i^R| - |V_i| > 0$. Thus $\mathbb{C} = 0$.   □

Clearly, user programs cannot subvert the access control
mechanisms. This approach appears to be practical because the
same operation can enforce different access predicates when
presented with different parameters. Moreover, the type mark
field grows only logarithmically with the number of views.
However, any malfunctioning of the subsystems' operations -
due to either hardware or software failures - may cause
breaches in the access restriction to the view representation.
Thus, this approach is vulnerable. Of course, the access control mechanisms of EXAMPLE 2 were vulnerable, too. Consequently, the option of redesigning the schema S , as mentioned above, is still necessary.

The above examples imply that the problem of designing
representations for a robust data base (i.e., invulnerable
to failure propagation) is relevant to other kinds of parti-
tionings, not just segmentation. The following observations
should help clarify this statement.

Data base entities cannot be named individually because
of their large numbers (e.g., millions). Hence, they are
grouped into records or files and, therefore, the number of
independently named groups of entities is reduced signifi-

cantly (e.g., hundreds or thousands). On the other hand, the access predicates - providing the view definitions - refer to the individual data base entities rather than to the indepently named groups of entities. Consequently, the need for having a robust system requires that each view, represented as a subset of all groups of entities, be the best approximation of its definition.

B. Minimization of Locking Conflicts

If several concurrent user programs try to access common data, then their access to the common data must be synchronized. In practice, the subschema defines the access synchronization by specifying various locking modes on a per view or subview bases (Chamberlin, et al., 1975; DEC, 1976). For example, while a user program updates the contents of a view defined by V_i, other user programs will be prevented from accessing their views defined by V_j if $V_i \cap V_j \neq \Phi$. Updates require exclusive access to common data; therefore, each concurrent program must lock its view exclusively. Thus, the possibility of locking conflicts is apparent.

An exclusive lock request on a view V_i issued by a program conflicts with an exclusive lock request on another view V_j issued concurrently by another program if $V_i \cap V_j \neq \Phi$. The predicates used in the view definitions must be simple so that the decision as to whether or not exclusive locks are in conflict, can be made in a straightforward way.

Locking conflicts are certain to degrade the performance of the concurrent programs of the data base system because only one of the programs which issued the concurrent lock request could be granted the lock.

Systems supporting segmented name spaces provide locking
on a per segment basis; this is because the segment is the
unit of sharing and access control. Locking in data base systems is done on a view or subview basis. Therefore, it may be
argued that data base locking facilities should be implemented
on the top of the operating system and need (should) not use
the segment locking facilities. However, the data base locks
must propagate to the segment level or else operating system
processes involved in segment maintenance may read inconsistent segments. Thus, subschema locking mechanisms are implemented by using the segment locking mechanisms already provided by the underlying operating system.

EXAMPLE 4. Consider a schema S which represents a data
base in a segmented system, and a subschema Σ . It is likely
that for some pairs of view definitions $\{V_i, V_j | V_i \cap V_j = \Phi\}$, the
representation will cause $V_i^R \cap V_j^R \neq \Phi$. In other words,
representing a data base in a segmented name space may
increase the chances of locking conflicts because the number
of segments is limited to K .

Consequently, the measure of the extent to which the requirements of the least privilege principle are violated
$\mathbb{C} = \overset{*}{\underset{i=1}{\overset{S}{\Sigma}}} (|V_i^R| - |V_i|)$, is also a measure of the increase in the
chances of locking conflicts. For this reason, the redesign
of schema S is necessary in order to decrease the cost $\mathbb{C}$. $\square$

It should be noticed that the design of schema S does
not depend on the mechanisms for implementing the subschema
specifications (e.g., protected subsystems, etc.), but only on
the specifications themselves (i.e., view definitions).

This example suggests that the problem of avoiding the introduction of locking conflicts is relevant not only to segments but also to <u>other kinds of locking units</u> such as records, sets, etc. The reason is similar to that mentioned in the access control case above: while the locking units may group data base entities together, the lock requests must be issued on a per view definition basis and, consequently, may refer to individual data base entities. Therefore, the need to avoid the introduction of locking conflicts requires that each view is the best approximation of its definition.

To summarize, the data base administrator is faced with the following problem:

Consider a data base $D = \{e_i\} i=1,\ldots,n$ and a set of view definitions $\{V_j | V_j \subseteq D \ j=1,\ldots,s\}$ provided by the subschema Σ. The problem is to design a schema S such that, if the data base is represented by a set of K segments $\{D_\ell\} \ell=1,\ldots,K$, then the cost $\mathbb{C} = \sum_{i=1}^{s} (|V_j^R| - |V_j|)$, incurred from representing the view definitions V_j as

$$V_j^R = \{\cup \ D_\ell | V_j \cap D_\ell \neq \Phi, \ \ell=1,\ldots,k \ , \text{ is minimal.}$$

The problem is well posed in the sense that: if $K=1$, then $\mathbb{C}$ is maximum and if $K=n$, then $\mathbb{C} = 0$. We will call it the <u>K-segmentation problem</u> for data bases.

III. THE K-SEGMENTATION PROBLEM FOR DATA BASES IS NP-COMPLETE

Consider a collection of subsets $S_1,\ldots,S_u$ of a set R. The <u>minimum disjoint set basis</u> for $S_1,\ldots,S_u$ is the coarsest partition $B_1,\ldots,B_p$ of R such that each S_i is the exact union of some of the B_j's. In other words,

$$S_i = \{\cup \ B_j | S_i \cap B_j \neq \Phi\} \ .$$

LEMMA. Given any K-segmentation $\{D_i\}i=1,\ldots,K$, of D ,
there is a K-segmentation $\overline{D}_1,\ldots,\overline{D}_K$ such that the minimum
disjoint set basis of a set of views defined by $\{V_i\}i=1,\ldots,s$
is a refinement of $\overline{D}_1,\ldots,\overline{D}_K$ and the cost of representing
$\{V_i\}i=1,\ldots,s$ from $\overline{D}_1,\ldots,\overline{D}_K$ is less than or equal to the
cost of representing the V_i from $\{D_i\}i=1,\ldots,K$.

This lemma implies that we need only consider segmentations in which the D_i are unions of some of the members of
the minimum disjoint set basis of the set of views. A proof
of this lemma can be found in Gligor and Maier (Gligor and
Maier, 1977).

Let us consider the 3-PARTITION PROBLEM of Garey and
Johnson (Garey and Johnson, 1976). The problem is: given
3n positive integers $m_1,\ldots,m_{3n}$, can we partition them into
n cells of three elements such that the sum of the integers
in each cell is the same, namely $(\sum_{i=1}^{3n} m_i)/n$?

Garey and Johnson have shown that this problem is NP-
complete in the strong sense. This means that there exists a
polynomial p such that the problem is still NP-complete
when restricted to instances I where $\max_i(m_i) \le p(\text{length}(I))$.
An alternate formulation of this states that the 3-partition
is NP-complete even when the m_i are written in unary.

In order to shown that the K-segmentation problem is NP-
complete, we will reduce the "unary" 3-partition problem to
the K-segmentation problem. In this reduction the length of
the instance I will be $O(\sum_i m_i)$ rather than $O(\sum_i \log m_i)$.

THEOREM. The K-segmentation problem for data bases is
NP-complete.

PROOF. Given an instance of the unary 3-partition problem $m_1, \ldots, m_{3n}$ we construct an instance of the K-segmentation problem as follows.

Let $M = \max_i (m_i)(20n)$

$f = 2M^2$

$\overline{m}_i = \{m_i + M | 1 \le i \le 3n\}$

$$M = \sum_{i=1}^{3n} \overline{m}_i$$

It should be noted that we can obtain a 3-partition of the $\overline{m}_i$
if and only if we can obtain a 3-partition of the m_i. Moreover, the transformation between m_i and $\overline{m}_i$ is performed in
time polynomial in the size of the 3-partition problem.
Using $\overline{m}_i$, let us construct the $\overline{m}_i + 1$ view definitions
shown in Figure 2.

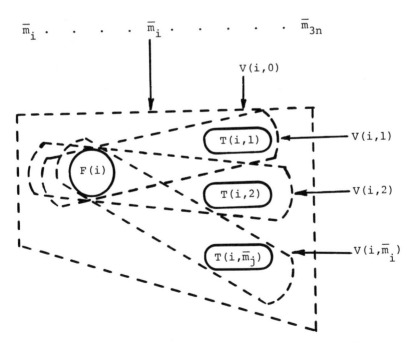

FIGURE 2. The view definitions corresponding to $\overline{m}_i$.

$$V(i,0) = F(i) \cup \bigcup_{j=1}^{\overline{m}_i} T(i,j)$$

$$V(i,j) = F(i) \cup T(i,j) \quad 1 \le j \le \overline{m}_i$$

In the above definitions, each $F(i)$ is a set of f elements (unnamed entities) which correspond to each $\overline{m}_i$; each $T(i,j), j=1,\ldots,\overline{m}_i$ is a singleton set of elements. It should be noticed again that the construction of the view definitions is done in time polynomial in M.

The total number of view definitions form the set

$$V = \{V(i,j) \mid 1 \le i \le 3n , 0 \le j \le \overline{m}_i\}$$

The set of elements of D is the union of the $\sum_{i=1}^{3n} \overline{m}_i + 3n$ view definitions in V. Thus, $D = \{\cup V(i,j) \mid 1 \le i \le 3n$ $1 \le j \le \overline{m}_i\}$. Furthermore, let the number of segments K be n.

CLAIM 1. If the cost of representing the view definitions of V from an optimal n-segmentation is $\frac{M^2}{n} + (2f+1) M + 6nf$, then a 3-partition can be obtained for the set $\{\overline{m}_i \mid 1 \le i \le 3n\}$.

CLAIM 2. If there exists a 3-partition of the $\overline{m}_i$, then there exists an n-segmentation $\{D_\ell\}$ of D such that the cost of representing the view definitions $V(i,j)$ using the D_ℓ $\ell=1,\ldots,n$ is $\frac{M^2}{n} + (2f+1) M + 6nf$.

CLAIM 3. The construction of the $V(i,j)$ can be done in time polynomial in M.

The proofs of the three claims, which conclude the proof of the theorem, can be found in Gligor and Maier (Gligor and Maier, 1977).

IV. SOME PRACTICAL IMPLICATIONS

There are two immediate implications of the K-segmentation
problem being NP-complete. The first refers to the nature of
the algorithms which a data base administrator may want to use
for the data base representation, and the second refers to the
kind of architectural support which may be needed.

The fact that the K-segmentation problem is NP-complete
means that it can be considered computationally intractable
(Karp , 1972).   It is known that either all or none
of the NP-complete problems can be solved by <u>polynomial-</u>
<u>time algorithms</u>. An algorithm is said to run in polynomial-
time if it terminates always in a number of steps which is
bounded by some polynomial in the size of the problem instance.
The class of P(NP) problems corresponds to the class of languages which can be recognized by deterministic (nondetermi-
nistic) Turing machines in polynomial-time. Therefore, if
$P \neq NP$, then none of the NP-complete problems can be solved by
polynomial-time algorithms. Since the class of NP-complete
problems contains many well-known problems which are notori-
ously difficult - such as the 0-1 integer programming problem,
the traveling salesman problem, and the graph coloring problem - it is believed that $P \neq NP$.

However, proving a problem NP-complete does not foreclose
the possibility of finding <u>polynomial-time approximation al-</u>
<u>gorithms</u>. A polynomial-time approximation algorithm, or sim-
ply an approximation algorithm, is guaranteed to find "near-
optimal" solutions i.e., within a constant factor of the optimal solution.

The Lemma of the previous section suggests the following approximation algorithm for the K-segmentation problem:

1. Given a set of view definitions $\{V_i\}$, $i=1,\ldots,s$ of data base $D = \{e_1,\ldots,e_n\}$, find the minimum disjoint set basis for the set $\{V_i\}$. Let the minimum disjoint set basis be the K_0-segmentation, and if its size $K_0 \leq K$, stop.

2. While $K_0 > K$, pick two segments B_i, B_j, $i \neq j$ of the K_0-segmentation and merge them if $\sum_\ell (|v_\ell^R| - |v_\ell|)$ is minimum for all V_ℓ and B_i, B_j such that $V_\ell \cap (B_i \cup B_j) \neq \Phi$. Then let $K_0 := K_0 - 1$.

Algorithms for finding the minimum disjoint set basis in $O(sn)$ steps have been proposed already (Shattuck, 1977). However, the above algorithm will run in $O(n^3)$. The reader can convince himself/herself that this algorithm produces a K-segmentation which is not always optimal. Although we have not evaluated how near to the optimal is this algorithm, it appears that the solutions of this algorithm differ from the optimal solutions by at least a factor of 2.

The fact that a problem is NP-complete in the strong sense bears some influence on the approximation algorithms closeness to the optimal and on their efficiency. An approximation algorithm A which operates in time bounded by the length (I) and error rate E, $0 < E \leq 1$ is called <u>fully polynomial</u> if $|A(I) - OPT(I)| / |OPT(I)| \leq E$, where $OPT(I)$ is the solution produced by the optimal algorithm with input I and $A(I)$ is the solution produced by A.

Garey and Johnson have pointed out in (Garey and Johnson, 1976) that the strong NP-completeness of a problem implies that no fully polynomial algorithm

can be found for it, unless P = NP . This means that as
E becomes close to zero the approximation algorithms for
strong NP-complete problems must become either very slow as a
function of 1/E or else very hard to find.

Finally, designing a data base representation so that each
view is the best approximation of its definition suggests that
the underlying architecture should support the existence of
large numbers of inexpensive, small segments. For many
reasons, known especially to operating system designers, this
requirement does not seem to be easy to meet.

ACKNOWLEDGMENTS

The authors would like to thank Professors M. P. Hecht and
J. D. Ullman for their suggestions on an earlier draft of this
paper.

REFERENCES

ACM (1971). CODASYL Data Base Task Group April 1971, New
York.

Chamberlin, D. C. et al. (1975). "Views, authorization and
locking in a relational data base system", Proc. AFIPS
1975 NCC, Vol. 44, pp. 425-430.

DEC (1976). Data Base Management System -- Programmer's
Procedures Manual, Order No. DEC-20-APPMB - A - D .

England, D. (1974). "Capability Concept Mechanism and Structure in System 250", IRIA, Int. Workshop on Protection in
Operating Systems, pp. 63-82.

Eswaran, K. E., et al. (1976). "The Notions of Consistency
and Predicate Locks in a Data Base System", Comm. ACM
Vol. 19, 11, pp. 624-633.

Garey, M. R. and Johnson, D. S. (1976). "Strong NP-Completeness Results: Motivation, Examples, and Implications",
Bell Laboratories, Murry Hill, N. J. (unpublished manuscript).

Gligor, V. D. (1977) "Architectural Aspects of Type Extendi-
bility", Proc. Trends and Applications: Computer Security and Integrity, NBS, Gaithersburg, Md., pp. 71-81.

Gligor, V. D. and Maier, D. (1977). "Representing Data Bases
in Segmented Name Spaces", Univ. of Maryland Technical
Report TR-605.

Griffith, P. P. and Wade, B. W. (1976). "An Authorization
Mechanism for a Relational Data Base System", ACM Trans.
Data Base Systems, 1, No. 3, pp. 242-255.

IBM (1972). Virtual Machine Facility/370: Introduction,
Doc. GC20-1800-0.

Jones, A. K. and Liskov, B. H. (1977). "A Language Extension
for Expressing Access Constraints on Data Access", to
appear in Comm. ACM.

Jones, A. K. and Wulf, W. A. (1975). "Towards the Design of
Secure Systems", Software Practice and Experience 5,
pp. 321-336.

Karp, R. M. (1972). "Reducibility Among Combinatorial Problems", in Complexity of Computer Computations (R.E.
Miller and J. W. Thatcher, eds.), Plenum Press, New York,
pp. 85-104.

Kou, L. T. (1977). "Polynomially Complete Consecutive
Retrieval Problems", SIAM J. on Comp. 6, pp. 67-76.

Minsky, N. (1976). "Intentional Resolution of Privacy Protection in Database Systems", Comm. ACM, Vol. 19, 3,
pp. 148-159.

Murphy, D. (1972). "Storage Organization and Management in
    TENEX", Proc. AFIPS 1972 FJCC, Vol. 41, AFIPS Press,
    Montvale, N.J., pp. 571-578.

Needham, R. M., et al. (1977). "Architecture of Cambridge CAP
    System and Its Protection Facilities", Proc. of 6th Symp.
    on Operating Syst. Principles, West Lafayette, Ind.

Organick, E. I. (1972). The Multics System: An Examination
    of Its Structure, M.I.T. Press, Cambridge, Mass.

Organick, E. I. (1973). Computer System Organization, the
    B5700/7600 Series, Academic Press, 1973.

Saltzer, H. J. and Schroeder, M. D. (1975) "The Protec-
    tion of Information in Computer Systems", Proc. IEEE
    Vol. 63, 9, pp. 1278-1308.

Shattuck, S., (1977). Personal communication.

Stonebraker, M. and Wong, E. (1974) "Access Control in a
    Relational Data Base Management System by Query Modifica-
    tion", Univ. of Calif., Berkeley Memorandum: ERL-M438.

Wong, C. K. and Yao, C. C. (1975). "A Combinatorial Optimi-
    zation Problem Related to Data Set Allocation", IBM
    Research Report: RC5392, Yorktown Heights.

STORAGE ALLOCATION FOR ACCESS PATH MINIMIZATION
IN NETWORK STRUCTURED DATA BASES

Johann P. Malmquist
Ehud Gudes
Edward L. Robertson

Department of Computer Science
The Pennsylvania State University
University Park, Pennsylvania

One problem in implementing a network (CODASYL) structured data base is the allocation of record occurrences to physical storage blocks. This paper presents a heuristic algorithm for performing this allocation for a stable network structured data base, in order to minimize the number of interblock references.

A network data base is mapped into a weighted directed graph such that record occurrences are mapped into nodes and set occurrences are mapped into edges. Nodes are partitioned attempting to minimize the total weight of those edges which connect nodes in distinct partition classes. Since edges correspond to access path components and partition classes to physical storage blocks, access time is reduced. Furthermore, an application of this algorithm could make use of query statistics in assigning edge weights.

The optimality criteria for this algorithm is the total weight of connecting edges (between distinct partition classes). The constraints are the given size of the partition classes (i.e. physical block sizes) and a packing factor of at least 1/2. The efficiency of the algorithm is considered, and the cost is shown to be quite affordable for a stable data base. It is highly unlikely that there exisits an efficient algorithm to find the optimal partition, since the general problem is NP-complete. However, the given algorithm performs quite well in reasonable cases.

I. INTRODUCTION

The CODASYL data base model is one of the most popular data base models today. The specifications of the CODASYL model were published in the well known 1971 Report of the CODASYL Data Base Task Group (DBTG) (5) and later modified and extended by the CODASYL Programming Language Committee (6) and The CODASYL Data Description Language Committee (7). The CODASYL proposal has already formed the basis of several commercial systems like the UNIVAC DMS 1100 (17) and the Integrated Data Management System (IDMS) (8). For more information on implementations using the CODASYL proposal, see the section on Vendor/CODASYL Developments in the paper by Fry and Sibley (9).

In all data base management systems, improving performance is very important. The four major categories of performance are space, insertion time, deletion time and retrieval time. This paper will deal with improving performance with respect to retrieval. Most of the research on improving performance has concentrated on relational data base systems, for example the work by Stonebraker et al. (18) on the INGRES Relational Data Base Management System and the work by Astrahan et al. (3) on System R. Some work has been done on performance optimization for the CODASYL model. Mitoma and Irani (14) deal with optimizing the design of DBTG-like schema structures. They are concerned primarily with the design of the logical schema which is at a higher level than ours, since we deal only with the physical data base design. Taylor (19) compares the pointer-array and chain implementations of the SET construct (see also section II in this paper).

Improving performance in a CODASYL based system is different from the other data base management systems, since the CODASYL schema Data Description Language (DDL) usually provides the ability to constrain the storage structure. For example, the SET construct in the CODASYL model predefines some preferred access paths in the data base system. Also the actual implementation of SETs is specified in the DDL for the schema in the MODE clause (e.g. the choice of CHAIN or POINTER-ARRAY). The CODASYL model is therefore not (currently) as data independent as, for example, the relational model (13). Even with these constraints there is still some freedom in the exact choice of storage structures, for example in determining block sizes and allocating record occurrences to blocks or pages. This paper is primarily concerned with the problem of allocating record occurrences to physical storage blocks or pages. A heuristic algorithm is presented for performing this allocation for a stable network structured data base, in order to minimize the number of interblock references.

Some work has been done on related subjects. For example Lukes (12) shows how to optimally partition a graph that is in the form of a tree. Kernighan (11) shows how to find a minimum cost partition of the nodes of a graph given the constraint that the sequence of the nodes may not be changed.

A clustering algorithm for hierarchical structures appears in Schkolnick (15). The most related work was done by Kernighan and Lin (10), where they give an algorithm to partition an arbitrary graph of 2n nodes into two even groups (2-way partition) with n nodes in each. However, they have constraints on the node sizes while we do not, and the running time of their algorithm for the general partition case is worse than ours. Clearly for a large data base the efficiency of the partitioning algorithm is important, even if it is performed only at times of creation or reorganization. The problem of finding an optimal partition can be shown to be NP-complete and therefore it is very unlikely that there exists a polynomial-time algorithm to find an optimal partition. Since achieving an optimal partition is, in general, intractable, finding efficient heuristic algorithm which approximates the optimal solution is very important.

The motivation for this research derives from a real-life data base problem. In 1965, work began on genetic information in Iceland under the supervision of the Genetic Committee of the University of Iceland (4). Iceland has records for most individuals born or living after 1703, giving a total population of approximately 670,000 individuals in 10 generations. The isolation of Iceland through the ages has resulted in insignificant immigration and emigration. An occurrence example of a small portion of this data base is shown in Figure 1. A possible query on the

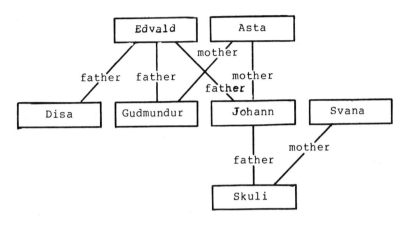

FIGURE 1   A Network Data Base Example

data base   in Figure   1 could be: "find all   descendants of

Edvald". To resolve this query   one will usually define SETs

named CHILD-OF and PARENT-OF and   then   use   these   sets

repeatedly to answer the query.   (The definition of SETs for

the example above is shown in the next section.) In the next

section, we use this example to explain the mapping   from a

network data base into a weighted directed graph.   In the

third section we present the partitioning algorithm and

comment on its time and space requirements.

II. NETWORK DATA BASE MAPPINGS

The general problem of mapping from the logical data base

structure into the storage structure is quite complicated and

has been investigated by several authors (see for example

Sibley and Taylor (16), and Astrahan et al. (2)).   The problem is somewhat simpler for a CODASYL data base, because some of the storage structure details are specified in the Schema DDL. The main tool for specifying this mapping is the SET construct. Although SETs represent logical relationships, the specification of their implementation defines clear access paths in storage. Another example is the specification of secondary indices. In this paper we do not deal with these indices although the algorithm can be generalized to include them.

There is still some freedom in choosing a storage structure for a CODASYL data base. Given a collection of record occurrences and their SET memberships, they can be partitioned into different blocks or pages. In order to improve performance, such partitioning should minimize the number of inter-page (inter-block) connections. This will then minimize the number of page faults while accessing records using the defined SETs. The frequency of various queries (i.e. of accessing different SET occurrences) could be taken into account by our algorithm but it will not be discussed here.

We assume a stable[1] network data base. Our algorithm partitions a given collection of record occurrences[2] and takes into account their logical relationships as defined in the Schema DDL. The first step is the translation from a

---

[1] If the data base is not stable then our algorithm should be applied at reorganization time.

[2] "Record" will stand for record occurrence.

collection of records into a weighted directed graph. For
the example in Figure 1 we define the data structure diagram
shown in Figure 2 (see Taylor and Frank (20) for explanation

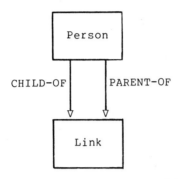

FIGURE 2   The Data Structure Diagram

of data structure diagrams). The data base model in the
example has two SET types, namely CHILD-OF and PARENT-OF.
The record type LINK is needed because of the restrictions in
CODASYL that one record type cannot be both the owner and the
member of the same SET (see also the "part explosion" example
in (20)). In Figure 3 the occurrences of the example in
Figure 1 are shown using the CHAIN mode of implementation and
in Figure 4 the same example is shown using POINTER-ARRAY
mode of implementation. Figures 3 and 4 are already in a
form of a directed graph. A node in the graph represents one
record. The size of the node is determined by the space it
takes to store the information contained in the record and
the pointers. An edge in the graph represents a pointer and
is given a weight of one, and in the case where there is more

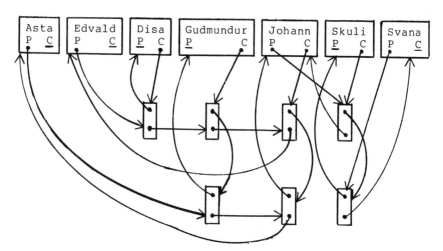

P stands for a pointer of an owner of PARENT-OF SET
C stands for a pointer of an owner of CHILD-OF SET
P and C are null pointers

FIGURE 3   A CHAIN Implementation

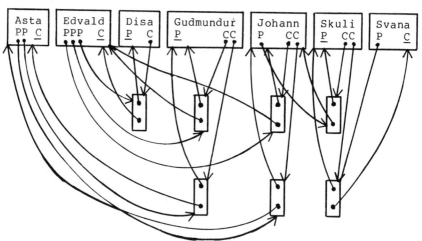

P stands for a pointer of an owner of PARENT-OF SET
C stands for a pointer of an owner of CHILD-OF SET
P and C are null pointers

FIGURE 4   A POINTER-ARRAY Implementation

than one direct edge from one node to another the weights are added. The assignment of weight of one represents our basic assumption that each record (node) and each pointer (edge) have the same probability of access. This also means that "navigation" in the data base can start at any point.

With the above construction, the data base problem has been abstracted into a graph problem. The heuristic algorithm in the next section partitions an arbitrary directed graph.

III. THE PARTITIONING ALGORITHM

The basic idea behind the algorithm is to 1) transform a weighted directed graph into a weighted undirected graph, 2) rank the edges of this graph corresponding to their likelihood of occurring in access paths, and 3) collapse the highest ranked (most likely) edges. A collapsed edge means an access path via that edge is (locally) on one page. The first step of the algorithm is to map the directed graph into an undirected one. This undirected graph is manipulated by the rest of the algorithm. The nodes in the graph represent pages, or in other words collections of nodes (records) from the original directed graph. Initially each node in the graph is assigned to a different page. An edge between two pages in the graph means that there is at least one edge between a node or nodes in one page and a node or nodes in the other page. The weight of an edge in the new graph represents the sum of the weights of all the edges in the original graph connecting some node in one page to some node in the other page. In the case where there exists an edge between two pages, but the size of the two pages does not allow them to be collapsed into one page, the edge is removed from the graph. At each basic step in the algorithm two nodes (pages), which are connected with an edge of greatest weight, are collapsed to form one node (page) and the graph is updated.

Partition Algorithm:

Input: Weighted directed graph with n nodes. Each node has
            a size associated with it.

Output: Vector A has one entry for each node and A(i)
            contains the page to which node i is assigned.

Data Structures:
            A(1,2,....,n) - Page assignment for each node.
            PC(1,2,...,n) - Page size for each page.
            Priority queue.
            Directed weighted graph.
            Reference vector.

Step 1:   Construct an undirected weighted graph from the
            directed weighted graph.
            Remove all edges from the undirected graph, which
            have the sum of the two connected node sizes greater
            than the page size.

Step 2:   Construct a priority queue of edges from the
            undirected graph.

Step 3:   Initially assign one node per page, such that for
            each i, $1 \leq i \leq n$, A(i)=i.

Step 4:   Assign the size of each node to PC, such that for
            each i, $1 \leq i \leq n$, PC(i)="size of node i".

Step 5:   Initialize a reference vector of size n to having
            all entries empty.

Step 6;   <u>While</u> priority queue is not empty <u>do</u>
           <u>begin</u>
             e := "the first edge on the priority queue"
             call procedure COLLAPSE(e)
             remove e from the priority queue
           <u>end</u>

Step 7:   For each i, $1 \leq i \leq n$, resolve indirection chain for
           A(i).

Step 8:   Merge pages which are less than half full.

In step one the weighted edges of the directed graph are changed to undirected edges. A single edge between two nodes has the same weight. Multiple edges between two nodes are replaced by one edge which carries the total weight of the directed edges. The edges connecting two nodes where the sum of the node sizes is greater than the page size are removed, since these two nodes can not belong to the same page. This step can be done in time proportional to the number of edges in the directed graph. An example of the above transformation is shown in Figure 6 which is the undirected weighted graph resulting from the directed weighted graph in Figure 5.

The undirected graph is stored in the following data structure: for every edge in the graph there is an entry containing the weight of the edge, and the two nodes n_1 and n_2 connected by the edge, and two pointers p_1 and p_2 pointing to other edges. The pointers join the edge in two circular linked lists. One list has node n_1 as a common node and the other has node n_2 as a common node. Figure 7 shows the undirected graph of figure 6 stored in this data structure.

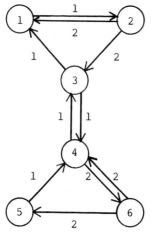

FIGURE 5   Directed Graph

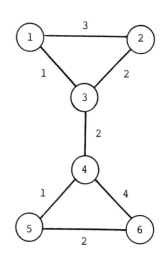

FIGURE 6   Undirected Graph

The second step constructs the priority queue in such a way that the first edge in the queue is the edge with the greatest weight.   When the weight of each directed edge is one, the maximum outdegree is D, and the maximum number of nodes that can fit on one page is ps, then the maximum weight between two pages can be shown to never exceed

   $2((D - 1)*ps + 1)$.

When the weight is always an integer number and the maximum weight between two pages is bounded by a relatively small integer, the priority queue can be constructed in the following way: double link the edges with the same weight together in arbitrary order. Use a vector H of size greater or equal to the maximum possible weight between two pages, in such a way that entry i in H points to the first edge on the double link list with weight i. See Figure 8 for better

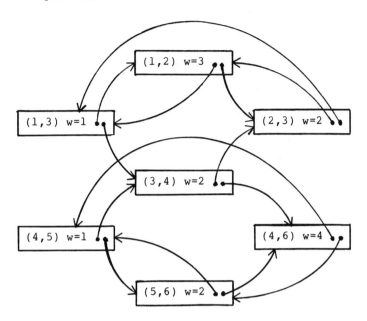

FIGURE 7   Data Structures for Edges

understanding of the above priority queue, where the undirected graph of Figure 6 is set up in the priority queue. The time it takes to construct this priority queue is proportional to the maximum possible weight (size of vector H) plus the number of edges in the undirected graph. In the case of a non-integer weight or a large range of possible integer weights, a different representation for the priority queue is required. Chapter 4 in Aho, Hopcroft and Ullman (1) explains several different methods of implementing priority queues. Note that the two data structures used in the algorithm, namely the undirected graph and the priority queue, have been presented as separate structures (as in the

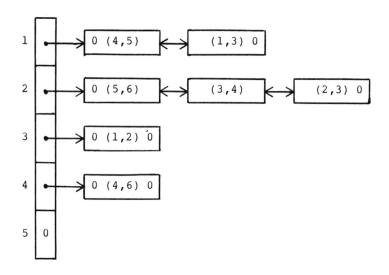

FIGURE 8   Priority Queue

examples of figures 7 and 8). In the actual implementation, these structures must be interlinked.

In step three the vector A is initialized. A is a vector of size n, that is one entry for each node which keeps track of the page to which the node is assigned. Initially there are n pages with one node in each.

Step four initializes PC, which is a vector of size n. PC(i) keeps track of the total size of all nodes assigned to page number i. Initially there is one node per page, therefore PC(i) contains the size of node i.

In step five a reference vector of size n is created. All entries in the reference vector are initially empty. The reference vector is used by COLLAPSE to temporarily store edges which might be merged with another edge, when two edges are connected to a common node, and is always restored to the empty state by COLLAPSE. If space is of concern a hash-addressed table, say of twice the page size, might be used instead.

Clearly, steps three, four and five each take time proportional to n.

Step six is the main step in the algorithm. While the priority queue is not empty, the edge with the greatest weight is selected, and its connected pages are merged into the page with smaller index by the procedure COLLAPSE and then removed from the priority queue. The number of times this step will be executed in the worst case is bounded by

$$n - \left\lceil \frac{\sum_{i=1}^{n} \text{node size}(i)}{\text{page size}} \right\rceil$$

Each iteration of step six takes time proportional to the running time of the procedure COLLAPSE (shown later in this section) plus the time it takes to remove an edge from the priority queue and retrieve the first edge on the priority queue. Depending on the priority queue used, the manipulation of the priority queue will usually take costant time.

In step seven of the algorithm, A(i) points, perhaps through a long chain of indirections, to the final assignment of i. Since A(i) is less than or equal to i, these pointers

may be resolved to direct addresses in a single linear pass
through A, of the form:

 <u>for</u> i := 1 <u>until</u> n <u>do</u> A(i) := A(A(i))

This step takes time proportional to n.

 Finally in step eight, the last step of the algorithm,
pages which are less than half full are merged together to
guarantee a packing factor of at least two.

 The COLLAPSE algorithm takes an edge e   and merges the
two pages which e connects into one page. The pages to be
merged are labeled f and s throughout the algorithm.

<u>Collapse Algorithm</u>:

COLLAPSE(e):   Let f and s be the two nodes (or pages)
connected by edge e and let f less than s.

Step 1: PC(f) := PC(f) + PC(s)
   PC(s) := 0
   A(s) := f

Step 2: Repeat this step for each e° on the list of f, where
   f and s° are the nodes connected by e°,
   <u>if</u> e° has been marked deleted <u>then</u>
    delete e° from the list of f,
   <u>else</u>
    <u>begin</u>
     <u>if</u> PC(f)+PC(s°) greater than "page size" <u>then</u>
      delete e° from the list, from the priority
      queue, and mark e° deleted
     <u>else</u> store the location of e° in position s° of
      the reference vector
    <u>end</u>.

Step 3:   Repeat this step for each edge   e° on the list of s,
          where s and f° are the nodes connected by e°.
          <u>if</u> e° has been marked as deleted <u>then</u> delete e° from
          the list of s
          <u>else</u>
            <u>begin</u>
              <u>if</u> PC(f)+PC(f°) greater than   "page size" <u>then</u>
                delete e° from the list, from the priority
                queue, and mark e° as deleted
              <u>else</u>
                <u>begin</u>
                  <u>if</u> the   position f° in the   reference vector
                    is not empty and   contains the location of
                    edge e" <u>then</u>
                    <u>begin</u>
                      set the weight of edge e" to the sum of
                      the weights of edges e° and e",
                      delete e° from the   list, from the
                      priority   queue, and   mark e°   as
                      deleted,
                      update the   priority queue with respect
                      to the new weight in e",
                    <u>end</u>
                  <u>else</u> change s to f in the edge e°
                <u>end</u>
            <u>end</u>.

Step 4:   Repeat this step for each edge   e° on the list where
          f is one of the node connected and s° is the other
          node connected by e°. Set entry s° in the reference
          vector to empty.

Step 5:   Combine the lists for f and s into one list and
          delete e from the list.

   Step one updates the page size vector and the page
assignment vector. This step takes a constant time[1].

   Step two scans all edges incident with the smaller
indexed connecting node for the collapsing edge, and the
following actions are taken: If the edge has been marked
deleted the edge is deleted from the scanned list.   In the
case where the combined size of the two connecting nodes does

―――――――――――――

[1] The times in this section refer to one call of COLLAPSE.

not allow them to be merged into one page, the edge is deleted from the scanned list and the priority queue. The edge is then marked deleted, since each edge is on two lists and can only be deleted in constant time from the currently scanned list[1]. If the edge is not deleted, then the edge is stored on the reference vector to be possibly merged with another edge, which is connected to a common node.

Step three scans all edges incident with the larger indexed connecting node for the collapsing edge, and the following actions are taken: If the edge has been marked deleted, the edge is deleted from the scanned list. In the case where the sizes of the connecting nodes do not allow them to be merged into one page, the edge is deleted. If the edge is not deleted, the reference vector is checked for an edge connected to a common node. If such an edge is found, the edge on the scanned list is merged into the edge on the reference vector by adding the weights and deleting the edge on the scaning list. The edge in the reference vector is moved in the priority queue according to the new weight. In the case where the edge on the scanned list is not deleted or merged, the index of its node which is common with the collapsing edge is changed to the smaller node index of the two connecting nodes for the collapsing edge.

---

[1] "Delete" will stand for deleting an edge from the currently scaned list, deleting the edge from the priority queue and marking the edge deleted.

The time for processing one edge in steps two and three is constant if the priority queue shown in this paper (see figure 8) is used. Therefore, the total time for steps two and three is proportional to the number of edges which have a node in common with the collapsing edge.

In step four the used entries in the reference vector are reset to empty. This step takes time proportional to the number of edges on the updated scanned list in step two.

In step five the updated scanned list from step two and the updated scanned list from step three are combined into one list. The collapsing edge is deleted from the combined list. This step takes a constant time.

Using the above timing for the collapse algorithm, the total expected running time of the partitioning algorithm can be shown to be time proportional to $n * D$, where n is the number of nodes and D is the maximum out degree. This algorithm is thus approximately linear in n (number of nodes), since for most data bases $n \gg D$. This result is similar to that derived by Schkolnick (15) for the special case of balanced trees.

The space requirements for this algorithm are approximately 7 words per edge and 3 words per node. (By assuming one word per pointer, index or weight.) Therefore the total space estimate is $3n + 7Dn$ (words). However, at any one point in the execution of the algorithm the main requirements are just the space needed for the priority queue header plus the space needed for one execution of the

COLLAPSE algorithm. This can be bounded by 30D * ps (words), which is very reasonable for most data bases. For example, for a page size of 100 records and out degree of 5, only 15K words are needed. The exact way in which this algorithm uses secondary storage is currently being investigated.

To test the heuristic we implemented the algorithm in APL and we applied it to several graphs of order up to 200 nodes. These test graphs were generated by simulation of the genetic data base mentioned in the introduction. The resulting partitons were compared to sequential and random partitions and in all cases had much superior cost. The sequential partition was derived from a "natural" order of the simulated data base, appearing similar to a breath-first-search ordering. On reasonable data the improvement was a factor of five. If the page size was absurdly small or large this factor decreased, while it increased for graphs unreasonably sparse. The resulting partitions were either optimal or very close to optimal.

IV. SUMMARY

A graph partitioning algorithm which can be used to improve the performance of network structured data base was presented. Although the number of nodes in such a data base may be very large, the time and space requirements of the algorithm are still reasonable. Future extensions of this

research will include: the inclusion of information about
query statistics, the extension of the algorithm to very
large number of nodes, the effect of page replacement and
buffering mechanisms on this and similar algorithms.

REFERENCES

(1)   Aho,A.V., Hopcroft,J.E., Ullman,J.D., The Design and
      Analysis of Computer Algorithms, (1974), Addison-Wesley,
      Reading Mass.

(2)   Astrahan,M.M., Altman,E.B., Fehder,P.L., Senko,M.E.,
      Concepts of a Data Independent Accessing Model, 1972 ACM
      SIGFIDET Workshop, Data Description, Access and Control,
      Denver, Colorado, (November 1972), pp.349-362.

(3)   Astrahan,M.M., Blasgen,M.W., Chamberlin,D.D.,
      Eswaran,K.P., Gray,J.N., Griffiths,P.P., King,W.F.,
      Lorie,R.A., McJones,P.R., Mehl,J.W., Putzolu,G.R.,
      Traiger,I.L., Wade,B.W., Watson,V., System R: Relational
      Approach to Database Management, ACM Transactions on
      Database Systems, 1, 2, (June 1976), pp.97-137.

(4)   Bjarnason,O., Fridriksson,S, Magnusson,M., Record
      Linkage in a Self-Contained Community, Record Linkage in
      Medicine, Oxford 1976.

(5)   CODASYL, Database Task Group Report, (April 1971), ACM.

(6)   CODASYL, Programming Language Committee Proposal,
      (February 1973).

(7)   CODASYL, CODASYL Data Description Language Committee
      Journal of Development, (June 1973).

(8)   Cullinane Corporation, Integrated Database Management
      System Program and Reference.

(9)   Fry,J.P., Sibley,E.H., Evolution of Data-Base Management
      Systems, ACM Computing Surveys, 8, 1, (March 1976),
      pp.7-42.

(10) Kernighan,B.W., Lin,S., An Efficient Heuristic Procedure
      for Partitioning Graphs, Bell System Technical Journal,
      49, 2, (February 1970), pp.291-307.

(11) Kernighan,B.W., Optimal Sequential Partitions of Graphs, Journal of ACM, 18, 1, (January 1971), pp.34-40.

(12) Lukes,J.A., Efficient Algorithm for the Partitioning of Trees, IBM Journal of Research and Development, 18, 3, (May 1974), pp.217-224.

(13) Michaels,A.S., Mittman,B.: Carlson,C.R., A Comparison of the Relational and CODASYL Approaches to Data-Base management, ACM Computing Surveys, 8, 1, (March 1976), pp.125-151.

(14) Mitoma,M.F., Irani,K.B., Automatic Data Base Schema Design and Optimization, Proceedings of the International Conference on Very Large Data Bases, 1, 1, (September 1975), pp.286-321.

(15) Schkolnick,M., A Clustering Algorithm for Hierarchical Structures, ACM Transactions on Database Systems, 2, 1, (March 1977), pp.27-44.

(16) Sibley,E.H., Taylor,R.W., A Data Definition and Mapping Language, Communication of ACM, 16, 12, (December 1973), pp.750-759.

(17) Sperry Rand Corp., UNIVAC 1100 Series, Data Management System (DMS 1100) Schema Definition, Data Administrator Reference, (1972,1973).

(18) Stonebraker,M., Wong,E., Kreps,P., Held,G., The Design and Implementation of INGRES, ACM Transactions on Database Systems, 1, 3, (September 1976), pp.189-222.

(19) Taylor,R.W., When are Pointer Arrays Better than Chains, Proc. ACM National Conference, (November 1974), p.735.

(20) Taylor,R.W., Frank,R.L., CODASYL Data-Base Management Systems, ACM Computing Surveys, 8, 1, (March 1976), pp.67-103.

Distributed Systems

MULTI-STAGE DATA DEFINITION
IN A MULTI-COMPONENT DBMS ARCHITECTURE

T. William Olle

T. William Olle Associates, Ltd.
West Byfleet, Surrey
England

I. BACKGROUND

The aim of this paper is to present an interpretation of
the multi-level architecture which was suggested in the 1975
and 1977 reports by ANSI/X3/SPARC (1,2) and also to comment on
the important ideas of a "conceptual schema". Since the
publication of these reports, there has been widespread discussion at conferences (3) about the idea of a conceptual
schema. The need for something along these lines appears to
be widely accepted and there is some measure of agreement on
its role. Nevertheless, there have been widely diverging
views presented about what it should contain.

Some of the controversy has arisen because the thinking in
each ANSI/X3/SPARC report can be given several different interpretations. Both reports are discursive and in many places
expository, but do not attempt to be definitive. This has
lead to a situation where there is indeed agreement on broad
concepts, but controversy on the interpretation of the somewhat narrower issues. The present paper focuses on some of
the narrower issues in an attempt to clarify them and thereby
expedite recognition of where consensus is called for.

II. TERMINOLOGY

The present paper adopts the ANSI/X3/SPARC 1975 terminology to a very large extent. The terms item, record type and

<u>relationship</u> are used to refer to the principal constructs at
each level (or stage) in the overall architecture. To distinguish between the elements at different levels, the name of a
construct may be qualified, using the name of the level - for
example conceptual record type.

To avoid imputing any difference between the words "<u>data</u>"
and "<u>information</u>" other than that implied in the IFIP glossary
(4), the word "data" is preferred throughout. "Information"
is noted as having the following definition:

> "In automatic data processing, the meaning that a human
> assigns to data by means of the known conventions used in
> its representation."

In less formal words, information, like beauty, is in the eyes
of the beholder.

In order to define the overall DBMS architecture more precisely, a number of "<u>formalisms</u>" will be needed. A formalism
is often a graphic formalism (one classic example being
Bachman diagrams), but not necessarily so.

The formalism of system schematics used in both ANSI/SPARC
reports is not used in the present paper. This is partly because the use of the formalism tends to be overloaded and
hence attempts to convey too much in one picture. Since this
paper attempts to present one interpretation rather than
several, a more rigid formalism is sought.

The word "<u>schema</u>" is used widely in all discussions on
data base management. In this paper it is taken to imply a
"description usually of data structure elements and their properties". One problem which arises with respect to "schema"
is whether it includes procedures or not. For the purpose of
this paper, a schema (on any level or at any stage) may include an invocation by name of a set of procedure statements,
but it does not include the procedure statements themselves.
Hence, the word "schema" must convey the idea of a template
used to form occurrences of what it describes. This is felt
to be consistent with the every day use of the word "schema"
in natural languages other than English.

Another word widely used in DBMS discussions is "<u>model</u>".
Generically speaking, the most important idea which this word

conveys is that of a representation of something, using material other than that in the original. It is proposed to use
this word only in 'its generic sense and with no special
meaning.

The role of a "data dictionary" is an issue which ANSI/X3/
SPARC alluded to in passing. Although the term has clearly
acquired a free-standing meaning in a non-DBMS oriented environment, in the framework of an overall DBMS architecture
the role is necessarily more integrated. In the context of
the present paper, a data dictionary is essentially a meta
data base containing data about data. This may be gathered
by translating the data definitions associated with the various schema levels and also from compiling application programs. It is noted that the first attempt to prepare a conceptual schema in an enterprise may be with a data dictionary
but not with a DBMS.

The word "mapping" is widely used in DBMS literature to
imply that some kind of transformation takes place. In this
paper, "mapping" is used only in the sense of something which
is defined in terms of a source image and a target image. If
a mapping is defined, then a transformation may take place.
One could say that a transformation is an instance of a
mapping. The different classes of mapping will be described
in the appropriate section.

III. HISTORICAL TRENDS

In the beginning (about 1959 to 1965), there was only one
component -- the now standardized programming languages for
commercial data processing. The definition of the data and
the definition of the process to be performed on the data were
all embodied or even interwoven in the one language.

Some users soon recognized the value of separating the
data definition out completely from the specification of the
"process to be performed on the data". Some did it by making
use of a library of file definitions (the COBOL COPY library)
and this trend was clear in some of the DBMS emerging around
1965 to 1968.

The next concept to emerge was that of a separate "sub-schema" which the CODASYL DBTG incorporated in their 1969 report, although it pre-dates that work. At the same time, the DBTG identified a capability referred to as the Device Media Control Language, thereby bringing the potential total number of components up to four. In 1975, the CODASYL DDLC working group based in the United Kingdom, namely DBAWG - Data Base Administration Working Group - in their report (5) defined the capabilities required in such a facility but changing the name to Data Storage Description Language (DSDL).

The ANSI/SPARC reports describe an architecture containing more components than ever previously suggested. In doing so, it created its own new terminology base which means that some effort is called for in relating to the combined components of CODASYL.

The components which ANSI/SPARC identify, of interest in the present paper, are the following:

```
Conceptual schema (interface 1)
Internal schema (interface 13)
External schema (interface 4)
Application programmer (interface 7).
```

The conceptual schema must be identified as the new corner-stone in any proposed overall DBMS architecture. Since an analogous concept is not provided in any DBMS in commercial use today, it is appropriate to examine its characteristics and potential uses in more detail.

IV. CHARACTERISTICS OF A CONCEPTUAL SCHEMA

A conceptual schema has the following characteristics.

1. It is independent of any consideration of how the data will be stored in computerized or non-computerized storage.

2. It is independent of any consideration of whether a commercial DBMS or conventional techniques will be used to manage the data in the data base. In the case of a commercial DBMS being used, therefore, it is independent of which one is involved.

3. It is as independent as possible of the programs or queries which will be prepared to process the data in the data base.

V. POTENTIAL ROLES FOR A CONCEPTUAL SCHEMA

It is intended to fulfil a number of roles in the enterprise in which it is used, as follows:

1. Provide a model of the enterprise's entity types of interest and possibly also of the attributes associated with each entity type.

2. Provide a description of the enterprise's data base in non-technical terms which can be used in discussions between data processing personnel and others in the enterprise.

3. Serve as an important stage in the overall data base design process as performed by the data base designer (normally a data administrator). In this role, it serves as a control point in the design process.

4. Serve as a point of reference in situations when an enterprise is either moving from conventional files towards a data base oriented approach or changing from one DBMS to another.

5. Serve as a point of reference in situations when the data base administrator wishes to redesign the access paths through his data structures. The conceptual schema serves as a definition of the original requirements rather than of how they were implemented.

6. Serve as a level of abstraction of the data base to those involved in the preparation of programs and queries, who do not wish to take advantage of more storage oriented, DBMS oriented or processing oriented views of other subsequent schema levels in the overall architecture.

These six roles will be referred to more succinctly in the remainder of this paper in the following terms:

1. Enterprise model
2. Non-technical description
3. Stage in design process
4. Aid at conversion time

5. Frame of reference for redesign

6. Programmer level of abstraction.

The above six roles bear comparison with the five benefits
listed in the cover memorandum to the ANSI/X3/SPARC 1975 report. These may be summarized as follows:

1. Formalized information model

2. Frame of reference, repository for information require-
    ments, beginnings of data dictionary

3. Authority for resolving security and integrity problems

4. Reducing number of possible mappings when other levels
    proliferate

5. Insulating other levels (specifically external schemas)
    from changes.

All five benefits are acknowledged, but the aim in citing
the above six roles has been to present a position on the
conceptual schema in terms which can be understood independently of the detailed discussion of the ensuing sections.
Each role of a conceptual schema will be discussed in turn.

V.1 Enterprise Model and Description in non-EDP Terms

These two roles are so closely related that it is useful
to discuss them together. It is considered to be a useful
activity for an enterprise to produce a conceptual schema.
Such an activity should be independent of the extent to which
the data concerning parts of the enterprise are computerized
and also independent of the techniques already used (conventional DP, DBMS, tub files, micro-fiche, notebooks).

For enterprises already using computers for data processing, parts of the conceptual schema often exist already,
buried in or interwoven with declarations which are concerned
with how the data is stored in computerized storage and how
the data is to be processed. The aim of the activity above in
such a situation would then often be one of distilling the
conceptual schema from the existing material rather than
creating something in a vacuum.

V.2 Stage in Design Process

A DBMS is usually regarded as a tool used in designing an
information system. Information systems design can be divided
into a number of stages (such as a feasibility study) depending on how the word "design" is interpreted. Nevertheless,
the phrase "stage in the design process" is meant to imply
that there may well be earlier stages and there would certainly be subsequent ones. Much of the controversy raging around
the composition of a conceptual schema can be attributed to
the fact that some observers feel that the term "conceptual
schema" as introduced by ANSI/X3/SPARC should in fact represent an even earlier stage in the design process than others
feel.

In simple terms, the process of information systems
design can be seen as gradually deciding on a number of
factors. For example, it is impossible to regard the term
"conceptual schema" as referring to what is generated at the
end of a stage during which representatives of the following
kinds of factors are chosen for inclusion.

1. Entity types with their attributes
2. Attributes of these entity types and their permitted values
3. Relationships between entity types
4. Validation criteria.

There could exist earlier stages than this example and the
intent is to recognize fully the viability of a point at which
less factors than the four in the above list are decided on.
There is a body of opinion which contends that assigning
attributes to entity types at the initial stage represents a
storage oriented decision. Hence, the term "conceptual schema"
should be used to refer to a stage earlier than the one in
which attributes are grouped into or assigned to entity types.

As another example, there is often a decision involved on
whether a given concept should be treated as an entity type,
an attribute of another entity type, or possibly a relationship between two entity types. At a design point preceding
the one associated herein with a conceptual schema, such decisions would not need to be made. Later in the design process, such decision would have been made.

The reason why a conceptual schema should be earlier in
the design process than that proposed by ANSI/SPARC in 1975 is
that the latter included explicit provision for a "conceptual
plex" in addition to the factors conceptual record type and
conceptual item (here called entity type and attribute). The
decisions called for in the development of a conceptual schema
containing such constructs are indeed influenced by processing
considerations. With this in mind, the potential value of a
conceptual level programming language is emphasized. Use of
such a language could occur during the same design stage as
that in which the conceptual schema is prepared.

It must be reasserted here that a conceptual schema is a
description and, furthermore, a description which is prepared
using a language and which can be translated into computerized
form. It is quite conceivable that an earlier stage, taking
into account only some of the factors necessary as input to
preparing the conceptual schema, could also have a language
and be computerizable. Furthermore, any kind of conceptual
schema could conceivably be computer generated. Such an
approach may emerge and become accepted by practitioners
during the coming decade.

V.3 Aid at Conversion Time

During the course of existence of an enterprise, the
approach to data processing may change several times. For
instance, a move may be made from the conventional data processing technology of the sixties, still in wide and successful use during the seventies, to a DBMS oriented approach.
At some point it may be felt desirable to change from one DBMS
oriented approach to another. It is felt that a conceptual
schema should be inviolate to such mutations, although clearly
it is much less independent of changes in the way the enterprise conducts its business.

If there is no conceptual schema, then any conversion
from one approach to another would tend to be more haphazard.
Unfortunately, the value of this assertion is likely to be

obscured by the fact that designers tend to take advantage of
the conversion process and introduce extensions. Such extensions can well be of the kind which causes the conceptual
schema itself to be extended.

V.4 Frame of Reference for Redesign

Business changes fairly frequently and as a result of this
it is natural to expect that the conceptual schema in its role
as a model of the enterprise will also change.

The conceptual schema plays an important role in the overall architecture in that it enables the non-technical person
to appreciate the significance of any change with the same
facility as he can assess the applicability of the conceptual
schema when it is presented to him as a stage in the design
process. The conceptual view is uncluttered by the kind of
storage and processing oriented factors which at present in-
hibit meaningful communication between DP technicians and non-
technical people.

V.5 Programmer Level of Abstraction

The role of the conceptual schema as a level of abstraction for the programmer or enquiry specifier is an important
role which hopefully will become clearer while elaborating
the place of a conceptual schema in the overall architecture
suggested here.

In proposing this as an important role, it is recognized
that it is beyond the state of practice today. At present,
all application programs written to process the data in a data
base have a perspective on that data which is dictated completely by the DBMS managing the data. A higher level of
interface appears technically feasible, as will be proposed.

It is also important to note that the word "programmer"
is used here in the very broadest possible sense. It includes
not only the programmer using a procedural language such as
COBOL or PL/I, but also the person using a query language or

non-procedural update specification language. This implies a
point of view that the procedurality level of a programming
language and the level of abstraction of the data base used
are essentially independent.

VI. FACETS OF AN ARCHITECTURE

Much of the controversy which arises in DBMS discussions
stems from interpretation of terminology and formalisms used.
Based on the debates which have ensued from interpretations
of the ANSI/X3/SPARC thinking, an attempt is made in the
interpretation given here to use tighter terminology and
formalisms.

With respect to the latter, one of the cornerstones in the
ANSI/X3/SPARC reports is the use of the so-called "system
schematics". These are certainly useful for giving an overview of what the components are called for in the overall
architecture, and where the critical man-machine interfaces
are. A double arrowed line between two graphics is claimed to
represent a "data, command, program or description flow". The
effect of this is that any diagram using the formalism is
grossly overloaded with ideas and subject to a range of
interpretations.

The description of the overall architecture is here broken
down into four compatible aspects. An architect designing a
house does not include everything in one diagram. He will
show floor plans, side elevations, site plans and so on. The
fact that all may be on one large sheet of paper is somewhat
incidental.

The four aspects of the overall architecture considered
here at the following:

1. Packaging of design decisions into components.

2. Sequences in which components may be used (ie. permitted
    sequences for feeding design decisions into the computer).

3. Static relationship among different classes of schema.

4. Mappings invoked during execution of application programs.

These four aspects are very much inter-related and the above sequence is felt to be the most useful for purposes of exposition.

VI.1 Packaging of Design Decisions

As one attempts to provide improved flexibility, there is a clear trend towards increasing the number of components in the overall architecture. However, there is a point of diminishing return in this exercise as if the number of components increases beyond a certain limit, the DBMS becomes over-compartmentalized and the relationships among components increase correspondingly.

The strategy adopted here is to increase the number beyond four, but not too far beyond. The conceptual schema itself is a new component. Since a level of programmer interface is associated with the conceptual schema, this introduces yet another.

It is necessary to take into account the number of commercially available data base management systems in worldwide use. While the ANSI/X3/SPARC work attempts this, it is open to interpretation whether it was achieved or not.

A component is defined in terms of its role in the overall architecture. It is useful to distinguish between components in which some properties of the data are described and components in which actions to be performed on the data are specified. This perpetuates the already traditional dichotomy between data definition and program (or procedure). It is further proposed to divide the data definition process into global and local, where global refers to the whole data base and local refers to the definition or selection of some subview for subsequent use by a programmer. These terms were used in the report (6) by the British Computer Society Data Dictionary Systems Working Party. The distinction is compatible with the CODASYL division conveyed by the terms schema and sub-schema. It could be what was intended by the ANSI/X3/SPARC terms internal and external schema, although some observers feel that the external schema is the CODASYL schema and that one can define external schema in terms of one already defined.

Further packaging strategy relates to the global view of the data definition stages. At least three such stages can be identified as follows:

1. Conceptual schema   Independent of any present day
                                                        DBMS.

2. Implementation schema)   Typically combined into one in a
3. Storage schema   )   present day DBMS.

The term "implementation schema" is preferred to "internal schema" in order to convey the implication of a present day data definition facility such as that in the Schema DDL of a CODASYL based system or in the IMS Data Base Description.

The possibility of splitting the conceptual schema into two stages should be mentioned again. It is also possible to conceive of splitting either the implementation schema or the storage schema into two or more stages, but one of these is discussed further in presenting this paper's packaging strategy.

Figure 1 shows which components are envisioned and how they are categorized with respect to the various packaging criteria in the overall strategy. In present day commercial DBMS there is considerable merging from among the nine components identified of two or more components into one component.

For example, the following components are not catered for in commercially available DBMS based on the CODASYL thinking as published up to 1975.

Conceptual sub-schema

Conceptual level program language

Storage sub-schema

Low level storage DML.

VII. DISCUSSION OF COMPONENTS

Each of the nine components will now be discussed in turn, following a row-wise sequence through the table.

	GLOBAL	LOCAL	
	DATA DEFINITION		PROGRAM SPECIFICATION
Independent of present day DBMS	Conceptual schema	Conceptual sub-schema	Procedural program. Non-procedural query or update.
Part of present day DBMS (explicitly or implicitly)	Implementation schema	Implementation sub-schema	Existing pro-gramming language/ DML pairing
	Storage schema	Storage sub-schema	Low level storage oriented DML

FIGURE 1.   Table of components in overall architecture.

VII.1 Conceptual Schema

In the rest of this paper, the term "conceptual schema" refers to a DBMS component used to define the entity types, the attributes of each, and the relationships required between pairs of entity types. It should include facilities for specifying the validation criteria which the data must satisfy. It is recognized that the definition of access control locks (or privacy locks) should be made on the conceptual level, but in view of the confidential nature of such locks, it is felt that their definition should be performed in a component separate from that for the conceptual schema definition.

Specifically excluded from the conceptual schema are factors such as the following:

Intra-record structures (eg. data aggregates, repeating groups.
Mappings to storage (eg. access method and location mode).
Search keys.
Control over physical contiguity in storage.
internal identifications (eg. data base keys).

VII.2 Conceptual Sub-schema

A conceptual sub-schema is best thought of as a special kind of ANSI/X3/SPARC external schema. It consists of some

(or possibly all) of the entity types defined in the conceptual
schema. For each entity type included in a sub-schema, it is
possible to include some or all of the attributes defined for
it in the conceptual schema. The same applies to relationships defined in the conceptual schema between any two entity
types included in the sub-schema.

VII.3 Conceptual Level Programming Language

Two classes of conceptual level programming language are
considered applicable here, referred to for convenience as the
procedural and the non-procedural. The first of these would
consist of a set of extensions to an existing programming
language. The second would consist of a set of self-contained
language features (independent of any programming language),
with which a pre-definable range of queries and updates could
be specified.

In the case of the non-procedural language, it could be
desirable to impose constraints on the sub-schema view permitted. If this is not done, the semantics of the non-
procedural language become so complex that the user would soon
learn to prefer the procedural.

VII.4 Implementation Schema

The implementation schema has already been mentioned as an
interpretation of the ANSI/X3/SPARC idea of an internal schema
(although some observers would equate it with an external
schema). The entity types. attributes and relationships of
the conceptual schema are used as a basis for defining a view
of the data base which is compatible with that of a commercially available present day DBMS.

There are at least two ways in which the progression from
conceptual schema to implementation schema could be handled.
One is that the conceptual schema processor translates input
declarations into an internal computerized form which could be
the foundations of a data dictionary. The implementation
schema definer must then base his input to the implementation
schema translator on the conceptual schema, taking

responsibility for compatibility and consistency. Another way
would be to have a conceptual schema translator which <u>auto-
matically</u> prepares input to the implementation schema translator using standard translation algorithms. In this latter
case, the conceptual schema translator would be essentially a
preprocessor to a present day DBMS.

This kind of mappings between a conceptual schema and an
implementation schema are illustrated in the following list
(with the commercial DBMS where they might apply indicated):

1. Two entity types related by a one to many relationship are
   coagulated to form a structured implementation record type
   (ADABAS, CODASYL, IMS).

2. An extra record type is introduced to handle a many to
   many conceptual relationship. Two one to many relationships replace the one many to many relationship (CODASYL,
   IMS, TOTAL).

3. Introduce and name a new construct (such as a hierarchy)
   built up from the implementation record types (IMS).

4. An extra record type and an extra relationship are introduced to handle a restriction on the number of implementation record types that a record type can be in a
   subordinate relationship to (IMS).

5. An extra implementation record type and an extra relationship are introduced to handle a situation when an entity
   type is defined as a subordinate in a one to many conceptual relationship and parent in another conceptual
   relationship (TOTAL).

6. One or more items in an implementation record type are
   defined as having a specific role with respect to the
   implementation record type such as prime key, search key,
   sequencer (all).

7. Each item is assigned a type which dictates how values of
   the item will be stored (all).

8. An entity type is split into two or more implementation
   record types (all).

The above list is not intended to be complete, but at least comprehensive enough to indicate the role played by an implementation schema. There could be as many implementation schemas as there are present day DBMS taken into account in the overall architecture.

An architectural problem is introduced if one wishes to cater for the situation where an enterprise is using two different DBMS. This in itself is no problem, but it becomes pertinent if and when the enterprise wishes to handle one collection of stored data using two (or more) DBMS. This is identified as a "cohabitation problem".

VII.5 Implementation Sub-schema

An implementation sub-schema is an interpretation of the ANSI/SPARC external schema. Some (or possibly all) of the implementation record types defined in the implementation schema are selected for inclusion. For each such record type selected, it is possible to include any sub-structure. Relationships may also be included implicitly (where they depend on item duplication) and explicitly.

VII.6 Implementation Level Manipulation Sub-language

This is the language provided in present day DBMS through typical DML facilities. As on the conceptual level, there could be two classes of interface applicable - the procedural and the non-procedural. However, there may not be any essential difference between a conceptual level non-procedural language and an implementation level non-procedural language.

It is noted that existing programming languages provide facilities for manipulating intra-record type structures.

VII.7 Storage Schema

If the implementation schema is treated as an interpretation of the ANSI/SPARC external schema, then the storage

schema must be regarded as an interpretation of their internal
schema. If the implementation schema is treated as an interpretation of the ANSI/SPARC internal schema, then this storage
schema is not catered for in ANSI/SPARC's thinking.

A storage schema contains a detailed definition of how the
data defined in an implementation schema would be stored.
A good example is the Data Storage Description Language of
DBAWG (5). It would include definition of such factors as
the following:

1. Control over physical contiguity of records of one type.

2. Control over physical contiguity of records of different
    types.

3. Item level storage control (packed decimal, binary).

4. Definition of compaction algorithms and the internal
    representation of null values.

5. Assignment of collections of record types to different
    classes of storage media.

The relationship between the implementation level sub--
language and the storage schema is an important one. It is
proposed that only factors which the implementation level
programmer does not need to be aware of may be included in the
storage schema. Hence, for a given DBMS, the design of a
storage schema facility is predicated on the design of the
implementation level programming sub-language. In present day
DBMS, those storage schema declarations provided are woven
into the implementation schema declarations.

VII.8 Storage Sub-schema and Storage Level
Manipulation Sub-language

These two must be discussed together because the merits of
their inclusion in an overall architecture is open to debate.
One could not be included without the other. If included,
they would provide a capability for the kind of user who is
prepared to sacrifice data independence for system performance
by preparing programs on a very physical level.

VIII. SEQUENCE OF DESIGN DECISIONS

There are several feasible sequences in which a selection
of nine components may be used. In order to depict these
sequences, some kind of graphic formalism is needed. It is
also important to depict the nature of the decision involved
when a given sequence is followed.

Such a graphic formalism needs to convey not only the
precedence succeedence aspect of critical path methods, but
also the decisions. The decisions involved in the overall
process are all human decisions and not the kind of decision
one could yet computerize. At the risk of introducing an
element of confusion with conventional programmers' flow
charts, a flow chart like formalism is used.

The permitted sequences are shown in Figure 2. It must be
noted that the following conventions are followed:

1. A rectangle represents a component in the overall
   architecture.

2. A diamond represents a human decision.

3. An arrow represents a precedence succeedence direction
   between two components, between two decisions or between
   one of each.

Each rectangle and diamond in Figure 2 is numbered. This
is to provide a shorthand for the definition of a number of
feasible paths through the chart.

Decision box 2 calls for explanation. Whether the decision is meaningful or not depends on how the conceptual schema
to implementation schema mapping is handled (see Section
VII.4). It is also possible that no present day DBMS is used
at all, in which case the path 1, 3, 4 is mandatory. If a
present day DBMS is used, and if a standard conceptual schema
to implementation schema mapping is built into the conceptual
schema translator, then this means that "define implementation
schema" (box 5) is implicit in box 1, and the "Yes" decision
line is followed. If there are no standard mappings built in to
the conceptual schema translator, then conceivably there is a
choice. One could go on to define the implementation schema
as if using a present day DBMS. Alternatively, there may be

the alternative to define conceptual level programs quite independently of the present day DBMS (even though one could go
that way if desired).

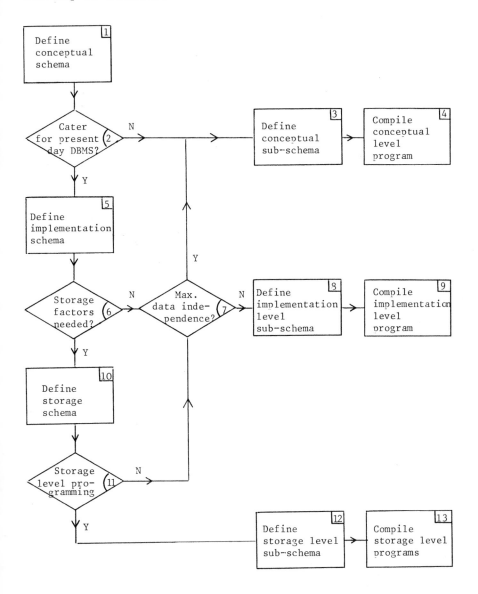

FIGURE 2.   Feasible sequences in the use of components

VIII.1 Path Independent of Present Day DBMS

This path (A) takes the sequence 1, 2, 3, 4.

It is possible that a DBMS (in today's sense) is being used but in a very real sense "behind the scenes". This means that the piece of software processing the conceptual schema has a "back end" which is allied to the DBMS being used. An implementation schema is generated automatically, because the conceptual to implementation mapping is "built in". The alternative is that one of today's DBMS is <u>not</u> being used in any sense. Effectively, one then has a three component system (conceptual schema, conceptual sub-schema and conceptual programming language).

In view of the fact that the conceptual level programmer's view involves cognizance by the programmer of the fewest possible factors, this is ipso facto a data independent path.

VIII.2 Path Dependent on Present Day DBMS
but Data Independent

This path takes one of the following sequences:

B = 1, 2, 5, 6, 7, 3, 4
or else
C = 1, 2, 5, 6, 10, 11, 7, 3, 4

These paths end up at the same level of programmer interface (namely the conceptual). However, in C, the storage schema is explicitly defined whereas in path B the system defaults for the factors otherwise defined in the storage schema would be accepted. From this aspect C is a more performance oriented path than A or B and is in fact the path which effectively offers the best of both worlds.

VIII.3 Path Dependent on Present Day DBMS
but Medium Data Independent

The two paths in this category would be:

D = 1, 2, 5, 6, 7, 8, 9
or

E = 1, 2, 5, 6, 10, 11, 7, 8, 9

with the difference being the same as that between B and C.
However, in these two, the implementation level programmer
interface is used, hence giving more programmer control over
performance at the expense of less data independence.

VIII.4 Path Dependent on Present Day DBMS
with Optimum Performance

This path follows the sequence:

F = 1, 2, 5, 6, 10, 11, 12, 13

and allows for the situation where the programmer is able to
use detailed knowledge of how the records are stored in order
to optimize system performance. Data independence is
sacrificed.

IX. RELATIONSHIPS AMONG DIFFERENT
CLASSES OF SCHEMA

It is assumed, purely for convenience, that for a given
enterprise there would be only one conceptual schema. Furthermore, if the enterprise does only conceptual level processing,
then there would be many conceptual sub-schemas, but no sub-
schemas on any other level.

The number of implementation schemas is a more difficult
question. If the enterprise uses one present day DBMS, then
it is convenient to say that there is only one implementation
schema. If the enterprise uses two or more DBMS, then it is
permissible for there to be a corresponding number of implementation schemas. Whether these may co-exist at application
program execution time depends on the approach taken to the
co-habitation problem.

This problem also affects the relationship between implementation schema and storage schema. For any one implementation schema, there may be defined one or more storage
schemas. No two storage schemas of the same implementation
schema would normally co-exist at application program
execution time.

IX.1 Co-habitation Problems

The co-habitation problem arises where two present day
DBMS are used in an enterprise either for internal non-
technical reasons or because one DBMS (and therefore one
implementation schema) is about to replace another. In either
case, it would be advantageous to handle the situation where
data stored under the aegis of one DBMS can be accessed
(possibly only for retrieval purposes) by the implementation
sub-language of another.

To handle this situation, one DBMS would clearly need to
play a dominant role and the other a subservient role. There
would need to be a "bridgeware" component associated with the
subservient DBMS to enable it to access the data which is
essentially under control of the dominant DBMS.

If the enterprise is replacing one DBMS by another, then
the one being replaced will be the dominant one until programs
written using the new DBMS are fully operational. If the
enterprise has an on-going commitment to use two DBMS, then
for any data base, one of the two must be dominant.

Further aspects of this co-habitation problem are considered later in the discussion of execution time mapping.

Another co-habitation problem arises when using only one
DBMS. This is on the storage schema level only. The capability for two storage schemas of a given implementation
schema to co-habit (at execution time) is needed in an information system providing uninterruptable on line query service.
When it is necessary to re-organize the stored data, that is
to say modify the storage schema, then the old and new storage
schemas must be able to co-habit.

IX.2 Sub-schema Relationships

For a given implementation schema there may be one or more
implementation sub-schemas. These may not only overlap, but
also they may co-exist at program execution time. A program
invokes one sub-schema only, but a given sub-schema may be
invoked by one or more programs even if these programs are

concurrently executing. Whether each executing program has
its own private copy of the sub-schema used is an implementation detail not considered here.

The relationships among a storage schema, its storage sub-
schemas and the programs which invoke the sub-schemas are
identical to that on the implementation level.

The complete picture of the relationships between different kinds of schemas is depicted graphically in Figure 3.
Each box represents some "schema type" and the relationships
are the typical kinds of relationships used in entity relationship models and Bachman diagrams.

X. MAPPINGS INVOKED DURING
EXECUTION OF PROGRAMS

There are two aspects which affect what a computer programmer "sees" of the data base. The first is the level (ie.
conceptual, implementation or storage) and the second is the
sub-schema. The level affects the kind of structural elements
he sees (and which of their properties) and the sub-schema
decides how many of the structure elements.

Between the programmer's view of the data and the data as
stored in the data base, there may be a number of transformation stages. A conceptual level view is probably furthest
away from the stored data and hence the most transformations
may occur. A storage level view, on the other hand, is quite
close to the storage and there would normally be no need for
transformations. Each view will be considered in turn.

X.1 Conceptual Level View

On this level, the programmer is cognizant of the following factors: entity types, the attributes of each, and the
relationships between entity types. The data base designer
may also have specified an implementation schema (if he used
path B) and possibly also a storage schema (if he used path
C). The programmer need have no cognizance of either of these
but if he does, he may be able to choose between differently
functioning DML constructs in an attempt to optimize performance.

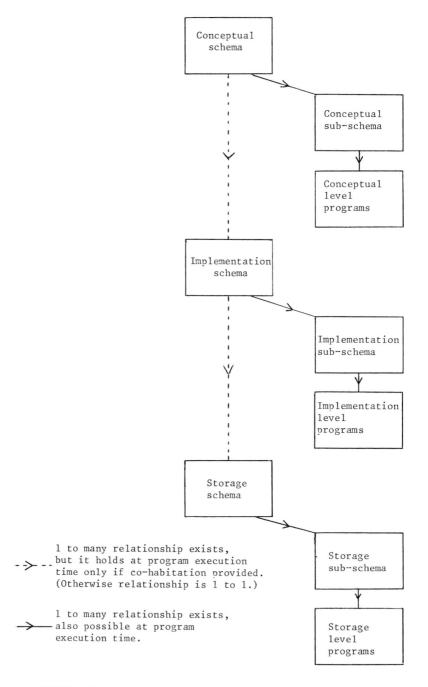

FIGURE 3.   Existence relationships among schema classes
                    and programs

The following aspects of the mapping between conceptual level and implementation level must be taken into account at execution time.

1. A conceptual entity type may be represented on the implementation level as part of an implementation record type. This means that the entity type has been defined to have some kind of conceptual relationship with the other entity type or types included in the implementation record type. Such a relationship would either be 1:1 or 1:M.

2. A conceptual entity type may be partitioned on the implementation level into two or more implementation record types. In view of the constraints on defining conceptual entity types, the relationship between any two such implementation record types must be 1:1. In other words, part of an entity type may be defined as an implementation record type. (The remaining part of the entity type may even be omitted from the implementation schema.)

3. The constraints of the present day DBMS associated with the implementation level may cause the creation of extra records at execution time when a new entity is added to the data base. An example of this phenomenon is the relationship record type needed in most DBMS to handle a M:N relationship. Coversely, when an entity is retrieved in a conceptual level program, the system may need to access other records, but the program should not be aware of this.

4. Item level mappings are dictated by the item type dictated in the implementation schema.

5. The system must ensure that the relationships defined in the conceptual schema are properly represented in storage when a new entity is added to the data base.

X.2 Implementation Level View

Each implementation level view corresponds to that of some DBMS which is commercially available today. However, no such DBMS includes a conceptual schema in its architecture. In today's DBMS, the conceptual schema declaration factors are

woven into the implementation schema. Hence, the implementation schema includes the factors which control how the entity
types, attributes and relationships are represented. There
is no execution time transformation called for other than that
implied in the mapping between the implementation sub-schema
and the implementation schema.

An illustration of the latter kind of mapping can be seen
in IMS, where the implementation schema must define the conceptual schema data base as a number of hierarchical structures (physical data bases) with extra relationships (so-
called logical relationships) permitted between different
hierarchies. In its implementation sub-schema, a sub-view
must consist of a number of hierarchical structures (logical
data bases) with no relationships allowed other than those
defined in the implementation schema.

X.3 Storage Level View

It must be emphasized that the storage level view is one
which is even more storage oriented than that of the implementation schema. Some of the implementation schemas of
existing DBMS are already considered by some to be very
storage oriented. However, the designers of these systems
with the two or three component packing strategy which they
have used, have tried to avoid providing manipulation facilities which are very storage oriented. In a nine component
architecture, this is less important and a storage level data
manipulation language facility could be provided. There
would probably be no execution time transformation for data
invoked at this level.

X.4 Co-habitation Problems

In the section discussing the relationships between the
different classes of schema, co-habitation problems were
identified on the implementation schema level and storage
schema level. Clearly, both of these call for specific
execution time mappings. The situations are depicted graphically in Figures 4 and 5.

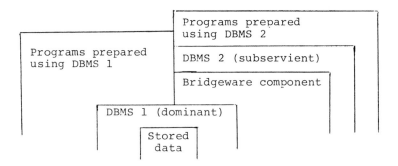

FIGURE 4.   Co-habitation problem at execution time
            (two implementation schemas)

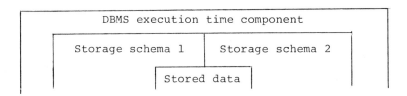

FIGURE 5.   Co-habitation problem at execution time
            (two storage schemas)

XI. CONCLUSIONS

This paper has attempted to suggest an evolution from the
two or three component systems in widespread use today towards
a multi-component system in which the cornerstone would be a
conceptual schema.   The way in which the multi-stage data
definition suggested could be used is illustrated by means of
a flow chart embodying all components.

A number of topics call for further analysis.   Most
significant among these is the question of splitting the
conceptual schema into two stages, one of which might provide
the ultimate in independence to any subsequent changes and the
other a reasonable improvement on and distillation from the
implementation Schema DDLs embodied in the DBMS currently in
use.

ACKNOWLEDGEMENTS

    This paper was initially prepared by the author as a
contribution to the work of the British Standards Institution
Working Group on DBMS (DPS/13 WG1). The paper has benefitted
from the perceptive comments of many colleagues in this group,
namely R. Boot, T.J. Bourne, M.H. King, J.R. Lucking, and
J.M. Sykes. In an earlier form, it was discussed at a meeting
of the ISO TC97/SC5 Study Group on DBMS and modifications
based on the comments made there have subsequently been incorporated. The views expressed herein are those of the
author and do not necessarily represent the current thinking
of the above mentioned BSI colleagues.

REFERENCES

1. ANSI/X3/SPARC Study Group on DBMS. Interim Report 75-02-
    08. Published as Vol. 7, No. 2, of ACM SIGMOD's Bulletin
    "FDT".

2. "The ANSI/X3/SPARC DBMS Framework". Report of the Study
    Group on DBMS, edited by D. Tsichritzis and A. Klug,
    July 1977.

3. "Modelling in Data Base Management Systems", edited by
    G.M. Nijssen. Proceedings of the IFIP Working Conference
    with same title, held in Freudenstadt, January 1976.
    Published by North Holland Publishing Company, 1976.

4. IFIP-ICC Vocabulary of Information Processing. Published
    1966 by North Holland Publishing Company.

5. Data Base Administration Working Group. June 1975 report.
    Available from British Computer Society, 29 Portland Place,
    London.

AN EXTERNAL SCHEMA FACILITY
TO SUPPORT DATA BASE UPDATE

Eric K. Clemons[1]

Department of Decision Sciences
University of Pennsylvania
Philadelphia, Pennsylvania

User views and multi-level schemata offer a very promising tool for coping with the increased logical complexity
of integrated data bases while maintaining efficiency of the
implemented system.

User views have been used as the basis of a user interface for data base retrieval, but it has not previously been
possible to extend this work to support data base update as
well. Maps to construct user records from the stored data
base are understood, but inverting these maps, to capture in
the stored data base the intention of changes to the user
records, has not been well understood.

In this paper we advocate explicit definition of maps to
support update, rather than using for update the inverse of
the maps used to perform retrieval. Relationships between
this idea and the concepts of extensible languages, abstract
data types, and SIMULA classes are observed.

I. INTRODUCTION

Data structures employed in an integrated data base

management system must address three goals: enterprise sup-

port, user support, and machine access for retrieval and stor-

age. Enterprise support requires logical completeness: if

data has been gathered and maintained at considerable cost,

then it is essential that it be possible to use this data to

respond to any meaningful query. User support requires

logical simplicity: regardless of the complexity of the

structures needed to support the enterprise, it is essential

___

[1]Supported in part by NSF grant MCS77-18108.

371

that the structures with which an individual user must interact be both simple and well suited to his programming needs.
And, for machine access to the physical data, data description must be provided at a level low enough to permit efficient operation by the physical devices.

Unfortunately, these requirements will usually be incompatible. A structure that is logically complete enough
for the enterprise is not sufficiently simple for convenient
use by most programmers. Likewise, as is shown by example in
the following section, a structure that is well designed for
one application will not be suitable for another.

A promising mechanism for resolving these difficulties is
the three schema model offered by ANSI/SPARC (ANSI/X3/SPARC
Study Group, 1975). Rather than attempt to define a single
class of data structures of universal applicability,
ANSI/SPARC proposes three levels of structures, one for the
enterprise, the users, and the machine itself.

Such a model requires not only the ability to declare
data structures of different classes, but to define maps
between these structures. We have considered in earlier
works the design of structures suitable for programming users
and the nature of maps to these structures (Clemons, 1976a
and 1976b); in this paper we address the more difficult
problem of mapping from user records to capture in the stored
data base changes resulting from user updates.

II. ANSI/SPARC ARCHITECTURE

In the proposed ANSI/SPARC architecture there are three separate but related levels of data base schema: conceptual schema, external schema, and internal schema. The conceptual schema must be complete; it supports the enterprise and its view of the data required for its operations. The external level includes many external schemata; each external schema supports one or more applications programmers and provides a set of data structures required by and designed for their applications. The internal schema is needed for data access at the device level; it will not be explicitly treated in this paper.

A. An ANSI/SPARC Example

We consider a simple university data base including six entity types and the relationships among them: Departments offer courses, employ both students and faculty, and have students taking a major concentration in the department's courses. Faculty members teach course sections and advise students. Students enroll in course sections, and for each course taken by each student there is a course grade. The conceptual schema for this data base is summarized in figure 1.

Several interesting external schemata can be defined on this conceptual schema; we offer three:

1. A grade report for each student, listing all courses and grades for courses taken

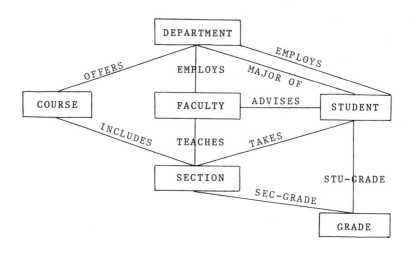

FIGURE 1.   A university data base with six record types
and the relationships between them.

2.   A course roster, giving for each course section the
     name of the faculty member who taught it and a list
     of students in the section and their grades

3.   A departmental roster, listing all student majors of
     each department and their grade average

These data structures are shown in figure 2.

We note that the structures of figures 2.a and 2.b appear
to be incompatible: for the first we want the data base organized as a hierarchy with courses listed for each student,
while for the second an organization with the students listed
for each course seems most appropriate.   Also, the grade point
average data in figure 2.c., while derivable from data in
figure 1, is not explicitly stored in the academic data base.
These observations can be summarized:

1.   None of the figures corresponds exactly to the data
     structure of figure 1 nor to a subset of this figure

```
STUDENT-NAME
               COURSE              GRADE
               COURSE              GRADE
                    .  .  .  .  .  .
               COURSE              GRADE
```

(a) a Student Grade Report based upon the data base shown in figure 1

```
FACULTY-NAME   COURSE
               STUDENT-NAME        GRADE
               STUDENT-NAME        GRADE
                    .  .  .  .  .  .
               STUDENT-NAME        GRADE
```

(b) a Course Roster based upon the data base shown in figure 1

```
DEPARTMENT
               STUDENT-NAME        GRADE-POINT-AVERAGE
               STUDENT-NAME        GRADE-POINT-AVERAGE
                    .  .  .  .  .  .
               STUDENT-NAME        GRADE-POINT-AVERAGE
```

(c) a Departmental Roster based upon the data base shown in figure 1

FIGURE 2. Three user views defined upon the university data base of figure 1.

2.   Each is a legitimate user view for a data processing application

3.   All are to be supported by the conceptual schema for the academic data base

4.   Each is to be supported by an appropriate external schema

B. Terminology

The following terms are required for the remainder of this paper. A base record is a record described in the internal schema and retrievable directly from secondary storage; the set of all base records is the stored data base.

A record described in an external schema is a <u>user</u>
<u>record</u>; the set of user record descriptions in a single
external schema is a <u>user</u> <u>view</u>; and the set of all user
records available through a single external schema is the
<u>user</u> <u>data</u> <u>base</u> corresponding to that schema.

C. Remarks

Capabilities of an external schema facility must be considerably more general than those proposed by the CODASYL
DBTG report (CODASYL DB Task Group, 1971) for their sub-
schema definitions. In particular:

1. General data access -- the combination of data from
    several base records -- is required

2. Selection of base records for inclusion in the user
    record may be determined by their content

3. Fully general data restructuring -- re-introduction
    of repeating items or combining detail entries into
    groups -- is required

4. Restructuring may also be controlled by content

5. Introduction of virtual items, derivable from the
    stored data base, may also be required

These requirements for an external schema facility have been
surveyed (Clemons, 1976b), as well as presented in detail
with discussion of implementation considerations (Clemons,
1976a). Implementation has begun at the University of
Pennsylvania.

III.   RELATIONSHIP BETWEEN USER VIEWS AND DATA BASE UPDATE

There is an essential relationship between user views and data base update. The user does not see the conceptual or internal schema, and is unaware of the underlying stored data base as distinct and different from his retrievable user data base. The user will, on occasion, be required by changes in his operating environment to make changes in the content of his user data base; although the user is unaware of the stored data base format and content, it is absolutely essential that changes made to his user records be captured as changes to the stored data base.[1]

Essential or not, maintaining the relationship between user records and base records while permitting update via user records is not yet possible.

IV.   FUNCTIONS BETWEEN SCHEMA LEVELS

A.   Mathematical Definitions

Review of the following standard mathematical definitions will prove useful. A _homomorphism_ is a function which pre-serves the structure of its arguments under given operations. For example, let S, T be vector spaces over a field F, s and v be elements of S, f an element of F. Then $\phi : S \to T$ is a homomorphism if and only if:

---

[1]Actually, as the ANSI/SPARC architecture is defined, changes to the user record must be mapped through the conceptual schema to changes in the stored data base. In the remainder of this paper we shall, for simplicity, refer to this map simply as a map from user data base to stored data base, without explicit reference to the two levels of mapping entailed.

$$\phi(u + v) = \phi(u) + \phi(v)$$

$$\phi(f \cdot u) = f \cdot \phi(u)$$

An isomorphism is a homomorphism which is one-to-one onto T.
In particular, this implies that for every element t in T
there is a unique element s in S such that

$$\phi(s) = t$$

Thus, if ϕ is an isomorphism, it is an invertible function;
we may then refer to s as $\phi^{-1}(t)$.

B.   Isomorphism and Update

It has been observed that update via user records is
ambiguous and hence impossible if the map from conceptual to
external schema is not invertible (Griffiths and Wade, 1976);
in consequence researchers have proposed restricting attention to user records which are constructed via isomorphisms.
We first illustrate the observation with an example; then,
attractive as the restriction may appear, we explain why it
must be rejected.

Consider a student whom the registrar erroneously
believes to have taken five courses and to have received
three A's and two B's, for a grade point average of 3.6.
The student, who has spoken to his professors and knows his
course grades, knows his average is a 3.8. It is not possible that a user in the student's departmental office,
whose view of the data is that shown in figure 2.c, could
correct the error in the average: This user has access to
student names and averages, but not to individual course
grades; a 3.6 can be changed to a 3.8 by changing either one
of the B's to an A, by dropping either of the courses with a

B grade and adding any other course offered by the university
with a grade of A, or through an infinite number of other
possibilities.

Since a tremendous number of combinations of courses and
grades map to the same average in the user record, the map
which constructs this record is not an isomorphism. Since
the map from the stored data base to this user data base is
not invertible, it is not possible to capture in the stored
data base the effects of a change to a single user record.
Thus update through user views is in general not yet
possible.

We note the following point:

Observation 1: If the function ϕ which maps from the stored
data base to the user data base is not invertible, update via
user views is not possible.

Accepting observation 1, we would like to restrict the
functions used to create the user records to be isomorphisms.
Unfortunately, this is neither sufficient to insure possibility of update nor compatible with an external schema of
adequate power and generality.

Consider an electronic mail routing system which includes
a stored data base comprising address records and message
records; address records are composed of a name and an office
address, while messages include a name and a text portion.
Combining a message with an address, the system constructs a
user record which we can call a letter.

If, at a given time there is a single address associated
with each name, then the function from address records to

letters appears to be invertible; that is, if the address of
a letter is changed, it is clear which base record must be
changed in order to produce the new letter. Unfortunately,
the intended action implied by the user's change of the
letter record cannot be uniquely determined; several actions
are possible:

1. Forward all mail to the new address -- for this
    intended action it is necessary to change the
    address base record, as suggested

2. Forward this letter but no others -- do not perma-
    nently change the address in the stored base

3. Note that the person named in the letter now has two
    offices -- add the second address and hereafter send
    all mail to both addresses

We note:

Observation 2: Although the function ϕ creating a user data
base may appear to be invertible, the structure of ϕ may not
uniquely determine the intention of an update to a user
record.

Finally, consider an inventory maintenance system. The
conceptual schema contains history records describing events
in the maintenance of stock -- for example, records of re-
stock quantities received or items shipped -- while a user
view might contain only current inventory quantities on hand
for all items. The choice of conceptual schema is reasonable; it permits unanticipated queries concerning rates of
dispersal or analysis of shipping trends; likewise an
external schema based on current levels is wholly adequate

for the inventory maintenance function. Clearly the map
which constructs these user records is not invertible: an
unlimited number of collections of re-stock and shipment
records could be found corresponding to any given stock
level, and there is no unique stored data base change corresponding to any update of the user data base.

We note:

Observation 3:   It is not possible to restrict the function
ϕ which defines a user data base so that it will be an invertible function; such restriction eliminates many, if not
most, useful user views.

The structure of the function ϕ tells us which data are
used and how they are processed to produce a user record.
The user may then alter the record in ways for which there
exist many corresponding updates to the stored data base.
Examination of the structure of ϕ can permit us to determine
which changes to the stored data base can possibly produce
the updated user record, but it cannot tell us which change
was intended.

We are thus forced to conclude:

Observation 4:   In general, update via ϕ^{-1} -- that is, update
based solely upon changes to the user record and structural
considerations of the function used to create the user data
base -- is not possible.

The user requirements for an external schema facility are
so varied that it is not possible to restrict maps from the
stored data base to the user data base to be isomorphisms.

Since the maps employed do not possess a unique inverse, in general there will exist an infinite number of stored data bases corresponding to a single user data base. Thus, there will exist an infinite number of possible changes to the stored data base corresponding to a single change to a user record. Therefore we must conclude that update based solely on structural considerations is not possible.

The semantically meaningful set of changes to any stored data base is quite limited. After illustrating this point we propose an alternate basis for data base update through user views, not requiring that the map ϕ possess a unique inverse.

V. SEMANTICS OF INTENDED UPDATES

Consider once again the inventory example introduced in section IV: the stored data base has a complete set of history records, while a user data base has only current inventory levels. As we recall, there is no map back from an inventory level to a unique set of corresponding history records. Thus we concluded that update via this user view was not possible.

The set of meaningful updates to this inventory data base is limited. Either items were received for re-stocking or returned by a customer, raising the inventory levels, or items were shipped or spoiled in inventory, lowering the levels.[2] And, for each form of update in the list, the changes to be performed upon the stored data base can be uniquely specified.

-----

[2]This list is not exhaustive. An exhaustive list, including a finite number of types of update required for this data base, can be prepared.

We wanted to start with a function

$$\phi: \text{Stored Data Base} \rightarrow \text{User Data Base}$$

and, based solely on structural considerations, derive a function

$$\phi^{-1}: \text{User Data Base} \rightarrow \text{Stored Data Base}$$

This was found to be impossible. Instead, by exploiting the semantics of the intended update, we can derive a set $\{f_i\}$ of functions

$$f_i: \text{User Data Base} \rightarrow \text{Stored Data Base}$$

representing the set of meaningful update operations. The set $\{f_i\}$ is derived by traditional systems analysis techniques, by studying the stored data base and the nature of the updates to it. When the update operations are understood, a map f_i is defined for each.

VI. EXAMPLES OF UPDATE THROUGH USER VIEWS

We now consider six classes of data base update and show how they may be performed by modifying records in the user data base. These six classes probably do not exhaust the possible forms of user update; however, they do represent many of the problems encountered in the design of an interface to support update. Significantly, for each problem, an implementatable solution is offered.

The discussion of each class has the following format:

1. A specific example representative of the class is introduced

2. The base records of S, the user record of U, and the mapping function ϕ from S to U are described

3. The desired updates are described

4. Changes to S, U, and ϕ, yielding S', U', and ϕ', are
    introduced which permit the definition of update
    functions f_i back to the stored date base

A. Change to a Virtual Sum

First consider a user record with a virtual sum, that is,
with a sum derivable from but not explicitly present in the
stored data base. It is necessary to determine the changes
to the stored data base required to capture correctly the intention of changes made to the sum in the user record. The
stored data base S has re-stock and shipment details for
items in inventory; the user data base U has merely current
levels for inventory quantities on hand:

          S: RESTOCK: (PART#, DATE, QTY)
               DETAIL: (INV#, LINE#, PART#, QTY)
               ϕ $\downarrow$

                          LEVEL: (PART#, QOH)

          where ϕ maps the sum of QTY of RESTOCK of a
          single part, minus the sum of QTY of DETAIL
          for a single part, to QOH of LEVEL for the part.

If changes must be made to the quantity on hand, this
may be for any of several reasons: Items may be returned by
a customer or damaged or lost in shipment and reshipped to a
customer. Items received from a supplier may be found to be
defective and returned. Finally, items may spoil in inventory or other adjustments may be required to reconcile the
data base with known inventory levels. Then the new data
bases and maps between them are:

```
S':   RESTOCK:          (PART#, DATE, QTY)
      RETURNED-RESTOCK:     (PART#, DATE, QTY)
      ADJUST:           (PART#, DATE, QTY, REASON)
      DETAIL:           (INV#, LINE#, PART#, QTY)
      RETURNED-DETAIL:  (INV#, LINE#, PART#, QTY)
      RESHIPPED-DETAIL: (INV#, LINE#, PART#, QTY)

         φ' ↓                    ↑  f
                                    i
      U':   LEVEL:   (PART#, QOH)
```

where φ' maps the sum of QTY of RESTOCK, minus the
sum of QTY of RETURNED-RESTOCK, plus the sum of QTY
of ADJUST, minus the sum of QTY of DETAIL, plus the
sum of QTY of RETURNED-DETAIL, minus the sum of QTY
of RESHIPPED-DETAIL, all sums taken over a single
part, to QOH of LEVEL for that part.

f_1 through f_4 create entries in RETURNED-RESTOCK,
ADJUST, RETURNED-DETAIL, and RESHIPPED-DETAIL.

The user does not simply change the quantity on hand.
Rather, he invokes one of the four update functions with
appropriate parameters, and the stored data base S is altered
in a manner that has the desired effect upon U.

B.   Changes to a Virtual Sum: User Record Consistency

Next consider a user record in which both details and a
virtual sum are present, for example, a user-invoice record
including details on items shipped and the total amount due
for the shipment. If it is desired to change the amount due,
because of a manager's discount or a discount for prepayment
of the order, it is necessary to capture this change. Changes
made must leave the invoice amount correct and the invoice
record consistent, in the sense that the invoice amount
remains computable from the details and their prices. Also
the stored data base must be correct, both in recording of
items shipped and recording of amounts receivable from
customers.

```
S:    CUSTOMER:    (CUST#, CNAME)
      INVOICE:     (INV#, CUST#, DATE)
      DETAIL:      (INV#, LINE#, PART#, QTY)
      CATALOG:     (PART#, PRICE)
         φ   ↓

            U:      USER-INVOICE:
                       (CUST#, CNAME,
                        INV#, DATE
                           LINE#, PART#, QTY, PRICE
                              .  .  .  .  .  .

                           LINE#, PART#, QTY, PRICE
                        TOTAL-DUE)
```

In order to permit the desired changes to be made, we alter the invoice record to include a discount rate ranging from 0 (no payment required) to 1 (no discount offered). The user-invoice record now includes the discount rate explicitly, and the rate is also used in the calculation of the total due. Changes to the total due are reflected in the stored data base as changes to the discount rate.

```
S':   CUSTOMER:    (CUST#, CNAME)
      INVOICE':    (INV#, CUST#, DATE, DISCOUNT-RATE)
      DETAIL:      (INV#, LINE#, PART#, QTY)
      CATALOG:     (PART#, PRICE)
         φ'  ↓            ↑    f
            U':     USER-INVOICE':
                       (CUST#, CNAME,
                        INV#, DATE
                           LINE#, PART#, QTY, PRICE
                              .  .  .  .  .  .

                           LINE#, PART#, QTY, PRICE
                        TOTAL-DUE)
```

φ' now uses the discount rate to calculate the total
due, f uses changes in the total due to calculate
the discount rate.

        C.   Changes to Item Description:
              Dependency Present

Once again we will use the user-invoice record of the previous section. A functional dependency (Bernstein, 1976) exists between part number and price, in that part number determines price uniquely; thus we have been able to associate a unique catalog price with each part in a detail record. Now we consider changing the price entered in the user-invoice record.

It may be necessary to alter permanently the association between a part number and price, that is, to alter the catalog entry for a part. This is easy to implement but probably should not be permitted; a user whose access to the data base is restricted to composite user-invoice records should not be empowered to alter pricing decisions.

Of greater interest, and increased implementation difficulty, is limited alteration of the relationship between a part number and a price. For example, if an ordered item is out of stock, it is sometimes necessary to substitute a similar but more expensive part for the item the customer has ordered. In this situation, the part number in the detail must be of the item shipped so that inventory records can be properly maintained. The part number in the user-invoice should also be of the part shipped, but the price in the user-invoice should be the price of the part originally ordered, thus over-riding for this user-invoice record only the functional relationship between part number and price.

This is made possible by changing the stored data base and the mapping function ϕ. In place of the original S, U, and ϕ:

```
S:    CUSTOMER:     (CUST#, CNAME)
      INVOICE:      (INV#, DATE)
      DETAIL:       (INV#, LINE#, PART#, QTY)
      CATALOG:      (PART#, PRICE)
         φ   ↓

              U:    USER-INVOICE:
                      (CUST#, CNAME,
                       INV#, DATE
                          LINE#, PART#, QTY, PRICE
                                · · · · · · ·
                          LINE#, PART#, QTY, PRICE
                       TOTAL-DUE)
```

we use S', U', and φ':

```
S':   CUSTOMER:     (CUST#, CNAME)
      INVOICE:      (INV#, DATE)
      DETAIL':      (INV#, LINE#, PART#, PART-SHIPPED,
                     QTY)
      CATALOG:      (PART#, PRICE)
         φ'  ↓           ↑  f
              U:    USER-INVOICE:
                      (CUST#, CNAME,
                       INV#, DATE
                          LINE#, PART#', QTY, PRICE
                                · · · · · · ·
                          LINE#, PART#', QTY, PRICE
                       TOTAL-DUE)
```

where φ' differs from φ only when part number of
detail differs from part shipped of detail; in this
case the part number of the user-invoice record is
that of the part actually shipped, the price is for
the part originally ordered.

The effect of f is, when a part substitution is
made, to alter the part shipped entry in the detail
base record.

D.   Changes to Item Description:
No Dependency Present

We next consider a data base in which entities have

descriptions of two types; for neither type is the descrip-

tion of an entity unique and thus no dependencies are assumed

to exist. User records are constructed from an entity identifier and a description of each type.

To make the ideas of this data base more concrete, consider an example. The entities are persons, descriptions of
of the first type are office addresses, and descriptions of
the second type are texts of messages; the user records,
which may be called letters, consist of a name, an office
address, and a message text.

<pre>
    S: ADDRESS: (ADDRESS-ID, NAME, OFFICE-ADDRESS)
        MESSAGE: (MESSAGE-ID, NAME, TEXT)

         φ ↓

        U: LETTER: (NAME, OFFICE-ADDRESS, TEXT)
</pre>

As noted in section IV, there may be three types of update associated with such a letter:

1. Change the address for this person

2. Add an address for this person

3. Change the address for this letter only

The first update is simple to implement. No changes to
the schema of S are required. It is necessary only that the
system use the new address from the letter to replace the
address originally used in the construction of the letter.

The second update also requires no changes to the schema
of S. It is here necessary that the system use the name and
the new office address to create an additional address
record, with address-id generated by the system.

The final update, which changes the address for a single
letter only, is more complex. In order to permit associations
to be made for a single letter, the schema of S must be

changed: an auxillary address record is created with
address-id and message-id identifying the unique letter to
which it is to be applied.

$$
\begin{array}{ll}
\text{S':} & \text{ADDRESS:} \quad (\underline{\text{ADDRESS-ID}}, \text{ NAME, OFFICE ADDRESS}) \\
& \text{MESSAGE:} \quad (\underline{\text{MESSAGE-ID}}, \text{ NAME, TEXT}) \\
& \text{AUX-ADDRESS:} \quad (\underline{\text{MESSAGE-ID}}, \underline{\text{ADDRESS-ID}}, \\
& \qquad\qquad\qquad \text{OFFICE-ADDRESS})
\end{array}
$$

$$
\phi \quad \downarrow \qquad\qquad\qquad \uparrow \quad f_i
$$

$$
\begin{array}{ll}
\text{U':} & \text{LETTER:} \quad (\text{NAME, OFFICE-ADDRESS,} \\
& \qquad\qquad\qquad \text{TEXT})
\end{array}
$$

Where ϕ' has the form:

for a given person
    for all messages to this person

        if there is a corresponding aux-address
        for this person and address, use it in
        the construction of the letter

        otherwise construct letter from message
        and address

There are three elements in $\{f_i\}$:

    f_1 maps letter address to change in address record
    f_2 maps letter address to new address record
    f_3 maps letter address to aux-address record

We note a difference between the methods of section VI.C
and VI.D. In the invoice system, over-riding the association
between a part number and price for a single invoice detail
involved changing the detail record but not the descriptive
catalog entry. In the mail system, over-riding the association between name and address for a single letter user record
is accomplished not by changing the message record but by
adding a descriptive aux-address record.

The catalog in the invoice system represents the set of
all valid item descriptions. Over-riding an association does
not alter the set of parts available, and hence does not

change the catalog; it does alter which catalog entry is to
be associated with a single detail and this is most easily
captured by changing the detail. In the mail system there is
no complete set of all valid addresses corresponding to the
catalog. Over-riding the address associated with a name can
introduce a new address; moreover, since this new address is
to be associated not with a single message or a single person
but only with a message to a person at an address, it must be
identified with both message and address identifiers and
placed in an auxillary address collection.

E. Deletion

The user-invoice record was constructed from customer,
invoice, detail, and catalog data. Deletion of the user-
invoice should delete the invoice and detail records, but
should not delete customer or catalog entries.

In the case of deletions our decisions are strongly influenced by structural considerations since they are for this
class of update closely related to the intended semantics.
Deleting a user-invoice should probably delete not just the
invoice record, but also all the associated detail records.
The deletion of details is suggested by their structure,
since the keys of details are composed in part of the key of
the deleted invoice record. Catalog records do not contain
references to details or invoices; they should not be
deleted.

These considerations guide but do not dictate the interpretation of updates. For example, when deleting a customer
record it is possible but not necessary to delete associated

invoice and detail records. Thus decisions about actions to
be taken when deletions are performed must still be made when
the external schema is designed.

Deletion of an invoice detail is straightforward and can
easily be included as a valid update if desired.

F. Insertion

A sales representative will need to retrieve customer
orders and to enter new orders as they are written. These
orders are constructed from the base relations in a fashion
similar to the construction of invoices.

```
S:  CUSTOMER:   (CUST#, CNAME)
    ORDER:      (ORD#, CUST#, DATE)
    O-DETAIL:   (ORD#, LINE#, PART#, QTY)
    CATALOG:    (PART#, PRICE)

        φ   ↓

    U:  ORDER:   (CUST#, CNAME
                 ORD#, DATE
                    LINE#, PART#, QTY, PRICE
                    · · · · · · · ·
                 LINE#, PART#, QTY, PRICE)
```

When a new order record is to be added, it is necessary
to map this user record back to new stored data base records.
Changes must be made to the stored data base. What action
is to be taken if there is no customer record corresponding
to the customer number? What if there is no catalog record
corresponding to part number? These decisions must be made
on semantic rather than structural consideration of the
update.

It is expected that the order will represent a new
order record, and one will be created.

It is possible that a salesman will make a sale to a new customer; when this occurs a new customer record is entered and additional actions (e.g., a credit check) are triggered.

It is not possible that the salesman develops new inventory items while taking an order; requests for items not in the catalog will not be entered as o-detail records. Prices entered by the salesman are ignored, since prices come from the catalog.

It is possible to alter an existing order by adding new order details. These will result in new o-detail records, provided they correspond to items listed in the catalog.

G.   Changes not Explicitly Supported By Maps Defined between Schemata

For many updates to user records the corresponding changes to be made to the stored data base will be clear. What action is to be taken if the update function required was not explicitly defined when the levels of schemata were prepared?

Consider yet again the relationship between the user-invoice record and the stored data base. The data base change associated with altering the invoice quantity of a part is clear: it is necessary simply to change the quantity entry in the uniquely associated detail record. This is not to say that the update should be permitted; if the invoice is for a shipment made months earlier and for which payment has already been received, then such alterations must be prohibited.

It is our position that all update operations not explicitly permitted are implicitly forbidden. If additional

forms of update through user records should later be required, no matter how simple they should prove to implement,
modification of the set of maps to support these updates will
be required.

VII. RELATION TO ABSTRACT DATA TYPES

We are familiar with the basic data types and operations
permitted upon them, as provided by current programming
languages; e.g., character data, operations are substring
and concatenation, or integer data, operations are addition,
subtraction, multiplication, and division.

COBOL records and PL/1 structures permit the construction
of more interesting data items, but neither restricts access
to or operations upon these items beyond the restrictions
placed on components based on type.

The use of mapping functions f_i may be considered an
application of abstract data types to data base processing.
Abstract data types comprise structured user records, the
function ϕ for their construction from the stored data base,
and the set of functions $\{f_i\}$ needed for their update. Just
as two character strings can be concatenated but not multi-
plied, so we restrict the operations that can alter defined
data types. Thus inventory stock can be increased or decreased by any of a set of defined operations, but it cannot
be altered arbitrarily.

While the concept of abstract data types has only
recently been applied to data base maintenance, it first appeared in programming languages several years ago. In
particular, the reader is referred to SIMULA (Dahl and Hoare,

1972), in which the programmer defines <u>classes</u>, structured
data types and the set of operations permitted to access or
alter them. Also, this work is related to work in extensible
languages (Cheatham, 1966; Galler, 1974; Thompson et al,
1969).

VIII.   CONCLUDING REMARKS

A.   Summary

User views and multi-level schemata offer a very promising tool for coping with increased logical complexity of
integrated data bases while maintaining efficiency of the
implemented system.

Update via views will be essential; this statement is
not altered by the fact that functions used to construct
user records are, in general, not invertible.

We attempt to exploit the fact that, while the possible
set of inverses associated with a user record update may be
infinite, the meaningful inverse for a given type of update
will usually be unique;   moreover, the set of meaningful
types of updates will also be quite limited. Therefore, we
propose that with the definition of each map from the stored
records to the user records an associated set of maps from
the user records to the stored data base also be defined.
Maps in this set correspond to the various forms of permitted
update.

B.   Work in Progress

We are continuing to study maps from the data base to
the stored data base. We seek to extend the classification
of maps introduced in section VI, to make it more formal and

more complete. If a set of maps based upon this classification can be shown to be complete, in the sense of being adequate and convenient for a large class of data processing
applications, then we will implement an interface based on a
general set of <u>templates</u> f_i^* from the user data base to the
stored data base.

As an example of the use of templates, consider once
again the mail system of section VI.D. S' contained:

    S':   ADDRESS: (<u>ADDRESS-ID</u>, NAME, OFFICE-ADDRESS)
          MESSAGE: (<u>MESSAGE-ID</u>, NAME, TEXT)
          AUX-ADDRESS: (<u>MESSAGE-ID</u>, <u>ADDRESS-ID</u>,
                         OFFICE-ADDRESS)

    f_1 changed an address
    f_2 added an address
    f_3 added an aux-address

S^* would include:

    S^*: TRANSIENT-TEXT: (<u>ENTITY-ID</u>, <u>TR-ID</u>, TR-TEXT)
           STATIC-TEXT: (<u>ENTITY-ID</u>, <u>ST-ID</u>, ST-TEXT)
           AUX-TEXT: (<u>TR-ID</u>, <u>ST-ID</u>, AUX-TEXT)

    f_1^* changes s-text

    f_2^* adds a static-text record

    f_3^* adds an aux-text record

These templates can readily be modified to support the mail
system presented above. And they can as readily be used to
support a customer order system which permits salesmen to
over-ride catalog prices when necessary. Definition of a
user data base would then consist of:

    1. designing the user records

    2. specifying ϕ needed to construct each record

3. specifying the set $\{f_i\}$ needed to support update of each user record -- wherever possible f_i will be based upon a template f_j^*

The implication of this work, and of three schema data base systems in general, for machine performance needs additional study. Definitive results will probably not be available until experience has been gained with a working prototype.

C. Contribution

Abstract data types appear to offer a solution to the problem of update through user records. We stress the fact that definition of a data type is not equivalent to subsuming the entire programming effort as part of schema definition. For example, the map from invoice to data base, reflecting actions to be taken when a substitution is made for an out of stock item, is part of the program to handle customer orders; it is independent of the program logic needed to determine that an item is out of stock, to determine if a substitute is available, or to determine if a substitution is actually to be made. Since preparation of schemata for a three schema system will now involve the specification of numerous maps from the external to the conceptual level, it is undeniable that the ideas proposed in this paper will complicate the process of schema design.

Finally, it is clear that use of an external schema facility for data base maintenance would greatly simplify all aspects of applications programming, from data access, algorithm design, program development, to program implementation and verification.

REFERENCES

ANSI/X3/SPARC Study Group on Data Base Management Systems
    Interim Report, 75-02-08. (1975). Vol. 7, No. 2, FDT--
    Bulletin of the ACM SIGMOD.
Bernstein, P. A. (1976). "Synthesizing Third Normal Form
    Relations from Functional Dependencies," Vol. 1, No. 4.
    ACM Transactions on Database Systems.
Cheatham, T. E. Jr. (1966). "The Introduction of Definitional
    Facilities into Higher Level Programming Languages,"
    Vol. 29, pp. 623-637. AFIPS Conference Proceedings.
Clemons, E. K. (1976a). Design of a User Interface for a
    Relational Data Base. Dissertation, Cornell University.
Clemons, E. K. (1976b). "An External Schema Facility for a
    Relational Data Base," Working Paper 76-11-03, Department
    of Decision Sciences, University of Pennsylvania.
CODASYL Data Base Task Group April 71 Report. (1971). ACM,
    New York.
Dahl, O., and Hoare, C. A. R. (1972). "Hierarchical Data
    Structures." In Structured Programming (C. A. R. Hoare,
    ed.), pp. 175-220. Academic Press, New York.
Galler, B. A. (1974). "Extensible Languages." Proceedings
    IFIP Congress, pp. 313-316. North Holland Publishing
    Company, Amsterdam, Netherlands.
Griffiths, P. O., and Wade, B. W. (1976). "An Authorization
    System for a Relational Data Base System," Vol. 1, No. 3,
    pp. 189-222. ACM Transactions on Database Systems.
Thompson, F. D., et al. (1969). "REL, A Rapidly Extensible
    Language," pp. 399-417. Proceedings ACM 24th National
    Conference. ACM, New York.

COMPARISON OF DIFFERENT ACCESS STRATEGIES IN A DISTRIBUTED DATABASE

BY

G.PELAGATTI AND F.A. SCHREIBER

ISTITUTO DI ELETTRONICA-POLITECNICO DI MILANO
P.ZA LEONARDO DA VINCI 32 - 20133 MILANO (ITALY)

A quantitative comparison of two different access strategies in a Distributed Database is made by treating a specific example. Cost comparison formulas and a statistical analysis of data are developed and comments on a further generalization are made.

1. INTRODUCTION

Distributed information systems have been favourably considered in the recent years owing to their flexibility, their intrinsic capabilities of non disruptive grow, their human engineered feature, etc. (1,2,3,4).

While in several works (5,6,7) issues related to the Distributed Database, on which the information system is based, have been discussed in terms of data distribution criteria, data models, and general strategies for data accessing, in this paper we want to examine two different distributed data access methods from a quantitative point of view, basing ourselves on a particular example which has been drawn from a feasibility study for a distributed university information system.

Even if the example is rather specific, its study has been made with the aim of reaching results which could be applied also in more general environments. However a general treatment of the problem would have required a more thorough examination of all the implications that complex interactions among files distributed in different locations could entail. Anyhow, at the end of the paper, we are discussing some more general cases.

Before discussing the example, we give here just some highlights about the information system and the requirements which originated the feasibility study.

Several minicomputers were available in the university, each of them located at a different department, their use being mainly for research and didactical purposes. However some departments were interested in keeping for local use administrative information about the teaching activities of the department itself. In this way different Databases were born containing nearly the same kind of information. At this time the need of managing common resource pools and the one of dealing with global information as, for instance, the distribution of the classrooms for the holding of the various courses, arose. Such a need requires the possibility of accessing the local Databases in a distributed way, since information on classroom utilization is stored at the different departments.

Looking at general classifications of distributed systems (3,4) we can say that, as much as our study is concerned, we deal with a homogeneous system with horizontally partitioned data.

A last remark is needed with respect to the question of terminology. The problem we are studying regards the choice of an access strategy to a set of distributed files. We found it very convenient to use the terminology of relational systems for the description of this problem, although the system is not relational.

2. ACCESS REQUIREMENT AND STRATEGY

The main result of this paper is to show on hand of a specific example that the choice of an access strategy in a distributed database may require a particular statistical

analysis even if the cardinalities of the files and the "selectivity" of the access-conditions are known (by "selectivi
ty" we mean the number of records that satisfy an access-con
dition divided by the total number of records of the file).

Independently from the creation of a network every department has its own files that we used for local processing.
One of the most important files is the COURSES file which
contains the following information :

COURSES (TEACHER,COURSE,ROOM,SUPPORT-MATERIAL,SCHEDULE)

Teacher and course are a compound identifier for this
file, because a Teacher can teach many courses and a course
is taught by more than one teacher. Every department has also
a file in which its own support-material and its available
quantity together with other relevant information is kept.
We will refer to these files as MATERIALS files containing
the following items: SUPPORT-MATERIAL, QUANTITY and omit
other information (of course, an implicit DEPT information
is also associated with the MATERIALS files).

If we consider now the whole problem from a network view
point, we can see two global COURSES and MATERIALS files
which are distributed over the departments. One of the results that is expected from the network approach is the possibility of using the Support-Materials that are available
at some department for all the courses that need them, even
if they depend from other departments. For reasons that may
appear not clear from the simplified description of the problem given above, it is not possible to plan the use of the
Support Materials in advance. Therefore we want to give the
person who is responsible of the preparation of some classrooms the possibility to ask on line the system for a list
of the Support-Materials that will be needed during the day,
and the departments that have these materials available.

The problem that we have to solve is to define the best
access strategy to satisfy the above requirement. The most
straightful solution would be to collect the COURSES and MATE-
RIALS files at one node and then access them in the desired
way, but this solution is clearly too expensive with respect

to transmission costs.

Let us therefore consider two different solutions which
take advantage of a distributed access possibility to some de
gree but differ in the amount of distributed versus centralized processing. We will call these two access strategies a
"more distributed" and a "less distributed" access strategy.

Both access strategies begin with sending all nodes the
command to select in the COURSES files the records which
contain the specified room values and to select the correspon
ding SUPPORT-MATERIAL values. As a result of this step a
list of required SUPPORT-MATERIALS is obtained at each node
of the network. From now on the two strategies are different.

In the "less-distributed" access strategy the obtained
SUPPORT-MATERIAL lists and the parts of the MATERIALS file
are sent from each node to one node (the requesting node).
The MATERIALS file is then searched to find all the departments that have the required materials available. In the "more distributed" access strategy, on the contrary, the selected SUPPORT-MATERIAL lists are sent from each node to every
other node. In this way every node is now in possess of a
complete list of all required materials. Each node can now
search its own part of the MATERIALS file and find the availability of the required materials. All this local results
have then to be collected and sent to the requesting node.
The two strategies are summarized in Table 1.

3. EVALUATION OF THE ACCESS STRATEGIES

In order to compare the two access strategies we make
the following assumptions:

1) The cost of transmitting commands is negligible compared
   with the cost of transmitting data
2) The cost of transmission between any two nodes is constant
3) Every file is distributed in equal parts over the nodes.

Assumptions 2) and 3) are made only to make simpler
the example which follows; therefore they can be released

without affecting the evaluation procedure, but only complica-
ting the mathematical notation. However the quantitative results might change.

    As to assumption 1), it certainly holds if by cost we
only mean the amount of $/bit for the use of transmission fa
cilities. It is still valid also in a broader sense, i.e.from
the point of view of the end-to-end transmission delays, if a
packet switching (V.A.N.) transmission facility is used with
a homogeneous end-to-end protocol. However, it could be que-
stionable and it should be carefully evaluated if the transmission network were composed of lines with very different
bandwith and different end-to-end protocols.

    Moreover, we will neglect the access and processing
costs and consider only the transmission costs. This assumption is done because the two strategies are identical from a
logical viewpoint and differ only from a distribution viewpoint and therefore the amount of processing needed in both
strategies is similar although not equal. Anyway, this assumption holds if the machines are comparatively inexpensive with
respect to transmission lines.

    An important aspect we have neglected in the above assum
ptions is the fact that the second strategy allows a high degree of processing parallelism; in fact one should take care
also of this aspect, which could play an important role in
the final evaluation. Admittedly, we have limited ourselves to
an analysis of how much data the two strategies required to
be transmitted around, which is not the only important
aspect of the optimization problem.

    The difference in transmission costs of the two solutions
can be found by inspection of Table 1. Let us define the following parameters :

ρ_F = number of records of file F
CTR = cost of transmitting one byte between two nodes
l_{DI} = length in bytes of the data item DI
N   = number of nodes. In our case N = 5.

Because of the assumption 3) above, the cardinality of the
part of a file F which resides on one node is ρ_F/N.

    The transmission costs of the "less distributed" solut-

"less distributed"	"more distributed"
1) Send command to each node. Select a list of Support-Materials at each node.	1) Send command to each node. Select a list of Support-Materials at each node.
2) Send the "selected lists" to one node(requesting node or execution node).	2) Send the "selected lists" of Support-Materials from each node to every other node.
3) Send the parts of the MATERIALS file from each node to execution node.	3) Select from (local parts of) MATERIALS file the partial results.
4) Select result from the MATERIALS file using the list of required materials at the execution node.	4) Collect the partial results.

TABLE 1 : Two different execution strategies.

ion is :

$$(\text{Cost of Step 2 + Cost of Step 3}) =$$
$$= \rho_{SELECTEDLIST} \cdot l_{SUPPORT\text{-}MATERIAL} \cdot CTR.(N-1) +$$
$$\rho_{MATERIALS} \cdot l_{SUPPORT\text{-}MATERIAL,DEPT,QUANTITY} \cdot CTR.(N-1)$$

while the cost of the "more distributed" solution is :

$$(\text{Cost of step 2 + Cost of step 4}) =$$
$$\rho_{SELECTEDLIST} \cdot l_{SUPPORT\text{-}MATERIAL} \cdot CTR.(N-1).N +$$
$$\rho_{RESULT} \cdot l_{SUPPORT\text{-}MATERIAL,DEPT,QUANTITY} \cdot CTR.(N-1)$$

If we subtract the first from the second cost we obtain the difference D between the two strategies; if this difference is positive the "less distributed" solution is more convenient, the opposite otherwise.

$$D = \text{cost of "more distributed" - cost of "less distributed"} =$$

$$= \rho_{SELECTEDLIST} \cdot l_{SUPPORT\text{-}MATERIAL} \cdot CTR.(N-1)^2 +$$

$$+ (\rho_{RESULT} - \rho_{MATERIALS}) \cdot l_{SUPPORT\text{-}MATERIAL,DEPT,QUANTITY} \cdot CTR.(N-1)$$

The first term is always positive and expresses the cost of

spreading the selected lists over all nodes compared to the cost of collecting them at one node. The second term is generally negative ($\rho_{MATERIALS} > \rho_{RESULT}$) and expresses the difference between the cost of collecting the MATERIALS file and the cost of collecting the result.

In order to evaluate D we must evaluate $\rho_{SELECTEDLIST}$ and ρ_{RESULT}.

$\rho_{SELECTEDLIST}$ is expecially important, because it multiplies the term $(N-1)^2$. Recall that the "Selected Lists" are the lists of Support Materials that are needed at a set of Rooms. In order to evaluate their cardinality we have to consider more in detail the selection process, at each node,which is the following:

- Select all records in the COURSE file that have the required ROOM numbers. The number of these records at each node,K, can be calculated by knowing the selectivity of the condition and the cardinality of the relation. In our case we have obtained K=8.
- Select from each record the corresponding SUPPORT-MATERIAL values.
- Eliminate duplicate values of the obtained SUPPORT MATERIALS. This last step should result in a reduction of the total number of values to transmit that is $\rho_{SELECTEDLIST}(\rho_{S.L.})$.

In the rest of this section we show how $\rho_{S.L.}$ can be calculated if we know the value of K, the total number of records ($\rho_{COURSES/N}$) and the number of different values that the selected domain (in our case SUPPORT MATERIALS) can assume ($\rho_{SUPPORT-MATERIALS}$).

The problem can be restated referring to figure 1 in the following general way. How many different values ρ_{SL} of a Data Item do we obtain if we select arbitrarily K records of a file F, if the cardinality of the file is ρ_F and the number of different, uniformly distributed values of the Data Item is ρ_{DI}?

This is an analogous problem to that of finding which is the mean number of different colours we can find by drawing K balls out of a urn containing ρ_F balls uniformly distributed over ρ_{DI} colours.

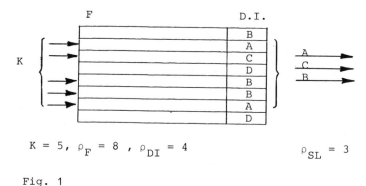

K = 5, ρ_F = 8 , ρ_{DI} = 4 ρ_{SL} = 3

Fig. 1

To solve such a problem we can rely on a theorem of
the combinatorial theory about mean (expected) values of con-
ditional events, that is (8):

$$E(x) = E(E(x|y))$$

i.e. the expected value of a random variable x is equal to the
mean value of the expected value of x conditioned by Y, when
y is another random variable.

In our case we can formulate this theorem in the following way:

$$E(\rho_{SL}(k+1)) = E(E(\rho_{SL}(k+1) | \rho_{SL}(k) = \alpha))$$

that is the expected number of different values ρ_{SL} after
K+1 drawings is conditioned by the number of different values $\rho_{SL} = \alpha$ resulting after k drawings. This formulation
leads to a recursive formula for calculating the value
$(E(\rho_{SL}(k+1))$, supposing that $\rho_{SL}(\emptyset) = \emptyset$, i.e. the number of
different values found in drawing no record at all is zero.

We must therefore evaluate the actual expression for
$E(\rho_{SL}(K+1) | \rho_{SL}(k) = \alpha)$. It will be given by the sum of the
mean value calculated for the case of getting a new value at
the K+1 drawing and the mean value calculated for the case
that at the K+1 drawing a value is found which is already pre
sent in the extracted set.It will result then in the following
expression

$$E(\rho_{SL}(k+1) \,|\, \rho_{SL}(k) = \alpha) = \alpha \cdot \underbrace{\frac{\left(\rho_F / \rho_{DI}\right) \cdot \alpha - k}{\rho_F - k}}_{\substack{\text{probability of} \\ \text{drawing an al-} \\ \text{ready present} \\ \text{value}}} + (\alpha+1) \cdot \underbrace{\frac{\left(\rho_F / \rho_{DI}\right) \cdot (\rho_{DI} - \alpha)}{\rho_F - k}}_{\substack{\text{probability of} \\ \text{drawing a new} \\ \text{value}}}$$

We can rewrite now this expression in a more useful form :

$$E(\rho_{SL}(k+1) \,|\, \rho_{SL}(k) = \alpha) = \frac{\rho_F}{\rho_F - k} + \frac{(\rho_F/\rho_{DI})(\rho_{DI} - 1) - k}{\rho_F - k} \cdot \alpha$$

However, the value α can be computed as $\alpha = E(\rho_{SL}(k))$, so leading to the final recursive expression of the form

$$E(\rho_{SL}(k+1)) = a + b \cdot E(\rho_{SL}(k))$$

$$E(\rho_{SL}(\emptyset)) = \emptyset$$

This value can be easily computed even on a programmable pocket calculator and in fig. 2 a diagram for the function is shown. It can be noticed that for very small values of K the number of different values found is nearly equal to K while for large values of K there is a saturation region in which the number of different values is equal to ρ_{DI}. This saturation region, the bounds of which are defined by

$$(\rho_F - \frac{\rho_F}{\rho_{DI}} + 1) \leqslant K \leqslant \rho_F$$

begins after having drawn all the K elements in ρ_F having $\rho_{DI}-1$ different values. Therefore the K+1 drawing will extract one element of the ρ_{DI}-th value and the number of different values will not change any more until all the K=ρ_F elements are extracted.

If DI is a key domain then $\rho_{DI}=\rho_F$, i.e. all the values in the file are different, therefore we shall always have ρ_{SL} = K. On the contrary if DI is a constant domain, i.e. ρ_{DI} = 1, we shall allways have ρ_{SL} = 1 for whatever k. Applying this analysis to our example, that is with

$$\rho_F = \frac{\rho_{COURSES}}{N} = 100, \quad \rho_{DI} = \rho_{SUPPORT-MATERIALS} = 10, \text{ and}$$

k = 8, we obtain a value ρ_{SL} = 5.83. Therefore the cardinali_
ty of the selected list is the 72.8% of the cardinality of k
with a reduction of 27.2%. We remember that ρ_{SL} is the mul-
tiplying factor of $(N-1)^2$ in the cost comparison expression,
so the more it is reduced, the more the "more distributed"
solution is likely to be convenient.

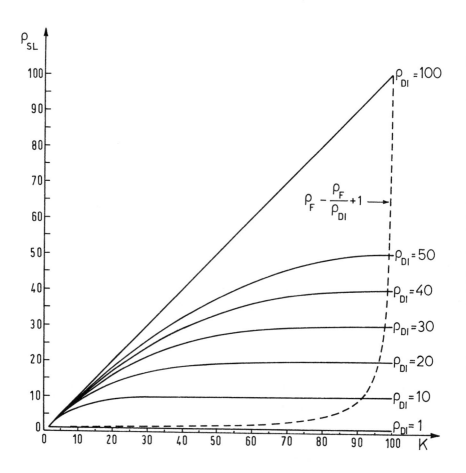

Fig. 2

4. GENERALIZATION AND CONCLUSIONS

A general access requirement to a set of files (assume
here a set of 2 files; the extension to n files is straightforward) can be conceptually decomposed into the following
operations:
a) Select a subset of the records of each file (intermediate
   files)
b) Build the Cartesian Product of the intermediate files
c) Select some elements from the Cartesian Product

If the data structures do not use links that represent
directly the required Cartesian Product (and this is often
the case in a distributed database, because distributed links
are difficult to maintain), the conceptual operations b) and
c) are combined by building the product of one element of one
file (possibly the smaller one) with the whole other file
and selecting the elements satisfying the condition; this
process is repeated for every element of the first file.

From the viewpoint of distribution the fact is important,
that the operation a) can be executed in a distributed way,
while the operation b) cannot, because the Cartesian Product
of two files is not the sum of the Cartesian Products of the
local subfiles. Therefore it is always possible (and convenient) to perform operations of type a) locally, but for operations of type b) this is not possible and one has to choose
between two alternative strategies:

1) Collect a complete copy of the files at one node and
   build the Cartesian Product here (collect operation); or
2) Send a complete copy of only one file to each node and
   build locally the Cartesian Product of this file with
   the parts of the other one (spread operation); the sum of
   the partial products is the required (complete) product.
As it has been shown in the example the cost of the first
solution is ($\frac{N-1}{N}$) times the cost of sending both complete
files; the cost of the second solution is (N-1) the cost of
sending one file. Therefore the second solution can be convenient only if one file is much smaller than the other one,

and this is for example the case if the access requirement has a strong selection condition on one file and no condition at all on the other one. Because of the cost of the <u>spread</u> operation, which is N times higher than the cost of the <u>collect</u> operation, the cardinality of the (intermediate) files to be spread must be accurately evaluated. The example has shown a case in which this evaluation requires the use of the statistical formulas given in section 3.

REFERENCES

1. Booth G.M. - "The use of Distributed Databases in information networks" - Proc. of 1st ICCC; Washington, Oct. 1972.

2. Booth G.M. - "Distributed Information Systems" - Proc. National Computer Conference - AFIPS 1976.

3. Giovacchini L., Schreiber F.A. - "Some Considerations on Distributed Management Information Systems" - Proc. of the International Symposium on Technology for Selective Dissemination of Information, IEEE Press, Sept. 1976.

4. Paolini P., Pelagatti G., Schreiber F.A. - "An application oriented approach to Distributed Databases" - Proc. Journées AFCET sur les Bases de données reparties, Paris, March 1977.

5. Stonebraker M., Neuhold E. - "A Distributed Database Version of INGRES" - Proc. 2nd Berkeley Workshop on Distributed Data Management & Computer Networks -1977.

6. Bucci G., Streeter D.N.- "A user oriented Approach to the design of distributed Information Systems" - IBM Research Report RC 5887 - March 1976.

7. Schreiber F.A. - "A Framework for distributed Database Systems" - Proc. ACM International Computing Symposium, 1977, North Holland Publ. Co. 1977

8. Dobb. J.L. - "Stochastic Processes" - John Wiley & Sons 1967.

EVENT DRIVEN PROTECTION FOR ENHANCING

DATA SHARING IN DATA BASE SYSTEMS[1]

David Cohen[2]
Ming T. Liu

Computer and Information Science
The Ohio State University
Columbus, Ohio, USA

In this paper, an event-driven protection mechanism is proposed for enhancing data sharing in a data base system without compromising its security. Functionally, the mechanism consists of three major processes: the authorization process (AP) that maintains protection specifications introduced by the owners of data resources; the monitoring process (MP) that monitors data base events specified in AP; and the enforcement process (EP) that makes logical access decision to deny or permit a user request according to the authorization policy dynamically maintained by AP and MP. The proposed mechanism supports two major activities: pattern enforcement and derivation protection, both of which are not supported by current systems. The mechanism developed can enforce any sequence of data base operations (finite or cyclic) from the moment such a protection requirement has been introduced into the system. Derivation protection (at the data attribute level) is also supported by using the user's access history as a representation of the knowledge he has acquired from the data base. The event-driven protection mechanism is compatible with current systems and can adjust its level of performance and degree of data sharing according to the availability of system's resources. The mechanism has been implemented on a DECsystem-10 so as to validate the model and to test design alternatives.

---

1. Supported in part by the Office of Naval Research under Contract N00014-75C-0573.

2. Present address: Bell Laboratories, Holmdel, New Jersey.

411

I. INTRODUCTION

In recent years data base systems have become increasingly central to the functioning of organized society. Information is deposited in a computer system to permit it to be shared among and to be used by various groups of users. Like other resources of an organization (e.g., funds, manpower and materials), the information stored in a data base has to be protected from unauthorized use and destruction.

Functionally, information protection involves two related activities. One specifies the access rights of the data base users, also known as the security policy, and the other en-

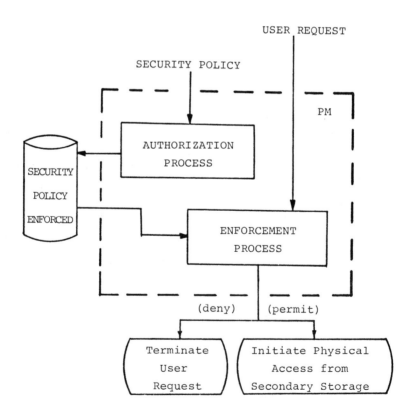

FIGURE 1. Protection mechanism in current systems.

forces the security policy specified. The protection mechanism is the agent responsible for both the update and enforcement of the security policy. Thus in current computer systems
the protection mechanism consists of an authorization process
and an enforcement process, as shown in Figure 1.

It is important to note that in a secure data base system,
authorization and enforcement have to be applied consistently
at three levels, as depicted in Figure 2. This is a simplified representation of "Threats and Their Usual Defense (1)."

At the third level, the logical protection process evaluates user requests for access to logical entries such as
files, records and fields (2). This level is handled by the
logical access control (LAC) mechanism. In this paper, we
present the design of an advanced LAC mechanism that can be
used to enhance information sharing in existing computer systems. In all our discussions it is assumed that protection
at the other two levels (physical protection and user identification) is adequate.

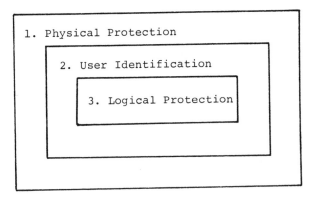

FIGURE 2. Three levels of protection.

II. MOTIVATION

Conceptually a LAC mechanism is a decision making process that generates an access decision (permit or deny) for every user request in compliance with a given security policy. There are two major characteristics of a decision making process: 1) timing of the decision in relation to timing of the request, and 2) information made available to the decision making process (the security policy).

With respect to 1) above, it is a well-known fact that in a dynamic environment the later the decision is made, the better the result is. This is referred to as the binding time problem in computer science (3). On the other hand, performance consideration may dictate an early decision in order to have the result instantly available when needed.

With respect to 2) above, the following information has to be made available to the LAC mechanism in a secure data base system:

1. the specifically protected information,

2. the user's knowledge relevant to deducing information to which he is not entitled, and

3. the semantic relations between the data elements (e.g., the salary of an employee, the price of a machine, etc.) with respect to which the user has some access right.

The user's knowledge is too large to be maintained in a computer system and its dynamic update is practically impossible. The same applies to semantic relations between data elements. It is estimated that the storage representation of these semantic relations alone would require a data base of three to four orders of magnitude larger than the information

data base itself. Thus current data base systems (e.g.,

INGRES (4) and SYSTEM R (5)) take a simplified approach in

which only the specifically protected information is provided

for the LAC mechanism to represent the security policy. To

prevent users from deriving specifically protected informa-

tion, existing systems must further restrict user's access

rights, thereby impeding data sharing, as demonstrated by the

following example.

**** EXAMPLE 1 ****

The data base has three files with the following information:

R1 (protected)			R2		R3	
NAME	AGE	ID	NAME	ID	AGE	
Jones	21	1	Smith	1	21	
Martin	35	8	Morgan	8	65	
Morgan	65	9	Peterson	9	22	
Peterson	22	15	Martin	15	35	
Smith	21	32	Jones	32	21	

A specific user is to be denied access to NAME-AGE relation

R1. Moreover, the user is permitted access either to R2 or

R3, but not both. If he were permitted access to both R2 and

R3, he would be able to derive the protected information

stored in R1 without directly accessing it. The ability of a

user to derive specifically protected information (R1) from

authorized access requests (R2 and R3) is called unauthorized

derivation. Thus the following three strategies can be used

to enforce the protection of R1:

1. Deny access to R1, R2 and R3.

2. Permit access to either R2 or R3, but not both. The

   decision is made a priori and arbitrarily.

3. Permit access to either R2 or R3, but not both. The

   decision is made at the time of request according to

the user's access history and not arbitrarily.

The first strategy is the most restrictive and impedes data
sharing. The second strategy permits the user to access one
of the two resources (R2 or R3), but the access decision has
to be made a priori and arbitrarily. All existing LAC mechanisms use the first or second strategy. In Section IV, we
will show that the event-driven protection mechanism developed
in this paper can use the third strategy, thereby enhancing
data sharing without compromising the security policy. Moreover, the logical access decision can be delayed to the last
practical moment (at the time of request) and utilizes dynamically updated event information.

* * * * * * *

The information made available to the protection mechanism
has a direct influence on its complexity. Conceptually, all
protection mechanisms are implementation of an access matrix
in which rows correspond to users and columns to data resources (6-9). Elements of the access matrix in its general
form contain functions that can be evaluate dynamically the
access rights of users with respect to resources. One known
attempt to identify these functions has been made by Hoffman
in his formulary model (10).

Most existing mechanisms are based on a simplified version
of the access matrix, where its elements are reduced from an
array of functions to an array of bits. The access matrix in
this case represents a degenerate form of the access decision
making process where decisions are made outside of the system
a priori (independent of the time of their utilization) and
only the results of the decision are stored inside the system.
Protection mechanisms supporting a security policy in this

format are referred to as <u>context</u> <u>free</u> (CF) or data independent mechanisms (7,8,11).

However, in many current applications protection specifications require that access decisions be dependent on a number of other things, such as the content of the requested information or user's access history (6,8,9,10,12-15). For example,

-User U1 cannot read records in the EMPLOYEE file if field SALARY is larger than $10,000.

-User U2 cannot update file R2 if user U1 has updated file R1.

Existing protection mechanisms cannot support such protection specifications. If needed, they are implemented by special application packages. Protection mechanisms capable of supporting these types of protection specifications[3] are called <u>context</u> <u>sensitive</u> (CS) or data dependent (8).

Context-sensitive protection mechanisms that can support protection specifications related to access history are called <u>event</u> <u>sensitive</u> (ES) or event driven.

There are three major reasons that justify the examination of event-driven protection mechanisms:

1. Data base activities are the logical elements handled by the LAC mechanism; therefore, their monitoring is easier.

2. Many applications in the real world require the en-

---

3. A protection specification identifies the conditions that have to be met in order to authorize a request.

IF (predicate) THEN [RQTi+]

RQTi is authorized (+) if and only if the value of the predicate is true. This also implies (by definition) that the request is denied if the value of the predicate is false.

forcement of specific event patterns (e.g., data base activities); therefore, these events are monitored anyway.

3. Access history may be used to represent the knowledge acquired by the user from the data base to support derivation protection, in addition to data resource protection (e.g., files). This will be an attempt to protect information instead of data resources in which it is packaged.

The objective of our research is to demonstrate that the event driven protection mechanism (EDPM) can enhance data sharing in data base systems without affecting the user's response time. This is achieved by utilizing access history information in making access decisions, which are delayed until the time of request.

III. FUNCTIONAL STRUCTURE

An event-driven protection mechanism consists of three major processes:

1. The authorization process (AP) organizes protection specifications introduced into the system by the owners of data resources in a format allowing efficient evaluation of user access requests. It also allocates space for the events to be monitored.

2. The monitoring process (MP) monitors data-base event values that have been identified by AP. Only events that might be needed to evaluate protection specifications are monitored by the system.

3. The enforcement process (EM) makes logical access decision to deny or permit a user request according to the

protection specifications introduced by AP and the

access history monitored by MP.

Figure 3 shows the information flow within EDPM in order

to support dynamic authorization and enforcement. Logical

access decisions (LADs) are evaluated based on context-free

and event-sensitive protection specifications, the objective

being to make the best decision before the retrieval of the

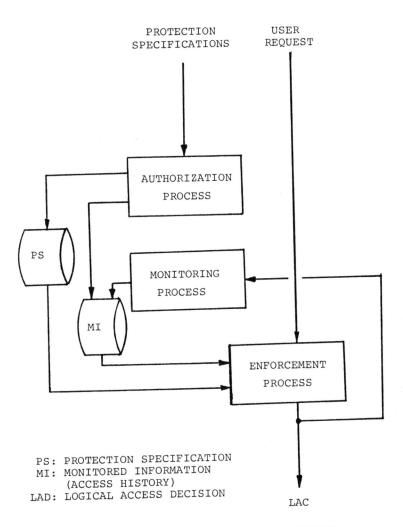

FIGURE 3. Functional structure of EDPM.

requested information from secondary storage.

The major advantage of this model is its capability of making more intelligent access decisions, thereby enhancing data sharing without compromising the security policy. The major disadvantage of this model is the additional overhead incurred by the logical protection. In our design, we overcome this disadvantage through the use of an adaptive policy that adjust the level of performance and degree of data sharing according to the availability of system's resources so as not to affect user's response time. At the same time we allow those users who do not need the enhanced protection capability to continue their activities in the restricted environment.

IV. AUTHORIZATION AND ENFORCEMENT

The nature of the authorization information determines both the capability and performance of the protection mechanism. Event-sensitive protection specifications are special cases of context-sensitive protection specifications where the predicate is evaluated based on past access history, also referred as event information. The protection specifications can be introduced into the system by the owners of the data resources. An authorization matrix is used to control the change in the security policy by the owners. Owners may change the security policy only with respect to their own resources. With respect to protection specifications the system examines the authorization matrix for both the affected request and the event information applied.

Several types of protection specification have been chosen to be supported by the system according two criteria. First, they should be able to support conditions that involve any boolean expression of event occurrences. Second, they should be restricted to a set of fixed formats in order to efficiently handle the activity of EP that makes access decisions based on this information. The fixed format of the protection specification will also allow the forecasting of expected performance, which is not possible in the formulary model, since each owner may utilize his own custom-made formularities (10).

The first type of event-sensitive protection specification examined is of type PS.ES.A:

$$IF \ (EVT1\underline{+}) \ THEN \ [RQTa\underline{+}]$$

RQTa is (or is not) authorized if EVT1 has (or has not) occurred since the protection specification was introduced by the owner into the system.

Analysis of this rule shows that the logic required to make an access decision can be simply represented by an access gate, as shown in Figure 4. The LAD is affected by the event occurrence and the request-event relation (RE = 1, if the signs of both event and request are the same; RE = 0, otherwise).

It is worth noting that an access gate can evaluate the logical access decision of a PS.ES.A type independently of the number of users, the number of data resources, and the number of data base operations supported by the system. A proof of this theorem is given in (17).

**** EXAMPLE 2 ****

The owner of the data resources given in Example 1 can enforce the third strategy for user U1 through the following security policy.

Let us define

$$EVT2 = RQT2 = (U1, R2, Read)$$
$$EVT3 = RQT3 = (U1, R3, Read)$$

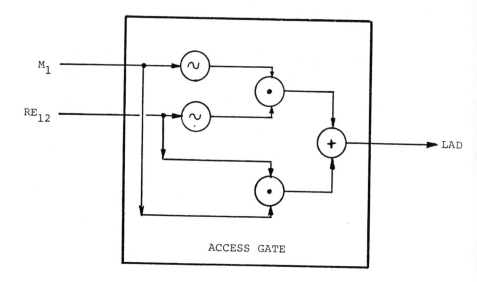

IF (EVT1±) THEN [RQT2±]

$$M_1 = \begin{cases} 0, \text{ if EVT1 did not occur} \\ 1, \text{ if EVT1 occured} \end{cases}$$

$$RE_{12} = \begin{cases} 1, \text{ if the signs are the same (++ or --)} \\ 0, \text{ if the signs are different} \end{cases}$$

FIGURE 4.   Logic for enforcing PS.ES.A rule type.

The security policy will be represented by the following protection specifications:

PS1:   IF (EVT2+) THEN [RQT3-]

PS2:   IF (EVT3+) THEN [RQT2-]

The enforcement of these rules will result in the denial of access to R1 (since it is not specifically authorized) and authorization of access to either R2 or R3 (but not both), depending on whether EVT2 or EVT3 occurs first.

* * * * * * *

IF ((EVT1'$\pm$) OR (EVT2'$\pm$) OR ... OR (EVTq'$\pm$)) THEN [RQTa'$\pm$]

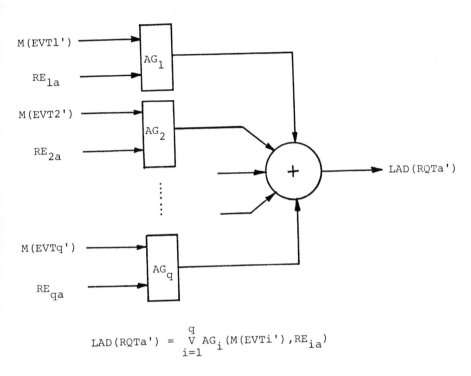

$$LAD(RQTa') = \overset{q}{\underset{i=1}{V}} AG_i(M(EVTi'),RE_{ia})$$

FIGURE 5. Logic for enforcing PS.ES.B rule type.

The second type of event-sensitive protection specification examined is of type PS.ES.B:

IF ((EVT1'$\pm$) OR (EVT2'$\pm$) OR ... OR (EVTq'$\pm$)) THEN [RQTa'$\pm$]

This can be viewed as an extension of the PS.ES.A type, where

(EVT1$\pm$) = (EVT1'$\pm$) OR (EVT2'$\pm$) OR ... OR (EVTq'$\pm$)

A PS.ES.B rule type can be evaluated by ORing the results of q access gates, as shown in Figure 5.

The two rule types above have been extended to support event counts (e.g., a user can update a resource only four times per week) and specific patterns of both successful and unsuccessful access attempts (which is needed for supporting dynamic threat monitoring). The choice of protection specifi-

cation types can be adjusted according to particular characteristics of a data base system. The event-driven protection
mechanism can enforce any pattern of event occurrence specified by the owners[4].

A security policy involving both event-sensitive and context-free protection specifications will authorize a request
if and only if the following two conditions are satisfied:

1. At least one protection specification explicitly
   authorizes the request.

2. All protection specifications related to the same
   request unanimously authorize it (a consistency
   requirement).

The consistency requirement enforced above introduces an AND
operation of all protection specifications' predicates with
respect to the same request. Through this requirement, we are
able to support multiple ownership of data resources. An
owner is allowed to remove or change only those protection
specifications that were previously introduced into the system.

All protection specifications related to the same request
can be evaluate simultaneously if appropriate multiprocessing
is available in the system, thereby allowing tight control
over performance. Because of the limited processing power
needed to evaluate one protection specification, we believe
that current microprocessor technology is very attractive for
implementation. This approach leads to the development of

---

4. The model has also been extended to support the enforcement of cyclic patterns. This property is particularily
   useful if we apply our model to implement the synchronizing
   function between processes in the operating system (16).

standard protection mechanisms (in hardware and firmware) with their own processing capability, interacting as the kernel with the operating system. Such a solution will allow up-grading of current systems to provide event-driven protection capability.

The protection mechanism is the agent responsible for carrying out owner's instructions to protect his resources. Thus in our mechanism all changes in the security policy (which are handled by AP) are given priority over user requests (which are handled by EP). On the other hand, the processing of a user request will not be interrupted until both its enforcement and monitoring have been completed. This is necessary in order to maintain at all time a consistent security policy. This critical sequential relationship between EP and MP is shown in Figure 6. The NEXT QUERY SIGNAL indicates the completion of an EP-MP cycle.

V. ADDITIONAL RESULTS

Due to space limitation, we will summarize in the following some of the additional characteristics of our design. Details are avialable in (17) and will be reported in future papers.

1. A scheme has been developed to centralize the monitoring of an event independently of the number of related protection specifications referring to it or the time they have been introduced into the system. This has important implications on the performance of the protection mechanism, since each data base operation may require an access history update.

2. Algorithms have been developed to consistently handle different granularity levels of subjects, objects, data base

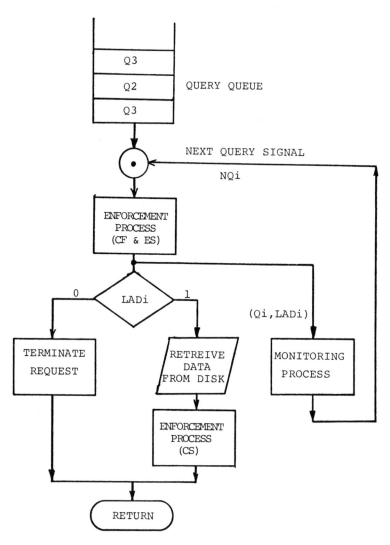

The logical access decision is based on context-free (CF)
and event-sensitive (ES) protection specifications. Once
the requested information is retreived from secondary
syorage, context-sensitive (CS) rules are then applied.

FIGURE 6.   Sequential relationship between EP and MP.

operations, events, and requests.

3. An equivalence relation on the user set has been defined as follows. Two user are <u>event</u> <u>related</u> (ER) in their
data base activities if they a) either share event information
in their protection specifications, or b) one's activity affects the other's access right. Two event-independent users
can be serviced by the protection mechanism simultaneously.
The ER relation can be used also to control migration of the
authorization information (protection specifications and
access history) between primary and secondary storage.

4. A set of utility packages have been developed to assist
owners in manipulating both protection specifications and
event information. The packages can be used concurrently with
regular activities of the data base. Each package involves
with a tradeoff between the completeness of the test (of the
security policy) and the level of interference with regular
data base activities.

5. Availability of current microprocessor technology has
motivated an examination of different hardware/software architectures to implement an event-driven protection mechanism.
The architectures developed take advantage of the inherent
parallelism at the system level, at the process level (EP, AP,
and MP), and at the subprocess level.

6. The model has also been upgraded to handle the enforcement of derivation protection. We use the event information
as a representation of the knowledge the user has acquired
from the data base. Using this information we can allow the
data base system to be even more responsive to the user's
information needs without compromising the security policy.
The model in its current format proved to be cumbersome to

apply and inefficient to enforce; therefore, we have developed
a different approach for enforcing derivation protection (18).
The solution is based on the reachablity algorithm in graph
theory (19).

7. A communication-theory based model has been developed
tp represent the level of information uncertainty in the data
base. The user and the data base are viewed as a two-way communication system (20). The communication channel is under
the control of the protection mechanism. The protection mechanism can now protect information not only through flow control but also through increases in the level of uncertainty in
the information transferred (a type of jamming). This is similar to Conway's suggestion (21), but we have concentrated on
the implications and not on the methods to introduce information uncertainty.

8. The introduction of protection specifications by owners
is a local activity that might have some global implications
to which the owners might not be aware of. We can easily en-
vision a situation where a set of requests are pending, each
waiting for the occurrence of the previous one in a cycle.
This phenomenon is called an access lockout. Algorithms have
been developed to identify its existence, its nature (permanent or temporary) and the users affected. Additionally, we
have compared the characteristics of access lockout with those
of deadlock in the operating system.

9. Finally, the requirements for implementing EDPM in
distributed data base systems have been examined. Strategies
have been developed to distribute the processes of EDPM and
the related authorization information as a function of the
active user-set in a computer network.

The event-driven protection mechanism has been implemented on a DECsystem-10 in order to validate the design and to test design alternatives. The implementation has also provided a rough estimate of storage requirement for a software implementation. The size of the current package is about 9K words (of 36 bits each). The code was written in ALGOL and contains a small number of assembler routines needed for interfacing with the operating system.

VI. CONCLUSIONS

The goal of this research is the development of an event-driven protection mechanism that can enhance data sharing in interactive data-secure systems. We have developed a unified model to handle access control as a decision making process. The major parameters to consider in such a process are a) the timing of the decision making and b) the information used in the decision making. Based on the information used in the access decision-making process, we have identified three types of protection mechanisms: context-free, event-sensitive, and context-sensitive. Our event-driven protection mechanism can support two major activities: pattern enforcement and derivation protection. In this paper, we have presented a solution to the first problem, pattern enforcement. Our solution to the second problem, derivation protection, is described in another paper (18). We also plan to report in future papers details of the results that have been summarized in Section V.

REFERENCES

1. "Security System Review Mamual," AFIPS Press, 1974.

2. D. K. Hsiao, "Logical Access Control Mechanism in Computer System," OSU-CISRC-TR-73-4, The Ohio State University, July 1973.

3. L. Presser and J. R. White, "Linkers and Loaders," ACM Computing Servey, Vol. 4, pp. 149-167, September 1972.

4. P. P. Griffiths and B. W. Wade, "An Authorization Mechanism for a Relational Data Base System," ACM TODS, Vol. 1, pp. 242-255, September 1976.

5. M. Stonebraker and E. Wong, "Access Control in a Relational Data Base System by Query Modification," Proc. ACM Annual Conf., pp. 180-186, October 1974.

6. B. W. Lampson, "Protection," reprinted in Operating Syst. Rev., Vol. 8, No. 1, January 1974.

7. G. S. Graham and P. J. Denning, "Protection: Principles and Practices," Proc. SJCC, Vol. 40, pp. 417-429, 1972.

8. R. Conway, W. Maxwell, and H. Morgan, "On the Implementation of Security Measures in Information Systems," CACM, Vol. 15, pp. 211-220, April 1972.

9. J. H. Saltzer and M. D. Schroeder, "The Protection of Information in Computer Systems," Proc. IEEE, Vol. 68, pp. 1278-1307, September 1975.

10. L. J. Hoffman, "The Formulary Model for Flexible Privacy and Access Control," Proc. FJCC, Vol. 39, pp. 587-601, 1971.

11. E. J. McCauley, "A Model for Data Secure Systems," Ph. D. dissertation, The Ohio State University, 1975.

12. T. D. Friedman, "The Authorization Problem in Shared Files," _IBM_ _Syst_. _J_., Vol. 7, pp. 258-280, December 1970.

13. R. C. Owens, "Primary Access Control in Large Scale Time Shared Decision Systems," M. S. Thesis, MIT, July 1971.

14. H. R. Hartson, "Languages for Specifying Protection Requirements in Data Base Systems - A Semantic Model," Ph. D. Dissertation, The Ohio State University, August 1975.

15. N. Minsky, "An Activate-Based Protection Scheme, TR-76-25, Rutgers University, July 1976.

16. R. K. Kanodia and D. P. Reed, "Event Counts: A New Model for Process Synchronization," Tech. Rept., MIT, January 1976.

17. D. Cohen, "Design of Event Driven Protection Mechanisms," Ph. D. Dissertation, The Ohio State University, August 1977.

18. D. Cohen and M. T. Liu, "Derivation Protection in Data Base Systems," submitted for publication.

19. N. Deo, _Graph_ _Theory_ _with_ _Applications_ _to_ _Engineering_ _and_ _Computer_ _Science_, Prentice-Hall, 1974.

20. C. E. Shannon, "A Mathematical Theory of Communication," _Bell_ _Syst_. _Tech_. _J_., Vol. 27, pp. 379-423, July 1948.

21. R. W. Conway and D. Strip, "Selective Partial Access to a Data Base," _Proc_. _ACM_ _Annual_ _Conf_., pp. 85-89, 1976.